Economic and Monetary Sovereignty in 21st Century Africa

'Opens the canvas to reflect on the economic and monetary dependence of the entire continent, picking up the unfinished business of economic and financial decolonization, updating it empirically and conceptually right up to the present conjuncture of the Covid-19 pandemic, which has further exposed inequalities.'

—Sabelo J. Ndlovu-Gatsheni, Professor and
Chair of Epistemologies of the Global South
at the University of Bayreuth

'A fresh and innovative view on Africa's entanglement in the world's financial and monetary system. Its point of departure – that Africa has long been a part of global finance – is absolutely necessary if we are to understand the future trajectory of Africa's political economy.'

—Randall Germain, Professor of Political Science
at Carleton University

'A timely and highly recommended contribution to the literature with well researched case studies and deep historical, theoretical and policy insights into the issue.'

—Howard Stein, Professor at the Department of Afroamerican
and African Studies, University of Michigan, Ann Arbor

'Insightful and diverse, it is crucial reading for anyone wanting to understand and engage with the theoretical and political debates about sovereignty and subordination in Africa.'

—Ingrid Kvangraven, Department of International
Development, King's College, London

'A powerful addition to a growing body of work aimed at enhancing our understanding of the ways in which, through the vector of finance, a transnational power regime controls the key levers of policy-making in Africa and undermines efforts at winning economic sovereignty. Readers will also find in the book, plenty of ideas for mobilizing alternatives for reversing the programmed reproduction of dependence and underdevelopment.'

—Adebayo O. Olukoshi, Distinguished Professor,
Wits School of Governance

# Economic and Monetary Sovereignty in 21st Century Africa

Edited by Maha Ben Gadha, Fadhel Kaboub,
Kai Koddenbrock, Ines Mahmoud, and
Ndongo Samba Sylla

Foreword by Prabhat Patnaik

PLUTO PRESS

First published 2022 by Pluto Press
New Wing, Somerset House, Strand, London WC2R 1LA

www.plutobooks.com



Open access to this publication is sponsored by the Rosa Luxemburg Stiftung with funds from the Federal Ministry for Economic Cooperation and Development of the Federal Republic of Germany. The content of the publication is the sole responsibility of the authors and does not necessarily reflect the positions of RLS.

ROSA
LUXEMBURG
STIFTUNG

British Library Cataloguing in Publication Data

A catalogue record for this book is available from the British Library

ISBN 978 0 7453 4408 9 Hardback
ISBN 978 0 7453 4407 2 Paperback
ISBN 978 0 7453 4411 9 PDF
ISBN 978 0 7453 4409 6 EPUB

This book is printed on paper suitable for recycling and made from fully managed and sustained forest sources. Logging, pulping and manufacturing processes are expected to conform to the environmental standards of the country of origin.

Typeset by Westchester Publishing Services

Simultaneously printed in the United Kingdom and United States of America

Illustration designed by http://www.ateliergliblett.com/

Printed and bound by CPI Group (UK) Ltd, Croydon, CR0 4YY

# Contents

# Foreword

*Prabhat Patnaik*

For Africa, as elsewhere in the third world, the need to go beyond neoliberalism has become a matter not just of desirability, but of practical urgency. This is because the regime of neoliberal globalisation has reached a dead-end, owing to the working out of its own immanent tendencies. Three tendencies in particular are important here.

The first is a de-segmentation of the world economy. Historically, labour from the Global South was never allowed to move freely to the Global North, and still is not; indeed recent efforts to circumvent restrictions on such movement have had tragic consequences, like the European refugee crisis. Capital from the Global North, though formally free to move to the Global South, never did so, except to sectors like minerals and plantations that only complemented the colonial pattern of the international division of labour; the low Southern wages were never enough to attract Northern capital to locate production in the south to meet global demand. And products of capital from the south were prevented by entry-barriers of various kinds from accessing global markets from low-wage Southern locations.

The world economy got segmented as a result: wages in the North rose along with labour productivity, while wages in the South remained tied to a subsistence level because of the vast labour reserves there, generated through the destruction of local craft production under colonialism.

This segmentation has been broken for the first time by the current neoliberal globalisation. Capital from the North is now willing to locate production in the third world so as to take advantage of low wages there and to meet global demand. True, it goes only to some destinations, and not to the third world in general, but this is sufficient to keep Northern wages in check, as the workers there now have to compete with third world workers and hence suffer the baneful consequences of third world labour reserves.

The overall vector of real wages therefore does not rise to any significant extent, since it is pulled down by massive third world labour reserves. However, the vector of labour productivity rises across the world, which results in a rise in the share of surplus in output, both in individual countries and for the world as a whole. It is this that underlies the rise in income inequality in almost every country that Piketty and others have been highlighting, though they adduce reasons for it that are erroneous.

This rise in the share of that surplus also has the effect of causing an ex ante tendency towards overproduction in the world economy. As the propensity to consume is higher for wage earners (and, more generally, for the working people) than for surplus earners, a shift from wages to surplus lowers the time profile of consumption, and hence of aggregate demand, for any given time-profile of investment. This pulls down the time-profile of investment itself, compounding the problem further.

This tendency towards rising surplus might have come to an end if the relocation of activities from the North to the south substantially used up the third world labour reserves. But here we come to the second immanent tendency. With capital, including finance, being globalised, while the state remains a nation-state, state policy everywhere must conform to the demands of finance. If a country defies the demands of finance, finance will leave that country en masse causing a financial crisis. Therefore, governments willy-nilly pursue policies in keeping with the demands of finance. This entails their withdrawing support from the petty production sector, including peasant agriculture, and opening up this sector to encroachment by big capital. A crisis in petty production ensues and an exodus of petty producers, including peasants, to urban areas where they swell the labour reserves.

Thus the relocation of activities from advanced countries to the third world does not lead to any exhaustion of labour reserves in the latter. On the contrary, the migration of distressed petty producers to urban areas, together with a natural growth in population, enlarges the relative size of the labour reserves in the total workforce. The rising share of surplus within each country and in the world as a whole thus continues unabated, as does the ex ante tendency towards overproduction.

This ex ante tendency would not become ex post if the state increased aggregate demand through raising its own expenditures. But, for state expenditure to counteract ex ante overproduction, it must be financed either by a fiscal deficit or by taxing the rich. A tax on the working people, who spend most of their income on consumption, would reduce their consumption by almost an equal amount, so that when the tax proceeds are spent by the state there would be hardly any net addition to aggregate demand. But if the tax is levied upon the rich, who save a large part of their income, there will be an increase in demand when the proceeds are spent. Likewise if larger government expenditure is financed by a fiscal deficit that does not reduce anyone's demand, there will obviously be a net increase in aggregate demand.

However, both these ways of financing larger state expenditure are an anathema for globalised finance capital. It will leave a country if its fiscal deficit is increased beyond a threshold, or if there is greater taxation of the rich. Indeed, and not surprisingly, the period of neoliberalism has been associated with 'fiscal responsibility' legislation limiting the ratio of fiscal deficits to GDP, and also with tax concessions for the rich. State expenditure, therefore, cannot provide a counter to the ex ante tendency towards overproduction, as it could in the years before the triumph of neoliberalism. This is its third tendency.

If the world economy did not slip into a recession earlier under neoliberalism, it was because asset price 'bubbles' in the United States, first the 'dot com bubble' and then the 'housing bubble', propped up demand in the world economy. But after the collapse of the 'housing bubble' there has been nothing to replace it. 'Bubbles' cannot be made to order, and people become wary of them because of past experience, which keeps 'bubbles' truncated.

The world economy therefore has entered a prolonged period of stagnation. This cul-de-sac is reflected in the rise of fascistic tendencies across the world, which are encouraged by international finance capital, both because they keep down resistance against its hegemony, and also because they bring about a discourse shift, so that it is not the economic system but the 'other', usually somewhat hapless minority, that is held responsible for the people's woes.

To rescue people from this cul-de-sac, a transcendence of the neoliberal order, which requires overcoming the hegemony of globalised finance capital, has become a matter of urgent practical necessity. Since a global solution does not seem possible (even the leading capitalist country, the United States, is trying to find its own 'national' solution to the crisis), different regions have to find their own solutions; that is, 'delink' from neoliberal globalisation and form their own alternative viable arrangements. The essays that follow in this volume acquire great importance in this context: between them they give an indication of the direction that Africa could follow in extricating itself from the current quagmire.

# Introduction

*By the editors*

In the face of the largest global pandemic in at least a century, the bifurcations of the world between the Global South and the Global North have become more visible than ever. 'Vaccine apartheid' separates the world into Europe and North America on one side, and most of Latin America, Asia, and, particularly, Africa – with a fraction of the available vaccines – on the other. At the same time, the ability to dole out massive fiscal stimuli is a staple of the North, with the United States taking the lead. The Global South, by contrast, and the African continent in particular, has run into a deeper looming debt crisis, while high public health expenditures are needed to combat the virus. This is illustrated by South Africa which witnessed the highest decline in GDP growth, -6 per cent, in 2020, followed by the North Africa region at -3.4 per cent.[1]

The meagre debt rescheduling initiatives pursued by the International Monetary Fund (IMF) and the G20 have been of little help. The need for Africa to increase its monetary and economic sovereignty in order to powerfully face the unequal international division of labour has rarely been more urgent, as being dependent on the 'benevolence' of foreign creditors, both public and private, is neither sustainable and beneficial. This book opens the discussion on how this could be done, which historical structures have to be faced and what has already been tried since independence.

To contribute to these urgent debates, this book delves into both the history and the present of African self-determination, and the particular roles monetary and financial systems have played in achieving or preventing it. Money and finance are no neutral instruments, but an integral part of the reproduction of unequal capitalist social relations. The international monetary system and the global and domestic financial markets partake in the regulation of social struggles and the distribution of profit. Yet, how exactly can money and finance work to constrain and empower has rarely been studied on the African continent. Because of this, there are few 'shoulders of giants' we can build on for this quest. Samir Amin, Joseph Pouemi, and Dani Nabudere have been among the few authors taking monetary and financial affairs seriously as part of Pan-African analysis.[2] The unique and singularly colonial currency arrangement, the CFA Franc, has received some attention over the decades,[3] but few attempts have been made to think about the question of monetary and financial sovereignty across the entire continent. This book partakes in the movement to make their analyses fruitful for today.[4]

We respond to three ongoing problems that have made the study of money and finance more urgent: first, the problem of debt denominated in foreign currency: The looming debt crises, and obvious differences in fiscal space between the North and the South have shown that debt crises are a structural problem of global capitalism since at least the debt crisis of the 1980s and the Asian financial crises. Second, the problem of capital flows: The North Atlantic financial crisis from 2007 to 2008 and the Eurozone crisis have shown that financial flows have multiplied and that no one is immune to the volatilities of global capital flows and the havoc they can wreak. Third, the problem of progressive policy: discussions about Modern Monetary Theory (MMT), which has animated policy debates on how best to make money and finance work for all and to use our resources to their full potential. The analytical perspectives adopted in this book speaks of three processes from the point of view of the African continent.

## THE IMMEDIATE CRISIS: COVID-19

In April 2020, at the beginning of the Covid-19 pandemic, while the world was experiencing the greatest health and subsequent economic crisis, the G20 announced an initiative to suspend the repayment of bilateral loans owed by a number of countries (most of them in Africa). These were faced with revenue losses stemming from a sharp decline in economic activity and, for many commodity exporter countries, a concurrent drop in commodity prices, trade, tourism revenues, and remittances that exacerbated their balance of payment crisis.

This was not a debt cancellation, however. The Debt Service Suspension Initiative (DSSI) only allowed 46 from 77 eligible countries to ask for a debt moratorium with their public, bilateral G20 creditors. The bulk of these countries' debt is held by multilateral institutions and private holders. For example, the Republic of Congo, Ethiopia, Senegal, and Zambia owed more than 50 per cent of their debt to commercial creditors during the period May 2020 to December 2020. Moreover, a report by Eurodad[5] found that DSSI-eligible countries were already scheduled to repay $115 billion of debt between 2022 and 2024, just at the time when their suspended 2020 payments are due.

In late 2020, the G20 extended this initiative to the 17 African governments who would have been eligible, but only three countries requested debt treatments: Ethiopia is seeking a flow rescheduling, while Chad and Zambia have requested debt restructurings.[6] The US- or UK-based credit rating agencies have made these initiatives costly for countries willing to ask for assistance. As soon as Ethiopia announced its willingness to take the G20 up on its offer, it was downgraded by Fitch ratings to the default risk zone 'CCC' and placed by Moody's under review for downgrade. Fitch's head of Middle East and Africa sovereign ratings stated quite openly to Reuters that 'it would be likely that any other countries applying under the G20 Common Framework would be considered along the same lines as Ethiopia'. The Eurobond contracts held by these countries already included a default clause that 'non-payment of external debt, including seeking a moratorium, would be considered as defaulting'. In the process, not only Ethiopia was downgraded, but all countries that responded to the G20's offer were punished for having attempted to use this poisoned gift.

Downgraded by credit rating agencies, they will have to pay higher interest rates on the same amount of existing debt, and access to capital markets will be more difficult. Additionally, during the programme, they will be not allowed to incur debt from any other creditors. Although they will benefit from a debt moratorium, the amount initially planned for debt service could only be used to address critical spending caused by the pandemic (such as spending on the prevention, containment, and management of pandemic) and not for their much needed economic recovery. Finally they will be forced to follow the usual austerity-based policy framework that was already imposed by the Bretton Woods institutions in charge of the implementation of the G20 programme.[7]

Across the Global South and the small and weakened internationalist left in the North some raised their voice to cancel Third World debt,[8] or to support the issuance and allocation of $3 trillion (US) special drawing rights (SDRs) by the IMF to permit countries in debt distress to tackle the health crisis, strengthen their health systems, and allow a long-term fiscal response for their economic recovery. Yet, in line with the prevailing constellations of forces, the Global North governments, the IMF, and the World Bank continue to promote the same conditions of fiscal tightening and further trade and capital account liberalisation.[9]

Waiting for international financial institutions or the Global North to show more solidarity seemed to be a losing strategy. There is no way around Africa taking its structural position in the international division of labour into its own hands, and to increase its monetary and economic sovereignty. While monetarily sovereign countries like the US, China, Russia, Japan and, to a lesser extent, the EU had the tools, and the means to limit the disastrous effects of the pandemic on their economies by combining monetary measures to avert the worst of the panic in financial markets, fiscal stimulus, and regulatory frameworks to preserve their productive capacity, the African continent had little of these; they wanted to refrain from asking their 'partners' in the North for help, but did not have the clout to do so.

## THE LONG-STANDING CRISIS: AFRICA AND THE QUEST FOR FINANCING DEVELOPMENT

Kwame Nkrumah's dictum that political sovereignty has not meant economic sovereignty was true in the early 1960s, and is true today.[10] There has been progress, but setbacks are frequent and, as this book will show, much remains to be fought for.

Most African countries gained political independence during the 1950s and early 1960s, with the Portuguese and Southern African colonies joining the fray later in the 1970s to 1990s. While the early decades were characterised by socio-economic reconstruction where many African countries successfully expanded their basic infrastructure, public expenditures, and social services, it did not succeed in delinking the continent from structural economic dependency on the European colonisers, or moving beyond existing capitalist relations of production and exploitation. Indeed, most of the infrastructure built by the colonisers was built for surplus extraction and capital accumulation, as we will see later in this book. Thus, the second oil price shock, falling commodity prices, and a succession of events in the 1980s[11] caused African economies, most of them exporters of unprocessed commodities and minerals, to incur external debts they could no longer afford to service. This outstanding debt crisis led to decades of growing multilateral debts and the famous Structural Adjustment Plans. The latter deepened intensive, extractive export-oriented development models. Moreover, by joining GATTS and EU Association agreements in the 1990s, African countries entered a vicious circle of opening borders to foreign investors that deepened their trade imbalances. Consequently, they are thus facing a continuous need for foreign currencies to service their accumulated foreign debt and to pay for imports of essential goods and energy, while continuing to export low value-added industrial products and raw materials.

Since the onset of the Global Financial Crisis in 2007, more than 15 African governments decided to sell US dollar denominated government bonds to Western banks for the first time since the debt crisis in the 1980s. Contrary to what the BRICS and particularly China did, which began to create alternative financial institutions and sought to internationalise the use of its currency, African countries further increased their dependency on Northern and Western capital markets, instead of decreasing it.[12]

Excess liquidity caused by quantitative easing and the search for yield in a low-interest environment pushed Northern banks towards African governments. The latter were interested because the interest rates of these bonds seemed low at first sight, and were thus a self-determined and promising way to finance their infrastructure investments. The Bretton Woods institutions' role in tightening fiscal space and pushing for conditions of financial and capital liberalisation were enabling conditions. Not being bound to the IMF, the World Bank, or other donors' conditions, appeared like an opportunity for policy space and more autonomy. However, with rising interest rates since 2015, and the slump in some export commodity prices, numerous countries have begun to face a debt trap. For Ghana, Kenya, Angola, and South Africa, debt levels have increased threefold between 2005 and 2015. For Mozambique, the situation is worse; its debt/GDP ratio increased from 38 per cent to 130 per cent between 2011 and 2016. In 2017,

Mozambique was forced to default on its debt. The situation faced by these countries shows a general trend throughout the continent. The future prospects, darkened by the Covid-19 crisis, look challenging as plenty of African sovereign Eurobonds, issued between 2016 and 2019, will come to maturity during the decade 2022–2032.[13] For most of the countries in distress, this represents a threatening wall of repayment which will be hard to confront.

At the same time, in countries where the debt to GDP ratio seems moderate, the real situation is sometimes masked by accounting tricks. Public Private Partnerships (PPPs) are often associated with 'hidden debts' which are not accounted for in standard evaluations of public debt.[14] Another disturbing trend is the increasing level of illicit financial flows exiting the African continent. This financial bleeding results mainly from accounting practices of multinationals (through what is called 'trade mispricing') and various criminal activities. It is responsible for the following paradox: while Africa is increasingly more indebted towards the rest of the world, Africa is nonetheless a net exporter of capital.[15]

## FROM STRUCTURAL CRISIS TOWARDS SOLUTIONS: FROM MONETARY DEPENDENCY TO MONETARY SOVEREIGNTY

Formal monetary sovereignty is defined in legal terms as the right of a state to issue its own currency, the right to determine and change the value of that currency, and the right to regulate the use of that currency or any other currency within its territory. But these principles are often challenged by international private law,[16] unequal power structures between reserve currency nations and developing countries, or by surplus/deficit positions in the global economy. Depending on their position in the currency hierarchy, countries in the centre are benefitting from more privileges and have more policy space than those in the periphery.[17] Monetary sovereignty is thus not only a question of rights and duties, it's a concept that indicates the ability to conduct the adequate monetary and fiscal policies, the degree of autonomy in choosing its objectives, and the legal and institutional capacity to implement them.

A lack of real monetary sovereignty, and thus a state of relative monetary dependency, is largely the result of a country's insertion into the international division of labour, and the status of a country in the global financial architecture. Several factors shape a country's monetary sovereignty: the degree of openness of a country to foreign capital, the degree of its integration into global value chains, and the institutional financial framework adopted; that is, whether the country has a central bank, the monetary policy of the central bank, an eventual integration into a monetary union, the government's chosen prerogatives in regulating domestic prices, and the shape of the banking and financial sectors. International conventions and binding IMF articles are key elements that shape the contours of monetary sovereignty. In the age of financial openness and the abolition of capital controls, the volatility of the financial cycle and exposure to it are important limiting factors, too.[18]

Monetary dependency in Africa has been a cause and an effect of the subordinate status of the continent in economic, political, and military domains. Monetary dependency remains a structural condition of the African continent as a whole, despite the great diversity of contexts, as will become clear in this book. All contributors agree that it is, to a great degree, a legacy of European colonialism.

Despite post-independence 'Africanisation' of monetary signs, and central bank staff in francophone West Africa's two monetary and economic unions – the West African Economic and Monetary Union (WAEMU) and the Central African Economic and Monetary Union (CEMAC) – the monetary mechanisms that were set up in the colonial period still operate without major changes. What is more, neoliberal ideology is solidly entrenched among African bureaucrats responsible for economic and monetary policy.[19] France, as their former colonial metropolis, continues to co-manage part of the foreign exchange reserves of these two blocs as well as their monetary and exchange rate policies. This lack of formal monetary sovereignty translates into a lack of an autonomous monetary policy and a situation of financial dependency. Over time, the economic and financial dependency of country members of the WAEMU and the CEMAC towards France has broadened and diversified to assume a more global character by including actors like the IMF, the European Union, and China.

The situation is not very different for the North African countries of Tunisia, Morocco, and Algeria. After independence they established their own central banks and began issuing their own currencies. Despite enjoying nominal monetary sovereignty, they face numerous facets of monetary, economic, and financial dependency.

Being a formally monetary sovereign does not mean that real economic sovereignty and self-determination have arrived. Nigeria's policy space has improved massively since becoming a substantial oil exporter, which came with the means to defend the currency and deal with its volatility. Debt crises could be averted for the recent decades; however, the exposure to global capital flows creates problems. How to delink as much as possible, and pursue policies tailored to the majority of the population, remains a riddle not yet solved by those countries with more policy space.

Economic problems have always been at the heart of African struggles for emancipation and liberation. Yet monetary and financial questions were for a long time monopolised by mainstream neoliberal discourse; presented as complex issues and abstract calculations, the experts' exclusive domain. This has facilitated the transfer of exclusive monetary powers to regional bodies (as in monetary unions) or to institutions like the IMF, with the objective of achieving 'financial stability'. Thus, little criticism has been raised against the 'central bank independence' principle, the 'monetary unions' model, or the 'inflation target' objective, and their effects on wages, labour and, most importantly, their role in removing government control over monetary policies, thus easily eluding political accountability. All these policy options work to facilitate the pillage of the resources of the continent as well as the super-exploitation of its workers, which are the fuel of what Samir Amin describes as the 'imperialist rent'.[20] A rent that can only be secured through militarised globalisation, protected technological innovation, and greater financial integration. Yet, more economic and monetary sovereignty is required to counter the structures that perpetuate the export of domestic economic surplus.

It is only recently that social movements and activists in Africa took up these important issues as a battlefield for a more socially just and autonomous economic development. Vocal anti-CFA Franc movements in Senegal and in the rest of the African franc zone, mobilisations against central bank domestic policies in Tunisia and Egypt, and protests in Mozambique against odious government debt are just a selection of recent popular movements.

There are lessons to be learnt from the debate on the future of Africa's decolonial struggle from the 2008 North Atlantic financial crisis, the Covid-19 virus pandemic and the monetary and fiscal response packages that were used to save financial capital at the expense of people and labour. The pandemic has raised fundamental questions about the way we should organise our society and the values that structure our lives. This book aims to be part of this urgent conversation.

## THE ORIGINS OF THIS BOOK AND ITS CONTRIBUTIONS

This book is the fruit of a collective effort to gather economists, scholars, journalists and activists from Africa, and the rest of the World in Tunis for a large international conference in in November 2019. Funded and hosted by the Rosa-Luxemburg Foundation's North Africa Office, the conference was organised in cooperation with the Politics of Money network from Germany and the Global Institute for Sustainable Prosperity from the US. We offer our thanks to the inspiring speakers who could not contribute a chapter to this book: Anthony Victor Obeng, Accra; Chibuike Uche, Leiden; Cédric Mbeng Mezui, Abidjan; Andrew Fisher, The Hague; Jan Kregel, New York; Jerome Roos, Amsterdam; Daniela Gabor, Bristol; Peter Doyle, Washington D.C.; Riaz Tayob, Johannesburg; Mehdi Ben Guirat, Tunis; Arndt Hopfman, Brussels; Enrique Martino, Berlin; Mokhtar Ftouh, Algiers; Rohan Grey, New York City; Patrick Bond, Cape Town; Ingrid Kvangraven, York; Okoli Chukwuma, Ibadan; Myriam Amri, Tunis; and Rym Kosi, Tunis.

Our collaboration began just before the Covid 19 outbreak, in November 2019. The pandemic has confirmed the diagnoses present at the conference and in the book: export-led development is vulnerable, banking on sectors like tourism can be uniquely volatile, and foreign denominated debt puts you at the mercy of investors not interested in the prosperity of your society. Finding alternatives to Africa's current development path is now widely debated among progressive thinkers, researchers, Pan-Africanists, and policymakers. Our book seeks to join this conversation with a particular focus on monetary and financial relations, giving serious attention to the historical structures and institutions so far preventing radical transformation.[21]

## PART I: THE CONTEMPORARY GLOBAL ECONOMIC AND MONETARY ORDER

As fears of a new Third World debt crisis mounted amid the pandemic, the G20 Debt Service Suspension Initiative (DSSI) postponed debt service on bilateral debt owed by more than 70 of the poorest countries.[22] As it did so, Third World and African debt became a new battleground between China and the West. How will the battle unfold? Will it land Africa in a new, even more ravaging debt crisis? Radhika Desai argues in Chapter 1 that China's presence on this scene means that the Third World debt crisis of the 2020s may unfold much less threateningly for Third World and African prospects. To understand this potential, we need to grasp the substantial differences between the Western dollar-denominated financial system and the Chinese one. Desai provides the historical background to this argument and shows how wrong it is to judge China's financial system by the standards of the dominant Western one, how both financial systems emerged through the uneven and combined development of capitalism, how the Western system is actually the more archaic and backward (and hence also the predatory and speculative one) and why, despite these liabilities, it has persisted until now.

## PART II: CHALLENGES TO MONETARY SOVEREIGNTY IN THE POSTCOLONIAL PERIPHERY

Governments that issue their own currency possess nominal monetary sovereignty. However, their degree of real monetary sovereignty is contested by commercial banks that create most of the means of payment through the loans they extend. In the postcolonial setting, governments' nominal monetary sovereignty is further eroded by their peripheral integration in the global economy as exporters of raw materials and users of hegemonic currencies they critically need, and which they do not issue. The history of banking and finance in Sudan, from independence in 1956 to the 2019 popular uprising, is an eloquent example of the gap between nominal and real monetary sovereignty. In Chapter 2, Harry Cross offers an account of successive forms of banking in Sudan – European multinationals, state-owned commercial banks, and private Islamic banks – as each sought to capture local and external flows of funds in a shifting international economy. He analyses how governments and political movements turned to the banking sector at particular historical moments in search of alliances. At the same time, he shows how the earlier efforts at building a nationally-controlled banking system were aborted due to the need to compensate nationalised foreign banks in foreign currency, and because of economic sanctions imposed by core countries. While the development of private Islamic banks and the forced 'delinking' of Sudan from the international payments system somehow constrained the country to follow a more endogenous development path, this proved unsustainable and ultimately resulted in a 're-integration' in the global economy, conditioned on the implementation of IMF-style austerity and liberalisation policies. Based on this case study, Harry Cross argues that the possibilities open to postcolonial states through their sovereign powers of local monetary creation are systematically disciplined by crises and imbalances produced by an international capitalist economy, in which states on the global periphery are 'rule takers' rather than 'rule makers'. According to him, this leaves two options for postcolonial states: Collective action to challenge the institutional structure of the international capitalist economy, or a strategy of 'delinking'/revolutionary exit from it.

Given the difficulties of such a collective action, most African states have suffered, alternately, the evils of deflation and inflation, and in very rare occurrences hyperinflation. Zimbabwe's record hyperinflation in 2008, and its subsequent issuance of the largest denomination in the history of money, has acquired legendary status, although most analyses so far have been rather superficial. Zimbabwe does not demonstrate the perils of monetary sovereignty and the so-called 'printing' of money, as most analysis insinuate. Rather, it shows that the monetary possibilities of nations are shaped and constrained by the nature of their insertion in the global economy, as well as their domestic economic structure.

In Chapter 3, Francis Garikayi provides us with a more profound understanding of the structural basis of Zimbabwean hyperinflation, which goes against the grain of mainstream accounts of economic mismanagement and corruption. He argues that Zimbabwe's monetary system has to be studied historically in relationship with how capital accumulation has tended to take place in the country. During the early colonial era, the monetary system served to facilitate the extraction of gold to the metropolis. With the transition from 'Chartered Company' rule to the white settlers' so-called 'Responsible Government', monetary relations shifted towards facilitating the 'draining off of surplus' – the export of local savings. As global conditions changed and the country started to industrialise, the monetary system transitioned towards facilitating trade. Since Zimbabwe's independence, money has mainly served to promote export-led growth in line with Washington Consensus policies. For Francis Garikayi, currency collapse and hyperinflation in Zimbabwe are not the result of mismanagement or fiscal indiscipline. They are an outcome of its particular economic structure. According to his account, the monetary system worked to maintain afloat extraverted sectors – mining, agricultural exports, and manufacturing – which would have collapsed without such support. With declining domestic capacity and export income, international sanctions compounded the economic and financial woes of a country where the consumption of critical goods are imported, while local production is mainly oriented towards the export market. To escape from this predicament, Francis Garikayi recommends a shift towards 'labour-centred industrial development', which presupposes the mobilisation of the monetary system for that purpose and a retreat from Washington Consensus policies that promote the reproduction of capital at the expense of labour.

In contrast to Zimbabwe, Algeria has done its best to limit its exposure to debt in foreign currencies, thanks to lavish hydrocarbon income receipts. However, given the limited diversification of its export base, government finance and monetary policy have been highly dependent on these proceeds from gas and oil. In Chapter 4, Fatiha Talahite analyses Algeria's monetary policy during the rule of long-standing president Bouteflika, from 1999 to 2018. Most of this period has been characterised by a boom in external revenues thanks to high hydrocarbon prices, which ended in 2014 with a large downward shock. The influx of hydrocarbon export revenues not absorbed by the economy has led, since 2002, to a situation of chronic excess liquidity of the banking system. Faced with this situation, the Bank of Algeria's policy, whose principal objective was to target inflation, consisted mainly in recovering liquidity from primary banks. The absence of any real credit market deprived the economy of the instruments needed to translate monetary policy measures into growth. The Revenue Regulation Fund, created in 2000 to cushion the effects of erratic oil price fluctuations on the economy, was used to freeze excess export revenues, fuelling idle savings in the context of structural underfinancing of the economy. Used since 2006 to finance growing budget deficits, the fund has contributed to the opaque leakage of public spending, leading to resource waste and widespread corruption. The economic downturn in 2014, following the drop in oil prices, caused a liquidity crisis that the Bank of Algeria tried to curb through an 'accommodating' monetary policy which proved ineffective due to the rigidity of the banking system. This impasse led the authorities to resort to quantitative easing, in a situation of political crisis that paralysed government initiatives. The two other solutions envisaged to curb the crisis in public revenues and the balance of payments were the devaluation of the dinar and external debt, thus reopening the nagging question of financial sovereignty, which the regime believed it had exorcised since the end of the structural adjustment programmes in 1999. Overall, even if Algeria managed to obtain more external stability than other hydrocarbon-rich countries, such as Venezuela, Nigeria, or Angola, this has not created the conditions for shared prosperity, given the lack of adequate policy tools and a clear development orientation in the context of weak political legitimacy, as exposed by the popular uprising of February 2019.

## PART III: INCREASING SOVEREIGNTY THROUGH MONETARY UNIONS?

In their quest for economic transformation conducive to shared prosperity, a favoured route is via regional integration at the continental level through the African Continental Free Trade Area (AfCFTA), as well as via Regional Economic Communities (RECs) that promote deeper integration through future monetary unions. The African Union envisions a single currency for the continent that will connect these

RECs into a larger monetary union. In this scenario, formal monetary sovereignty will progressively move from the national to the continental level of governance. Are monetary unions the way to go in order to help the African continent achieve more economic and monetary sovereignty?

The four following chapters caution against excessive optimism. Monetary unions, even as they epitomise the ideal of pan-African unity, can become straightjackets that are detrimental to both economic development and democracy. What is more, although they may be desirable, feasibility is often in question. As a matter of fact, current global financial trends do not seem to favour the move towards monetary unions beyond the two existing ones in the African continent – the West African Economic and Monetary Union (WAEMU) and the Central African Economic and Monetary Community (WAEMU). Both currency areas are a vestige of French colonialism and are still under French control.

Chapter 5, by Carla Coburger, shows how the WAEMU has still not broken from its colonial origins, and continues to be a constraint for the prosperity of its members. This currency area has the particularity of being a 'double monetary union' – a monetary union between its currently eight member countries and also a 'monetary union' with the Eurozone through the CFA franc peg to the euro, and the WAEMU special institutional and financial relationships with the French treasury. Coburger explores the three key promises of a fixed currency regime in this context: (i) lower inflation and higher economic growth, (ii) decreased coordination costs via one monetary policy and increased solidarity and trade integration, and (iii) higher economic attractiveness and long-term development. Using a mechanism-based analysis, she demonstrates that all three theoretical promises do not offset the loss in monetary sovereignty for the WAEMU and its member countries individually. Her evidence suggests that the peg to the euro should be replaced with a more flexible peg, similar to the SDR (Standard Drawing Rights) peg. To move beyond the status quo and avoid a simple rebranding of the CFA franc, she also contemplates an alternative regional integration project of mutually supportive national currencies to foster regional trade, develop regional financial systems, and diversify regional production pattern with the help of radical industrial policy.

The WAEMU is also the focus of Chapter 6 by Hannah Cross who examines its monetary policy from the perspective of labour struggles.

As elsewhere, the development during the last four decades of a neoliberal monetary regime based on inflation targeting and central bank independence brought new dynamics to economic and political dominance in the WAEMU. Within the framework of this so-called 'new monetary policy consensus', employment and the regulation of labour are removed from government responsibility and political control. They instead became factors that must adjust to the imperatives of the market. For Hannah Cross, the CFA franc has long been linked with the losses and gains of the labouring classes, while the introduction of a macroeconomic framework that ideologically seeks to suppress labour has reinforced the significance of monetary policy to the wider project of social transformation. A labour-centred development is therefore needed as an alternative to the neoliberal macroeconomic paradigm. However, it should be embedded in a political project that goes beyond traditional Keynesianism.

In Chapter 7, Thomas Fazi makes the point that current discussions on how to strengthen the economic and monetary sovereignty of African countries cannot afford to ignore the dramatic consequences that monetary unification has had on the countries of Europe. According to him, monetary unions are no panacea. This observation matters to Africa as their monetary integration projects at regional and continental levels try to emulate the Eurozone 'model'. For him, African countries would be well-advised to learn from the shortcomings of the Eurozone rather than uncritically drawing inspiration from it. A Eurozone type of monetary integration, he argues, would not enlarge their policy space and would not be tailored to their specific challenges. More worryingly, it could compromise national independence and democratic self-determination, including the capacity by national authorities to implement coherent development policies that have lasting effects for their populations. Indeed, in the case of Europe, monetary unification, according to Thomas Fazi, has cemented the unchecked power of neoliberal unelected bureaucrats over elected governments and national constituencies.

The issue of the desirability of monetary unions in Africa has to be distinguished from their feasibility. Granted they are desirable, the political will might be lacking. The single currency project for the 15 countries of West Africa is a good example of this predicament. While Nigeria, which represents two-thirds of the regional GDP and half of its population, is not interested in a monetary union in which it would not have the last say, other countries, such as those using the CFA franc, fear the might of the oil giant and have until now preferred to integrate monetarily with France and the Eurozone. Beyond political rivalries and leadership contests, there is another reason why the creation of new monetary unions seems highly unlikely.

In Chapter 8, Elisabeth Cobbett argues, with the help of an analysis of the shifting geography of global finance, that formal monetary sovereignty will most likely remain at the domestic level of governance in Africa. This is because powerful African states are reaching out to embed financial networks within their economic hubs as they establish international financial centres (IFCs). And to do this, they need to hold on to their monetary sovereignty instead of delegating it to a sub-regional or continental level of public authority. Therefore, according to her, Africa's financial geography will likely replicate that of the current global financial structure organised through a hierarchy of IFCs, where formal monetary sovereignty is retained at the domestic level, rather than a European Union model where formal monetary sovereignty is transferred to the supranational level of governance through the creation of a single currency. She predicts the development of financial centres or hubs instead of monetary unions.

## PART IV: ALTERNATIVES

How to increase the economic and monetary sovereignty of African countries? Various answers were offered during the Tunis conference in 2019. The current volume focuses on four avenues: rejecting the Washington Consensus policies and the neoclassical paradigm on which they are grounded; promoting a peasant path to peripheral development; reforming the international financial system; and being cautious about the agenda of global finance, especially the likely illusory promise of local currency bond markets.

During the last four decades, under the aegis of the international financial institutions, developing countries have been applying the 'Washington Consensus' as a recipe for 'catching-up' with rich countries. For Heiner Flassbeck (Chapter 9), these neoliberal, ideology-driven approaches have failed bitterly wherever they have been implemented.

Africa, with its extremely restrictive monetary conditions, has been suffering more than most other developing regions. While under the Bretton Woods regime, inclusive growth had been the rule rather than the exception in the North and in the South; the neoliberal counter-revolution had decoupled economic growth from welfare gains for the masses. Although based on flimsy theoretical grounds, the neoclassical economic doctrine became mainstream and dominated economic policymaking in the North and in the South for the last four decades.

For Flassbeck, only emancipation from these flawed ideas will allow Africa to prosper and achieve significant economic progress. A new paradigm for macroeconomic policy is indeed urgently needed for Africa. According to him, the neoclassical dogma, grounded in the idea of comparative advantage, flexible labour markets, and efficient capital markets, has to be replaced by an approach based on stability of wages, rising domestic demand, and control of the monetary conditions. Furthermore, the sectoral financial balances have to guide government policies and make sure that governments provide demand stimuli in case the private sector fails to provide enough investment to close demand gaps.

According to Max Ajl, in Chapter 10, progress in terms of economic sovereignty implies the gradual elimination of structures of dependency; that is, the mechanisms of value transfer from peripheral countries to centres of capitalist accumulation. The value transfer operates mainly through the super exploitation of workers at the periphery, namely the peasantry, which represents the bulk of the labour force in Africa in particular, and in the Global South in general. Capitalist development in this context is manifested in the lack of control by peripheral governments over the reproduction of their labour force, lack of food sovereignty, a disarticulation between manufacturing and agriculture, declining terms of trade, unequal ecological exchange, and a reliance on imported technologies – to the detriment of local systems of knowledge and agro-ecological practices. As an epiphenomenon of this overall structure, balance of payment crises and resulting political blackmailing by international financial institutions and imperialist countries further weakens the socio-economic status of peripheral workers in an unending vicious circle. To break this pattern of dependency, Max Ajl advocates a peasant path to peripheral development. According to him, it's the only environmentally and socially sustainable, yet untried, model that can deliver prosperity for the many in Africa and the rest of the Global South. He makes his case by unearthing the towering work of dependency scholars like Tunisian agronomist, Slaheddine el-Amami, who argued for a self-centred development strategy based on agroecology, food sovereignty, and the valorisation of local technological creativity and innovation. As a key foundation for economic and financial sovereignty, food sovereignty is, for Max Ajl, a constitutive element of a politics of national and popular liberation.

Economic and monetary sovereignty is not a national affair. Its global underpinnings have to be factored in, especially in the current context marked by highly mobile and volatile capital flows. Peripheral countries, including many African ones, face a number of macroeconomic challenges, such as balance of payment difficulties, high external indebtedness, volatile exchange rates, and high interest rates. The consequences include domestic boom and bust cycles, recessions, high unemployment and limited policy space. Because these challenges are connected to the current international monetary system, the plethora of calls for reforms can be understood against this background.

In Chapter 11, Anne Löscher gives an overview of variously radical reform proposals focusing on the current international payment system. While some want to reform the management of external debt, and call for reparation funds and the reintroduction or normalisation of capital controls, others aim to decouple their domestic economy from the macroeconomic implications of a country's balance of payments by improving its position in the international currency hierarchy, or by applying extensive public work programmes under import-substituting industrial policies financed in domestic currency. A third set of reforms targets the financial cycle itself by tightening financial regulation in centre countries, and by introducing a truly international currency not subject to any national monetary policy decisions or a central bank of central banks which administers cross-border transactions at fixed exchange rates. After presenting these reform proposals, Anne Löscher discusses them with regard to the issue of monetary sovereignty.

Bonds in local currencies are seen by some critical minds as an important element for achieving economic sovereignty in Africa. In principle, they can help reduce dependency on foreign currencies and hence avoid the risks of currency devaluation for debt servicing. In Chapter 12, Frauke Banse examines this claim and situates the push for local currency bond markets (LCBMs) in Africa in a broad geopolitical and geo-economic perspective. She shows that bonds in domestic currency have a commodity character and have become a critical instrument that allows the worldwide deployment of speculative and globalised finance in peripheral countries. In the myriad of external interests in establishing Local Currency Bond Markets (LCBMs) in Africa, Frauke Banse takes a closer look at the outstanding activities of diverse German state institutions and discusses to what extent the recycling of Germany's economic surplus, and an increased economic footprint in Africa, might have played a role. While underlining the class character of German surplus recycling, Frauke Banse argues that LCBMs, when scrutinised in relation to the global context, are not conducive to greater policy space. Instead, they are more likely to create renewed patterns of economic dependency and to aggravate social inequalities. She concludes by identifying some entry points for international solidarity.

## NOTES

1 UNCTAD, Trade and Development Report 2020, from global pandemic to prosperity for all: Avoiding another lost decade. United Nations conference on trade and development Available at: unctad.org/system/files/official-document/tdr2020_en.pdf

2 Amin, S., 1974. *Accumulation on a world scale: A critique of the theory of underdevelopment*. Vols. 1 and 2. New York: Monthly Review Press; Amin, S., 1976. Zone franc et développement in *Impérialisme et sous-développement en Afrique*. Paris: Anthropos Institute, pp. 409–19; Pouemi, J.T., 2004 *Monnaie, servitude et liberté: La répression monétaire de l'Afrique*. Paris: Menaibuc; Nabudere, D.W., 1990. *The rise and fall of Money-capital*. London: Africa in Transition; Nabudere, D.W., 2009. *The crash of international finance and its implication for the Third World*. 2nd ed. Cape Town: Pambazuka Press.

3 Pigeaud, F. and Sylla, N.S., 2021. *Africa's last colonial currency: The CFA franc story*. London: Pluto Press.

4 Koddenbrock, K.S. and Sylla, N.S., 2019. Towards a political Economy of Monetary Dependency: The Case of the Franc CFA in West Africa. MaxPo Discussion Paper, Paris. Koddenbrock, K.S., Kvangraven, I.H., and Sylla, N.S., 2020. Beyond financialisation: The need for a longue durée understanding of finance in imperialism. OSF Preprints. September 25. doi: 10.31219/osf.io/pjt7x

5 Fresnillo, I., 2020. Shadow report on the limitations of the G20 Debt Service Suspension Initiative: Draining out the Titanic with a bucket? Eurodad.

Available at: d3n8a8pro7vhmx.cloudfront.net/eurodad/pages/768/attachments/original/1610355046/DSSI-briefing-final.pdf?1610355046 [Access date: March 25, 2021].

6 IMF, Regional economic outlook for Sub-Saharan Africa, navigating a long pandemic. Accessed April 2021. Available at: www.imf.org/-/media/Files/Publications/REO/AFR/2021/April/English/text.ashx

7 IMF. 2020. Joint IMF-WBG staff note: Implementation and extension of the debt service suspension initiative. Available at: www.devcommittee.org/sites/dc/files/download/Documents/2020-10/Final%20DC2020-0007%20DSSI.pdf [Access date: March 25, 2021].

8 Declaration of African intellectuals concerning Covid-19 crisis, 30 April 2020. Available at: darajapress.com/2020/04/30/declaration-of-african-intellectuals-concerning-Covid-19-crisis [Access date: March 25, 2021]; African feminist post-Covid-19 economic recovery statement. Available at: africanfeminism.com/african-feminist-post-Covid-19-economic-recovery-statement/ [Access date: March 25. 2021]; Africa's pandemic response calls for reclaiming economic and monetary sovereignty: An open letter. Available at: mes-africa.org/

9 Gadha, M.B., 2020. Tunisia joins forces to save global capital. Available at: news.barralaman.tn/tunisia-joins-forces-to-save-global-capital-maha-ben-gadha/ [Access date: March 25, 2021].

10 Nkrumah, K., 1965. *Neo-colonialism: The last stage of imperialism*. London: Thomas Nelson & Sons.

11 For more detail, see Ezenwe, U., 1993: The African debt crisis and the challenge of development. *Intereconomics* ISSN 0020-5346, Nomos Verlagsgesellschaft, Baden-Baden 28, no. 1, pp. 35–43. doi: 10.1007/BF02928100 [Access date: March 25. 2021].

12 See Kvangraven, I.H., 2016. The changing character of financial flows to Sub-Saharan Africa. In Aleksandr V. Gevorkyan, and Otaviano Canuto (eds), *Financial Deepening and Post-Crisis Development in Emerging Markets: Current Perils and Future Dawns*, pp. 223–45. doi: 10.1057/978-1-137-52246-7_11; and Sylla, N.S. and Koddenbrock, K., 2019. Financialization in the WAEMU Available at: twnafrica.org/wp/2017/wp-content/uploads/2019/06/WAEMU.pdf, *African Agenda*. 22(2), pp. 7–9. Published under: twnafrica.org/wp/2017/wp-content/uploads/2019/06/WAEMU.pdf [Access date: March 25, 2021].

13 Smith, G., 2020. Can Africa's wall of Eurobond repayments be dismantled? Available at: www.bondvigilantes.com/insights/2020/01/can-africas-wall-of-eurobond-repayments-be-dismantled [Access date: March 25, 2021].

14 Gabor, D. and Sylla, N.S., 2020. Planting budgetary time bombs in Africa: The Macron doctrine en Marche. Available at: geopolitique.eu/en/2020/12/23/macron-doctrine-africa/ [Access date: March 25, 2021].

15 Boyce, J.K. and Ndikumana, L., 2011. *Africa's odious debts: How foreign loans and capital flight bled a continent*. London: Zed Books.

16 Gianviti, F. Current legal aspects of monetary sovereignty. May 2004. Available at: www.imf.org/external/np/leg/sem/2004/cdmfl/eng/gianvi.pdf; Zimmermann, C.D., 2013.The Concept of Monetary Sovereignty Revisited, *European Journal of International Law*, 24(3), pp. 797–818. doi: 10.1093/ejil/cht041 [Access date March 25, 2021].

17 Daniela Magalhães Prates, and MAM CINTRA, Monetary sovereignty, currency hierarchy and policy space: A post-Keynesian approach. Textos Para Discussão, Campinas 315 (2017). Alami, I., Alvares, C., Bonizzi B., Koodenbrock, K., Kaltenbrunne,r A., Kvangraven, I., Powell, J., (2021) International Financial Subordination – A critical research agenda, https://gala.gre.ac.uk/id/eprint/33233/1/%23GPERC85.pdf

18 Dafe, F., 2019. Fuelled power: Oil, financiers and central bank policy in Nigeria. *New Political Economy* 24(5), pp. 641–58. Naqvi, N., 2018. Manias, panics and crashes in emerging markets: An empirical investigation of the post-2008 crisis period. *New Political Economy*. Published online October 2, 2018. doi: 10.1080/13563467.2018.1526263

19 Boris, S. and Kako, N., 2020. The neoliberal turn and the consolidation of a transnational bureaucracy. *Actes de la recherche en sciences sociales*, 234(4) pp. 50–65.

20 Amin, S., 2010. *The Law of Worldwide Value*, 2nd ed. New York: Monthly Review Press.

21 Sylla, N.S., 2020. Modern monetary theory in the periphery. Rosa-Luxemburg-Stiftung. Available at: www.rosalux.de/en/news/id/41764/modern-monetary-theory-in-the-periphery. Kaboub, F., 2019, Modern Monetary Theory: A Tool for the Global South: www.rosalux.de/en/publication/id/41284/modern-monetary-theory-a-tool-for-the-global-south [Access date: March 25, 2021].

22 Word Bank, April 2021, Covid-19: Debt service suspension initiative. Available at: www.worldbank.org/en/topic/debt/brief/Covid-19-debt-service-suspension-initiative [Access date: March 25, 2021].

# PART I
# The contemporary global economic and monetary order

# 1
# China's Finance and Africa's Economic and Monetary Sovereignty

*Radhika Desai*

African debt began making headlines once again in the Covid-19 pandemic. As lockdowns induced economic crisis, fears of a new Third World debt crisis mounted, reviving memories of the horrific economic devastation of the last one. With great fanfare, the G20 announced the Debt Service Suspension Initiative (DSSI) in mid-April 2020, postponing debt service for eight months on debt owed by the seventy-three poorest countries to governments.[1] At the November 2020 G20 meeting, after Zambia had defaulted, the DSSI was extended it until mid-2021. However, more ambitious proposals were not taken up, including the call to issue up to $4 trillion in Special Drawing Rights (SDRs) to provide all governments unconditional international liquidity in proportion to their International Monetary Fund (IMF) quotas. This would have provided meaningful relief to the poorest countries.[2] Not only will the DSSI lead to higher debt when the debt service suspension ends, it leaves debt owed to the IMF, the World Bank, and private creditors out of account. That debt must still be paid unless re-scheduled.[3] The majority of these seventy-three countries are located in Africa.

The 1980s debt crisis had led to one or two 'lost decades' of development in indebted countries under the IMF and the World Banks's infamous Structural Adjustment Programs (SAPs). Designed to rescue creditors from their irresponsible lending decisions, they squeezed incomes, investment, social spending, and state capacities in indebted countries. Despite owning most of its debt to official sources, African suffering was greater, not less. Today, however, Africa's debt is owed not just to the traditional Western creditors, but also to China. Given the culmination of rising hostilities between the US and China in the US's new cold war against that country, Africa and its debt will inevitably number among its major theatres.

The West complains that China does not participate in the DSSI. Extending long-standing accusations about China's 'debt trap diplomacy', David Malpass, president of the World Bank, claims that Chinese debt constitutes 'a major drain on the poorest countries' and comes with 'high interest rates and very little transparency'.[4] Those familiar with China's credit and aid practices point out that this criticism exempts the World Bank and Western private credit while counting all Chinese credit as bilateral, whether it was concessional or commercial. Little is said about Western non-transparency or about the still yawning gap between Chinese and Western per capita incomes that puts the greater onus on the richer West to forgive debt. Finally, China's established record of openness to debt cancellation and restructuring on a case-by-case basis is entirely ignored.[5] No wonder the Chinese Finance Minister, Liu Kun, shrugged off these accusations, suggesting, instead, that the World Bank 'should lead by example in suspending debt service'.[6] How will the battle unfold, and will it land Africa into a new, even more ravaging debt crisis? Will we witness the same or worse? The answer is complex.

There are certainly similarities. As before, this debt crisis was triggered by collapsing export prices following a build up of debt encouraged by the international dollar-denominated financial system and its touts, the IMF and the World Bank,[7] because, amid the 'Long Downturn' that began in the 1970s, domestic opportunities could no longer satisfy the Western financial sector's hunger for returns. The situation is, if anything, worse today. The Long Downturn was never resolved and Western stagnation since 2008 has been even worse. To the already high cash hoards it has left with Western lenders, central banks, particularly the Federal Reserve and, to a lesser extent, the European Central Bank, have added massive liquidity issuance, most of which has ended up in financial institutions rather than being invested productively. With fewer opportunities for profit domestically, these lenders have turned to lending to Third World governments. The resulting increase in Third World debt as a proportion of GDP is more than twice as high as it was in the early 1980s. Worse, it consists of complex elements, including private credit from shadow banks.[8] As before, the African scene has its differences since private lenders have never been too keen on lending to Africa. Most African debt is still owed to official development agencies and, this time around, also to China.[9]

China's presence on this scene means that the Third World debt crisis of the 2020s can unfold more benignly for Third World and African sovereignty and their development prospects. This potentiality will be more fully realised once the momentous differences between the Western dollar-denominated financial system and the Chinese are widely understood. However, such understanding faces three obstacles. First, there is Western, US and US-sponsored obfuscation. Second, there is the tendency of Western scholars to discuss China's financial system as if it were merely a backward version of the dollar-denominated financial system headquartered in the US and the UK rather than, as we shall see, a contrasting system and a vastly more beneficial one. Finally, the historical development of these contrasting financial systems holds the key to their differences, which is rarely appreciated.

In this paper, I provide the essential historical perspective that shows just how wrong it is to judge and measure China's financial system by the standards of the dominant Western one. I trace how these opposed financial systems emerged through the uneven and combined development of capitalism, how the Western system is actually the more archaic and backward (and hence also the predatory and speculative) one and why, despite these liabilities, it still persists.

I begin with an overview of African development until the setback of the debt crisis of the 1980s. I then outline the turn to neoliberalism and financialisation behind the disasters of the 1980s and 1990s, before going on to provide a historical perspective on the US and Chinese financial systems, and explain their contrasts. We end the paper with an expose of three prominent tropes in Western discourses about China's financial system, which obfuscate the contrasts that reflect so badly on the Western system. They relate to the internationalisation of the renminbi, the allegedly impending crash of China's property bubble, and China's 'debt trap diplomacy'. We conclude by taking note of the factors that might change the Chinese system and of how the peoples of Africa and the developing world can best draw on the development potentialities of China's distinctive financial sector and its international engagement.

## A PERSPECTIVE ON AFRICA'S DEVELOPMENT

African development in the early years of independence was fired by the left-leaning and popular visions – such as Nyerere's, Nkrumah's or Lumumba's – of autonomous national development, subjecting market forces to state and social direction, much as in the USSR and in other developing countries embarked on 'socialistic' development, such as India.

This project faced major obstacles. Externally, there was imperial pressure, particularly from the United States 'for whom any assertion of national self-determination was "communism", to be hounded and destroyed, by force if necessary, by manipulation and deception if possible'. It was behind 'the gruesome assassination of Patrice Lumumba and the overthrow of Kwame Nkrumah' and behind most of 'the continuing story of military coups, assassinations, and resistance to national liberation wars; and the civil strife in Africa'.[10] Domestically, the inability of nascent domestic capitalist classes and the unwillingness of foreign capital to advance development left matters to states and bureaucracies. They, however, did not have the requisite resources and skills and fell increasingly under the spell of Western 'Modernisation' discourses.

Inevitably, the results of the early years of development fell short of the optimistic 5 and 6 per cent per annum growth rates originally projected.[11] The chief limitation was that African countries' growth remained dependent on primary commodities. Post-war recovery and growth in the imperial core kept demand buoyant and reliance on them was an all-too-easy option, reducing the urgency of structural transformation and industrialisation necessary for faster and self-sustaining development. Inequality also rose. The limitations of this path were revealed in the 1970s, when world growth slowed, terms of trade moved against (most) commodities, and African growth rates plummeted. Amid accompanying social and political crises, African countries, encouraged by the World Bank, borrowed from abroad. However, when the Volcker Shock jacked up interest rates to unprecedented heights, debt crises erupted and delivered most African countries into the deadly embrace of the IMF and the World Bank, and their SAPs.

The tragedy of the next decades is well known. Standard one-size-fits-all economic policies were designed to extract as much as possible from African economies in terms of money and resources while investing as little as possible in society and economy. Worse, they destroyed hitherto created state capacity for economic development. If the first two decades after decolonisation were disappointing, the next two were horrendous. Sub-Saharan African economies had grown by 36 per cent between 1960 and 1980; they shrank by 15 per cent over the next two decades.[12] Per capita incomes shrank even more. Poverty mounted until it engulfed more than half of Africans. Human development and health indicators could only go south amid the Structural Adjustment-dictated cuts in social expenditures.

Perhaps the most eye-watering statistic related to financial flows. As Asad Ismi noted in 2004, 'Africa's external debt has increased by more than 500 per cent since 1980 to $333 billion' and 'transferred $229 billion in debt payments from Sub-Saharan Africa to the West since 1980 . . . four times the region's 1980 debt. In the past decade alone African countries have paid their debt three times over, yet they are three times as indebted as ten years ago'.[13]

While this devastation undoubtedly had domestic determinants, the international change in the character of imperialism, along with that of metropolitan capitalism itself, was arguably decisive. When the prodigious, if uneven, productive expansion of the imperial core, its 'Long Boom' ended in the early 1970s; it was followed by the Long Downturn,[14] a decline in growth and investment rates. Western governments led by the UK and the US adopted neoliberal policies to address this and, despite their failures, have persisted with them over the past four decades. Rather than reviving their economies, neoliberalism has fostered the predatory and speculative financial system, a veritable world creditocracy, centred on the dollar that has visited debt and currency crises and accompanying economic misery around the world.

## NEOLIBERALISM AND THE FORMATION OF THE WORLD CREDITOCRACY

Neoliberal policies of deregulation, privatisation, cutbacks on social services and attacks on unions and working class wages, starting in the 1980s, were supposed to restart growth, restore capitalism's mojo and revive the 'animal spirits' of its entrepreneurs by removing the 'dead hand of the state' and the constraints of trade unions that allegedly ailed them. They failed to do so. The virtues of competition they invoked were irrelevant to a capitalism that had entered its monopoly phase already before the First World War.

Freedom from regulation was not going to make this capitalism vigorous and could only exacerbate the vices and irrationalities of its monopoly form. Indeed, lowering taxes on corporate capital and feeding it lucrative state assets and contracts through privatisation and contracting out only implicated the state in increasing the degree of monopoly. Without the spur of competition towards investment, deregulated and coddled monopoly capitalism could only become financialised capitalism. Profits made, but not invested productively, could only seek to profit from financial speculation. Inevitably, under neoliberalism, productive activity languished and financial activity exploded.

Scholars have studied this explosion of financial activity extensively under the rubric of financialisation. However, few have pointed to its reliance on the dollar-denominated international financial system that emerged in the previous decade.[15] Most take the existence of this system for granted, arguing on the one hand that money is inherently difficult to regulate and, on the other, that the dollar serves stably, if not beneficially, as the world's money. In reality, as we see below, on the one hand, the dollar system rests on financial deregulation by neoliberal capitalist states, led by the US. On the other, it defies the laws of the geopolitical economy of capitalism and is, as a result, contradictory and volatile.

## THE GEOPOLITICAL ECONOMY OF WORLD MONEY

To begin with basics, money is not a commodity but a political institution created by states and the financial systems they regulate. At the international level, the dynamic of uneven and combined development that governs the international relations of capitalism, generating international competition and struggles, prevents the formation of a world state and thus world money.

Dominant capitalist states compete to externalise their capitalism's contradictions, such as excess commodities and capital, the need for cheap raw material and labour and idle capital seeking financial returns. They seek to impose a *complementarity* between subordinated states' low-value production and debtor status and their own high-value production and creditor status. Subordinated or threatened states can and have struggled to resist or escape this fate by industrialising purposively. This involves directing their economies and controlling trade and financial flows to achieve productive and financial *similarity*.[16] It was not markets, but such combined or contender development that spread productive capacity around the world. It can be capitalist, as in the cases of countries that challenged Britain's industrial supremacy in the nineteenth century, the US, Germany, and Japan, or 'Communist', as in the cases of the Soviet Union and Communist China. Since the 1870s, combined development has made the world progressively more multipolar.

Such competition and struggles also make attempts by dominant national governments to foist their national currency on the world volatile and unstable. The UK's and the US's attempts to do this, in the nineteenth and twentieth centuries respectively, resulted in creating only destructive and unstable systems. Domestically, they entail maintaining or re-creating archaic, short-term, speculative and predatory financial systems incapable of financing productive expansion with long-term capital. Internationally, they are subject to resistance from states competing with and struggling against them.

The development of today's developing countries in Africa and elsewhere depends on combined development, also known as autonomous national development. Serious attempts to pursue it have historically required the fashioning of financial systems capable of supporting productive expansion, as Karl Marx anticipated. Rudolf Hilferding, developed Marx's analysis in his famous publication *Finance Capital*. Writing in the early twentieth century, Hilferding distinguished sharply between the archaic financial system of the UK, unfit for the purposes of modern industrial expansion, and those of the 'model states' of finance capital, such as Germany and, at that time, the US.

## THE ORIGIN OF FINANCIAL CONTRASTS

The UK's early capitalism inherited pre-modern financial institutions based on short-term credit and speculation. Marx correctly anticipated that capitalist development would transform them, and it did. When the competitive capitalism of small firms matured into massive concentrations of capital and labour in planned productive enterprises, the 'conditions and requirements of modern industry' faced a new borrower: no longer a supplicant in financial straits but a capitalist to whom money is lent 'in the expectation that he . . . will use [it] to appropriate unpaid labour', that is, increase production and make profits from which to pay interest. This new credit system, capitalism's 'own creation', would aid its productive expansion.[17]

In Hilferding's later analysis, this historical evolution became part of capitalism's *geopolitical economy*. Britain could industrialise despite its archaic financial system because individual fortunes could cover the investment needs of small firms. Later, more capital-intensive industrialisation by large firms in contender countries needed a modernised credit system. Hilferding dubbed it 'finance capital', contrasting its 'model countries', Germany and the US, with Britain.

Although competitive pressure began forcing Britain to adopt the finance capital model, the British Empire blocked this process. Once critical to Britain's industrial success,[18] it now absorbed uncompetitive British exports and yielded colonial tribute and vast trade surpluses with the rest of the world.[19] These flows supported the fabled international gold-sterling system. Britain provided international liquidity in the form of her capital exports to her settler colonies and the US, aiding their capital-intensive industrialisation, using the surpluses from her non-settler colonies, pre-eminently India.[20] Domestically, a quiescent working class on whom high levels of unemployment could be inflicted every time credit conditions needed to tighten to preserve sterling's gold value was also important.

The system, which required short-term capital flows responding to changes in interest rates to keep sterling's gold value, undermined Britain's industry and productive economy, setting off its still-unarrested (relative) industrial decline.[21] Moreover, it was not automatic, pervasive and stable as nostalgia portrays it. Keynes exposed its managed character, and reliance on financial flows from India, on the eve of the First World War.[22] Decades later, Marcello De Cecco replaced the inaccurate 'Ricardian' or free trade-based interpretation with the more realistic Listian one, showing how an international system rocked by rising new industrial powers competing for markets and colonies could hardly fail to destabilise the sterling system.

While colonies such as India could be dragooned into bearing its burdens and rulers of smaller independent countries adopted it opportunistically, powerful new industrialisers such as Germany 'adopted the Gold Standard . . . to deprive Britain of her last power, that of control over international financial flows'. As their power grew, the system 'began to oscillate more and more dangerously, till its final collapse in July 1914.'[23] By then also, increasingly organised working classes prevented governments from inflicting periodic bouts of unemployment on it to keep sterling's gold value stable,[24] Russians Bolsheviks made their revolution and colonies mobilised for war became more organised and demanding. Welfare states, actually existing socialisms (now including China) and developmental states in newly independent countries were the results after 1945.

## THE US FINANCIAL SYSTEM

This was the context in which the US began pursuing the goal of replacing the sterling system with a dollar system. In the inter-war period, US efforts to do this were highly destabilising. When it exploited its creditor status and demanded repayment of allied war debt at Versailles, it only prompted the allies, in turn, to demand reparations from Germany, which then needed and received US lending. This financial merry-go-round and its collapse contributed to the Second World War and was also implicated in the US stock market bubble and crash. Depression era banking legislation, including the Glass Steagall Act, made the US financial system among most tightly regulated in the world – until the 1970s.

At Bretton Woods, the US once again exploited its economic and financial dominance by rejecting proposals for multilateral international monetary arrangements, including Keynes's, leaving the world with no alternative to the dollar though it had to be backed with gold. The dollar's rocky career until 1971 is well known: unable to export capital the US ran deficits to provide liquidity, a method that was subject to the Triffin Dilemma: deficits made the dollar unattractive, putting downward pressure on the currency, and leading those earning dollars to demand gold instead. The process could only culminate in the 1971 breaking of the dollar-gold link.

### *The US Dollar and its Financialisations*

Only now did the US financial system begin its transformation into a British style short-term, predatory and speculative one. Only now it began fostering the series of financialisations, each more volatile and dangerous, that counteracted the downward pressure US deficits exerted on the dollar. The transformation began when the US lifted capital controls to permit OPEC surpluses to be recycled through US financial institutions. As US financial institutions competed to lend internationally thanks to a stagnating domestic economy, they created a veritable 'magic liquidity machine'[25] enabling Third World governments to borrow, apparently without limit, while the dollar devalued. Paul Volcker, appointed Federal Reserve Chairman to deal with this intolerable situation, permitted the infamous recession-inducing spike in interest rates that put creditors firmly in command.

Capital mobility and creditor-oriented finance laid the foundations for the dollar-denominated world creditocracy that delivered the disasters of 1980s and 1990s in Africa and the Third World. This creditocracy grew larger as other countries lifted their capital controls and the US financial system was progressively deregulated. Alan Greenspan, appointed Chairman of the Federal Reserve in 1987, also began rewarding the very institutions that created asset bubbles by rescuing them with liquidity after crashes so they could resume speculative activity.

The series of international dollar-denominated financialisations or asset bubbles left a trail of destruction, beginning with the 1982 Third World Debt Crisis. It included the currency and financial crises of the 1990s, the East Asian Financial Crisis of 1997–98 and the dot com bubble. After Greenspan sponsored the repeal of the Glass Steagall act in 1999, he set the stage for the mother of all financialisations, the housing and credit bubbles of the 2000s that burst in 2008.

### *US Dollar Financialisations and the Rest of the World*

The dollar creditocracy is headquartered in New York and, because until the 1980s the US financial system remained heavily regulated, London, with its historically far greater financial freedoms increased by Prime Minister Thatcher's 'Big Bang' reforms of 1987.

The financial systems of major regulated contender economies, pre-eminently Germany, Japan, South Korea, Taiwan, and China, largely remained within their original production-oriented 'finance capital' mould and financed successful export engines. Many point to their large dollar reserves to explain the dollar's continuing world role after 1971. However, they are tiny compared to the torrents of money that actually flow in and out of the dollar system in each successive financialisation, creating the updrafts that hold up the dollar's value. These flows originate in financial institutions, corporations and individuals in countries open to the dollar system through a combination of free capital flows and deregulation and are often routed via tax-haven 'Treasure Islands', the largest of which is the UK.[26]

Though most advanced countries, including some historic contender economies, lifted capital controls, banking regulation kept their financial systems focused on financing domestic production. Their export surpluses yielded massive reserves and, after Japan benefited from keeping them in high-interest Treasury securities in the early 1980s, the dollar sank to another nadir in the early 1990s. Then the Clinton administration launched its drive to get more countries, particularly in Asia, to lift capital controls. Though it promised them much needed capital investment, they only got short-term return-hungry hot money from investors ignorant of the realities of destination economies,[27] including entirely different bank-industry relations. Stampeding in, herd-like, such capital also stampeded out at the first hint of trouble, triggering the biggest of financial crises seen hitherto, the East Asian Financial Crisis of 1997-98.

The Europeans got burned next with financial deregulation accompanying German unification and the launch of the euro. It was Eurozone financial institutions' massive investment in the 'toxic securities' that contributed to inflating the US housing and credit bubbles of the 2000s, not the 'global' or 'Asian' Savings glut blamed by Federal Reserve Chairman, Ben Bernanke, and President Bush.[28] 2008 was a North Atlantic financial crisis, not a global one.

The contradictions and destructiveness of the dollar system and resistance to it are now mounting. The progressive weakening of the dollar in the twenty-first century, renewed during the pandemic, is forcing already reluctant holders of reserves in dollars to look for alternatives. Weaker economies without capital controls are exposed to economically damaging levels of currency volatility and elite political will to keep capital flows open in these countries is likely to weaken as the economic damage becomes politically unsustainable. The dollar system is also losing its semblance of neutrality. Its legal regime increasingly favours US corporations, as the infamous case of the vulture funds and Argentina showed.[29] Its payments system, SWIFT, has been weaponised in the aggressive pursuit of US foreign policy goals in ways that make rivals and targets such as Russia and Iran, as well as long-standing allies such as Western European countries wary. To top it all, the pandemic has witnessed the Federal Reserve crossing another line and lending not just to US and foreign financial institutions, but also to US non-financial corporations, undermining further its pretence of being the world's money and credit supplier.[30] Though the recent EU fiscal deal may not resurrect the euro as a rival to the dollar, it continues to subtract the Eurozone from the dollar payments system.

Other countries are seeking three types of ways out. First, Russia, the EU, and China are building alternative payments systems in the form of SPFS, INSTEX, and CIPS respectively. Second, other countries are choosing to trade in each other's currencies in order to avoid the rigged dollar system, while Sino-Russian monetary and financial cooperation is widening even further. Third, China, with its Asian Infrastructure Investment Bank and Belt and Road Initiative, increasingly constitutes an alternative source of finance.

Although, the dollar system has in the past defied anticipations of its demise, unless this analysis of its volatility is wrong, its maturing contradictions, multiplying conflicts, and the availability of alternatives mean that 2008 represented the peak of the cycle of dollar-denominated financialisations, and heralded its demise. The recovery of international capital flows thereafter remained 65 per cent short of their 2007 peak a decade later.[31] Moreover, the dollar's management by the Federal Reserve became captive of a contradiction. While the Federal Reserve needs to issue cheap liquidity into the financial system after each crisis, the sheer scale of liquidity issuance after 2008, dubbed 'quantitative easing', has put downward pressure on the dollar and the even greater liquidity issuance necessitated by the pandemic has put the dollar on a steep downward trajectory.[32]

## THE CHINESE FINANCIAL SYSTEM AND DEVELOPING WORLD ECONOMIC AND MONETARY SOVEREIGNTY

Internationally, Chinese finance outshines the dollar system. Against its short-term predatory and speculative capital, the Chinese system offers long-term patient capital for productive investment. Whereas Western capital comes with demands for free capital flows and liberalisation of banking (turning it away from productive investment and toward speculation), and even stricter conditionalities when the IMF or the World Bank became involved, Chinese finance comes without policy constraints. China's cooperative stance could not contrast more with that of the US system when we consider the wars launched by the US against countries seeking to exit the dollar system.

China's financial system has come a long and complex way in the last several decades. Well into the reform period, Western analysts considered it – essentially a banking system without asset markets – near to being insolvent. Today, however, China is home to three of the world's five biggest banks and enjoys a remarkably low rate of non-performing loans, and Western investors are lining up to invest in them.[33] As the reform of China's banking system picked up pace, so did Western interest. However, Western scholars on the Chinese financial system judge it 'according to the degree of implementation of free market policies'[34] complete with the full paraphernalia of elements associated with neoliberal financialisation: central bank independence (essentially regulatory capture of the regulators by the regulated), private ownership, stock markets, unrestricted foreign ownership, and greater 'financial inclusion' (of anyone who can profitably be indebted). They do not criticise the extensive damage done by the US-dominated financial system, nor do they discuss the critical importance of long-term 'patient finance' in China's spectacular industrialisation and development.[35]

Western discourse on China's financial system must also be placed amid the explosion of Western scholarly and journalistic writing on China's increasing centrality to the world economy in the twenty-first century and its twists and turns. Perhaps after the North Atlantic Financial Crisis of 2008, and certainly after Obama's 2012 'Pivot to Asia', it underwent a distinct change of tone. It had been ambiguous, if not enthusiastic, about China as long as the West and the US believed that enfolding China into their embrace was making it neoliberal and capitalist. This phase climaxed in talk of 'Chimerica', referring to the alleged trade and financial inter-dependence of the Chinese and US economies.[36]

However, the economic relationship proved one-sided as the US remained mired in stagnation after 2008, while China resumed robust growth after a nasty but short trade shock. Moreover, it soon became clear that China had its own ideas about its development path and neoliberalism was not among them. Nor did its party state intend to throw in the towel, as the Soviet leadership did[37]. Indeed, it was anxious to avoid that fate.[38] As this realisation sank in and the economic contrast between US debility and Chinese dynamism sharpened, President Obama announced his 'Pivot to Asia', and Western commentary on China turned distinctly hostile, culminating in President Trump's declaration of a 'New Cold War' against China, a policy from which the incoming Biden administration has found it difficult to deviate. Today, not only are sections of the capitalist class threatened by China's increasing technological prowess, the need to win the votes of large swathes of the working class hurt by the neoliberal policies of the past four decades has made China-baiting a regular feature of US political discourse. These are the parameters that shape Western and US discourses about China in general, and its financial system in particular.

For instance, Walter and Howie praise the reforms that culminated in China's entry into the WTO, and criticise limitations and reversals. The resulting financial system, they say, is still largely confined to banks with underdeveloped asset markets. It underserves 'China's heroic savers' who have to accept low interest rates. Since China's large banks typically focus on financing the state-owned and/or closely monitored corporations that remain at the commanding heights of China's economy, it leaves many smaller businesses without any reliable source of capital. Not only do Walter and Howie fault the party-state for protecting this system from competition or failure, particularly by keeping foreign banks confined to a marginal role, they complain further that:

> Beyond the pressures of competition, the Party treats its banks as basic utilities that provide unlimited capital to the cherished state-owned

> enterprises. With all aspects of banking under the Party's control, risk is thought to be manageable. Even so, at the end of each of the last three decades, these banks have faced virtual, if not actual, bankruptcy, surviving only because they have had the full, unstinting, and costly support of the Party.[39]

These 'virtual' bankruptcies have been resolved, Walter and Howie note, by the 'traditional problem-solving approach of simply shifting money from one pocket to another and letting time and fading memory do the rest'. This, they believe, cannot go on forever. They look forward to the moment when, '[t]ied up as it is in financial knots, the system's size, scale, and access to seemingly limitless capital can [no longer] solve the problems of the banks'. This would, they argue, provide the opening for further market reforms abandoned after 2005. Western financial institutions also generate similar criticisms: a chapter of a World Bank report on the Chinese economy, for instance, later redacted under Chinese government protest, 'gave warning that 'the poor performance of the financial system' had confirmed previous assessments that the system was 'unbalanced, repressed, costly to maintain and potentially unstable'.'[40]

Such writers ignore many rather obvious facts. Stock markets have rarely provided long-term patient capital. While high interest rates strangle industry, public services and investment should obviate ordinary people's need for savings. Providing small businesses with capital will likely require the expansion of China's financial system from its present basis downwards into the economy, not neoliberal reform. Above all, commentators blithely ignore the regularity with which Western countries have bailed out their banks, and done so in return for socially, economically and politically destructive asset bubbles, not patient productive investment.

To understand the Chinese system, we need to understand it historically and in relation to the very different role that the Chinese banking system has played in China's economy and its impressive expansion of recent years. China's banking system was long dominated by a single bank, the People's Bank of China. After the official adoption of a socialist market economy in the early 1990s, market reforms were gradually introduced to liberalise it.[41] However, contrary to Western views, liberalisation did not have neoliberal aims. To be sure, reformers have learned and borrowed a great deal from Western banking techniques and institutions as they introduced competition; reduced the inevitable moral hazard in a system ultimately protected by the state; allowed carefully calibrated private ownership, including some foreign ownership; and imposed prudential limits on lending and risk-taking.[42] However, reformers have proceeded with caution, bearing in mind the Chinese adage about 'crossing the river by feeling the stones'. Their borrowings have been governed by the party-state's aims, usually articulated as principles arising from an understanding of China's economic needs and history. Reform has sought to 'transform the banking system to a market-oriented one that is viable in the long run thereby better serving the economic development of the country',[43] that is, serving the needs of the productive economy rather than of a tiny financial elite.[44] Unlike the neoliberal financialised banking systems, China's banks have played a critical role in maintaining the remarkably high investment rate that has been so critical to China's economic success.[45]

The recent suspension of the Ant Group's initial public offering shows that this principle has not been suspended. The geopolitical rivalry between the US and China, which will put a greater premium on steady industrial growth, requires finance to be more like China's than the US's (with many even in the US speaking of the need for industrial policy and banking regulation). When the Ant Group tried to defy Beijing's tougher prudential requirements for consumer lending by going ahead with its IPO, it was forced to suspend its IPO abruptly. It was an instance of Beijing curtailing the political power of defiant capitalists as well as opposing any trend towards profit-driven expansion of consumer borrowing[46] that detracted from the productive focus of the financial system. Given its commitment to raising wages, the last thing China needs is ballooning consumer credit to replace low wages. As we have seen in the US and many other neoliberal countries, that has only indebted ordinary people, lowering their disposable incomes and bankrupting many. Regulators are also wary that financialisation may lower growth.

With this background, we are now ready to tackle the three major themes that dominate Western discussion of China's financial system.

## INTERNATIONALISATION OF THE RENMINBI

Like the Chinese financial system, the internationalisation of the renminbi is also found wanting against the benchmark of the unstable, predatory, and volatile dollar system.[47] The dominant claim here is that, since the renminbi is not being internationalised in the same way as the dollar – whether because the party state is unable or unwilling to do so – the dollar's position is secure. Benjamin Cohen, for instance, assuming that currency internationalisation is desirable in itself, finds that Beijing's internationalising ambitions are checked by episodes like the outflow of nearly a trillion dollars in 2015 that forced devaluation,[48] and by the fear that it will undermine the party's political hold. Thus, Cohen concludes that the dollar remains 'the *indispensable currency* – the one money the world cannot do without' thanks to the 'depth of US financial markets',[49] along with 'still broad network externalities in trade, a wide range of political ties, and vast military reach'. While Cohen is careful not to doubt China's ability to internationalise the renminbi, and even agrees that it has 'achieved tangible results, particularly along the trade track', he concludes that progress is doubtful. 'On its own the 'gravitational pull of China's economic size will not suffice. Other factors – above all, *a well-developed and open financial structure* – must also come into play' and China is unlikely to be willing to engage in the necessary financial liberalisation because it would entail 'a significant modification of Beijing's authoritarian economic model'.[50] The financial structure Cohen implies China needs is precisely the archaic, short-term, speculative, and predatory one sported by the US and the UK. Adopting it would bring an end to the spectacular growth China has experienced precisely because it is home to the contrasting financial system.

As we have seen, however, much of this is beside the point. The dollar has pushed the contradictions of national money posing as world money to its limits and the renminbi is unlikely to follow in its footsteps. US authorities had already overestimated the dollar's prospects when they blocked multilateral agreements of the sort Keynes proposed in 1944. Only such arrangements can create a stable and viable world money capable of serving the needs of productive economies in a multipolar world. Barring them, regional, bi- and multi-lateral agreements will be the realistic options. Interestingly, in the US, since at least the 2008 financial crisis, critical voices pointing to the costs the US itself has had to pay for its financialised dollar internationalisation are becoming louder.[51] Indeed, financial systems of the finance capital type have historically been reluctant to internationalise their currencies in the same manner[52] for good reason.

The reality is that the internationalisation of the renminbi is proceeding according to the domestic and international needs of China's productive economy and it is likely to proceed further along the same path. It is, however, radically different from that taken by sterling and the dollar in the past. Precisely for that reason, the path China takes to internationalising the renminbi will be attractive to Africa and the developing world. There is certainly no evidence that the China's party state is willing to tread the path of the dollar; the cost to its productive system would be too high.

China's financial system is designed for financing production with long-term credit, not speculation with short-term credit. It is not loaded in favour of creditors against debtors, lends very little for non-productive purposes, and facilitates national autonomy (its own and that of other countries) not international domination. While the US and Chinese states govern, and bail out, their respective financial systems, the priorities that each imposes on their financial system could not be further apart. China's party-state requires that its financial system serve the wider, productive, job-creating economy, not a set of private interests. Further, China manages and controls capital flows rather than permitting their free flow, especially to tax havens. This means that its financial system is not designed to siphon off productive incomes into the coffers of financial institutions and the high net worth individuals who own and control them.

These differences illuminate the real dynamics of China's monetary and financial relations with Africa. They also account in critical ways for China's economic success and contain critical lessons for African countries in their pursuit of broad-based prosperity, while developing the tremendous human potential of that continent to the fullest.

## CHINA'S PROPERTY BUBBLE

The same differences also ensure that, while Chinese asset and property prices are undoubtedly rising, it is unlikely, as many fear,[53] that China will suffer from the 'bursting' of a property bubble causing an economic crisis like that in the US after 2008 or in Japan after 1990. Walden

Bello fears not only this, but also decades of Japan or US-like economic stagnation. He warns that though workers complain of unaffordable housing, authorities are loath to end the bubble given that 'China's real-estate sector accounts for an estimated 15 per cent of gross domestic product (GDP) and 20 per cent of the national demand for loans'. Shutting down this economic engine is not done lightly.[54]

Surprisingly for a critical writer, Bello fingers financial repression as the culprit. According to him, low returns on savers' deposits lead them to speculate in assets, and the financial system's focus on large, state-owned and, critically for Bello, export-oriented enterprises leads investors into the property market and to the pervasive shadow banking system. Only 'a fundamental reform in the country's national credit system to end the virtual monopoly by the export-oriented economic complex of the banking system', which creates the 'strong demand for these *sub rosa* entities'[55] can resolve the problem. He blames the 'export lobby' for hijacking the post 2008 stimulus 'that had been intended to place money and resources in the hands of consumers' and for preventing further liberalisation which would end financial repression and orient the financial sector towards financing small investor and firms producing for the domestic market.[56]

However, there are at least three major problems with this diagnosis. First, in naturalising savers' search for high returns, it misses the opportunity to criticise the rising inequality and gaps in social provision that really lie behind those households engaging in property speculation, not to mention the key role of land sales in raising revenues for local authorities.[57] Second, in framing the export sector as the culprit, he ignores the extent to which, since 2008, the Chinese economy, never as reliant on export as was widely believed anyway, was reorienting towards domestic investment and consumption, a development that has culminated in the 'Dual Circulation' strategy, emphasising the increasing importance of the domestic market as a growth stimulant.[58] Finally, by blaming financial repression, this diagnosis appears to be implying that China's financial system should become more like the speculative Western one.

In any case, sober observers, even Western ones, reject Bello-style alarmism. While acknowledging that some Chinese banks, particularly regional ones, are in trouble thanks to their involvement in the real estate market, they caution against interpreting these troubles 'as indications of an imminent financial crisis'. Chinese authorities are approaching the problem through a pincer movement. They are putting pressure on banks to 'clean up their balance sheets, raise new capital, and dispose of bad loans' and lending 'to struggling companies at nonmarket rates to forestall a further slowdown in the pace of economic growth'. This indicates that 'PBOC and the CCP leadership remain committed to ensuring stability. Authorities have so far successfully contained isolated bank failures and prevented sector-wide contagion'.[59]

## 'DEBT TRAP DIPLOMACY'

So, if China is not about to endanger its productive economy and rising prosperity by internationalising the renminbi on the US model or liberalising its financial sector, is it preying upon the developing world with its alleged 'debt trap diplomacy'? How are we going to make sense of the war of words emanating from Western countries and institutions, such as the World Bank on China's lending to the Third World?

Despite a decade and more of scholarly work exploring the distinctive, and largely beneficial, Chinese pattern of trade and financial engagement with the developing world,[60] tendentious accusations about China being a 'rogue donor', 'freeriding on Western debt forgiveness' and engaged in 'debt trap diplomacy' continue to proliferate. It was recently given high-profile definition by an Indian defence expert, Brahma Chellany.[61]

The accusations are that China extends loans for infrastructure projects 'not to support the local economy but to facilitate access to natural resources or open the market for its low-cost and shoddy export goods', often not even creating local employment but sending 'its own construction workers' instead. These projects 'bleed money' and only add to the debt burden. China leverages it to get additional projects and loans with which to take over assets, as in the case of the Hambantota port in Sri Lanka, and to force countries to accept its questionable international positions and territorial claims. By locating the roots of the problem in developing countries' unmet infrastructure needs '[n]eglected by [Western] institutional investors', Chellany also appeals to Western financial institutions to not leave this breach for China to step into. He concludes by warning countries 'not yet ensnared in China's debt trap' to 'take whatever steps they can to avoid it.[62]

The reality is very different, as Deborah Brautigam's extensive work at the China Africa Research Initiative at Johns Hopkins University shows. While, as with all countries, China's aid and economic engagement are bound up with its foreign policy, its conception of aid, economic engagement and their purposes are radically different from those of the neoliberal West. They are based on China's long-standing principles of peaceful coexistence, including non-interference and respect for sovereignty. China has had a decades-long engagement, going back to its pre-reform days, with the Third World, Africa in particular, based on Third World solidarity.

Accusations that China is a rogue donor are beside the point since only a small part of Chinese financial flows to Africa is aid. Indeed, as Brautigam points out, it would hardly be fair for China, given its own modest per capita income levels, to give much aid. China's practices of international economic engagement are, moreover, often versions of the Western and Japanese trade and investment practices in China that the Chinese government found particularly beneficial and China has a record of long-term commitment to the success of its projects, including by training personnel.

China invests in infrastructure and manufacturing as well as in resources. While resource-related FDI stock amounted to 11.2 per cent of total Chinese outbound FDI in 2017, that for manufacturing, construction, the production and supply of electricity, gas, and water amounted to 12.3 per cent.[63] While at 24.8 per cent in 2019, mining FDI stock accounts for a greater proportion of Chinese FDI stock in Africa; manufacturing and construction together still loom large 43.2 per cent.[64] Finally, and perhaps most importantly, what developing countries, including African countries, appreciate is that Chinese aid and credit giving capacities are vast and they are exercised without conditionalities affecting their economic autonomy, unlike Western donors. Brautigam also emphasises that China does not claim to know what policies African countries should follow.

Specifically on the subject of debt trap diplomacy, in his recent survey of the literature on the subject, Ajit Singh makes a number of helpful clarifications.[65] The extent of Chinese loans to debt-distressed countries is overstated. They constitute a major share of the debt in just three of seventeen such countries. Since a great deal of Chinese credit is actually lent to the Chinese firms undertaking the investment,[66] the overwhelming majority of the debts owed by African governments are owed to the World Bank and non-Chinese private creditors. Not only are most Chinese loans not connected to resources, China does not lock in low resource prices or take repayment in physical resources or strategic assets.[67] Instead, it arranges repayments from sales at current spot prices. Finally, Singh clarifies that most of China's loans are extended at low or commercial rates, and China has a record of being willing to renegotiate loans in distress cases.[68]

## CONCLUSION

It should now be clear that China is not only a major source of external finance for Africa and the developing world more generally, it is a qualitatively different kind of source. Its historical evolution and place in the geopolitical economy of capitalism, where it has retained the characteristics of a productively superior contender socialist market economy with a financial sector that serves rather than strangulates production both at home and abroad, account for this difference.

We conclude with two caveats, one relating to China, the other to Africa. Since China embarked on its reforms, constituencies that have an interest in pushing China towards greater liberalisation, and possibly full-blown capitalism, have grown in size and power. They include China's sizeable capitalist class and large sections of the bureaucracy, many of whose more talented layers have imbibed the neoliberal and neoclassical economics taught in nearly all Chinese universities, and as foreign students abroad. So far, however, despite these pressures the Chinese party-state has kept up its commitment to the 'socialist' part of the label 'socialist market economy', a commitment that can only be strengthened by the dismal performance of Western economies, particularly the US economy, both in general and on the pandemic front. However, should the forces of neoliberalism gain the upper hand, both China and its international engagement could change quite radically for the worse.

However, short of that as yet unlikely eventuality, African countries can continue to benefit from their engagement with China. However, that benefit will be the greater the more they see China not only as a trade and investment partner, but also as a model.

As a partner, China affords developing countries greater policy latitude and places on partnering governments the responsibility of using it wisely to ensure that trade and investment relations work well and to mutual benefit. To exploit to the fullest the benign potential this has for the development of African countries, partnering with China requires them to consider China a model to critically adapt to Africa's needs and capacities. For instance, trade with China without proper planning and industrial policy could endanger fledging manufacturing in African countries. While hardly without faults, China is as close to a model of autonomous national development as it is possible to have today. It involves an intelligent combination of public and private initiative in planning national development rationally via appropriate policies for the major sectors, a productively oriented financial sector and management of external economic relations of trade and finance with a view to optimising the national economy rather than a slavish devotion to free markets and free trade. They only guarantee that rich countries remain rich and poor countries remain poor. It also involves a state that is committed, broadly speaking, to public welfare, rather than being committed to a tiny and unproductive financial elite as Western countries, particularly the most neoliberal ones such as the US and the UK, are. Learning from China how to refashion their economies and financial systems for production, employment and productivity growth requires that African states endeavour to acquire that broad and deep political legitimacy that gives China's party-state the political capacity that has permitted it to undertake the scale of the economic transformation it has since the revolution.

## NOTES

1 Word Bank, April 2021, COVID 19: Debt service suspension initiative. Available at: www.worldbank.org/en/topic/debt/brief/Covid-19-debt-service-suspension-initiative [Accessed March 25, 2021].

2 Adler, D. and Araus, A., March 2020, It's time to end the Fed's monetary triage. *The Nation*. Available at: www.thenation.com/article/economy/economy-fed-imf/ [Access date: March 25, 2021].

3 Patnaik, P., June 2020, The problem of external debt. *International Development Economics Associates*. Available at: www.networkideas.org/news-analysis/2020/06/the-problem-of-external-debt/ [Access date: March 25, 2021].

4 Wheatley, J. and Joseph Cotterill, J., October 2020, African debt to China. *Financial Times.*

5 Acker, K., Brautigam, D., and Huang, Y., 2020, Debt relief with Chinese characteristics, *SAIS-CARI Policy Brief.* Washington DC: China Africa Research Initiative; Nyabiage, J., August 2020, Coronavirus: China under pressure to detail debt relief before G20 talks. *South China Morning Post.* Available at: www.scmp.com/news/china/diplomacy/article/3098431/coronavirus-china-under-pressure-detail-debt-relief-g20-talks [Access date: March 25, 2021]; Olander, O., October 2020, When it comes to G20's DSSI, China's playing by a different set of rules. *The China Africa Project.* Available at: chinaafricaproject.com/analysis/when-it-comes-to-the-g20s-dssi-chinas-playing-by-a-different-set-of-rules/ [Access date: March 25, 2021].

6 Nyabiage, Coronavirus.

7 Toussaint, E., 2020, The World Bank saw the debt crisis looming. Committee for the Abolition of Illegitimate Debt (CADTM).

8 UNCTAD, 2020, *From the Great Lockdown to the Great Meltdown.* Geneva: United Nations Conference on Trade and Development, p. 3.

9 Jubilee Debt Campaign, October 2018, Africa's growing debt crisis: Who is the debt owed to? Available at: jubileedebt.org.uk/wp/wp-content/uploads/2018/10/Who-is-Africa-debt-owed-to_10.18.pdf; Arekzi, R. and Erce, A., 2020. How to reignite Africa's growth and avoid the need for future debt jubilee. Washington DC: Brookings Institution, December 8 [Access date: March 25, 2021].

10 Shivji, I., 2016, National autonomous development in Africa. In R. Reinert, J. Ghosh, and R. Kattell, eds 2018, *Handbook of Alternative Theories of Development.* Cheltenham: Edward Elgar Publishing, p. 241.

11 Leys, C. 1996, *The rise and fall of development theory.* London: James Currey, p. 108.

12 Ismi, A. 2004, *Impoverishing a continent: The World Bank and the IMF in Africa.* Halifax: The Halifax Initiative, p. 11. Available at: www.policyalternatives.ca/sites/default/files/uploads/publications/National_Office_Pubs/africa.pdf [Access date: March 25, 2021].

13 *Ibid.*, p. 12.

14 Brenner, R., 1998, The Economics of Global Turbulence. *New Left Review,* I/229 (May–June), pp. 1–265.

15 Desai, R., 2019, The Past and Future of the International Monetary System. ЭКОНОМИЧЕСКОЕ ВОЗРОЖДЕНИЕ РОССИИ 3 (Economic Revival of Russia) (61) 2019 периодическое научное Издание (Scientific Periodical), EKONOMICHESKOYe VOZROZHDENIYe ROSSII 3 (61) 2019 periodicheskoye nauchnoye Izdaniye, pp. 35–54. Available at: scholar.google.ru/scholar?hl=ru&as_sdt=0%2C5&q=radhika+desai+THE+PAST+AND+FUTURE+OF+THE+INTERNATIONAL+MONETARY+SYSTEM&btnG [Access date: March 25, 2021].

16 For more on uneven and combined development, see Desai, R., 2013, *Geopolitical economy: After US hegemony, globalization and empire*. London: Pluto Press.

17 Marx, K. 1894/1981. *Capital*, Volume III. London: Penguin, pp. 567–68.

18 Patnaik, U., 2006, The free lunch: Transfers from the tropical colonies and their role in capital formation in Britain during the Industrial Revolution. In K.S. Jomo, ed., *Globalization under Hegemony*. Delhi: Oxford University Press.

19 Desai, R. (2018), 'John Maynard Pangloss: *Indian currency and Finance* in Imperial Context'. In S. Dow, J. Jespersen, and G. Tily (eds), *The general theory and Keynes for the 21st century*, Cheltenham: Edward Elgar Publishing, pp. 116–31. Patnaik, U. and Prabhat, P., 2016. *A theory of imperialism*. New York: Columbia University Press.

20 *Ibid.*

21 Gamble, A., 1994. *Britain in Decline*. London: Macmillan.

22 Keynes, J.M., 1913. *Indian currency and finance*. London: Macmillan. Desai, John Maynard Pangloss.

23 De Cecco, M., 1984. *The international gold standard: Money and empire*, 2nd ed. London: Pinter.

24 Block, F., 1977. *The origins of international economic disorder: A study of United States international monetary policy from World War II to the present*. Berkeley, CA: University of California Press.

25 Calleo, D.P., 1982. *The imperious economy*. Cambridge, MA: Harvard University Press, p. 138.

26 Shaxon, N., 2011. *Treasure islands: Tax Havens and the men who stole the world*. London: Vintage.

27 F. Rohatyn provided a prescient early warning in World capital: The needs and the risks. *New York Review of Books*, 14 June 1994.

28 Borio, C. and Disyatat, P., 2011. Global imbalances and the financial crisis: Link or no Link. *Bank for International Settlements Working Paper*, No. 346, May 2011; Desai, *Geopolitical Economy*, pp. 249–51. Desai, The Past and Future.

29 Wolf, M., 2014. Holdouts give vultures a bad name. *Financial Times*, September 2. Available at: www.ft.com/content/bf3bd3f2-31ef-11e4-b929-00144feabdc0

30 Brenner, R., 2020. Escalating Plunder. *New Left Review*, II/123 (May–June), pp. 5–22 [Access date: March 25, 2021].

31 McKinsey Global Institute. 2017. The *new dynamics of financial globalization*. Washington DC.

32 Roach, S., 2020. The vise tightens on the dollar. *Project Syndicate*, September 25. Available at www.project-syndicate.org/commentary/saving-rate-and-current-account-imply-dollar-depreciation-by-stephen-s-roach-2020-09 [Access date: September 9, 2021]; Cohen, B., 2020. The pandemic is shaking the dollar's supremacy. *Project Syndicate*, May 18. Available at www.project-syndicate.org/commentary/covid19-trump-failures-shaking

-dollar-supremacy-by-benjamin-cohen-2020-05?barrier=accesspaylog [Accessed March 25, 2021].

33 Guy Williams, G., 2020. *The evolution of China's banking system, 1993–2017*. London: Routledge, pp. 1–2.

34 *Ibid.*

35 Byrd, W., 1983. *China's financial system*. London: Routledge, is an early example, while Amstad, M., Sun, G., and Xiong, W. eds., 2020. *The handbook of China's financial system*. Princeton, NJ: Princeton University Press, is a more recent one.

36 Ferguson, N. and Schularick, M., 2007. 'Chimerica' and the Global Asset Market Boom. *International Finance* 10 (3), pp. 215–39.

37 Kotz, D., 1997. *Revolution from above: The demise of the Soviet system*. London: Routledge.

38 Tsang, S. Consolidating political and governance strength. In Tsang, S. and Men H. eds, 2016. *China in the Xi Jingping Era*. Nottingham: School of Contemporary Chinese Studies, The Nottingham China Policy Institute Series. pp. 17–40

39 Walter, C. and Howie, F., 2012. *Red capitalism: The fragile financial foundations of China's extraordinary rise*. New York: Wiley, p. 27.

40 Donnan, S. and Wildau, G., 2015. World Bank denies China sought to have critical report censored. *Financial Times*, July 3. Available at: www.ft.com/content/5bc2d58c-21c2-11e5-aa5a-398b2169cf79

41 For the early history, see Jiang, C. and Yao, S., 2017. *Chinese banking reform: From the pre-WTO period to the financial crisis and beyond*. The Nottingham China Policy Institute Series. London: Palgrave Macmillan, pp. 15–20.

42 *Ibid.*, 35–8.

43 *Ibid.*, 55.

44 Williams, G. 2020, *The evolution of China's banking system, 1993–2017*. London: Routledge.

45 Ross, J., 2020. Why China maintained its strong economic growth. *LearningfromChina.net*. Available at: www.learningfromchina.net/why-china-maintained-its-strong-economic-growth/

46 Kynge, J. Sender, H., and Yu, S., 2020. 'The Party is pushing back': Why Beijing reined in Jack Ma and Ant. *Financial Times*, November 4. Available at: www.ft.com/content/3d2f174d-aa73-44fc-8c90-45c2a554e97b [Issued March 25, 2021].

47 Prasad, E.S. 2017, '*Currency* Power', *Gaining Currency: The Rise of the Renminbi*. Oxford: Oxford University Press. Guo K. et al., 2020. RMB Internationalization. In Marlene Amstad, Guofeng Sun and Wei Xiong, eds, *The handbook of China's financial system*. Princeton, NJ: Princeton University Press. (The above are typical works.)

48 McDowell, D., 2019. From tailwinds to headwinds: The troubled internationalization of the Renminbi. In K. Zeng, ed., *Handbook on the International Political Economy of China*. Cheltenham: Edward Elgar Publishing, p. 194.

49 Cohen, *Currency Power*, p. 6.

50 *Ibid.*, 236, emphasis added.

51 Bergsten, F. The dollar and the deficits: How Washington can prevent the next crisis. *Foreign Affairs* 88(6) (November/December 2009); Bergsten, F., 2011. Why the world needs three global currencies. *Financial Times*, February 15. Available at: www.ft.com/content/d4845702-3946-11e0-97ca-00144feabdco [Accessed March 25, 2021].

52 See, for instance, Henning, R.C., 1994. *Currencies and politics in the United States, Germany and Japan*. Washington DC: Institute for International Economics; Helleiner E. and Malkin, A., 2012. Sectoral interests and global money: Renminbi dollars and the domestic foundations of international currency policy. *Open Economic Review* 23, pp. 33–55. For a good overview, see Chey, H.-K. and Li, Y.W.V., 2020. Chinese domestic politics and the internationalization of the renminbi. *Political Science Quarterly* 135/I, pp. 37–65.

53 Glaeser, E., Huang, W., Ma, Y, and Shleifer, A., 2016. A Real Estate Boom with Chinese Characteristics. NBER Working Papers 22789, National Bureau of Economic Research; Song, Z. and Xiong, W., 2018. Risks in China's Financial System. *Annual Review of Financial Economics* 10, pp. 330–44.

54 Bello, W., 2019. *Paper Dragons: China and the Next Crash*. London: Zed Books, p. 4; Glaeser et al., make a similar point.

55 *Ibid.*, p. 6.

56 *Ibid.*, p. 180.

57 Liu, C. and Xiong., 2020. China's Real Estate Market. In Marlene Amstad, Guofeng Sun, and Wei Xiong, eds, *The Handbook of China's Financial System*. Princeton, NJ: Princeton University Press.

58 Tang, F., 2020. What is China's dual circulation strategy and why is it important. *South China Morning Post*, November 19. Available at: www.scmp.com/economy/china-economy/article/3110184/what-chinas-dual-circulation-economic-strategy-and-why-it [Accessed March 25, 2021].

59 Bisio, V., 2020. China's Banking Sector Risks and Implications for the United States. Staff Research Report. Washington DC: US-China Economic and Security Commission, p. 19. Available at: www.uscc.gov/research/chinas-banking-sector-risks-and-implications-united-states [Accessed March 25, 2021.

60 Brautigam, D., 2010. *The Dragon's Gift: The Real Story of China in Africa*. Oxford: Oxford University Press, is the best known on Africa.

61 Chellany, B., 2017. China's Debt-Trap Diplomacy. *Project Syndicate*, January 23, Available at: www.project-syndicate.org/commentary/china-one-belt-one-road-loans-debtby-brahma-chellaney-2017-01 [Accessed March 25, 2021].

62 *Ibid.*

63 Wang, B. and Gao, K., 2019. Forty Years' of China's Outward Foreign Direct Investment: Retrospect and Challenges Ahead. *China and the World Economy*, 27(3), p. 8.

64 China-Africa Research Initiative, China-Africa Foreign Direct Investment Date. Available at: www.sais-cari.org/chinese-investment-in-africa [Accessed March 25, 2021].

65 Singh, A., 2020. The myth of 'debt-trap diplomacy' and realities of Chinese development finance. *Third World Quarterly* 42(2): pp. 1-15

66 Brautigam, *Dragon's Gift*, p. 142.

67 On this see also, Brautigam, D. and Kidane, W., 2020. China, Africa and Debt distress: Fact and fiction about asset seizures. *CARI Policy Brief*, no. 47.

68 This point is also elaborated by Acker, Brautigam and Huang in 'Debt relief with Chinese characteristics' and C. P. Chandrashekhar's, 'Branding debt as a Chinese weapon', *Frontline*, 14 September 2020.

# PART II
# Challenges to monetary sovereignty in the postcolonial periphery

# 2
# Banking, Business, and Sovereignty in Sudan (1956–2019)

*Harry Cross*

## INTRODUCTION

This chapter examines the history of banking and finance in Sudan from independence in 1956 until the aftermath of the Sudanese revolution of 2019. Discussions of monetary sovereignty rightly consider the monetary powers of sovereign states. However, most monetary creation in contemporary capitalist economies is carried out not by states, but by the loan-issuing activities of commercial banks.[1] Furthermore, banks play a crucial role in the routine operation of the payment systems, flows of funds and 'market' mechanisms that shape and constrain the sovereign monetary power of states.

This chapter provides an historical analysis of banking in one African country, Sudan, to explore the successive ways in which banks have negotiated strategic positions at the intersection between national economies, regulatory regimes and international flows of funds and capital. The chapter highlights many instances of collusion between private finance and political authorities. However, it will also be argued that it is the *routine* business activities of banks and the payments system that produce the possibilities and constraints faced by states within the international capitalist economy. Whereas other contributions to this volume emphasise the possibilities open to postcolonial states through their sovereign powers of local monetary creation, I argue that these powers are systematically disciplined to crises and imbalances produced by an international capitalist economy in which these states are 'rule takers' rather than 'rule makers'. This presents the political choice instead as one of collective action by postcolonial states to challenge the institutional architecture of the international capitalist economy, or else a strategy of 'delinking' or revolutionary exit from this economy.

This chapter begins by analysing the history of banking in Sudan. It then discusses the state's consecutive policy choices with a view to monetary and economic sovereignty. It concludes by considering Sudan at a crossroads after the fall of its long-standing military government in 2019.

## IMPERIAL AND POST-IMPERIAL BANKING IN SUDAN

Sudan was ruled from 1899 until 1955 as an Anglo-Egyptian condominium, nominally administered by both Egypt and the United Kingdom. In practice, Egypt was sidelined in most aspects of Sudan's internal administration, and Sudan resembled a British colony. The creation of the condominium was followed shortly by the arrival of European-owned banks in Sudan, beginning with the National Bank of Egypt (NBE) in 1901.[2] These banks provided a financial infrastructure with which to measure, circulate, and accumulate wealth in Sudan as part of a larger capitalist economy.

European colonisation did not, of course, introduce money or markets to Africa (though these were much less important in East Africa in the nineteenth century compared with West Africa) and European merchants frequently used, imported, manufactured, and counterfeited African forms of currency. However, these local embodiments of value 'were not convertible, could not be banked, and were not applicable to the acquisition of European assets'.[3] (Or, rather, assets in the international capitalist economy). Toby Green has argued that the rejection by European merchants, colonial administrations, and financial payment systems of monies and currencies historically used on the African continent, led to the devaluation of African wealth within global capitalism.[4] The activities of banks within national and international payments systems are crucial in enforcing what constitutes value within capitalist economies – ultimately, ledger entries issued by finance capital itself – and the rules by which value operates. Much of this chapter is about how national and international bank ledgers have interacted.

When Sudan became independent in 1956, all of the banks operating in the country were local branches of foreign institutions that were managed from offices in London, Paris, or Cairo. The largest bank in Sudan was the British-owned Barclays Dominions, Colonial and Overseas (DCO). The lending policies of European multinational banks became the object of anti-colonial critiques, both in academia and Sudanese political discourse after independence, which charged these banks with overwhelmingly focusing on short-term finance for fellow multinationals engaged in external trade, especially the extractive export of primary products, while simultaneously neglecting the small-scale and long-term financing needs of local business and industry.[5] These charges had a significant grounding in fact, though some qualification is required. Following Sudan's accession to independence, the Sudanese who could access bank branches (which were rare in rural areas, but well-established in most urban settlements) had no difficulty in opening deposit accounts. Furthermore, foreign banks did lend to (wealthy) Sudanese and issued (some) long-term local finance, and lending to Sudanese increased markedly after independence.[6] In other periods of colonial and postcolonial history, multinational banks participated in explicitly racist endeavours to exclude local populations from sectors of the economy. However, in Sudan in the 1950s and 1960s, this was not the case. Although European banks remained conservative in their lending ratios relative to deposits, and favoured the business of multinational corporations over small-scale local businesses, this followed an internally coherent market logic that sought to protect banks from an excess of local liabilities (customers' bank balances arising from bank loans) relative to liquid assets (notably cash reserves).

Other banks in this period, such as the Egyptian Banque Misr which operated branches in Sudan, and the Agricultural and Industrial Banks created by the Sudanese state, deliberately engaged in small-scale, long-term, and under-collateralised lending that foreign commercial banks had traditionally neglected. These endeavours successfully fostered new forms of business and social organisation. However, in moments of crisis (such as a collapse in cotton prices in 1958 and the withdrawal of US aid to Sudan in 1967), these banks suffered greater pressure on their liquid resources than the financially conservative European banks. The ultimate limit to banks pursuing redistributive lending policies lay not with the imperial chauvinism of these multinational institutions, but with the disciplining effects of the routine 'market' mechanisms of national and international capitalism.

## NATIONALISATION AND AFTER

In 1969, a coup by junior army officers brought to power a reforming government in Sudan, led by Colonel Jaafar Nimeiri and ministers who were socialists, Arab nationalists and members of Sudan's powerful Communist party. The following year, the government implemented its most radical policy, namely a sweeping programme of nationalisations (which offered compensation to company owners), and sequestrations and confiscations (which did not). All private banks were nationalised in 1970, including the country's foreign banks and the Sudan Commercial Bank, which had been established by a consortium of local investors in 1959.[7] Compensation to shareholders of local nationalised companies was a relatively straightforward affair. Sudanese residents were subject to the legal sovereignty of the Sudanese state, which could determine the method of calculating compensation, or even deny it (as occurred with sequestered and confiscated companies, whose owners were accused of criminal activities such as economic sabotage and currency smuggling). Furthermore, local shareholders could be compensated in Sudanese currency and government bonds, of which the Sudanese government was the sovereign issuer.

In contrast, the nationalisation of assets belonging to foreign investors raised the question of compensation in foreign currencies. Financial obligations in foreign currencies compromise monetary sovereignty as states face an external constraint in their supply of such currencies.[8] Bank nationalisation triggered protracted negotiations between the Sudanese government and foreign investors over the valuation and compensation for the latter's nationalised local businesses. This section focuses on the largest national group of investors, those from Sudan's former imperial power, Great Britain.[9]

In the early 1970s, international law governing transnational investments and mutual rights following nationalisation was little developed, reflecting the fact that many of these investments had initially been made within imperial legal jurisdictions. Decolonisation caused these imperial jurisdictions to splinter so that the laws governing an investment could no longer be decided solely in the former metropoles, and nationalisations by newly-independent states were becoming a common occurrence. A debate existed in legal scholarship regarding the rights of transnational investors subject to nationalisation, with positions ranging from support for the 'prompt, adequate, and effective' compensation payments (see below), to a position contending a 'community of fortunes', according to which foreign investors were said to have merged their fortunes with residents of a jurisdiction upon investing, making their investments subject to the sovereign legal authority of host jurisdictions without external legal recourse.[10]

The Sudanese government did not question companies' rights to compensation and offered payment in 15-year Sudanese government bonds based on net asset values. Meanwhile, British corporations did not contest Sudan's sovereign right to nationalise. However, they made little reference to the nuanced debates in international law regarding the rights of nationalised investors and, unsurprisingly, insisted that 'prompt, adequate, and effective' compensation was their unassailable legal right. The provenance of this phrase was a demand made by the US Secretary of State, Cordell Hull, to the government of Mexico in 1938 following the nationalisation of US-owned oil firms in the country. Subsequently, multinational investors and creditors in capital-exporting countries attempted to uphold this language as a precedent in international law.[11] British investors in Sudan interpreted this as a requirement for compensation in the form of a (prompt) down payment that included compensation for goodwill[12] as well as (adequate) net assets, and be paid in sterling rather than Sudanese currency or securities.[13] Accordingly, negotiations between the Sudanese government and British investors were not merely a debate over the nominal level of valuation, but also, and primarily, over which political, legal, and accounting principles should apply.

The public position of the British companies was that 'the basic principle should be that what one is trying to find is the sum of money that would be paid for the assets in question by a willing buyer to a willing seller in the open market'.[14] This was a somewhat remarkable expectation, that an anti-colonial government engaged in nationalisation and a corporate purchaser in an 'open' market might be expected to pay the same price. Other company directors conceded privately that their initial claims would undergo a significant markdown.[15] This was a reflection of Sudan's objective shortage of foreign exchange with which to compensate foreign firms at the levels they demanded, a position of apparent weakness that, in fact, served to temper the demands made by British firms in negotiations.

This reveals how insolvency and the threat of default subverts the typical power relationship between debtors and creditors. Precedents existed in Russia in 1917, China in 1949, and Cuba in 1959 for governments to simply refuse compensation for foreign investors following nationalisation, based on a revolutionary rejection of the financial commitments of previous regimes that returned the problem of recovering investments squarely to foreign company owners. Such measures also invited hostile commercial, financial, and military responses that these revolutionary governments were prepared to accept as the price of implementing their political programmes. In Sudan, the UK Foreign Office noted internally that aid from the Soviet Union after 1969 made it difficult for Western nations to use economic sanctions to pressure the government towards generous compensation settlements, as Sudan now had access to an alternative means of external supply.[16]

However, the more radical options of partial or total refusal to pay were not contemplated by Nimeiri's governments. For Nimeiri, nationalisation was not a revolutionary challenge to the capitalist organisation of Sudanese society but, rather, a nationalist and technocratic society that sought to wrest public control over the sources of local financing and exchange activities that were eroding Sudan's external balance of payments. The latter included remittance of profits in foreign currency by multinational banks and their alleged facilitation of exchange control violations for their customers. As a contemporary journalist observed, 'Behind the ideological screen raised by the authors of the [1969] coup lies the hand of the nationalist technocrats'.[17] From late 1969, Nimeiri had begun sidelining and repressing his erstwhile communist allies, who supported building economic alternatives to capitalism in Sudan. This culminated in the bloody liquidation of communist cadres and sympathisers by Nimeiri in July 1971.[18]

Political counter-revolution was accompanied by Sudan's capitulation in negotiations with foreign representatives of nationalised firms. After nationalisation, Sudan lost its creditworthiness in international markets, which viewed the outstanding demands for compensation by foreign companies as unsettled creditor claims on the Sudanese state. This prompted the withdrawal of commercial credit and official capital aid. Although Sudan had the option of exiting these systems and deepening its commercial relationship with the Soviet Union in a model of 'socialist globalisation', this was not the desire of Nimeiri's purged government.[19] To regain international creditworthiness, Sudan was obliged to concede to compensation payments largely on terms demanded by the firms in question, regardless of how spuriously they invoked accounting and legal principles to justify their claims. This occurred in June 1973.

The 1970s were a period of transition in Sudan, and the international political economy. Financial liberalisation and US dollar dominance eroded the international importance of sterling and the imperial organisation of the global monetary system.[20] Meanwhile, the OPEC oil price shocks directed substantial revenue flows ('petrodollars') into the postcolonial world. Many petrodollars accumulated by Arab Gulf states were recycled through intra-regional investment, including in Sudan through utopian projects to develop agricultural schemes that would make the Arab World nutritionally self-sufficient.[21] After 1970, commercial banking in Sudan was carried out by the nationalised successors of the foreign banks that had operated before that date. These banks pursued progressive policies, such as increasing long-term financing and expanding branch networks into unbanked areas in the far West and South of the country. These banks could pursue liberal credit policies in local currency as they were backed by the liquidity of the Sudanese state, though access to foreign exchange for external transactions presented a more significant challenge.

With the socialist aspirations of Nimeiri's government decidedly checked in the early 1970s, Sudan implemented an 'open door' policy to foreign investment. This attracted investment in Sudan from the United States, Western Europe, Japan, and the Middle East, reflecting the increasingly globalised financial flows of the period. Foreign banks returned to Sudan in the form of the Abu Dhabi National Bank, the Bank of Credit and Commerce International (both in 1976), and Citibank (1978).[22] These banks all operated out of single branches in the national capital, Khartoum, and extended corporate banking services, such as foreign exchange provision to foreign investors and wealthy domestic clients. However, a different form of bank would soon seek out the branch banking requirements of the Sudanese populace.

## THE ISLAMIC BANKING REVOLUTION

Islamic banking in Sudan has received more attention from historians and political scientists, which they have compared with other financial institutions in the country's history.[23] This is because the links between finance and organised politics have been much more explicit within Sudan's Islamic banks than under previous organisations of banking and finance in that country.

Islamic banking advances a moral and practical alternative to Western finance, founded on the Islamic prohibition of usury. In contrast to loans-at-interest, Islamic financing is carried out through profit shares, forward purchases, and other innovative arrangements between banks and their customers. It is commonly debated whether Islamic banks merely provide a different accounting presentation for loans-at-interest, but, in principle, Islamic financing precludes the possibility of compounding debts that exceed customers' eventual means of repayment, and resulting insolvency and financial ruin.[24]

The first Islamic bank to open in Sudan was the Faisal Islamic Bank of Sudan (FIBS) in 1978. FIBS was part of the group of banks owned by Prince Muhammad bin Faisal of Saudi Arabia, which were financed in no small part by the petrodollar earnings of that Kingdom.[25] Unlike the other foreign-owned banks that had opened in Sudan in the 1970s, FIBS pursued a strategy of provincial branch expansion that sought provincial clients and depositors. FIBS was soon joined by other Islamic banks pursuing similar strategies, such as the Tadamon Islamic Bank and the Al-Baraka Investment and Development Company, with its shareholdings divided between Sudan and the Arabian Gulf.

One scholar has explained the success of these banks by 'the extent to which an appeal to Islamic principles in banking can result in the accumulation of enormous financial reserves'.[26] This is no doubt part of the explanation. However, the dizzying success of these banks in raising deposits – FIBS secured over £S.10 million ($20 million) within four hours of opening in Khartoum[27] – suggests that they could promise superior facilities and international connections compared with their state-owned competitors. Significantly, the Islamic banks' Gulf connections gave them access to foreign exchanges that the state-owned commercial banks lacked.[28]

Islamic banks became active political operators in Sudan in support of the Sudanese chapter of the Muslim Brotherhood. Islamic banks employed members of this party among their staff, and one interviewee told me that the banks' computer systems were used for party membership lists and other party activities.[29] Furthermore, preferential access to bank credit was a means of rewarding and recruiting party members. Other religious and political bodies in Sudan soon established rival Islamic banks to counter the growing influence of the Muslim Brotherhood, such as the Sudanese Islamic Bank founded by the Khatmiyya Islamic order in 1982, which was associated in Sudanese politics with the Democratic Unionist Party.[30]

In the early 1980s, Nimeiri's government was facing severe local and external imbalances and was increasingly dependent on the support of local Islamic banks, and Sudan's Islamist movement was able to leverage this influence for political ends. In 1983, Nimeiri implemented Sudan's 'September laws', which were a substantial Islamisation of the country's legal system, thereby igniting a civil war in Sudan's non-Muslim south.[31] These laws remained in place after the fall of Nimeiri during a brief restoration of parliamentary rule in Sudan from 1986 to 1989.

In 1989, a new military coup brought the Muslim Brotherhood to power, which refounded itself as the National Congress Party (NCP). The NCP ruled Sudan for the following 30 years under the presidency of Umar al-Bashir. The NCP learned from the failure of Sudan's previous military governments and sought to break the economic power of the country's existing political, religious, and business elite (categories which overlapped).[32] Simultaneously, the NCP sought to remake Sudanese society based on Islamic principles. This included presiding over a small-business revolution in Sudan that allegedly saw as many companies registered between 1989 and 1994, as in the entire period between 1925 and 1989.[33] This institutionalised the long-standing political, social, and business strategies of the Islamic banks, with which the NCP in government remained in close alliance.[34]

## SANCTIONS AND A SIEGE ECONOMY

In 1997, the United States organised a system of stringent economic sanctions against Sudan due to the NCP government's alleged support for Islamist political violence outside of its borders. Because US-registered technology is used to operate international payments, Sudan was frozen out of international finance. This imposed great material suffering on the

Sudanese people but, like sanctions elsewhere, the measures also provided an exogenously imposed protectionist boost to local businesses, thereby reinforcing the social and economic base of the government in power.[35]

In the long run, Sudan's state of siege had its desired effect of eroding living standards and placing external pressure on the government's policies. Starved of external resources, the ideological fervour of the NCP's foreign policy of the 1990s had long vanished by the 2000s. Despite its early independence in foreign policy, al-Bashir's government had always been a faithful student of the orthodoxies of the IMF and World Bank recommendations and conditionalities. After 1997, this adherence was continued in the sustained hope of readmission to international systems of trade and finance.[36] Notwithstanding the dissipation of the original causes of sanctions against Sudan, it suited Western states to maintain them as a status quo so that the country's external reserves remained on drip feed. This ensured the besieged government's ready compliance to any external actor willing to extend short-term liquidity to the country. By the 2010s, al-Bashir's foreign policy had become entirely pragmatic, with examples of its purchased cooperation, including Sudan's role in the policing of migrant corridors in Africa in coordination with the European Union; its sale and lease of land by the Red Sea to Turkey as part of that country's investment in strategic regional arteries; its support for Ethiopia against Egypt for a dam on the Blue Nile that would capture scarce water resources in the upper Nile valley; and, most tragically, Sudan's deployment of ground troops for Saudi Arabia's war in Yemen.[37]

Academic and popular commentary, including within Sudan, frequently point to NCP corruption and mismanagement in explanation of the country's economic travails. This no doubt has a basis in fact, but these simplistic and frequently caricaturised accounts fail to account for the enormous staying power of Sudan's Islamist government across three decades. The NCP succeeded in cultivating a constituency of small- and medium-sized businesses financed by Islamic banks. Simultaneously, the declining external value of the Sudanese currency, due to shortages of foreign reserves, boosted the local revenues of exporters of primary goods (notably cotton, livestock, and crude oil). In short, the NCP was built on an alliance with those who lived from local revenues rather than foreign currency receipts, in contrast with the political economies of economically liberal export-oriented African countries.

So far, this chapter has described what appear to be successive discrete periods, but it should be noted in closing that there are important continuities in the history of banking in Sudan, including, most notably, local banking staff. Sudanese employed in junior positions in foreign banks and the government civil service in the 1950s and 1960s went on to hold senior managerial positions in subsequent decades, despite there being a transformed financial sector. By placing their technical financial training at the service of different projects, they both navigated and created successive phases of Sudan's political economy.

## FINANCIAL SYSTEMS AND MONETARY SOVEREIGNTY

Wealth and value in capitalism is measured, stored, and enforced through the symbols and accounting entries issued by the financial sector. In the period of capitalism's global and imperial expansion, finance capital was centred on Western Europe, while in the twentieth century its centre of gravity shifted to the United States.[38] By excluding non-capitalist measures of value from their payment systems, banks devalued accumulated African wealth in the global capitalist economy.[39] In the twenty-first century, it is the capitalist system of value that receives spontaneous or enforced adherence across the globe. States that issue currencies used for international trade – a privilege whose geographic distribution has clearly been decided by the history of empires – have significant means to pursue a sovereign monetary policy. Those that do not have the means have to challenge the rules of the game governing the global distribution of wealth, terms of credit, and accepted forms of payment under capitalism.

European imperialism incorporated colonial territories into relationships of free trade and free financial flows with metropolitan economies, and often with the global economy more widely. Postcolonial states that retained economic openness towards the rest of the world after independence must take measures to avoid their residents' balances in local currency being converted into external reserves – through remittances and imports – beyond the finite limits of these reserves. These measures include demand reduction in countries that are impoverished by global standards, and through budgetary austerity and conservative credit policies, combined with export-oriented support for external reserves. In the absence of local industries, this often implies the intensification of extractive exports of primary commodities. In other words, these are policies that extend those of colonial administrations and imperial banks which themselves typically operated in open economies with institutionalised scarce money constraints. This policy option was pursued by Sudanese governments in the 1950s and early 1960s.

In response to the dependence on primary commodity exports, late colonial states in Africa initiated a turn to 'developmentalism', which was continued after independence.[40] This advocated building countries' productive and export capacities through local capital investments. This utopian ideal of economic independence had the immediate effect of increasing countries' dependence on external finance, which contributed to balance of payments crises in Sudan from the 1960s, and a public debt crisis across the postcolonial world in the 1980s. People advocating the progressive potential of sovereign monetary creation on the African continent, who include as precondition judicious capital investments to build economic capacity, should be cautious not to admit by the backdoor the failed technocratic developmentalism of the twentieth century.

If local money supplies expand through bank lending or expansionary public budgets, either following or stimulating local business activity, then this creates an excess of domestic balances relative to external reserves. Success in growing local business activity consequently becomes self-defeating as growing demand from local balances for the purchase of external reserves results in chronic external deficits. This either prompts the deflationary policies described above, or else trends asymptotically towards external insolvency, currency crisis, and the intervention of external creditors in a situation of highly unequal negotiation positions.[41] This latter scenario can be said to have characterised Sudan in the late 1970s and 1980s.

Conversely, it is possible to limit openness towards the international economy, either through the (post)Keynesian policy of capital controls, or Samir Amin's more radical policy of 'delinking' from global capitalism and building autonomous bases for production and exchange in the postcolonial world.[42] The former route was taken in Sudan in the late 1960s under the auspices of al-Sharif Hussain al-Hindi as Minister of Finance, whose policies I examine at greater length in my doctoral research. Such policies transform a crisis in external reserves into one of domestic inflation and public enforcement of exchange controls.

Delinking from global capitalism was briefly contemplated by the more radical elements of Nimeiri's political coalition following Sudan's programme of nationalisations in 1970. 'Socialist globalisation' in the form of economic cooperation between socialist states and postcolonial governments provided an alternative to global capitalism in the second half of the twentieth century.[43] Within such a system, domestic money supply and external trade could be organised through non-market mechanisms such as payment agreements. Naturally, it was difficult to pursue such a policy by degrees, and it required a popular and political commitment to building a different form of society. In Sudan, this political commitment was lacking.

Each of the scenarios described, other than the radical options of delinking or socialist globalisation, bestows vast strategic influence on external creditors. The argument that external finance can be an effective and socially neutral arbitrator of these imbalances has been debunked by historical experience, as is demonstrated throughout this volume.

## CONCLUSION: SUDAN AT A CROSSROADS

From the 1990s, Sudan has undergone a forced 'delinking' from much of the international economy. US sanctions were nominally lifted in 2017, but Sudan's status as a designated state sponsor of terrorism by the US State Department meant that few external actors sought to do business with Sudan. In the last twenty years, Sudan's economy had entirely adapted to a state of siege, meaning that little changed on the ground and the country remained under a system of 'sanctions by default'. In 2017, the withdrawal of government wheat subsidies (under IMF recommendations)[44] was the proximate cause of street protests in Sudan, which soon gave way to a popular uprising against declining living conditions and political repression, calling for the departure of the NCP and the army from government. In April 2019, army officers responded to pressure from the streets by arresting and deposing President al-Bashir. At the time of writing, Sudan is ruled by a Transitional Military Council (TMC), containing both military and civilian ministerial appointments, and elections are scheduled for 2022.

Sudan's popular revolution will have succeeded if it puts an end to the violent repression that characterised al-Bashir's rule. Restoring political and monetary sovereignty will be more challenging. The NCP's alienation from the West caused many participants in Sudan's 2019 revolution to view Europe and the United States as natural allies in their uprising. However, with al-Bashir duly toppled, it appears that Sudan's readmission to international systems of trade and credit will only come at a punitive price. During a three-year transition to scheduled elections, Western states and creditors have already exacted from the TMC the continued implementation of IMF diktats, notably withdrawing fuel subsidies,[45] the resurrection of junk bonds defaulted on by Sudan in the 1990s and earlier,[46] a privatisation programme of state assets,[47] and 'compensation' payments for US victims of Islamic terrorism in the 1990s – without parallel compensation for Sudanese civilian victims of separate aerial strikes by the United States and Israel in the intervening period.[48] While the abdication of a sovereign economic and foreign policy is proving to be the preimposed condition of Sudan's reintegration into international trade and finance, the alternative is for Sudan's public finances to remain on a drip feed of liquidity under a state of siege, leaving any Sudanese government open to influence by any interest willing to supply short-term infusions of external liquidity.

If a radical third course exists, it is to be found in the fact that Sudan has undergone a forced delinking from an international economy that stacks legal, economic, and coercive powers behind the interests of creditors, perhaps more so than ever before. A state of siege has forced much of production, consumption, and financial circulation in Sudan to be organised nationally. Sudan could use this to adopt a more sovereign economic model, seek partners for payment agreements and alternative trading networks, and pursue a vision of social progress beyond one of capitalist growth. This would not come with the guarantee of immediate and rapid increases in material wealth. However, this may not be attainable by chasing reintegration into external capitalist markets at any price. If external investment is restored, then economic success should not be measured by the arrival of Western retail outlets in Khartoum while the material and social emancipation of the Sudanese people remains a more elusive object. The route is difficult, in all circumstances.

## NOTES

1 John Maynard Keynes, *A Treatise on Money* (1930).
2 Abd al-Hameed Muhammad Jameel, Abd al-Moneim Muhammad al-Tayyeb, and Abd al-Basit Muhammad al-ustafa, 2008. *Al-qata'a al-mustafi fii al-sudan*. Khartoum: Union of Sudanese Banks, p. 22.

3 Guyer, J., 1995. Introduction. In J. Guyer. ed. *Money matters: Instability, value and social payments in the modern history of West African currencies.* London: James Currey, p. 8.

4 Green, T., 2020. *A fistful of shells: West Africa from the rise of the slave trade to the age of revolution.* London: Penguin.

5 Odle, M., 1981. *Multinational banks and underdevelopment.* Oxford: Pergamon Press. Newspapers and political parties in Sudan were known to criticise foreign banks as imperialist agents, even if this was rarely matched by a political programme to respond to this diagnosis.

6 This section is based on the author's thesis project on the history of banking in Sudan between independence and nationalisation in 1970. This research is based primarily on the archives of Barclays DCO, held by Barclays Bank in Manchester, UK; Credit Lyonnais, held by Credit Agricole in Montrouge, France; and the National Records Office in Khartoum, Sudan.

7 Suleiman, A.M., 2016. *Al-tameem wa al-musadrah.* Khartoum: Abdel-Karim Mirghani Cultural Centre.

8 These include the terms of financing in this currency by financial institutions, as well as the global supply of this currency supplied by its issuing authority and available to the debtor state in trade receipts.

9 The UK Foreign & Commonwealth Office (FCO) helped to coordinate British investors' negotiations with the Sudanese government following nationalisation. Primary sources cited in this section are from FCO files 39/700 to 706; 39/917 to 924; and 39/1165 to 1168; all held in the National Archives, Kew, UK.

10 Francioni, F., 1975. Compensation for nationalisation of foreign property: the borderland between law and equity. *The International and Comparative Law Quarterly* 24(2), pp. 255–83.

11 *Ibid.*, pp. 263–4.

12 Goodwill is an accounting concept that represents payment for foregone future profits.

13 British Embassy, Khartoum, Note verbale to Sudanese government (28 May 1970). FCO 39/700.

14 J.K. Dick, Chairman, Mitchell Cotts (trading company). Letter to the Confederation of British Industry (7 July 1970). FCO 39/703.

15 Emblematic was National and Grindlays Bank, which informed the FCO that its compensation claim included 'ten years' profits before tax'. However, 'Ten years' profits may, in practice, be an unrealistically high amount to claim in these particular circumstances and we would naturally be prepared to envisage a somewhat more modest figure. For your private information we might well come down to eight years' profits and, possibly, even slightly less. (29 May 1970). FCO 39/701.

16 'The big difference between Uganda and the Sudan is that Uganda is still dependent on Western aid, and private investment and the threat of

sanctions are taken seriously. The Sudan has almost entirely switched to Soviet bloc aid'. Annotation on archived extract of 'Request for state action on Uganda'. *The Times (business supplement)* (26 July 1970). FCO 39/704.

17 Eric Rouleau, *Le Monde* (5 September 1969). Cited in Alain Gresh, 1989.The Free Officers and the comrades: the Sudanese Communist Party and Nimeiri face-to-face, 1969–1971. *International Journal of Middle East Studies* 21(3), p. 404.

18 *Ibid.*

19 James Mark, J., Artemy M. Kalinovsky, and Steffi Marung, S., eds., 2020. *Alternative globalizations: Eastern Europe and the postcolonial world.* Bloomington, IN: Indiana University Press.

20 Sudan left the sterling area in 1947, but it invoiced trade, pegged its exchange rate, and invested most of its reserves in this currency until 1967.

21 Jay O'Brien, J., 1981. Sudan: An Arab breadbasket? *MERIP Reports* 99, pp. 20–6.

22 Jameel (et al.), *al-qata'a al-musrafi*, p. 84.

23 Stiansen, E., 2004. Interest politics: Islamic finance in the Sudan, 1977–2001. In Clement M. Henry and Rodney Wilson, Rodney, eds, *The politics of Islamic finance.* Edinburgh: Edinburgh University Press, pp. 155–67. Edward Thomas, E., 2017. Patterns of growth and inequality in Sudan, 1977–2017. Working Paper. Institute for Middle East and Islamic Studies, Durham University, p. 26. Available at: www.dur.ac.uk/resources/sgia/imeis/lucefund/Luce-Fellowship-Paper-2017_Sudan-Thomas.pdf

24 Tripp, C., 2010. *Islam and the moral economy: the challenge of capitalism.* Cambridge: Cambridge University Press, pp. 103–49.

25 Shaaeldin, E. and Brown, R., 1985. Towards an understanding of Islamic banking in Sudan: the case of Faisal Islamic Bank. *Development Studies and Research Centre Monograph Series.* Khartoum: Khartoum University Press.

26 O'Neill, N., 1983. Recent trends in foreign investment and uneven development in Sudan. *Review of African Political Economy* 10(26), p. 61.

27 *Ibid.*

28 Abbashar Jamal, A., 1991. Funding fundamentalism: the political economy of an Islamist state. *Middle East Report* 172, pp. 14–17.

29 Interview conducted in Omdurman, Sudan (24 February 2018).

30 Stiansen, 'Interest politics'.

31 *Ibid.*

32 The Democratic Unionist Party in Sudan was backed by the Khatmiyya and Hindiyya Islamic orders with important support from merchants engaged in trade with Egypt. The National Umma Party was backed by the Ansar Islamic movement with support from exporting agricultural capitalists.

33 Information from a seminar by Atta al-Battahani in CEDEJ, Khartoum, (14 December 2017).

34 Jamal, Political economy of an Islamist state, pp. 14–17.

35 Tim Niblock, 2001. *Pariah states and sanctions in the Middle East: Iraq, Libya, Sudan.* London: Lynne Rienner.

36 Thomas, Growth and inequality in Sudan, pp. 23–7.

37 Cross, H., 2019. Sudan's struggle for democracy. *Tribune*. April 26. Available at: tribunemag.co.uk/2019/04/sudans-struggle-for-democracy

38 Arrighi, G., 2010. *The long twentieth century: money, power and the origins of our times*. New York, Verso.

39 Green, *A Fistful of Shells*, London: Penguin.

40 Cooper, F., 2002. *Africa Since 1950*. Cambridge: Cambridge University Press.

41 Fixed exchange rates can enable a depletion of external reserves. However, floating exchange rates often merely delay this outcome if there is a structural demand for remitting local funds and if capital flows are procyclical, as are both the case in postcolonial societies.

42 Amin, S., *Delinking. Towards a Polycentric World*, London: Zed books, 1989.

43 Mark, Kalinovsky, and Marung, *Alternative globalizations*, Indiana, IN: Indiana University Press.

44 IMF, Sudan: Selected issues (December 2017). Available at: www.imf.org/en/Publications/CR/Issues/2017/12/11/Sudan-Selected-Issues-45457

45 Mirghani, A., 2019. Sudan to lift fuel subsidies gradually in 2020: minister. *Reuters*, December 27. Available at: www.reuters.com/article/us-sudan-economy-idUSKBN1YV1LY

46 Strohecker, K., 2019. Bashir ouster rekindles interest in long-defaulted Sudan loans. *Reuters*, April 12. Available at: fr.reuters.com/article/uk-sudan-politics-debt-idUKKCN1RO28B

47 Abdelaziz, K., 2020. Sudan approves plan to liquidate, privatise state firms. *Reuters*, June 18. Available at: www.reuters.com/article/us-sudan-economy/sudan-approves-plan-to-liquidate-privatise-state-firms-idUSKBN23P32I

48 Robinson, N., 2016. Bill Clinton's act of terrorism. *Jacobin*, October 12. Available at: www.jacobinmag.com/2016/10/bill-clinton-al-shifa-sudan-bombing-khartoum/. Toi Staff, 2020. Netanyahu hints at Israel role in past Sudan raids. *Times of Israel*, October 24. Available at: www.timesofisrael.com/netanyahu-hints-at-israeli-role-in-sudan-bombings-predicts-more-peace-deals/

# 3
# Money, Finance, and Capital Accumulation in Zimbabwe

*Francis Garikayi*

## INTRODUCTION

The Southern African nation of Zimbabwe became the first country in the world to record hyperinflation in the twenty-first century. In November 2008, the country's month-over-month inflation reached 79.6 billion per cent.[1] In early 2009, the country's central bank issued a record-breaking one hundred trillion dollar bill.[2] This latest attempt at taming runaway inflation was followed by the official dollarisation[3] of the economy in April 2009.[4] Since then, Zimbabwe has struggled to manage its currency arrangements.

Like most studies on social phenomena in contemporary Africa, dominant literature on Zimbabwe's monetary woes has tended to follow a technicist and neoclassical approach (see for instance McIndoe-Calder).[5] In neoclassical theory, money is considered neutral; the notion that in the economy money only affects prices, wages, and inflation[6]. In this light, Zimbabwe's currency has mainly been analysed based on its ability to work as a medium of exchange,[7] as a store of value[8] and as a unit of account.[9] Studies have therefore tended to emphasise the importance of the following causal factors: fiscal policy,[10] institutions, corruption, poor economic growth, dwindling foreign direct investment (FDI), and good governance.[11] Consequently, the deceptive 'appearances'[12] of inflation and currency instability have been approached as financial management problems.

For this reason, policymakers and academics have mostly sought technical solutions to Zimbabwe's monetary problems. Moreover, relatively little attention has been paid to the impact of social relations, interests, and social forces behind Zimbabwe's currency collapse and hyperinflation. To be more precise, no regard has been given to how Zimbabwe's economic structure might have influenced its monetary relations. In broad terms, economic structure refers to the configuration of economic sectors as conceptualised through the system of national accounts (SNA); i.e. manufacturing, mining, agriculture, services, and so on. Besides this, literature on Zimbabwe's monetary sovereignty is a rarity. To fill this gap in the literature, I will explore two questions. First: is there an alternative conception of money capable of throwing light on Zimbabwe's monetary sovereignty? Second, what role has money played in the processes of capital accumulation throughout Zimbabwe's history?

Answering these questions might reveal why Zimbabwe's hyperinflation is not merely an aberration but an outcome of the country's economic structure. I will argue that Zimbabwe's monetary system is and has been related to its historically specific processes of capital accumulation. To support my argument, I will analyse the relationship between capital accumulation and the evolution of Zimbabwe's monetary system.

During the imperial period, Southern Rhodesia's[13] monetary system served to facilitate the extraction of gold. With the transition in 1923 from Chartered Company rule to a 'Responsible Government'[14] monetary relations shifted towards facilitating the 'draining-off of surplus'. The idea of a monetary system geared towards draining-off surplus was propounded by Loxley.[15] In his study of the Tanzanian monetary and financial system, Loxley argued that, in the first place, Tanzania's colonial financial and monetary system was geared towards 'the unimpeded creaming-off of surplus'. And that, secondly, the main objective of Tanzania's colonial monetary institutions was to export surpluses.

A similar situation could be observed in inter-war Rhodesia. However, as global conditions changed, Rhodesia became industrialised. At that stage, the monetary system moved towards facilitating the export of processed agricultural and mining products to global markets, as well as manufactured goods to neighbouring countries. Since Zimbabwe's independence in 1980, the function of the monetary and financial system has strengthened its role in promoting exports in concert with the Washington Consensus (WC). Zimbabwe has, therefore, not been spared from financialisation processes. Financialisation in this instance being understood as the 'increasing power of the owners of money in the management of economic affairs'.[16] This conjuncture has undermined the country's sovereignty.

The rest of this chapter is structured as follows. To begin with, I outline an alternative theoretical framework for understanding currencies and monetary relations. The second part provides an empirical account of the historical broad changes and continuities between money and capital accumulation in Zimbabwe. The last part provides concluding remarks and some recommendations on how Zimbabwe might attain more sovereignty.

## THE RELATIONSHIP BETWEEN MONETARY RELATIONS AND CAPITAL ACCUMULATION

Processes of capital accumulation have a close relationship with the nature and form of monetary relations. The function and forms of money are closely related to the underlying structure and functioning of an economy.[17] As a result, monetary relations cannot be separated from relations of capital accumulation. Moreover, processes of capital accumulation differ in time and space. Therefore, different situations of monetary sovereignty exist.[18]

In this light, the type and nature of a country's monetary system are contingent upon specific historical processes of capital accumulation.[19] Money does not emerge independently of any social setting, nor does it spontaneously appear out of the market exchange process. Rather, a monetary system shapes and is shaped by a country's political and economic history. Moreover, a monetary system is not simply banks, currency, and transactions. Instead, it encompasses 'the interaction between financial and other institutions and how they mutually undertake financial functions'.[20] Whether a monetary system is supportive of the extraction of surpluses, developmental processes, general commodity exchanges or capital flow is subject to change and is 'historically and socioeconomically specific'.[21] How then can we understand money and financial systems in relation to the structure and functioning on an economy? In this chapter I will argue that the idea of a system of accumulation provides a powerful framework for this purpose.

The concept of a system of accumulation[22] was pioneered by Fine and Rustomjee.[23] It refers to historically determined linkages of capital accumulation that develop between different fractions of capital[24] within a particular situation. Such linkages are both concrete and dynamic. Though the concept emerged from an analysis of the South African economy, it does not necessarily pertain to a 'national entity'.[25] Instead, it integrates:

> spatial scales of analysis in a manner which recognises that national capital relations are conditioned by global capital relations, but that they also contribute to and are constitutive of the global whole.[26]

A system of accumulation framework commences from capitalist development as a process of capital accumulation. Capital is an abstract concept encompassing certain powerful tendencies. From a Marxist political economy vantage point, the central question is how to move from abstract to concrete situations – unfolding from the simple or abstract, to the complex or totality.[27] Thus, the penetration of capital[28] tends to produce universal development features; for instance, the creation of an excess population. However, capitalist reproduction differs across specific concrete situations because there are differences in the interaction between class forces, the state, and productive forces.[29] A system of accumulation is therefore an articulation of how capitalist value relations are constructed, organised, and reproduced.[30] Here, the role of the state is emphasised, but not as an independent arm of society. State and market are instead considered as constitutive of the capitalist whole. For this reason, state and market are viewed as a reflection of social relations.[31]

Accordingly, the evolution and development of a national financial system is theorised as occurring in relation to the character of a country's capital accumulation processes. Most significantly, the framework recognises that a monetary system is 'built in relation to existing [political and economic] structures in a contested, frustrated, and co-constitutive manner'.[32] Moreover, a system of accumulation conception of money rejects the dichotomisation of the real economy and the monetary system – the so-called classical dichotomy.[33] By contrast, mainstream economics accounts conceptualise money as a technical phenomenon. Therefore, in analysing Zimbabwe's monetary relations, I do not conceptualise the financial system as simply an independently evolving intermediary between lenders and borrowers. With this understanding, I now proceed to apply the systems of accumulation framework to the specific case of Zimbabwe.

## A HISTORICAL VIEW OF MONEY AND CAPITAL ACCUMULATION IN ZIMBABWE

### *Early colonial capital accumulation and monetary relations*

The most significant determinant of political-economic development in southern Africa was the discovery of diamond and gold in South Africa in the late nineteenth century.[34] Thus, it was in the wake of failures on the Transvaal Rand[35] that Southern Rhodesia was established by Cecil John Rhodes's British South Africa Company (BSAC) in 1890. In this context, the BSAC was set up to represent the interests of international capital[36] whose goal was to extract as many internationally tradeable commodities as possible.[37] The Chartered Company sought to pursue a 'Second Rand' in the area North of the Limpopo River.[38] Just like in South Africa, Rhodesian gold mining relied on metropolitan finance. Because of this, the BSAC had to compete with the Witwatersrand of South Africa for foreign capital. And so, early optimism in the prospects of gold in the territory saw an explosion of mining stocks on the London Stock Exchange. By April 1900 almost one hundred mining stocks and shares had been listed on the London bourse.[39] Therefore, at the very outset, the imperial colonial financial system evolved to facilitate the flow of metropolitan finance to gold mining operations. Indeed, it was share trading and not banks that formed the bedrock of the early financial system.

The relative poverty of mineral resources in Rhodesia induced change in development strategy. Most importantly, the BSAC needed to recover its outlays on the railway system, mining claims, and developed land.[40] For this reason, in the early 1900s settlers (the first of which were some of the displaced employees of De Beers[41] after its amalgamation with Kimberly Company[42]), and companies were impelled to transition from mining towards agriculture and other economic activities. By the 1930s, a state-supported white agrarian bourgeoisie[43] had emerged. The subsequent increase in commercial activity in mining and agriculture accentuated the demand for currency. To lessen coinage shortages, a banknotes ordinance was passed in 1922 authorising Barclays Bank and Standard Bank ('expatriate banks') to issue some notes.[44] But the rapidly growing agricultural sector could not be sustained by privately issued notes, such that by 1938 the Southern Rhodesia Currency Board (SRCB) had been established.[45] Certainly, the notion of a Currency Board was aimed at 'draining-off surplus'.[46] The expatriate banks were simply hoarding money without spurring local industrial development.[47]

Furthermore, Currency Board arrangements reflected the speculative nature of white agriculture at the time. Farmers tended to switch from crop to crop depending on expected returns.[48] Consequently, the expatriate banks endeavoured to drain-off surpluses emanating from those speculative ventures. Unsurprisingly, the 1930s economy resembled typical colonial conditions, notwithstanding twenty years of self-government.[49] Capitalist relations were concentrated in the foreign-owned mining and agricultural primary products sectors. In turn, the primary products sector was heavily oriented towards the world market. In fact, most economic activity revolved around gold mining and tobacco-growing, which was destined for the export market. This conjuncture assembled an intricate relationship between domestic and international capital. The outcome was decisive in shaping an externally oriented form of capital accumulation that has endured to this day, albeit in different forms.

In the 1930s, the growing influence of settler-led production in mining and tobacco farming meant that domestic capital was earning a surplus from internationally tradable commodities. So, any reinvested surpluses in the export sectors amounted to the real growth of domestic capital. But the external orientation of domestic capital meant that it was de facto international, not least because its reproduction was dependent on importing inputs and exporting output.[50] For this reason, the expansion of domestic capital heightened the demand for imports. Consequently, import substitution industries emerged. Logically, this called for a system of managing imports and exports. Hence, the Rhodesian state evolved to manage the distribution of international purchasing power earned in the territory. In this light, the monetary system simply served to 'divert' a portion of the international purchasing power earned from gold and agricultural products for the benefit of the country's white population.[51] It is important to note that Rhodesia's pre-war white population comprised a rural bourgeoisie involved in agriculture and mining, wage workers, and a trading petty bourgeoisie.[52]

## WAR AND POST-WAR CAPITAL ACCUMULATION AND MONETARY RELATIONS

The outbreak of the Second World War revolutionised capital accumulation processes in Southern Rhodesia. Most significantly, it stimulated a process of remarkable economic growth.[53] In the 1930s the economy had been underdeveloped, and stagnant in part, because of a lack of internal demand. However, with the war taking up most of the world's resources, imported goods became scarce.[54] Furthermore, a global shortage of agricultural produce created a huge market for local farmers.[55] This created demand for local industries. Most impactful though was an air training scheme implemented in the country in conjunction with the British government.[56] Under the scheme, Rhodesia supplied air stations, quarters, land, buildings, and labour to build aerodromes.[57] Again, this expanded the market for farmers and industrial firms, resulting in the tripling of gross manufacturing output between 1939 and 1946.[58] The upshot was the emergence of a 'manufacturing capitalist class' heavily controlled by British and South African capital.[59]

After the war, new external stimulants sustained economic buoyancy.[60] Most notably, a post-war high demand for raw materials, an influx of British and South African immigrants, and capital flow into the territory. Added to this were the effects of the collapse of the Gold Standard, which secured Rhodesia a pole position in supplying Britain with tobacco.[61] Further, the Federation of Rhodesia and Nyasaland which existed from 1954 to 1963 widened the market for southern Rhodesian industries.[62] As a result, monetary arrangements evolved to support the booming capitalist economy. Local banking started to take root such that the share of local assets to total assets held by the two expatriate banks increased by 56 per cent in 1946, and 71 per cent in 1947.[63]

But most influential after the war was the role of South African and British capital inflows. British capital comprised immigrant remittances, loan repayments, and proceeds from London issued debt.[64] South African capital flows, on the other hand, reflected the heightened apprehension by international capital in the wake of the 1948 victory of the National Party. Southern Rhodesia thus became an alternative investment destination. Unlike in the past whereby London investments passed through Johannesburg, from the late 1940s London started to invest directly in Southern Rhodesia. Because of this, foreign investment tripled between 1947 and 1949, reaching £51 million by 1951.[65]

The confluence of rapid industrial led economic growth and heightened capital inflow could no longer be sustained by a Currency Board.[66] Moreover, the rapid expansion of the manufacturing industry brought about economic complexity. This was exacerbated by a shortage of American dollars and an impending sterling devaluation. Hence, the Southern Rhodesian authorities recognised that if industrialisation were to proceed smoothly, there was a need to control money supply.[67] The ensuing debate revolved around whether financial institutions were allocating resources towards the most productive sectors and how they could be regulated.[68] In the end, a central bank was established in 1956 because it was viewed as more effective at influencing development as well as asserting sovereignty over money compared to a Currency Board.[69] In other words, a central bank was deemed fit for efficiently managing international purchasing power.

Although the manufacturing industry was the most influential factor in Rhodesia's capitalist economic development in the post-war period,[70] it harboured two major contradictions. First, due to its infancy, it could not compete on a global scale. For this reason, its success was dependent on an expanded local market. Yet, if demand was to be increased, there was a need to improve the buying power of the majority black population. To do this would have meant reforms to the agricultural sector which, in turn, would have disadvantaged the politically influential white nationalist class.[71] Second, the expansion of manufacturing industry relied on foreign currency from the export of primary products. It could thus be said Rhodesia had a form of dependent industrialisation.[72] In sum, Rhodesia's 'manufacturing capitalism required for its expansion the relative worsening of living conditions of the very classes on which it still heavily depended'.[73]

Socially, war and post-war economic development were accompanied by widespread change. First, among the country's white population, there was a shift in power from petty commodity producers towards wage workers. In the late 1950s, Rhodesian white wage workers rose to become some of the best paid globally thanks to the 'over-full-employment' in skilled occupations. This conjuncture gave white workers a strong bargaining position. Second, economic growth accelerated the rise of an African proletariat. In turn, this brought about African nationalism and demands for higher wages and improved working conditions. Third, mass, and capital-intensive production shifted labour demands from unskilled migrant labour of the farming type toward skilled labour. There was thus an interest by the manufacturing class to weaken the bargaining power of white workers by supporting the expansion of African skilled and non-manual labour.[74]

## RHODESIA'S ECONOMY AFTER THE UNILATERAL DECLARATION OF INDEPENDENCE

To safeguard their interests against manufacturers, white middle-class and white working-class voters elected the Rhodesian Front (RF) in 1962.[75] After getting into power, the RF unilaterally declared independence from Britain in 1965 – an event referred to as the Unilateral Declaration of Independence (UDI).[76] Britain's response to the UDI was an imposition of financial sanctions. British sanctions meant Rhodesia's expulsion from the sterling area, denial of access to gold and financial reserves held in London as well as access to the London money and capital markets. Furthermore, under the Southern Rhodesian Act of 1965, the United Kingdom (UK) banned the import of Rhodesian tobacco and sugar.[77] The UDI thus marked a rupture of the system of distributing international purchasing power that had existed hitherto.

British financial sanctions also caused significant shifts in the processes of accumulation; for instance, import substitution manufacturing increased, foreign trade's economic impact declined, mining industry output increased, dependency on Britain ebbed, and the economy became more integrated into the southern African region.

Moreover, the state took an even more active role in investment.[78] These changes resulted in an economic boom. Between 1966 and 1974, Rhodesia's yearly GDP growth averaged 9.5 per cent,[79] thanks to the rapid expansion of manufacturing industry. Up to a quarter of gross fixed capital formation originated from manufacturing industries.[80] In addition, the ratio of Manufacturing Value Added (MVA) rose from 16 per cent in 1966 to about 21 per cent in 1974, spurred by mostly domestic demand.[81] Interestingly, however, is that under conditions of relative sovereignty brought about by sanctions, Southern Rhodesia's economy thrived. Figure 3.1 shows the annual GDP growth rate in Zimbabwe since 1960.

Besides trapping local finance and corporate profits, sanctions also forced the Southern Rhodesian authorities to implement stringent exchange controls, and to restrict the repatriation of non-resident deposits.[82] Whereas in the past surpluses would have been repatriated to the metropole under the Exchange Control Act, No. 62, 1964,[83] companies were forced to reinvest profits locally.[84] The resulting excess liquidity spawned the development of a white housing sector thanks to high-net-worth white immigration. Increased mortgage demand set in

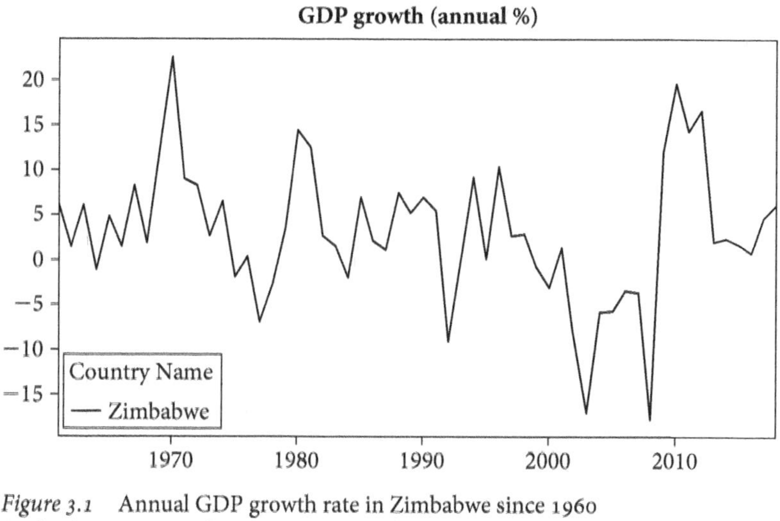


*Figure 3.1* Annual GDP growth rate in Zimbabwe since 1960
Author's conception from World Development Indicators (WDI) data
Source: World Development Indicators

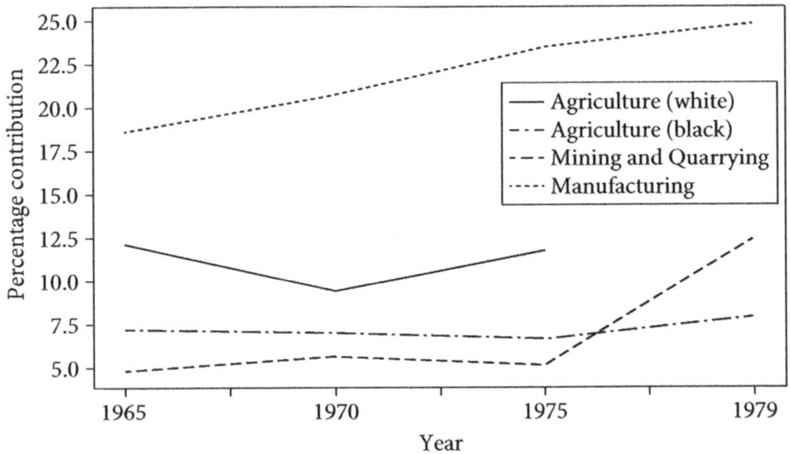


*Figure 3.2* Selected sectors of Rhodesia's economic structure (percentage contribution to GDP)
Source: Stoneman 1981

train a boom in both residential and commercial property. Furthermore, the rapid industrial development associated with increased buying power in the economy greatly increased the demand for hire purchase and leasing facilities. This was accompanied by growth in the primary sectors which increased the demand for financing.[85] As illustrated in Figure 3.2, between 1965 and 1974, manufacturing and services boomed relative to other sectors.

## MANUFACTURING-CENTRIC ACCUMULATION: 1965 TO 1974

Another significant outcome of UDI was the strengthening of a system of externally oriented manufacturing-centric capital accumulation. Between 1966 and 1974 the volume of manufacturing grew by 9.6 per cent,[86] but because of a policy of import substitution, the manufacturing sector became tightly integrated with the primary sectors. For instance, in 1965, up to 13 per cent of agricultural output was used as manufacturing inputs, increasing to 44 per cent by 1981/82. In turn, 42 per cent of agricultural inputs came from domestic manufacturers.

By the early 1980s, this had increased to 48 per cent.[87] Trade statistics also reflected the increasing strength of manufacturing. From the time of colonial conquest until UDI, mineral exports, especially gold, had accounted for 50 per cent of Gross National Income. However, during the same period, there was a shift in major exports from mining to agricultural products (mainly tobacco), and then to manufactured goods.[88]

At the point of UDI, manufactured goods accounted for 40 per cent of exports. Two major commodities were exported: processed mineral and agricultural products destined for the world market (cigarettes, ferrochrome, copper, sugar, meats), and manufactured products (clothing, textiles, radios, footwear, iron and steel, fertilisers, etc.). The latter was sold to neighbouring Zambia, Malawi, and South Africa. After sanctions, South Africa rose to take over 25 per cent of Rhodesia's manufactured exports.[89] Most significantly, because South African firms were not subject to the restrictions of the Exchange Control Act, they came to dominate Rhodesia's manufacturing industry.[90] After 1974, however, manufacturing started to experience significant strains. Production volume declined by 27 per cent between 1974 and 1978.[91] Both internal and external forces caused this slump. In terms of the former, the exigencies of the liberation struggle were a notable factor. For the latter, global gluts and the oil crisis of 1973 played a major role.[92]

## ZIMBABWE'S 1980 INHERITANCE

At its independence in 1980, Zimbabwe inherited an economy that was dominated by manufacturing industry, mining, and agriculture.[93] Most notably, the economy was externally oriented because output was mainly exported. Figure 3.3 shows that, apart from services, manufacturing industry was the single most significant contributor to GDP in 1979.

So, despite manufacturing having started to decline in the mid-1970s, Zimbabwe inherited a system of manufacturing-centric accumulation. But as discussed earlier, manufacturing processes were externally oriented. For this reason, the manufacturing industry mainly existed in support of the extraction and production of internationally tradeable

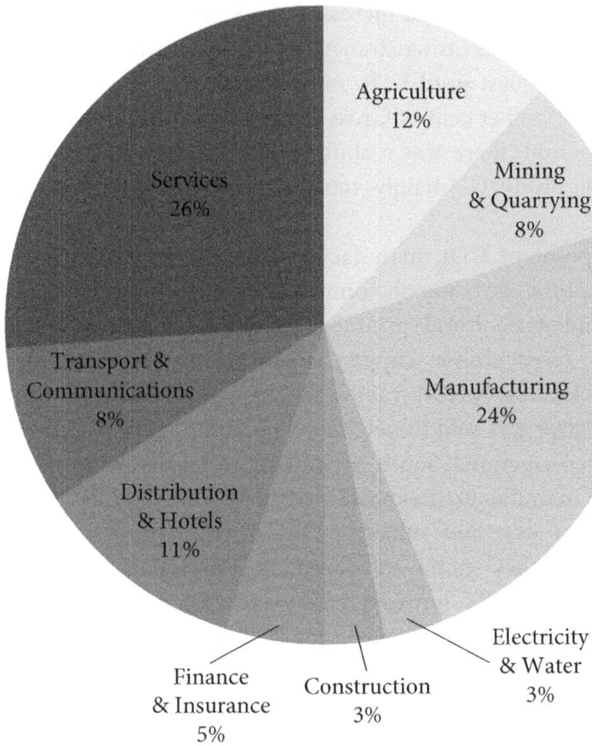


*Figure 3.3* Rhodesia's economic structure in 1979
Source: Stoneman 1981

commodities. UDI-era sanctions had brought about a shortage of foreign currency and, in turn, import substitution industrialisation. But that did not mean the diminution in the demand for foreign currency, even though the economy had become almost self-sufficient.[94] Facing this constraint, the Southern Rhodesian government sought to tightly manage the distribution of international purchasing power through the Exchange Control Act.

It is, therefore, crucial to note that independence negotiations were held in this context. Existing economic realities, in part, forced the Zimbabwe African National Union Party (ZANU) to ditch its liberation struggle socialist policies in favour of programmatic socialism. This later morphed into growth with equity.[95] The idea was to harness international finance in the form of aid and balance of payments support to achieve socialist transformation, however stupid that might have been.[96] The outcome was a class compromise that left the colonial structure of wealth and income inequality intact. Most constraining were the provisions of the 1979 Lancaster House agreement between the colonial government and the two liberation movements, ZANU and the Zimbabwe African People's Union (ZAPU), which blocked radical land reform even as the country faced a severe land problem.[97] In the circumstances, greater attention was now paid to racial and rival reconciliation instead of economic transformation. And for the peasantry who had been at the forefront of the liberation struggle, an era of neocolonialism commenced; how were their social conditions to be improved if capital was to remain untouched? As mentioned earlier, at the very outset, ZANU was forced to jettison the idea of economic transformation although it maintained it rhetorically.[98] For this reason, an externally oriented system of accumulation persisted.

## STABILISATION AND STRUCTURAL ADJUSTMENT: 1980 TO 1990

The easing of sanctions after legal independence expanded foreign trade, although imports increased more than exports. As a result, Zimbabwe recorded enormous current account deficits between 1981 and 1982.[99] Exports were further hurt by the global recession of 1981–1983 which negatively affected the prices and demand of exports.[100] Because of this and other exogenous shocks,[101] the country started experiencing a balance of payments crisis. Inevitably, the country accepted an IMF stabilisation package and World Bank loans. According to Stoneman,[102] in the first few years after independence, Zimbabwe received nine loans from the World Bank and four [International Development Assistance] (IDA) credits, totalling US$646 million. Of the nine loans, two were specifically targeted towards the promotion of manufactured exports.

Considering that at independence the concrete system of accumulation was centred on manufacturing, manufacturing sector loans from the World Bank were indeed geared towards influencing existing relations of capital accumulation.[103] Zimbabwe's manufacturing class had been successful not because of its global competitiveness, but rather because of state protection against international competition.[104] As is common with IMF/World Bank assistance, the funds came with conditions curtailing the role of the state in managing investment.[105] In this regard, Zimbabwe's 1982–1983 IMF/World Bank package was conditional on the elimination of budget deficits, the scrapping of food subsidies, export promotion, and currency devaluation.[106] Because UDI had partially isolated Zimbabwe, it was the aim of international financial institutions (IFIs) to firmly integrate Zimbabwe into the global economy. But this policy stance was antagonistic to ZANU's earlier quest to redress colonial imbalances.[107]

Because of this tension, beginning in the mid-1980s, the contentious economic policy issue concerned the degree of openness or market-based reforms that the government ought to undertake. Two extremes emerged. On the one hand, the agrarian class resented the preferential treatment of manufacturers in accessing foreign currency.[108] In addition, agriculturalists were dissatisfied with the exorbitant costs of inputs from local manufacturers. Hence, for the agrarian classes, deregulation meant cheaper inputs and an expanded market for their produce. On the other hand, the manufacturing class and ruling elites adopted an intermediate position. Indeed, the government had recognised the importance of manufacturing in its First Five-Year National Development Plan (1986–1990) albeit narrowly conceived to promote export-led growth.[109]

With low economic growth (see Figure 3.1), unemployment, burgeoning external debt, and a fiscal deficit, Zimbabwe acquiesced to an Economic Structural Adjustment Programme (ESAP) in 1991. ESAP marked a watershed moment in Zimbabwe's history and a turning point in monetary relations. It emphasised:

> [...] moving away from a highly regulated economy to one where market forces were allowed to play a more decisive role, while concurrently taking steps to alleviate any transitional social hardships which may arise from this transition,[110] citing Government of Zimbabwe.[111]

ESAP which, according to Bond,[112] became known as 'Eternal Suffering for the African People' also deregulated finance, eased exchange controls, and liberalised trade. In the banking sector, new entrants were encouraged.[113] The government set out to meet a certain inflation target.[114] And high positive interest rates were to be maintained. But in reality, ESAP was a class compromise between international capital, the manufacturing class, the ruling elites, and the agrarian elites. For the government, market-based reforms provided an opportunity to revive industry given the high levels of unemployment. Whereas for the manufacturing class, reforms had the potential of solving production hampering foreign currency shortages.[115]

In terms of finance, the government intervened in the sector to promote an emerging black elite along the lines of neoliberal orthodoxy. The idea was to modernise by furthering the reach and depth of finance.[116] Key financial institutions in support of black accumulation were either acquired or established. Some of the new financial institutions were funded by the World Bank Group, the International Financial Corporation (IFC), and the Commonwealth Development Corporation (CDC). To cite some examples: the Zimbabwe Investment Centre in 1987, the Indigenous Business Development Centre in 1990,[117] and Zimtrade and the Venture Capital Company of Zimbabwe in 1991.[118]

As a result of this, during the 1990s Zimbabwe's financial sector went through rapid expansion, as shown in Figure 3.4. The graph

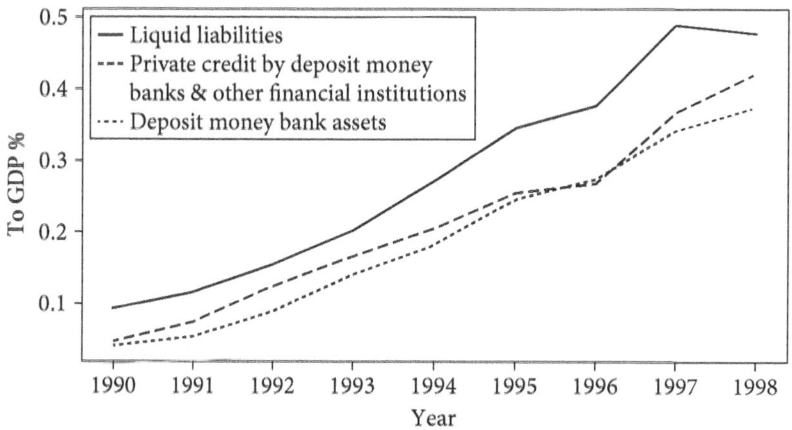


*Figure 3.4* Selected indicators of financial structure during ESAP
Source: World Bank financial infrastructure database

shows that between 1990 and 2000 there was a substantial increase in firm indebtedness[119] and that finance deepened.[120] However, because Zimbabwe's financial sector liberalisation did not have a pro-poor inclination, it benefited those who were already integrated into the market economy.[121] An unintended outcome was that the social conditions for war veterans and peasants who had been at the forefront of the liberation struggle worsened.[122] But since the war veterans represented a formidable social force in the balance of power within ZANU-PF, they exacted financial compensation for their participation in the liberation struggle.[123] Moreover, revelations that the War Victims' Compensation fund had been looted by the ruling elites made it harder for Mugabe's government to refuse to compensate ordinary war veterans.[124]

In the circumstances, in August 1997 the government conceded to paying an unbudgeted lump sum of Z$50,000 (approximately US$3,000) to each war veteran; in total, the pay-out represented 3 per cent of GDP.[125] In addition to this, the government committed to paying Z$2,000 (approximately US$125) as a monthly pension.[126] The World Bank reacted by withdrawing US$62.5 million in balance of payments support amid fears Zimbabwe would breach its projected budget deficit.[127] To compound matters, on 5 November 1997, Britain notified Zimbabwe that it did not feel duty bound to meet the costs of land reform as agreed at Lancaster House.[128] Subsequently, on 14 November 1997 (now known as 'Black Friday'), the Zimbabwe dollar lost 75 per cent of its value against the US dollar in four hours.[129] The 1997 conjuncture showed that, without monetary sovereignty, Zimbabwe could not radically intervene in the economy without attracting backlash. Furthermore, it signified the climax of a crisis whose roots could be traced to the 1970s, as well as the collapse of the Lancaster House class compromise.[130]

## CURRENCY COLLAPSE AND HYPERINFLATION

### *Early 2000 era*

The turn of the new millennium witnessed agitation by classes that hitherto had been subjugated by neocolonialism.[131] The independence class compromise,[132] which had resulted in 'elite accommodation' started to unravel rapidly.[133] To this end, war veterans and peasants organised for a radical reform of agrarian relations.[134] In fear of losing power, ZANU-PF 'co-opted and adopted' the land occupation movement in 2000.[135] A negative short-term effect of land reform was its adverse effect on tobacco production – one of the country's biggest foreign currency earners.[136] Before 2000, the country produced approximately 200 million kilograms per annum; however, by 2008 production had plummeted to 48.7 million kilograms per annum.[137]

The collapse of export revenues and the imposition of financial sanctions by the United States (US) accelerated the further collapse of the Zimbabwe dollar. The Zimbabwe Democracy and Economic Recovery Act of 2001 (ZIDERA), as amended in 2018, prohibits 'support that is intended to promote Zimbabwe's economic recovery and development, the stabilisation of Zimbabwean currency, and the viability of Zimbabwe's democratic institutions' until Zimbabwe meets certain political conditions.[138] According to Gono,[139] Zimbabwe had maintained foreign currency reserves worth three months of imports in 1996, but this had fallen to cover of less than one month by 2007. Hence, the convergence of foreign currency shortages, financial sanctions, current account deficits, and low capital inflows shifted capital accumulation processes towards speculative activities. For the majority of the country's citizens, a new economic logic of '*kukiya-kiya*' or 'making do' to 'get by' became the only means of subsistence.[140]

## THE ERA OF BANK FAILURES IN ZIMBABWE: 2003 TO 2005

Between 2003 and 2008, Zimbabwe's economy effectively became a 'casino'.[141] Money laundering activities became endemic, and a series of 'indigenous' banks and financial institutions failed.[142] Corporations could profit more from dealing in foreign currency instead of engaging in productive activities. For instance, in 2006, the Reserve Bank of Zimbabwe (RBZ) governor, Gideon Gono, revealed that less than 25 per cent of the issued currency was operating in the official financial system.[143] Firms and individuals were thus engaged in, inter-alia, one-way exporting, offshoring executive management employment

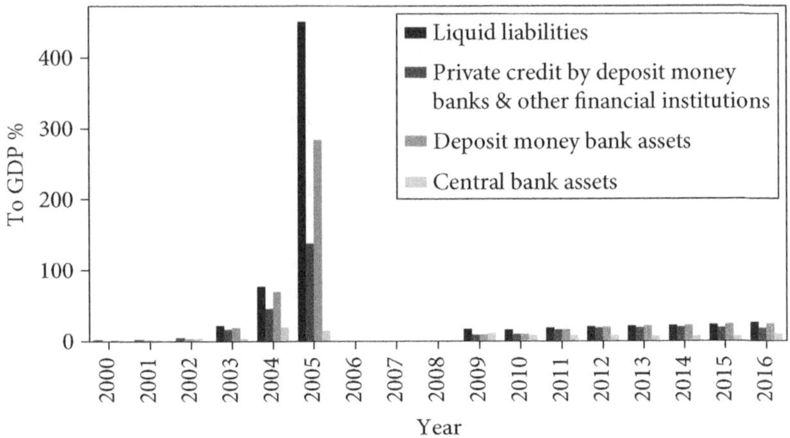


*Figure 3.5* Selected indicators of financial structure 2000–2016
Source: World Bank financial structure database

benefits, over-invoicing imports, transfer pricing, diamond smuggling, and externalising funds from hunting conventions.[144] The upshot was a dramatic expansion of the financial sector, as illustrated in Figure 3.5.

As shown in Figure 3.5, in the early 2000 period, broad money, as represented by the ratio of liquid liabilities to GDP, rose remarkably. Simultaneously, the ratio of central bank assets to GDP remained virtually constant whilst banks and other financial institutions increased their claims on the non-financial sector. This is reflected in Figure 3.5 by the spike in the ratio of deposit bank money assets to GDP. Most notable, however, is that financial sector expansion went hand in glove with runaway inflation. By the end of August 2006, inflation had reached 1,204 per cent, a world record at the time.[145] Because of high inflation, most bank assets were now comprised of illiquid investments in properties and equities (as a way of hedging).[146] As a result of this, the Zimbabwe Stock Exchange (ZSE) boomed.[147] Zimbabwe was now awash with worthless money. While many factors contributed to this, including, for example, the decline in real output, the exposition of the actual mechanics is beyond the scope of this chapter – suffice it to say that the World Bank attributed the 2002–2003 crisis to inappropriate policies.[148]

By late 2003, the hubris of financial enterprise became a nemesis, especially as inflation continued to rise.[149] Acute foreign currency shortages, exacerbated by the country's inability to borrow from the IFIs, affected the central bank's ability to import paper and ink for printing banknotes.[150] For this reason, a cash crisis ensued.[151] This compelled the central bank to tighten liquidity by hiking interest rates; by March 2004 interest rates had risen to 5,242 per cent. Because of this, many banks struggled to cover their positions, resulting in, mostly indigenous, banks failing.[152] Part of the reason why indigenous banks failed was because they tended to provide loans to low-income groups. Because of this, their default rate was higher compared to those of multinational banks.[153] After many bank failures, the central bank became actively involved in almost all sectors of the economy through Quasi-Fiscal Activities (QFAs).[154] Mackenzie and Stella[155] define a QFA as:

> an operation or measure carried out by a central bank or other public financial institution with an effect that can, in principle, be duplicated by budgetary measures in the form of an explicit tax, subsidy, or direct expenditure and that has or may have an impact on the financial operations of the central bank, other public financial institutions, or government.

## HYPERINFLATION AND THE QUEST FOR FOREIGN CURRENCY: 2006 TO 2008

To fund QFAs, the central bank expropriated foreign currency accounts of corporations, Non-Governmental Organisations (NGOs), and banks.[156] To recompense the affected parties, the Reserve Bank of Zimbabwe (RBZ) issued debt instruments. By January 2009, debt from QFAs had reached approximately US$200 million.[157] Described by former central bank governor Gideon[158] as 'extraordinary measures for extraordinary challenges', QFAs comprised subsidies, foreign exchange trading, and the interest expense of sterilisation operations.[159] These measures were only 'extraordinary' because of Zimbabwe's weak monetary sovereignty. Without foreign currency, the country's economy would have totally collapsed.

To this end, four schemes were implemented. First, the central bank provided 'free' foreign currency to parastatals for the importation of grain, fuel, and electricity on behalf of the government. The foreign currency was free in the sense that the transaction was treated as an interest-free loan to the government.[160] Second, the RBZ provided subsidies to private sector exporters as compensation for an overvalued exchange rate. Third, the central bank availed funds to failed financial institutions under the Troubled Bank Fund. Fourth, the RBZ subsidised commercial bank lending to farmers, manufacturers, and public enterprises under the Productive Sector Facility (PSF) and the Agricultural Sector Productivity Enhancement Facility (ASPEF). These schemes were highly inflationary, not least because the money that was created to fund them did not stimulate production. Instead, it was used to acquire foreign currency for the importation of consumptive goods.[161]

The nature of QFAs also demonstrated the strength of the manufacturing and exporting class. The strain of international financial sanctions meant that the state had to be more assertive in managing the distribution of international purchasing power. Consequently, in 2004, the central bank introduced a foreign currency auction system. This was followed by tighter regulation of international transactions.[162] Additionally, a retention scheme in terms of which exporters were obliged to surrender 25 per cent of export proceeds to the central bank at a prescribed exchange rate was introduced. These measures were augmented by a scheme of multiple exchange rates. A higher than market exchange rate for diaspora remittances was maintained[163]. Accordingly, members of the public could only buy foreign currency from the highly controlled foreign currency 'auction' system. Meanwhile, exporters were paid the higher of the auction-rate or diaspora rate while importers had currency sold to them at the auction rate.[164]

By directly intervening in the foreign exchange market, the central bank balanced the interests of exporters and the state. The former could benefit by retaining 75 per cent of their proceeds offshore. In addition, they received a higher rate for the 25 per cent mandatory surrender. Thus, locally denominated transactions were effectively subsidised by the central bank through the higher exchange rate. The public sector, on the other hand, purchased foreign currency at the below-market exchange rate.[165] Any realised exchange losses from these transactions were funded by printing currency. To curb the subsequent money growth, the central bank issued bills with interest rates of more than 900 per cent per annum. Because of this, the central bank incurred massive inflationary domestic debt related to sterilisation operations. By 2005, the interest expense of sterilisation operations had reached 40 per cent of GDP.[166] What this shows is that the central bank engaged in inflationary activities to balance the interests of exporters, manufacturers, and the state. Under sanctions, international purchasing power had to be carefully managed, notwithstanding the consequent inflation.

In 2015, Parliament passed a bill to assume RBZ debt of US$1.4 billion, most of which related to the QFAs.[167] A significant portion of this foreign currency-denominated debt is owed to financial institutions, banks, and companies in the mining and agricultural sectors.[168] It is therefore apparent that Zimbabwe's hyperinflation and currency collapse was not a progenitor of mismanagement or fiscal indiscipline. Rather, the country's central bank successfully managed the distribution of international purchasing power among the state, manufacturers, and primary producers. Put differently, externally oriented capital accumulation under sanctions-induced financial asphyxiation fuelled hyperinflation. Without inflationary foreign currency subsidies, capital accumulation in mining, agriculture, and manufacturing would have grounded to a halt. It is well established in the literature that inflation is beneficial to manufacturers, producers, and exporters because wages, taxes, and mortgage debts never keep up with inflation.[169]

In Zimbabwe, the negative outcomes of hyperinflation were borne by ordinary citizens who were forced to '*kiya-kiya*' or eke out a living.[170] During the period 2000–2008, there were job losses, basic commodities became unaffordable, hunger and poverty increased, health and educational outcomes worsened, and school enrolment declined.[171] All this in a bid to protect manufacturers and exporters of primary products. Although some social protection schemes were launched by the central bank, their success was ambivalent.[172]

In March 2007, Zimbabwean prices had reached hyperinflation, and by mid-November 2008 inflation was calculated at 79.6 billion per cent – a position second to Hungary in world record terms.[173] At this stage, the country's currency effectively collapsed. Many Zimbabweans refused to accept the Zimbabwean dollar as legal tender. For this reason, in 2009, Zimbabwe phased out its currency in favour of a basket of currencies led by the US dollar.[174] If Zimbabwe was productively sovereign, then increasing money supply might have resulted in different outcomes. Instead, money supply was channelled towards accessing foreign currency rather than promoting production. As I have argued earlier, Zimbabwe's economy revolves around the production and extraction of internationally tradeable commodities from manufacturing, mining, and agriculture. Most significantly, Zimbabwe's manufacturing industry mainly exists in service of mining and agriculture instead of providing basic consumer goods. A situation therefore persists whereby consumption needs are imported, and local production is almost entirely geared towards the export market. Under such circumstances it is hard to be sovereign.

## CONCLUSION AND RECOMMENDATIONS

This chapter has argued that Zimbabwe's monetary system is and has been related to its processes of externally oriented capital accumulation. During the imperial period, Zimbabwe's monetary system served to facilitate the extraction of gold from the colony. To this end, foreign finance flowed through the stock exchange system to facilitate mining infrastructural development. When the so-called Responsible Government took over in 1923, monetary relations shifted towards facilitating the 'draining-off of surplus' from speculative agricultural and mining ventures. During the war and post-war period, Rhodesia became industrialised and manufacturing capitalism became dominant. Consequently, the monetary system shifted towards facilitating trade and increasing local demand.

Since Zimbabwe's independence, the function of money has strengthened its focus on promoting exports, in concert with the Washington Consensus. In the early 1990s, Zimbabwe deregulated finance and promoted the establishment of new financial institutions and instruments. These policies were supported by international and manufacturing capital.[175] By the early 2000s, most of the established financial institutions had failed, leading to a financial crisis. To compound matters, Zimbabwe was officially cut off from accessing balance of payments support by US government sanctions. This called for a much more assertive management of international purchasing power by the central bank. To overcome the crisis, Zimbabwean authorities, in conjunction with miners, manufacturers, and tobacco exporters, turned to finance. However, in the absence of local productive capacity the result was hyperinflation and eventual currency collapse. Too much money chased too few goods.

The Zimbabwe dollar was reintroduced in 2019.[176] Regardless of this, earning foreign currency remains a major economic policy objective.[177] It is fair to conclude that the enduring importance of primary commodities in Zimbabwe's political economy means that prospects of economic sovereignty are distant. This is not to argue that there are no options. To overcome its socio-economic problems, Zimbabwe must embark on a radical industrialisation programme. This would entail altering the existing externally oriented productive structure. Such a programme would strive for worker participation in the organisation of production.[178] One can't help but imagine that if Zimbabwe's QFAs had focused on the reproduction of labour and not capital, the outcomes could have been quite different.

## NOTES

1 Hanke, S.H. and Kwok, A.K.F., 2009. On the Measurement of Zimbabwe's Hyperinflation. *Cato Journal*, 29(2), pp. 353–64. doi: 10.1007/978-1-4684-8848-7_7
2 Pilossof, R., 2009. 'Dollarisation' in Zimbabwe and the Death of an Industry, *Review of African Political Economy*, 36(120), pp. 294-99
3 Understood here as the use of the United States dollar as legal tender.
4 Tara McIndoe-Calder, T., 2018. Hyperinflation in Zimbabwe: Money demand, seigniorage and aid shocks. *Applied Economics*, 50(15), pp. 1659–75. doi: 10.1080/00036846.2017.1371840
5 pp. 1659–1675
6 Hughes, P. and Annina Kaltenbrunner, A. What Is the role of money in economics? In Kevin Deane and Elisa Van Waeyenberge, eds, 2020. *Recharting the history of economic thought*. London: Red Globe Press, pp. 131–47.
7 Commodity acceptable for exchanging goods and services
8 Commodity able to maintain purchasing power
9 A commodity that is the basis of pricing
10 Terrence Kairiza, T., 2009. *Unbundling Zimbabwe's journey to hyperinflation and official dollarization*. Available at: https://ideas.repec.org/p/ngi/dpaper/09-12.html [Accessed 30 July 2021].
11 Mitchell, B., 2009. *Zimbabwe for Hyperventilators 101*. Available at: http://bilbo.economicoutlook.net/blog/?p=3773 [Accessed 21 March 2021].

12 It is trite that in bourgeois society, reality is remarkably to the way things appear – see Harvey, D., 2018. *A companion to Marx's Capital: The complete edition*. London: Verso. doi: 10.2307/1956786

13 Southern Rhodesia (now Zimbabwe) was established by the nineteenth century British imperialist Cecil Rhodes's British South Africa Company (BSAC) in 1890. In 1964, the territory's name changed to Rhodesia after the collapse of the Federation of Rhodesia and Nyasaland: see for instance, Verrier, A., 1986. *The road to Zimbabwe*. London: Jonathan Cape.

14 Responsible government was the administrative apparatus of Southern Rhodesia which established it as a settler state: Phimister, I., 1988. *An economic and social history of Zimbabwe 1890–1948: Capital accumulation and class struggle*. New York: Longman Inc.

15 Loxley, J., 1972. Financial Planning and Control in Tanzania, *Development and Change*, 3(3), pp. 43–61. doi: 10.1111/j.1467-7660.1972.tb00623.x

16 Bracking, S., 2016. *The financialisation of power: How financiers rule Africa*, New York: Routledge, p. 1.

17 Hughes, P. and Annina Kaltenbrunner, A. What Is the role of money in economics? pp. 131–47.

18 In Modern Monetary Theory (MMT), this idea is understood in terms of a 'spectrum of monetary sovereignty'. In basic terms, this means that the positionality of nation states in the international trading and financial systems affects their monetary policy autonomy. See: Tankus, N., 2018. Monetary Sovereignty and Our Dollar World. Manchester International Law Centre Speaker Series, June 6, www.youtube.com/watch?v=xZnEDrVfcHU

19 Newman, S., 2020. Finance and Development in Sub-Saharan Africa. In Janelle Knox-Hayes and Dariusz Wójcik, eds, *The Routledge Handbook of Financial Geography*. New York: Routledge, pp. 587-619.

20 Ashman. S. and Fine, B., 2013. Neoliberalism, varieties of capitalism, and the shifting contours of South Africa's financial System. *Transformation Critical Perspectives on Southern Africa*, 81(1), 172, 144–78.

21 *Ibid*., 58.

22 This is different to the *Regulation School or Social Structures of Accumulation*. The distinguishing feature being its departure from overemphasising the role of institutions. See: Ashman, S., Fine, B., and Newman S.. Systems of Accumulation and the Evolving MEC, in B. Fine, J. Saraswati, and D. Tavasci (eds), 2012.*Beyond the developmental state: Industrial policy into the 21st Century*. London: Pluto Press, pp. 1–20. Available at: www.google.com/%5Cnpapers2://publication/uuid/B4124AE4-1285-4C1C-B21F-0E33F3CE306F [Accessed 25 March 2021].

23 Fine, B. and Rustomjee, Z., 1996. *The political economy of South Africa: From minerals-energy complex to industrialisation*. London: C. Hurst & Co. (Publishers) Ltd.

24 According to Clarke, S. (1978). Capital, Fractions of Capital and the State: 'Neo-Marxist' Analysis of the South African State. *Capital &*

*Class*, 2(2), pp. 32–77. https://doi.org/10.1177/030981687800500103, p. 35, 'a fraction of capital is the product of the political organisation of a number of individual capitals who have an interest or interests in common, whether that organisation takes the form of a pressure group, or a political party. [...], or some other part of the state apparatus [...]'.

25 Ashman, S., 2012. Systems of Accumulation and the Evolving MEC. In S. Ashman, B. Fine, and S. Newman, 2012. *Beyond the Development State: Industrial Policy into the 21st Century*. London: Pluto Press.

26 *Ibid.* 1.

27 *Ibid.* 2.

28 This idea originates from Bill Freund's conception of modern African history. Freund, B., 2016. *The making of contemporary Africa: The development of African society since 1800*. London: Palgrave.

29 Palma, G., 1978. Dependency: A formal theory of underdevelopment or a methodology for the analysis of concrete situations of underdevelopment? *World Development*, 6(7–8) pp. 881–924. doi: 10.1016/0305-750X(78)90051-7

30 Ashman, Fine, and Newman, Systems of Accumulation, p.4.

31 Ashman, B., Fine, B., and Newman, S., 2010. The development state and post-liberation South Africa. In Neeta Misra-Dexter and Judith February, eds, *Testing democracy: Which way is South Africa going?* Cape Town: Idasa, pp. 23–45.

32 Newman, S., Finance and Development in Sub-Saharan Africa, p. 604.

33 Hughes and Kaltenbrunner, What is the role of money in economics? pp. 131–47.

34 Farnie, D.A., 1952. The Mineral Revolution in South Africa. *South African Journal of Economics*, 24(2), pp. 125–34.

35 Transvaal was a provincial area in the then South African Republic in which major gold deposits were discovered in 1886.

36 20 per cent of the company's initial capital in 1889 was provided by De Beers Farnie.

37 Bienefeld, M. and Innes, D., 1976. Capital Accumulation and South Africa. *Review of African Political Economy*, 3(7), pp. 31–55. doi: 10.1080/03056247608703299

38 Phimister, I.R., 1974. Rhodes, Rhodesia and the rand. *Journal of Southern African Studies*, 1(1), pp. 74–90.

39 Karekwaivenani, G., 2004. A history of the Rhodesian stock exchange: The formative years, 1946–1952. *Zambezia*, 30(1), pp. 9–34. doi: 10.4314/zjh.v30i1.6734

40 Arrighi, G., 1967. *The Political Economy of Rhodesia*. The Hague: Mouton & Co. N.V. doi: 10.1207/S15326934CRJ1504

41 Farnie. The Mineral Revolution in South Africa, pp.125–35.

42 Bienefeld and Innes. Capital Accumulation and South Africa, pp. 31–55.

43 Two pieces of legislation buttressed the white bourgeoisie class: The Land Apportionment Act and the Native Registration Act – both helped supply cheap labour to the white farmers, Arrighi, G,. *The Political Economy of Rhodesia.*

44 Nyamunda, T., 2017. Money, Banking and Rhodesia's Unilateral Declaration of Independence. *Journal of Imperial and Commonwealth History*, 45(5), pp. 746–76. doi: 10.1080/03086534.2017.1370220

45 *Ibid.*, p. 752

46 The notion of draining off surplus was used by Loxley to describe how the East African Currency Board, as the major conduit for surpluses originating in Tanzania, did not invest locally, but rather exported the gains to the metropole. The motivating principle was to remit most of what was gained locally abroad instead of reinvesting in local assets.

47 Nyamunda, Money, Banking, pp. 746–76.

48 Rupert, S., 1998. *A Most Promising Weed: A History of Tobacco Farming and Labor in Colonial Zimbabwe, 1890–1945*, 1998. doi: 10.2307/525260

49 Arrighi, 1967. *The Political Economy of Rhodesia.*

50 Bienefeld and Innes, 1976. Capital Accumulation and South Africa, pp. 31–55.

51 Stoneman, C., 1978. Foreign Capital and the Reconstruction of Zimbabwe. *Review of African Political Economy*, 5(11), pp. 62–83. doi: 10.1080/03056247808703351

52 Arrighi, 1967. *The Political Economy of Rhodesia.*

53 Vickery, K.P., 1989. The Second World War revival of forced labor in the Rhodesias. *The International Journal of African Historical Studies*, 22(3), pp. 423–37.

54 Phimister, I., 2000. From preference towards Protection: Manufacturing in Southern Rhodesia, 1940–1965, in A.S. Mlambo, E.S., Pangeti, and I. Phimister (eds) *Zimbabwe: A history of manufacturing, 1890–1995*. Harare: University of Zimbabwe Publications, pp. 31–50.

55 Arrighi, 1967. *The Political Economy of Rhodesia.*

56 Phimister, I., 2000. From preference towards Protection: Manufacturing in Southern Rhodesia, 1940–1965.

57 Vickery, 1989. The Second World War revival of forced labor in the Rhodesias.

58 Stoneman, Foreign Capital and the Reconstruction of Zimbabwe, p. 64.

59 Arrighi, 1967. *The Political Economy of Rhodesia.*

60 Arrighi, 1967. *The Political Economy of Rhodesia.*

61 Stoneman, C. 1978. Foreign capital and the reconstruction of Zimbabwe, Review of African Political Economy, 5 (11) doi: 10.1080 /03056247808703351, pp. 62–83.

62 *Ibid.*

63 Bond, P., 1998. *Uneven Zimbabwe: A study of finance, development and underdevelopment*. Trenton: African World Press.

64 *Ibid.*, 68.

65 Arrighi, 1967. *The Political Economy of Rhodesia.*

66 Nyamunda, T., 2015. Financing rebellion : The Rhodesian state, financial policy and exchange control, 1962–1979. Doctoral thesis.

67 Phimister, I. 'From preference towards protection: Manufacturing in Southern Rhodesia, 1940–1965', in *Zimbabwe: A History of Manufacturing, 1890–1995*, (ed.) A.S. Mlambo, E.S. Pangeti, and I. Phimister. Harare: University of Zimbabwe Publications, 2000, pp. 32–3.

68 Bond, *Uneven Zimbabwe,* pp. 64

69 Nyamunda, Money and banking, pp. 746–76.

70 Clarke, D.G., 1975. *The political economy of discrimination and underdevelopment in Rhodesia with special reference to African workers, 1940–1973*. St Andrews: St Andrews Research Repository. http://hdl.handle.net/10023/2812 [Accessed 25 March 2021].

71 Stoneman, C., 1990. The industrialisation of Zimbabwe - Past, present and future. *Afrika Focus*, 6(3–4), pp. 245–82. doi: 10.21825/af.v6i3-4.6126

72 Skalnes, T., 1995. *The politics of economic reform in Zimbabwe: Continuity and change in development*, London and Basingstoke: Macmillan Press.

73 Arrighi, 1967. *The Political Economy of Rhodesia*, p. 51.

74 *Ibid.*, p. 51.

75 Stoneman, C., 1990. The industrialisation of Zimbabwe - Past, present and future. Pp. 245.282

76 Nyamunda, Money and banking, pp. 746–76.

77 Central Intelligence Agency, 2002. *UK financial sanctions in the Rhodesian crisis.* Available at: www.cia.gov/library/readingroom/docs/CIA-RDP79T01003A002500030001-0.pdf [Accessed 30 July 2021].

78 Stoneman, Foreign capital and the reconstruction of Zimbabwe, pp. 62-8380.

79 Bond, *Uneven Zimbabwe*

80 Wield, D., 1981. Manufacturing industry. In T. Bowyer-Bower and C. Stoneman, (eds), *Zimbabwe's Inheritance*, London and Basingstoke: The Macmillan Press Ltd, pp.151–73

81 Riddell, R., 1988. Industrialisation in Sub-Saharan Africa: Country case study, Zimbabwe. Overseas Development Institute, p. 5.

82 Bond, *Uneven Zimbabwe.*

83 The Act is still in force although in a revised form. It stipulates that it is: 'AN ACT to confer powers and impose duties and restrictions in relation to gold, currency, securities, exchange transactions, payments and debts, and the import, export, transfer and settlement of property, and for purposes connected with the matters aforesaid' Government of Zimbabwe, Exchange Control Act 2004. Available at: www.rbz.co.zw/documents/acts/exchangecontrol_act.pdf [Accessed 25 March 2021].

84 Pangeti, E.S., 2000. The economy under siege: Sanctions and the manufacturing sector, 1965–1979. In A.S. Mlambo, E.S., Pangeti, and I Phimister, I. (eds), *Zimbabwe: A History of Manufacturing 1890–1995*, Harare: University of Zimbabwe Publications, pp. 51–79.

85 Bond, *Uneven Zimbabwe.*

86 Wield, Manufacturing industry, pp. 151–73
87 Skalnes, *The politics of economic reform in Zimbabwe.*
88 Rob Davies, R., 1981. Foreign trade and external economic relations. In Colin Stoneman (ed.), *Zimbabwe's Inheritance*, London and Basingstoke: The Macmillan Press Ltd, pp. 195–227
89 Wield, 'Manufacturing industry', pp.151–73.
90 Pangeti, 'The economy under siege', pp. 51–79.
91 Wield, 'Manufacturing industry', pp. 151–73.
92 Pangeti, 'The economy under siege', pp. 51–79
93 Stoneman, C. and Rob Davies, R. The economy: An overview. In Colin Stoneman, ed., *Zimbabwe's inheritance*, London and Basingstoke: The Macmillan Press Ltd, pp. 95–126.
94 Stoneman, Foreign capital, pp. 62–83
95 Skalnes, *The politics of economic reform in Zimbabwe*, pp. 97–149.
96 Stoneman, C. 'The World Bank and the IMF in Zimbabwe'. In Campbell, B. K., and Loxley, J. *Structural Adjustment in Africa*, Basingstoke: Palgrave Macmillan., pp. 37–66.
97 Stoneman, The World Bank, pp. 37–66.
98 Dawson M. and Kelsall, T., 2012. Anti-developmental patrimonialism in Zimbabwe. *Journal of Contemporary African Studies*, 30(1), pp. 49–66. doi: 10.1080/02589001.2012.643010
99 Skalnes, *The politics of economic reform in Zimbabwe*, pp.104–5.
100 Stoneman, The World Bank, pp. 37–66.
101 Notably, drought and South African sponsored insurgency in the southwestern part of the country – see Scarnecchia, T., 2011. Rationalizing Gukurahundi: Cold War and South African foreign relations with Zimbabwe, 1981–1983. *Kronos*, 37(1), pp. 87–103 doi: 10.2307/41502446 – on South Africa's destabilization efforts in Zimbabwe.
102 Stoneman, 'The World Bank', p. 39.
103 Stoneman, 'The World Bank', pp. 37–66.
104 Bond, P. and Manyanya, S., 2002. *Zimbabwe's plunge: Exhausted nationalism, neoliberalism and the search for social justice*. Africa World Press.
105 Newman, 'Finance and development', pp. 587–619.
106 Skalnes, *The politics of economic reform in Zimbabwe*, p.105.
107 Stoneman, 'The World Bank', pp. 37–66.
108 In 1987, the World Bank provided US$70m under the Export Revolving Fund which was exclusively for the benefit of producers of manufactured exports. Dashwood, H.S., 2000. *Zimbabwe: The Political Economy of Transformation*. Toronto: University of Toronto Press.
109 Dashwood, H.S., 1996. The relevance of class to the evolution of Zimbabwe's development strategy. *Journal of Southern African Studies*, 22(1), pp. 27–48.
110 Simpson, M. and Hawkins, T., 2018. *The primacy of regime survival: State fragility and economic destruction in Zimbabwe*. Cham: Palgrave Macmillan, p. 65. doi: 10.1007/978-3-319-72520-8

111 GOZ. 1991. *Zimbabwe: A framework for economic reform 1991–1995*, Harare, p. 4.
112 Bond, P., *Uneven Zimbabwe.*
113 Tembo, J., 2016, Bank failures in Zimbabwe. In George Kararach and Raphael O. Otieno, eds, *Economic Management in a Hyperinflationary Environment: The Political Economy of Zimbabwe, 1980–2008*, Oxford Scholarship Online. doi: 10.1093/acprof
114 Simpson and Hawkins, *The primacy of regime survival*, pp. 65.
115 Dashwood, *Zimbabwe*, pp. 191–192.
116 Moyo, T., 2010. *Financial sector liberalization and the poor: A critical appraisal. SAPRI-Zimbabwe Initiative Poverty Reduction Forum.* www.saprin.org/zimbabwe/research/zim_fin_sect.pdf [Accessed 25 March 2021].
117 Zimbabwean billionaire Strive Masiyiwa is a product of the IBDC, together with notable figures like Philip Chiyangwa, Chemist Siziba, and Mutumwa Mawere. Fidelity Mhlanga, *Zimbabwe Tycoons Sink into Oblivion*, 2015. Available at: www.theindependent.co.zw/2015/03/27/zimbabwe-tycoons-sink-into-oblivion [Accessed 25 March 2021].
118 Bond, *Uneven Zimbabwe*, p. 366.
119 Measured by private credit by deposit money banks and other financial institutions to GDP: defined as claims on the private sector by deposit money banks and other financial institutions divided by GDP (Beck et. al., 'Financial institutions and markets across countries and over time' 2009, p. 5).
120 As measured by the ratio of liquid liabilities to GDP. Thorsten Beck, Asli Demirguc-Kunt, and Ross Levine, 2009. *Financial Institutions and Markets across Countries and over Time.* Available at: documents.worldbank.org/curated/en/2009/05/10682384/financial-institutions-markets-across-countries-over-time-data-analysis
121 Moyo, 'Financial Sector Liberalization and the Poor', pp. 1–2.
122 Chitiyo, K., 2000. *Land violence and compensation: Reconceptualising Zimbabwe's land and veterans' debate.* Available at: idl-bnc-idrc.dspacedirect.org/handle/10625/28393 [Accessed 25 March 2021].
123 Carver, R., 2000. *Zimbabwe: A Strategy of Tension.* WRITENET. Available at: www.refworld.org/pdfid/3ae6a6c70.pdf
124 Dashwood, *Zimbabwe*, p. 194
125 Kairiza, 'Unbundling Zimbabwe's Journey to Hyperinflation and Official Dollarization', pp. 4.
126 Carver, 'Zimbabwe: A strategy of tension', p.11.
127 Kairiza, 'Unbundling Zimbabwe's Journey to Hyperinflation and Official Dollarization', p. 4.
128 Gono, G., 2008. *Zimbabwe's casino economy: Extraordinary measures for extraordinary challenges.* Harare: ZPH Publishers (Pvt) Ltd.
129 Bond, P., 2007. Competing explanations of Zimbabwe's long economic crisis. *Safundi*, 8(2), pp. 149–81. doi: org/10.1080/17533170701370976
130 Bond and Manyanya, 'Zimbabwe's plunge', pp. 28–63.

131 Moyo, S. and Yeros, P., 2007. The radicalised state: Zimbabwe's interrupted evolution. *Review of African Political Economy*, 34(111), pp. 103–21. doi.org/10.1080/03056240701340431
132 Zimbabwe's independence was a negotiated settlement between international capital, white agrarian elites, and nationalists at Lancaster House.
133 Dawson and Kelsall, 'Anti-developmental patrimonialism in Zimbabwe', p. 55.
134 Moyo and Yeros, 'The Radicalised State', p. 105.
135 *Ibid.*
136 Kairiza, 'Unbundling Zimbabwe's Journey to Hyperinflation and Official Dollarization', p. 7.
137 Scoones, I. et al., 2018. Tobacco, contract farming, and agrarian change in Zimbabwe. *Journal of Agrarian Change*, 18(1), pp. 22–42. doi: org/10.1111/joac.12210
138 United States Congress, 2001. *S.494 – Zimbabwe Democracy and Economic Recovery Act of 2001*, p. 115. STAT. 963. Available at: www.congress.gov/107/plaws/publ99/PLAW-107publ99.pdf
139 Gono, G. *Zimbabwe's casino economy: Extraordinary measures for extraordinary challenges* (Harare: ZPH Publishers (Pvt) Ltd, 2008).
140 Jones, J.L., 2010. Nothing is straight in Zimbabwe: The rise of the Kukiya-Kiya economy 2000–2008. *Journal of Southern African Studies*, 36(2), pp. 285–99. doi.org/10.1080/03057070.2010.485784
141 Gono, Zimbabwe's casino economy, p. xi.
142 Tembo, 'Bank failures in Zimbabwe', p. 13.
143 Fundira, B., 2007. Money Laundering in Zimbabwe, 2004 to 2006. In Charles Goredema, ed., *Confronting the proceeds of crime in Southern Africa*. Pretoria: Institute for Security Studies. Available at: oldsite.issafrica.org/uploads/M132FULL.PDF
144 Gono, 'Zimbabwe's casion economy', pp. 65–72.
145 Fundira, 'Money laundering in Zimbabwe', p. 47.
146 Tembo, 'Bank failures in Zimbabwe', p. 14.
147 Nyamadzawo, J., 2016. Operations, regulation, and practices of the Zimbabwe stock exchange during the hyperinflationary period, 2000–2008. In George Kararach and Raphael O. Otieno, eds., Economic management in a hyperinflationary environment: the political economy of Zimbabwe 1980-2008, Oxford University Press. doi: org/10.1093/acprof
148 IMF, Staff Report for the 2003 Article IV Consultation, July 2003, 03/224. Available at: www.imf.org/external/pubs/ft/scr/2003/cr03224.pdf [Accessed 25 March 2021].
149 Makoni, A.T., 2006. *Aetiology of Zimbabwe banking crisis 2003–2004*. University forum. http://universityofzimbabwenews.blogspot.com/2006/08/aetiology-of-zimbabwe-banking-crisis.html. [Accessed 25 March 2021].
150 Kairiza, 'Unbundling Zimbabwe's Journey to Hyperinflation and Official Dollarization', p. 9.

151 Unfortunately, published Zimbabwean financial statistics do not break down access level by income groups, making it harder to determine the level of access to financial services across various social groups
152 Makoni, 'Aetiology of Zimbabwe Banking Crisis', para. 1.
153 Moyo, 'Financial Sector Liberalization and the Poor', p.16 .
154 Sibanda, G.J., 2017. *Institutional responses to the Zimbabwe economic crisis: The case of the Reserve Bank of Zimbabwe's quasi-fiscal activities, 1997–2009.* (Dissertation)
155 Mackenzie, G.A. and Stella, P., 1996. *Quasi-fiscal operations of public financial institutions, IMF Occasional Papers.* MCMXCVI, p. 17.
156 Parliament of Zimbabwe, 2015. *National Assembly Hansard 17 February 2015 Vol 41 No 17.* Available at: www.parlzim.gov.zw/national-assembly-hansard/national-assembly-hansard-17-february-2015-vol-41-no-17
157 Parliament of Zimbabwe, 2015. *Reserve Bank of Zimbabwe (Debt Assumption) Act, 2015.* Available at: zimlii.org/zw/legislation/act/2015/22015
158 Gono, 'Zimbabwe's casino economy', p. xv
159 Munoz, S., 2007. *Central bank quasi-Fiscal losses and high inflation in Zimbabwe: A Note.* Available at: www.imf.org/en/Publications/WP/Issues/2016/12/31/Central-Bank-Quasi-Fiscal-Losses-and-High-Inflation-in-Zimbabwe-A-Note-20630 [Accessed 25 March 2021].
160 *Ibid.*, 6.
161 Sibanda, 'Institutional Responses to the Zimbabwe Economic Crisis', p. 49
162 Munoz, 'Central bank quasi-fiscal losses and high inflation in Zimbabwe', p.10.
163 *Ibid.*, p. 10
164 *Ibid.*, p. 10
165 *Ibid.*, p. 10
166 *Ibid.*, 6.
167 Parliament of Zimbabwe. *Reserve Bank of Zimbabwe (Debt Assumption) Act 2015.*
168 *Ibid.*, 20–72.
169 Coomer, J. and Gstraunthaler, T., 2011. The Hyperinflation in Zimbabwe. *The Quarterly Journal of Austrian Economics*, 14(3), pp. 311–46. doi.org/10.5055/ajrt.2011.0028
170 Jones, J.L., 2010, 'Nothing is straight in Zimbabwe: The rise of the Kukiya-Kiya economy 2000–2008', *Journal of Southern African Studies*, 36(2), pp. 285–99. doi: .org/10.1080/03057070.2010.485784Jones.
171 Sanderson, A. Social Challenges of Hyperinflation. In George Kararach and Raphael O. Otieno, eds, *Economic management in a hyperinflationary environment.* Oxford Scholarship Online: Oxford University Press. doi.org/10.1093/acprof
172 Sibanda, 'Institutional Responses to the Zimbabwe Economic Crisis', p. 57.
173 Hanke and Kwok, 'On the measurement of Zimbabwe's hyperinflation', p. 354.

174 Noko, J., 2011. Dollarization: The case of Zimbabwe. *Cato Journal*, 31(2), pp. 339–66. doi.org/10.3868/s050-004-015-0003-8

175 Skalnes, The politics of economic reform in Zimbabwe, p. 137.

176 BBC News, 2019. *Zimbabwe dollar notes issued for first time in a decade.* Available at: www.bbc.co.uk/news/world-africa-50374402

177 Government of Zimbabwe, 2019. The 2019 National Budget Statement.

178 Ashman, S., Newman, S.A., and Tregenna, T. Radical Perspectives on Industrial Policy. In Arkebe Oqubay et al., 2020. *The Oxford Handbook of Industrial Policy*. Oxford: OUP.

# 4
# Monetary Policy in Algeria (1999–2019): An economic and monetary history approach

*Fatiha Talahite*

## INTRODUCTION

In Algeria, where 132 years of French colonisation destroyed indigenous institutions, and independence was won at the price of a long war of liberation (1954–1962), sovereignty is a particularly sensitive issue. Indeed, the slightest vulnerability stokes fears of falling once again under the yoke of the former colonial power, or of another dominant nation. Independent, the country gained the trappings of political sovereignty: a state, a flag, a national anthem, an army.

Derogating from the Evian Agreements (1962),[1] in April 1964, Algeria decided to leave the Franc zone and created its own currency, the Algerian Dinar (DA), thus regaining its monetary sovereignty,[2] following the example of Morocco and Tunisia.[3] The DA, which was non-convertible, maintained a fixed parity with the Franc (1 DA for 1 Franc), and an exchange rate of about 1 USD for 5 DA, until the devaluation of the dollar in 1971 and the collapse of the Bretton Woods system. In 1974, the Algerians decided to have the value of the dinar depend on a basket of 14 currencies, the definition of which remains secret. This allowed them to stabilise the DA and to carry out a vast economic development programme sheltered from monetary storms, until the downward oil shock of 1985–1986.[4]

The purpose of this chapter is to provide an account of the evolution of monetary policy in Algeria as it relates to the issue of sovereignty. I will investigate how, subject to strong external financial, political, and economic constraints, the authorities created room for manoeuvre, the means they used, and the extent to which they succeeded in preserving the country's monetary sovereignty. I will look at the role played by the Income Regulation Fund (FRR) in this context. The period of time under consideration coincides with the reign of President Bouteflika (1999–2019). This timeline makes it possible to study this policy; first, from a situation of abundant fossil fuel revenues (1999–2014), to a downward shock (2014) and, finally, up to the resignation of Bouteflika on April 2019, amid heavy contests from the streets against the regime and its policies.

The literature review paints a paradoxical picture, pointing on the one hand to the failure, or at least the inadequacy, of this policy, and on the other to a certain resilience of the monetary and financial system, when compared to other similar countries, like Venezuela.[5] Indeed, inflation seems to have been brought under control and the purchasing power of the dinar has been preserved, while the economic collapse forecast several years ago by experts has not (yet) materialised. However, this observation must be qualified, insofar as the lack or even absence of reliable statistical data makes it impossible to know the true state of the economy. After a brief review of the literature on banking and financial reforms in the Middle East and North Africa (Mena) region and a presentation of the context, which preceded the period under study, I will analyse this policy in a situation of abundant resources (1999–2014) and then after a bearish shock (2014–2019).

## THE DEBATE OVER BANKING AND FINANCIAL REFORMS IN THE MENA REGION

*Reform and sovereignty:* In the 1970s and 1980s the external debt crisis led many developing countries to conditionally submit to IMF and World Bank structural adjustment programs (SAPs). These countries lost their sovereignty over economic and monetary policy for a time through forced budget cuts and sharply devalued currencies in order to restore financial equilibria. It is within this framework that reforms were recommended to them. These were not aimed at avoiding using debt to finance development, but rather at transforming its terms and conditions so that it would be more rational and efficient, notably by replacing bank-based financing with financial market and active debt management. Most of the literature on banking and financial reforms in the Mena focus on the link between financial liberalisation and economic development. The question of sovereignty has not been central, although it re-emerges through the debate on the place and role of the state in this process, particularly in the monetary field.

*Financial liberalisation and development*: For several decades now, research on the development of the Mena has shown that these countries are not taking off when compared to those in South-East Asia. Among the reasons put forth to explain the region's growth deficit is the controversial link between financial liberalisation and development. In the years leading up to the 2008 financial crisis, some had come to believe that the development gap was not so much a matter of lacking financial resources as a misallocation of resources, with the weak performance of financial systems hampering development funding.[6] This seemed even more true for hydrocarbon exporting countries such as Algeria, which displayed a weak capacity to absorb external revenues.

The debate turned to the liberalisation of the financial sector. For some, financial reform, one of the most significant measures prescribed by the IMF under the Washington Consensus, should have been implemented prior to opening up to FDI, as its positive impacts depend on the economy's absorption capacity, which in turn is directly linked to its financial development. For others, on the contrary, it should only be implemented in the final stage of economic liberalisation. Beji sets thresholds for institutional development at which financial openness can deliver financial development. He concludes that in Mena, trade liberalisation should precede financial opening due to an unfavourable institutional and legal environment.[7]

This debate was settled, at least temporarily, by the financial crisis of 2008. The Arab economies' resilience, which was attributed to weak integration into the world financial system, lent credence to the claims of those who feared the opening up of financial systems and called for a gradual approach. Whereas previously reforming the banking system meant liberalising it, a progressive approach was now favoured, separating the 'modernisation' of national financial institutions from their opening to international finance. The priority shifted to the necessary upgrading of banks and financial institutions, both in terms of governance and of technical innovation. These reforms were implemented with the help and expertise of the Bretton Woods institutions and the European Union, within the framework of association agreements. According to Ayadi et al.,[8] one of the main objectives of the reforms should have been to decrease the role of the state in the banking sector, while ensuring that the regulatory framework and institutional development adequately address market imperfections. They believe that standards, such as Basel II capital standards, were designed for developed countries and may not be appropriate due to various gaps in information sharing and institutional mechanisms. Others question the relevance of this model for the Mena, arguing that none of these countries have the monetary architecture necessary for a 'modern' policy of the inflation targeting type.[9] Implementing such a system comes at a cost in terms of capital and already scarce intellectual and physical resources. The cost would first have to be estimated and compared with the likely benefits. From this point of view, the strategic choice made by some countries, particularly the smaller ones, to fix the exchange rate because of their inability to conduct an effective monetary policy may, indeed, be appropriate.[10]

## MONETARY REFORM AND STRUCTURAL ADJUSTMENT IN ALGERIA

*The 1989–1991 reform:* Following the 1985–1986 fall in oil prices, the economic system that had been built up through costly investment programmes proved to be rigid, with little resistance capacity to the external shocks to which it was particularly exposed.[11] In the wake of the riots of October 1988, in a context of worrying internal[12] and external debt, the appointment of a 'reformist' government (1989–1991) marked the start of a comprehensive reform project explicitly aimed at reinstating market rules into the economy and, in particular, at restoring financial constraints on banks[13] and public companies. The project was drawn up in a public sector-dominated economic environment largely dependent on exporting hydrocarbons, where the banking and monetary system, including the central bank, was administered on the model of the Soviet Gosbank, under the supervision of the Ministry of Finance. The priority was then to provide the government with the economic policy tools that the administered system had deprived it of. Although it was a decided break with the previous policy, this process of reform was gradual and was to be progressively extended to the entire economy.

The Law on Currency and Credit (*Loi sur la monnaie et le crédit* or LMC, April 1990), one of the first to be promulgated by the government of Mouloud Hamrouche without waiting for the election of the new national assembly,[14] transformed the former Central Bank of Algeria (CBA), renamed Bank of Algeria (BA), into a 'commercial' bank and asserted its independence. The bank was now headed by a governor appointed by the President of the Republic, whose mandate exceeds the latter's by one year, and a Money and Credit Council chaired by the governor.[15]

The independence of the central bank was, at the time, at the very core of the European monetary debate[16] in the run-up to the creation of the Euro. At stake was the transfer of monetary sovereignty from the level of nations to that of the European Union.[17] Algerian reformers put it on their own agenda. In a context in which economic and political changes (end of the single party system and introduction of multipartism, creation of representative institutions) were going to transform the institutional landscape, officials wanted to make the central bank an independent institution to safeguard it and protect it from the uncertainty of political reform.[18] The LMC restricted and strictly regulated the possibility for the central bank to advance funds to the Treasury, which the previous regime had abused. It stipulated that the Treasury had to repay the liabilities within 15 years. This was included in the law in order to make it a dogma that can only be understood in light of previous excesses.

The issue of sovereignty then arose crucially, in regard to Algeria's loss of solvency and the risk of a suspension of payments that would have led to a rescheduling of the external debt. For the reformers, regaining financial sovereignty required the revival of economic growth by the rehabilitation of the market and its institutions within the national economy, recognising in particular the place and role of private enterprise, which the previous system had totally marginalised. On the other hand, external opening and integration into the world economy was considered as a very gradual process and had to remain under control.

In order to avoid a rescheduling, a prospect dreaded as an unacceptable attack on national sovereignty, the government was negotiating with its creditors a 'reprofiling' of its debts without the mediation of the International Financial Institutions (IFIs).[19] This was made possible both by Algeria's solvency as a hydrocarbon exporter and by the fact that these loans were mostly short-term. The objective was to gain time while waiting for growth to resume, so as to carry out its own adjustment within the framework of a reform project independent of rescheduling conditionality.[20] The buyback of 60 per cent of the short-term debt to convert it into indirect investments, through equity investments, was proposed to institutional investors. This meant speeding up reforms to open the capital of certain public companies to foreign investment. Investors were reluctant to embrace this proposal because of the lack of a financial market and the uncertainty of the reforms.

The reformist government, which had been committed to transparency[21] and open public debate,[22] faced strong opposition on the proposed reforms and the issue of external debt. While some opposed both reform and rescheduling and advocated rather for austerity policies to get the country out of the crisis,[23] others downplayed rescheduling, believing that structural adjustment under IMF leadership would provide an opportunity to overcome internal resistance and accelerate reforms. After the coup d'état of January 1992, these two options were tested in turn, the first in 1992–1993, the second during the SAPs, 1994–1999.

Political liberalisation unleashed a powerful social and political dynamic that caused the withdrawal of military support for the reformist team, which led to the fall of the government in June 1991, a few months before the first pluralist legislative elections. In September 1991, the dinar was depreciated by 22 per cent with a view to opening up foreign trade. Algeria obtained credit from the IMF, conditional on performance criteria that were essentially aimed at limiting monetary creation. To comply with the statutes of the Bretton Woods institution, the monetary authorities had to pledge to eliminate the multiple exchange regime and move towards abolishing exchange controls. Indeed, as in most socialist countries, there were several exchange rates for the dinar depending on how they were used.

*'War economy' (1992–1993) and Structural adjustment (1994–1998)*: The interruption and subsequent cancellation of the legislative elections followed by the coup d'état of January 1992 marked the end of the reform process, both politically and economically. Parallel to the state of emergency, the 'war economy', in the words of the head of government Belaid Abdessalem, was set up. The LMC was revised and the Central Bank, which changed governor, was brought back under government control. The decision to return to multiple exchange rates was rejected by the IMF. As a result, and particularly after structural adjustment, the authorities relied on the parallel currency market as a substitute for the legal multiple exchange rate, replacing it with a tolerated legal/illegal double exchange rate. This market, which already existed as a corollary of exchange controls and the non-convertibility of the dinar, took on such proportions with the opening of foreign trade that it became a de facto informal institution within the Algerian monetary system. Unchecked by the authorities it became integrated into monetary policy.[24]

In 1994, faced with a suspension of payments, Algeria requested the rescheduling of its external debt and was obliged to negotiate a SAP with the IFIs. Discussions stumbled over the issues of the public sector, its restructuring and privatisation, the role of the state as an economic actor, and the liberalisation of foreign trade. The low bargaining power of a regime with no legitimacy resulted in it agreeing to standard structural adjustment measures lacking continuity and consistency with the previously initiated reform process. From then on, 'transition' was largely subject to the requirements of SAPs.

Debt rescheduling agreements brought in $20–22 billion in new money. In return, the government committed Algeria to a structural adjustment plan with its creditors, including macro-financial stabilisation measures (reducing inflation, devaluation[25] and convertibility of the dinar in foreign trade transactions, price liberalisation, liberalisation of foreign trade, and a return to internal and external equilibrium) as a precondition for structural reforms. Privatisation was a centrepiece of the IFI's reform agenda.

While the second SAP ended in a period with a depressed oil price,[26] a salutary reversal of the world oil market at the beginning of 1999 saved Algeria in extremis from a third rescheduling, which had been considered inevitable a few months earlier. After seven years of violence and destruction, the anticipated presidential elections of April 1999 brought Bouteflika to power.

## MONETARY POLICY IN A TIME OF RESOURCE BOOM (1999–2014)

*The monetary issue in oil countries:* One aspect of this issue was theorised by the Dutch disease effect on the exchange rate. This effect is a special case of the Balassa-Samuelson effect,[27] which holds that, in a catching-up economy exposed to international competition, productivity in the 'tradable' goods sector (on external markets) tends on average to increase faster than that in the 'non-tradable' sector (domestic market). As wages adjust broadly to this increase, labour costs in the non-tradable sector rise relative to productivity. The price of non-tradables relative to tradables then tends to rise relative to foreign countries, and the real exchange rate tends to rise. In an oil economy, the tradable goods sector is the oil sector. The increase in the value of oil exports is reflected in a tendency for the currency to appreciate (in real terms), which leads to a decline in the competitiveness of local industry (non-tradable) because of high labour costs relative to productivity. The latter loses market shares on the export or on the domestic market, when it is subjected to international competition, which can go as far as deindustrialisation. In order to defend local industry, the exchange rate policy can aim to limit this appreciation. However, in the context of free movement of capital and international integration, the use of exchange rate controls is incompatible with an autonomous monetary policy,[28] so that traditional instruments (the constitution of foreign exchange reserves, sterilisation, and interest rate control) prove ineffective in achieving internal objectives, particularly in terms of economic growth. Faced with these constraints, a government may be tempted to control capital flows in a way that favours their exit or restricts their entry, and thus hinder integration into the world economy. The main recommendation to avoid Dutch Disease syndrome is to diversify production and exports. But this solution is hampered by the low competitiveness of the local industry, itself an effect of the Dutch Disease.[29] It is theoretically easier to implement when hydrocarbon export revenues fall, which leads to a depreciation in real terms of the local currency and, therefore, allows exports to become more competitive in regaining market shares.

Finally, there are other problems facing oil-producing countries, notably the volatility of oil prices and the amplitude of their fluctuations, which subject these economies to shocks that can sometimes be very violent.

*Dealing with external shocks*: The Algerian economy faces two types of external shocks: oil price shocks and euro and dollar exchange rate shocks.[30] They can act in the same way or, on the contrary, cancel each other out. In the face of this vulnerability, the economic policy pursued by governments will aim at stabilisation. On the one hand, monetary policy consistently targets a priority objective of limited inflation (Table 4.1) to ensure the stability of the dinar;[31] on the other hand, fiscal policy is subject to a new mechanism, the Income Stabilisation Fund (*Fonds de Stabilisation des Recettes*, FRR), which aims to stabilise state revenues and expenditure.

*Table 4.1* Inflation rate (2000-2014) %

| Year | Inflation rate |
|---|---|
| 2000 | 0,3 |
| 2001 | 4,2 |
| 2002 | 1,4 |
| 2003 | 2,4 |
| 2004 | 3,6 |
| 2005 | 1,6 |
| 2006 | 2,5 |
| 2007 | 3,5 |
| 2008 | 4,4 |
| 2009 | 5,7 |
| 2010 | 3,9 |
| 2011 | 4,52 |
| 2012 | 8,9 |
| 2013 | 3,2 |
| 2014 | 2,9 |

Source: Ministry of Finance.

It had been argued that this monetary policy, this monetary policy was not adapted to cope with oil shocks.[32] They showed that, over the period 1990–2010, the core (long-term) inflation target would have been the best policy to stabilise output and inflation, and the best way to improve social welfare. The adoption of a core inflation targeting framework requires certain preconditions, such as central bank independence and reliance on interest rates as the main instrument of monetary policy. These authors argue that, on both these points, Algeria lags behind other upper-middle income countries, including the MENA countries. Strengthening the interest rate as a channel for monetary policy transmission involves encouraging bank credit to the private sector and developing the capital market. But, as the authors acknowledge, the model does not consider fiscal policy, in particular the FRR, which aims to reduce the sensitivity of fiscal policy to fluctuations in hydrocarbon revenues.

*The Income Stabilisation Fund (FRR)*: Disruptions in oil prices immediately affect public revenue, a phenomenon which is accentuated in Algeria where the amount of income (especially from fossil fuels) is more unpredictable than public spending, and the revenue variables are more volatile than those of expenditure.[33] Empirical studies show that oil exporting countries often pursue pro-cyclical budgetary policies. In boom times, windfall revenues from exports are mainly used to boost investment in infrastructure and the public wage bill, through wage increases and public sector job creation;[34] whereas, after a downward resource shock, policies to reduce public spending, especially on subsidies, public employment, and wages, are socially and politically difficult to implement. Governments then tend to favour monetary measures (currency depreciation or devaluation, and inflation).

In order to force itself into a countercyclical fiscal policy, the government introduced a mechanism to insulate public finances from oil price volatility.[35] This framework has two components:

(A) A fiscal reference price of the barrel (FRP/B), set by the authorities, is introduced for the calculation of oil taxation as part of the forecast revenue of the state budget;[36] this notional barrel price is intended to smooth out the effects of oil price volatility;
(B) A special Treasury account, the FRR, is created (complementary finance law of 2000), which records in revenue the fiscal gains resulting from a level of oil price higher than the budget forecasts

> and, in expenditure, the compensation of the part of the budget deficit 'resulting from a level of oil tax revenue lower than the finance law forecast' (finance law, 2004), excluding deficits linked to other factors. The latter clarification reflects a preoccupation with maintaining FRR revenue and expenditure in line with the same logic linked to the strict cyclical fluctuations in oil market prices. It also expresses the authorities' intention to diversify the state's resources and is a signal against the propensity for uncontrolled increases in public spending, typical of oil economies in boom periods.

The FRR is a special allocation account of the Treasury. A legacy of the French system of national accounting, these accounts were designed to deal with exceptional targeted and specific expenditure, by temporarily derogating from the democratic principle of the universality of the budget, which requires that revenues be calculated globally and then allocated to the various expenditure items. The budget, as a part of the annual finance law, has to be discussed, amended, and voted on by the National Assembly and the Senate, and then published in the Official Journal. This derogation is limited and regulated, and must not in any case exceed one year.

However, the FRR is not adapted to this framework. First, its objective of 'regulating the budget balance' is not a one-off. Second, as soon as it was set up, it was assigned a second objective, the early repayment of the public debt.[37] But above all, the 2006 finance law allowed the FRR to fund budget deficits that no longer result solely from cyclical variations in the price of oil, opening the way to a systematic transgression of the principle of the universality of the budget.

By keeping the fiscal reference price per barrel (FRP/B) far below the average annual market price (AMP/B), the government imposed a policy of budgetary austerity, in a context where the oil price remained at exceptionally high levels.[38] However, since the 1994–98 SAPs, wages have hardly increased,[39] and there has been very little public job creation. Apart from temporary measures to promote youth employment, no major policy has been implemented to create jobs in industry and services. The accumulation of growing surpluses in the FRR was becoming less and less justified in the eyes of the public, given the tremendous needs of society and the economy. Eventually, protests led authorities to gradually ease their control over spending.

But it is mainly to avoid the contagion of the 'Arab springs' that the government let public spending blow up from 2011. In fact, wage increases and job creation in the public sector, as well as the rise in the National Guaranteed Minimum Wage,[40] which are seen as a way to buy social peace, barely make up for some of the delay accumulated since the SAPs in the evolution of employment and purchasing power. This increase in public expenditure generated artificial budget deficits, compensated by the FFR (Table 4.2). These amounts, subtracted from the calculation of the budget, escape any control. Through this subterfuge, a large part of the state's revenue is allocated in a discretionary manner and in the greatest opacity, opening the way to an unprecedented expansion of bribery and corruption.

The Treasury's special accounts were not designed to carry out strategic tasks such as financing the budget deficit or early repayment of the public debt. Internal control procedures are not adequate, given the amounts involved.[41] In reality, the FRR has never been audited. As a simple account managed by the Ministry of Finance, it has no autonomous institutional existence. As it is not remunerated, it is impossible to calculate the profitability of the use of the oil tax surpluses allocated to it. It cannot be assimilated to a sovereign wealth fund, insofar as it does not aim to constitute savings, invest them and make them bear fruit for future generations, or invest in development, or for any other public utility purpose.

The question of giving an institutional status to the FRR has been debated and several solutions have been proposed, including: converting it 'into a savings and financing account fully integrated into the budget';[42] or by creating a *Caisse des Dépôts et Consignations* on the French model,[43] already adopted by Morocco; or a sovereign wealth fund,[44] without any decision having been taken by the authorities to regularise the status of this fund.[45]

The FRR played a role in monetary policy as well. The volatility of oil prices also has an impact on the money supply. A high price can create excess liquidity in the economy, while a price fall can lead to a situation of tight liquidity. In this regard, the FRR was used to stem the surplus in dinars, matched by foreign exchange reserves held by the central bank. Through its capacity to withdraw or, conversely, reinject huge quantities of money into the economy, it weighs on the money supply and the determination of variables such as the inflation rate, the interest

*Table 4.2* Resources and uses of the FRR 2000–2016 (billions DA)

| Years | 2000 | 2001 | 2002 | 2003 | 2004 | 2005 | 2006 | 2007 | 2008 | 2009 | 2010 | 2011 | 2012 | 2013 | 2014 | 2015 | 2016 |
|---|---|---|---|---|---|---|---|---|---|---|---|---|---|---|---|---|---|
| Remaining at 01/01 | 0 | 232 | 249 | 276 | 568 | 722 | 1843 | 2931 | 3216 | 4280 | 4317 | 4843 | 5382 | 5634 | 5564 | 408 | 2074 |
| Oil tax (Finance Law calculation) | 720 | 841 | 916 | 836 | 862 | 899 | 916 | 973 | 1715 | 1927 | 1502 | 1529 | 1519 | 1616 | 1578 | 1722 | 1683 |
| Oil tax recovered | 1173 | 964 | 943 | 1285 | 1486 | 2268 | 2714 | 2712 | 4004 | 2828 | 2820 | 3830 | 4054 | 3678 | 3388 | 2275 | 1781 |
| Capital gain on oil tax | 453 | 124 | 27 | 449 | 623 | 1369 | 1798 | 1739 | 2288 | 401 | 1318 | 2300 | 2535 | 2062 | 1811 | 552 | 99 |
| Advance of BA | – | – | – | – | 0 | 0 | 0 | 0 | 0 | 0 | 0 | 0 | 0 | 0 | 0 | 0 | 0 |
| Availability before withdrawals | 453 | 356 | 198 | 477 | 944 | 2090 | 3641 | 4670 | 5504 | 4681 | 5635 | 7143 | 7917 | 7696 | 7374 | 4960 | 2172 |
| % of GDP | 10,9 | 8,4 | 4,4 | 9,1 | 15,3 | 37,5 | 42,7 | 49,9 | 49,6 | 46,6 | 46,5 | 49,6 | 48,8 | 46,2 | 42,8 | 29,9 | 12,6 |
| Public debt repayments | 221 | 107 | 0 | 156 | 470 | 248 | 618 | 314 | 465 | 0 | 0 | 0 | 0 | 0 | 0 | 0 | 0 |
| Advance of BA repayments | – | – | – | – | 0 | 0 | 0 | 608 | 0 | 0 | 0 | 0 | 0 | 0 | 0 | 0 | 0 |
| Treasury Deficit Financing | 0 | 0 | 0 | 0 | 0 | 0 | 92 | 532 | 758 | 365 | 792 | 1761 | 2283 | 2132 | 2966 | 2886 | 1388 |
| Total withdrawals | 221 | 184 | 170 | 156 | 223 | 248 | 710 | 1454 | 1224 | 364 | 792 | 1761 | 2283 | 2132 | 2966 | 2886 | 1388 |
| Remaining at 31/12 | 232 | 249 | 276 | 568 | 722 | 1843 | 2931 | 3216 | 4280 | 4316 | 4843 | 5382 | 5634 | 5564 | 4408 | 2074 | 794 |
| % of GDP | 5,6 | 5,9 | 6,1 | 10,8 | 11,7 | 33,1 | 34,4 | 34,3 | 38,6 | 43 | 40 | 37,4 | 34,7 | 33,4 | 25,6 | 12,5 | 4,6 |

Sources: FMI; Ministry of Finance, ONS, Algiers

rate, and the exchange rate. Even if it can converge with the objectives pursued by the BA, its action disrupts the BA's policy, if only because of a dual decision-making centre, and because it does not fit into the same agenda. Thus, a BA report states that 'the emergence of net claims of the Treasury on the banking system has a profound influence on the conduct of monetary policy'.[46] The Treasury has been a net creditor of the banking system since late 2004, even though in 2006 it resorted to exceptional advances from the BA to prepay the rescheduled debt. The report notes that part of this debt was transformed into Treasury debt to the BA without drawing on the FRR, thus increasing domestic public debt. This debt is also fuelled by the Treasury's repurchase of non-performing public bank[47] debt, which explains the decline in demand for liquidity on the interbank market.

The compensation of growing budget deficits by the FRR led to the injection of previously 'sterilised' funds into the economy. This only aggravated the crisis of excess bank liquidity, so that most of the monetary policy consisted in trying to mop it up.[48] The absorption of primary bank liquidity by the Central Bank at a high rate with no corresponding risk encouraged banks to build up idle resources and discouraged credit activity, at the expense of production. This is the paradox of excess bank liquidity and the underfunding of the economy.[49] Imports, which are tantamount to destroying dinars through the purchase of foreign currency, are favoured. Throughout this period, the rediscounting system was put on hold. Neither the interbank market nor the open market was operational.

## MONETARY POLICY FOLLOWING A BEARISH RESOURCE SHOCK (2014–2019)

In late June 2014, a sharp fall in the price of oil caused a sudden turnaround in the economic outlook, which very quickly resulted in a drastic drop in external resources and state revenue, and the widening of twin deficits: the current account deficit of the balance of payments and the budget deficit. The authorities continued to draw on the savings accumulated in the FRR. Due to the size of the budget deficits to be filled and the lack of oil tax surpluses to replenish it, this fund was depleted in 2017 (see Table 4.2).

At the monetary level, the fall in hydrocarbon export revenues had the dual outcome of reducing foreign exchange reserves and squeezing the main engine of monetary creation, the dinar exchange of external revenues, thus putting the banks in a situation of illiquidity. The monetary authorities regularly depreciated the dinar, but without going as far as to devalue it, as requested by the IMF.

The 'orthodox' management of the dinar was abandoned in 2016. The international context had become more favourable to so-called 'accommodating' monetary policies, since their adoption by Western central banks (the Fed and the ECB) to support their economies. A study on Algerian monetary policy between 2007 and 2014[50] questioned whether this policy was transposable to the Algerian post-oil shock context, where the weakness of credit is linked to structural causes. After the chronic excess liquidity of banks had rendered the transmission of monetary policies to growth inoperative, the author wonders whether the fall in hydrocarbon prices and the quasi-structural illiquidity that followed was favourable to the accommodative open-market monetary policy adopted by the Bank of Algeria in September 2016. The author deplores the lack of macroeconomic impact studies to assess the effects of this policy, resulting in the central bank 'flying blind'.

The monetary authorities adopted measures to help refinance the banks: lowering the rate of compulsory reserves from 12 to 8 per cent in 2014; the refinancing of Treasury bills in excess of three years; and the rediscounting of private claims (the rediscounting rate went from 4 to 3.5 per cent in 2015). New regulations aim to fluidify the banks' liquidity. This unconventional policy of qualitative easing quickly finds its limits in the rigidity of the banking system. Obstacles to the transmission of these actions on the volume and quality of credit include the lack of a real credit market and the delayed reaction time of economic agents.[51] These instruments can take up to three years to have an impact, making them ineffective in responding to the economic situation, and even likely to have delayed effects contrary to those intended.[52]

The Central Bank tried without much success to encourage banks to use the interbank market and the open market, both of which had become obsolete due to a prolonged period of excess liquidity. Public bankers lacked the expertise to handle these instruments but, more importantly, the liquidity shortage had affected the entire system, which required deeper measures. To draw money to the banks, a voluntary tax compliance programme was launched in early August 2016. Targeting the money of the informal sector, it granted a kind of tax amnesty to fraudsters to place their money in banks at rates that were meant to be attractive. The government also launched a large national bond issue,[53] and announced an Islamic bond (*sukuk*) called a 'participative loan'. Finally, the authorities increased administrative constraints with the sole aim of getting money into the banks, thereby aggravating market distortions and deepening the mistrust felt by economic agents.

These measures failed for two main reasons: the first relates to the deep crisis of confidence between economic agents on the one hand, and the state and the banking system on the other; the second is the fact that the authorities probably overestimated the importance of liquid savings hoarded by economic agents, the liquidity crisis stemming primarily from the fall in oil revenues and their counterpart in dinars. Indeed, the shortfall in dinars was due to the current account deficit in the balance of payments. Foreign exchange reserves fell from $194 billion in December 2013 to $102 billion at the beginning of November 2017, a drop of $92 billion. This meant that the dinar counterpart of these currencies had been depleted.

From 2017 onwards, and despite the warnings of many economic and financial experts, the unconventional financing policy crossed the threshold of quantitative easing. This consisted mainly of advances from the Central Bank to the Treasury for financing the budget deficit, as well as other extra-budgetary expenditure such as investment or pension funds. This required a further amendment to the Law on Currency and Credit. Once again, the banking system remained on the sidelines, and the Central Bank's rescue of the economy allowed the state to continue its spending spree in a context where no government could afford to curb it.

At the time, for the experts, the two remaining solutions were currency devaluation and foreign loans, a taboo under Bouteflika's reign. Paralysed by the political crisis that led to the resignation of the President in April 2019, and the organisation of a widely disputed presidential election nine months later, the authorities did not define a clear monetary policy. This period was marked by unstable governance at the Bank of Algeria, which had had three governors between May 2016 and November 2019.[54]

## CONCLUSION

Algeria's monetary policy during the two decades of Bouteflika's rule was marked by the decisive role of the FRR. Although it converged with the task assigned to the BA, focused on inflation targeting at the cost of creating a liquidity shortage, the massive nature of this fund disrupted the central bank's handling of the instruments of a more complex monetary policy capable of transmitting impulses to growth. The FRR strengthened the financial weight of the Treasury through the accumulation of oil tax surpluses, thus enabling it to circumvent the constraints of the monetary policy by emptying it of its content.

In doing so, the finance administration regained its monetary power, which had been limited by the 1990 reform. There was a kind of sharing of roles: while the Bank of Algeria served as a formal interface with the IFIs, whose advice is literally applied, most of the monetary power shifted to a special Treasury account whose management was opaque. This strategy, which is more a matter of cunning than the policy of a sovereign state, was made possible by financial manna in a resource boom situation, but it did not led to the establishment of a sustainable institutional mechanism. Throughout this period, the authorities froze any reform of the banking system, which would have meant the loss of their control over these resources. But this strategy lost its effectiveness when the oil price collapsed, exposing the vulnerabilities of the economy and its increased dependence on hydrocarbon revenues. All the more so as these revenues experienced a structural decline, beyond that caused by the fall in prices, linked to factors affecting both demand (energy transition in client countries; emergence of new, more aggressive competitors; etc.) as well as supply (a drop in production capacity due to non-renewal of equipment; depletion of wells; delays in prospecting; and uncontrolled increase in local consumption at subsidised prices; etc.). Can it be said that Algeria has recovered its financial sovereignty, if this has been done to the detriment of the entire economy? And was it necessary to go through this? Wouldn't a different policy have made it possible to alleviate the burden of the external debt thanks to the resource boom, while strengthening and diversifying the economy?

In February 2019, millions of Algerians peacefully took to the streets in many cities across the country to challenge the legitimacy of the regime. In addition to rejecting a fifth term for President Bouteflika, who has been ill and impotent since 2014, they are demanding a radical change to the 'system', in particular an end to electoral masquerades and the army's control over institutions. The *hirak* accused Bouteflika's government of squandering oil revenues and allowing the *issaba* (literally the ruling 'gang') to enrich itself shamelessly. No longer considered an exclusive matter for experts, the FRR entered the public debate as the instrument of this squandering, a kitty from which the authorities have drawn from with impunity and without limit. But, what the *hirak* raises, beyond denunciation of corruption and mismanagement of public funds, is the issue of democratic control over the state budget and its implementation. While the FRR was designed to preserve the financial sovereignty of the state by safegarding oil revenues, the *hirak* challenges the government's legitimacy in implementing such a policy in the absence of democratic control over its management of the country's resources. By brandishing Article 7 of the Constitution[55] to forcefully demand a re-foundation of the state and institutions on the basis of the principle of popular sovereignty, a prerequisite for restoring trust between the people and political power, it reminds us that sovereignty of the state is based first and foremost on its legitimacy as the expression of the nation. Beyond technical and ideological choices, this crisis of confidence is the main cause of the failure of monetary and financial policy.

## NOTES

1 'Algeria will be part of the Franc zone. It will have its own currency and its own foreign currency assets. There will be freedom of transfer between France and Algeria under conditions compatible with the economic and social development of Algeria' (Evian Agreement, 1962). For a year and a half after independence, the "Algerian Franc" was a local currency only valid within the boarders, pegged by a fixed exchange rate to the French Franc, which was its reference currency for external payments. Foreign exchange reserves were managed by the French Treasury.

2 Benissad, M. E., 1972. Du satellisme à l'indépendance monétaire. *Revue algérienne des sciences économiques, politiques et juridiques* (1972).

3 Pigeaud F. and Sylla N. S., 2021. Africa's Last Colonial Currency: The CFA Franc Story, London, Pluto Press.

4 Between December 1985 and July 1986, the price of OPEC crude oil fell by 58%, causing an exogenous shock to oil exporting economies. I prefer to

speak of a downward oil "shock" rather than a "counter-shock", which is the accepted term when viewed from the perspective of importing countries.

5 To limit the comparison to the hydrocarbon sector, like Algeria, Venezuela is largely dependent on oil revenues, which account for almost all of its export earnings, half of government revenues and a quarter of GDP (respectively 96, 43% and 21% for Algeria in 2004-18. https://www.tresor.economie.gouv.fr/Pays/DZ/indicateurs-et-conjonctures [Accessed March 25, 2021]). Like the Algerian Sonatrach, PDVSA is a state-owned company that dominates the sector. As in Algeria, production in this sector has stagnated in recent years due to low investment in infrastructure and exploration. But there are other similarities to be made between the two countries, especially in terms of political regimes. See Vasquez-Lezama, P., 2019. *Pays hors service. Venezuela, de l'utopie au chaos*, Paris, Buchet/Chastel.

6 Ayadi, R., Arbak, E., Ben Naceur S. et al., 2011. Convergence of banking sector regulations and its impact on bank performances and growth: The case for Algeria, Egypt, Morocco and Tunisia, Research (33)04, Femise.

7 Beji S., 2007. "Financial openness and financial development in the South Mediterranean Sea countries: Institutional approach and calculation of development thresholds", *European Research Studies Journal*, 10, nos. 3–4 (2007): 107–127.

8 Ayadi, R., Arbak E., Ben Naceur S. et al., 2011, *op.cit.*

9 Boughzala, M. and Cobham, D. eds., 2011. *Inflation targeting in Mena countries: An unfinished journey.* Basingstoke: Palgrave Macmillan.

10 Cobham, D., 2010. Monetary policy strategies, financial institutions and financial markets in the Middle East and North Africa: An overview. In D. Cobham and G. Dibeh, eds., *Money in the Middle East and North Africa: Monetary policy frameworks and strategies.* London: Routledge.

11 Algeria exports more gas than oil, but the price of gas is indexed to that of oil. The fall in the price of oil is compounded by that of the dollar, the currency in which hydrocarbons are sold. At the time, some exporters (Iraq, Libya) considered changing the currency in which they sold their oil to avoid the manipulation of the dollar by the Fed.

12 In addition to the large debt owed by the Treasury to the Central Bank as a result of systematic advances, there was an inextricable network of debts owed by public companies to public banks and to each other. Laksaci, M., 1986. La monnaie dans le financement des investissements des entreprises publiques en Algérie. *Recherches Économiques de Louvain / Louvain Economic Review*, 52(2) pp. 173–98.

13 There was then in Algeria neither private bank nor foreign banks.

14 The new Constitution (1989), adopted by referendum, was silent on the issues of currency and the Central Bank but granted the future National Assembly the prerogative to legislate on 'the banking, credit, and insurance regime'.

15 Henni A., 2009. La réforme monétaire et financière en Algérie : enseignements pour une transition vers le marché dans un pays en voie de développement.

*Confluences Méditerranée*, No 7, pp. 27–40. Talahite F., 2000. La réforme bancaire et financière en Algérie, *Cahiers du Cread*, No 52, pp. 93–122.

16 In the European debate, on the eve of the creation of the euro and the ECB, the issue at stake was the transfer of monetary sovereignty from the nation-states to the European Union.

17 This debate would rather refer to the project of Maghreb regional economic integration, which would entail a transfer of sovereignty but "should lead to greater sovereignty vis-à-vis the international community", Oulmane N., 2009. Politique commerciale, intégration régionale sud-sud et souveraineté économique en Algérie. *Confluences Méditerranée*, No 7, pp.119–33. Unlikely at the time, given the tensions between Algeria and Morocco, this prospect has since become even more remote.

18 This aspect was missed by Zouache and Ilmane who only deplore the fact that the BA's independence is *de jure* and not *de facto*. Zouache, A. and Ilmane, M. C., "Central bank independence in a MENA transition economy. The experience of Algeria, In D. Cobham and G. Dibeh eds., *Monetary Policy and Central Banking in the Middle East and North Africa*. London: Routledge, pp. 85–105.

19 An approach led by the governor of the Bank of Algeria and supported by Japan, Algeria's second largest creditor after France, which set the condition that Algeria would not reschedule, Hadj-Nacer A., 2011. *La martingale algérienne: réflexions sur une crise*. Alger: Barzakh.

20 After an initial refinancing on an unconditional IMF loan (stand-by agreement May 1989-May 1990), an international call for tenders to share in a balance of payments assistance credit of 1.5 billion dinars issued by the *Crédit Populaire d'Algérie* and managed by the *Crédit Lyonnais*, was not successful until 1992, after the interruption of the democratic process.

21 The reform project, before its official adoption, was set out in five issues of the Cahiers de la Réforme, available in bookstores, an innovation that overturned current governmental practices.

22 Following the 1989 constitution guaranteeing freedom of expression and opening up press pluralism, the government encouraged the establishment of dozens of privately owned newspapers.

23 Some were betting on the Libyan proposal to pay Algeria's foreign debt in return for a political rapprochement or even a union between the two countries.

24 Gamache N. and Mebirouk M.B., 2020. Une (re)classification du régime de change en Algérie : que disent les données du marché parallèle des changes ? *Cahiers du Cread*, 36(01), pp. 5–40.

25 In 1994, a 40.17 percent devaluation was approved by the IMF in order to stabilize the external accounts and halt the fall of the dinar. *Le Monde*, April 12.

26 In the second half of 1998, the price per barrel fell to its lowest level since the 1970s (US$10–12).

27 Balassa, B., 1964. The Purchasing Power Parity Doctrine: A Reappraisal. *Journal of Political Economy*, 72(6), pp. 584–96. Samuelson, P.A., 1964. Theoretical Notes on Trade Problems, Review of Economics and Statistics, 46(2), pp. 145–154.

28 This incompatibility has been theorized by the 'triangle of incompatibilities'. Mundell, R. A., 1960. The monetary dynamics of international adjustment under fixed and flexible exchange rates. *Quarterly Journal of Economics* 74(2), pp. 227–57.

29 This reason was put forward by the World Bank to advise Algeria to develop other mineral resources export in which it abounds, thus pushing the country into the dead end of extractivism. World Bank, 2008. Export Diversification in Algeria. Policy Note. Washington D.C., August. So far, despite announcements to this effect, Algeria has not really taken this route. It would seem that the industrialist current still has an influence on decision-makers, even if it has not succeeded in obtaining a return to a proactive industrial policy.

30 Dib A., 2008. Oil Prices, US Dollar Fluctuations and Monetary Policy in a Small Open Exporting Economy. *Cahiers du Cread*, 24(85/86), pp. 5–44.

31 Boumghar M. Y., Miniaoui H. and Smida. M., 2009. La stabilité financière, une mission pour la banque centrale? *Cahiers du Cread*, No.87, pp. 69–89. Bank of Algeria, 2013. Rapport sur la stabilité financière du système bancaire algérien, 2009–2011.

32 Allegret, J.P. and Benkhodja, M.T., 2015. External shocks and monetary policy in an oil exporting economy (Algeria). *Journal of Policy Modeling*, 37(4), pp. 652–667.

33 A World Bank study on Algeria covering the period 1990–2005 also shows that non-oil GDP is less volatile than total GDP and operating and investment expenditure is more stable than GDP. World Bank, 2007. À la recherche d'un investissement public de qualité. Une revue des dépenses publiques, volume I, Rapport n° 36270, Algeria.

34 Zakharova, D.Z. and Medas, P.A., 2009. A primer on fiscal analysis in oil-producing countries. IMF Working Papers, pp. 1–39.

35 At the same time is adopted the dogma of not resorting to external borrowing, under any circumstances whatsoever.

36 The taxation of hydrocarbons represents around 2/3 of total budget revenue.

37 It could be understood as a temporary measure aimed at remedying a situation inherited from the past. However, the 2004 decision to allow the FRR to receive advances from the Bank of Algeria for the 'active management of external debt' paved the way for it financing the state's debt.

38 The subprime crisis in July 2007 in the United States, and its propagation to the world economy, caused a fall in the price of oil, which affected Algerian exports in early 2009, raising the spectre of an oil shock. The authorities, who had begun to relax budgetary discipline under the pressure of social

demand, saw this signal as a stinging reminder, even if this fall does not appear in the annual statistics, as the Chinese stimulus policy had caused an upturn in oil prices that same year, which were to remain at exceptionally high levels until 2014. Mezouaghi, M. and Talahite F., 2009. Les paradoxes de la souveraineté économique en Algérie. *Confluences Méditerranée*, No. 7, pp. 9–26.

39 FCE, 2013. Éléments de réflexion sur l'évolution des salaires et du pouvoir d'achat en Algérie, 2000–2011. Available at : http://www.fce.dz/wp-content/uploads/2015/08/note-de-conjoncture-evolution-des-salaires.pdf [Accessed March 25, 2021]

40 Muzette M.S., Bazizi Y., Buoyacoub A. and al., 2003. Impact économique et social du SNMG en Algérie, Cread Working Paper, Algiers, décember https://www.researchgate.net/publication/266199992_le_salaire_minimum_en_Algerie_Minimum_Wage_in_Algeria [Accessed March 25, 2021]

41 In 2007, 2008, 2011 and 2012, the availability before drawdowns reached half of GDP (see Table 4.2).

42 World Bank, 2007. À la recherche d'un investissement public de qualité. Une revue des dépenses publiques, volume I, Rapport no 36270 Algeria.

43 El Mouhoub M., Plihon D. and Thieu C., 2006. Les carences du financement à long terme de l'économie algérienne. *Finance et Développement*. Study conducted within the framework of the Programme to support the modernisation of the Algerian financial sector, MEDA, BQ/2004/47.

44 Hadj Nacer A., 2009. Les défis de la création d'un fonds souverain en Algérie. *Revue d'Economie Financière*, 9(1), pp. 121–124.

45 For a more in-depth analysis of the FRR, see Talahite, F. and Beji, S., 2013. Accumulation of Foreign Exchange Reserves and its Effects on Domestic Economies. Algeria and Tunisia Comparative Case Studies. In M. Peeters and N.R. Sabri, eds., *Financial Integration. A Focus on the Mediterranean Region*, The Netherlands, Springer, pp. 27–60.

46 Bank of Algeria, 2008. Rapport 2007. Évolution économique et monétaire en Algérie, July.

47 The Algerian banking system is dominated by six public banks "which, at the end of 2012, held 86 percent of total banking system assets and continue to play a key role as a provider of funds for priority public projects. Private banks, all foreign-owned, are more focused on international trade credits". IMF Algérie. Évaluation de la stabilité du système financier. Rapport No. 14/161

48 IMF (2014) (*ibid.)* calls on the BA to 'create a structural liquidity shortage in order to facilitate the implementation of monetary policy.

49 Doumbia S., 2011. Surliquidité bancaire et 'sous-financement de l'économie'. Une analyse du paradoxe de l'UEMOA. *Tiers Monde*, 1(205), pp. 151–70.

50 Boudjani M., 2017. La Banque d'Algérie : vers une politique monétaire accommodante en 2016? Analyse de la période 2007–2014. *Cahiers du Cread,* No. 118(3), pp. 3–28.

51 Afroune, N. and Achouche, M., 2017. Le taux d'intérêt à court terme et la politique monétaire en Algérie. *Cahiers du Cread*, 33(119/120), pp. 71–103.

52 Boumghar, M.Y., 2018. Conduite de la politique monétaire en Algérie : une stratégie à découvrir. *Revue d'Économie & de Gestion*, 2(2), pp. 92–113.

53 'This loan will not go through the Algiers stock market, although it was hoped that the government would take action to revive the Algiers stock market', Azzaoui, K. and Tabta, L., 2018. L'emprunt obligataire en Algérie. *Revue des Réformes économiques et Intégration En économie Mondiale*, 12(25), pp. 33–53. Established in 1998, the Algerian bond market is barely emerging. Guendouzi, M. and Bia, C., 2019. La Place du financement obligataire dans la croissance économique en Algérie. *Revue des réformes économiques et intégration en économie mondiale*, 13(1), pp. 161–171.

54 This instability stands in contrast to the stability of the previous period under the same governor, from 2001 to 2016.

55 Art. 7 – 'The people is the source of all power. National sovereignty belongs exclusively to the people.'

# PART III
# Increasing sovereignty through monetary unions?

# 5
# The West African CFA Franc Zone as a Double Monetary Union: Loss of economic competitiveness and anti-developmental path-dependencies

*Carla Coburger*[1]

## INTRODUCTION

One of the very last colonial currency regimes was meant to be abolished in 2020: The CFA franc. Born during the colonial period, the CFA franc describes a unique and lasting monetary regime that lacks any comparability with other currency regimes. It incorporates a particularly severe loss of monetary sovereignty for each member state through a *double monetary union*. The double character originates in the fact that each member state's monetary policy space is restricted twice: first, by being part of a monetary union, and second via the fixed exchange rate between the CFA franc and the euro.

Critical voices portraying this currency regime as neocolonial and anti-developmental have gained momentum in recent years. In 2015, late Chad's President Idriss Deby found strong words for the CFA franc and its particular set-up, including the neocolonial 'cooperation agreement clauses' that 'are dragging Africa's economy down' and 'will not allow it to develop with this currency'.[2]

To address this kind of criticism, the Ivorian president, Alassane Ouattara, and the French president, Emmanuel Macron announced in

2019 that the West African CFA franc would be renamed the ECO in 2020, which was postponed due to the Covid-19 pandemic. Despite the purported name change, the ECO[3] would preserve key fundamentals of the current CFA franc regime, including the fixed peg to the euro.[4]

This chapter will provide a framework to understand the exceptionality of the current CFA franc currency regime, and the loss of monetary sovereignty it implies via Kamrany et al. (1974) concept of a double monetary union[5]. Crucially, it will also assess the three key promises of a fixed peg currency regime on economic benefits through gained 'stability' and their actual realisation in CFA franc using countries.

First, I depict the mechanism through which a fixed currency regime influences inflation and sets in motion a dynamic that eventually counteracts its own growth imperative. Second, I ask whether the solidarity and trade integration between CFA franc using countries and the euro area are strong enough to offset losses occurring from giving up an adjustable exchange rate tool to counteract external economic shocks. Lastly, I introduce a hypothesis that needs further modelling investigation on how neocolonial path dependencies are fostered and reinforced by the CFA franc regime and how financial dependency is created.

The concluding suggestion for achieving greater monetary sovereignty will be twofold: (1) the fixed peg to the euro needs to be replaced with an alternative currency regime and (2) the continuation of the West and Central African monetary unions should be critically assessed due to the large heterogeneity of their member states.

## THE CFA FRANC ARRANGEMENT: A UNIQUE DOUBLE MONETARY UNION

Following the collapse of the international monetary order based on the gold standard during the interwar period, different colonial powers established their own currency areas. Britain established the sterling area after it left the gold standard in 1931, while France created the franc zone in 1939 on the eve of the Second World War. The primary function of the latter was to serve as a 'trade and monetary defence zone'[6] to unite its colonial territories in Africa, Asia, the Pacific, and the Americas.

After the end of the Second World War, inflation and economic collapse in France led to uneven devaluations of the metropolitan franc which circulated across most parts of its colonial empire. This gave rise to the so-called 'colonial francs', which included the *franc of the French colonies in Africa (franc des colonies françaises d'Afrique).* At its birth, on 26 December 1945, the CFA franc was the single currency of the sub-Saharan Africa part of the French empire.

In the process of former colonies gaining independence, other colonial currency zones such as the pound sterling area, the Spanish peseta zone, the Portuguese escudo zone, and the Belgium monetary zone were dismantled, and their member states started to issue their own national currencies.

This had not been the case for the member states of the CFA franc zone, which split into two monetary blocs: 1) today's West African Economic and Monetary Union (WAEMU) – Benin, Burkina Faso, Cote d'Ivoire, Guinea-Bissau (joined in 1997), Mali, Niger, Senegal, and Togo – using the *franc of the African financial community* (West African CFA franc) issued by the Central Bank of West African States (BCEAO), and 2) today's Central African Economic and Monetary Community (CEMAC) – Cameroon, Chad, Congo, Gabon, Equatorial Guinea (joined in 1985), and the Central African Republic – using the *franc of African financial cooperation* (Central African CFA franc) issued by the Bank of Central African States (BEAC).

The continued use of the CFA franc by former French colonised countries was, in most cases, not a voluntary choice, but a contractual demand by France:

> Before granting them independence, France had required sub-Saharan African countries to sign 'cooperation agreements' in various fields: foreign affairs, foreign trade, raw materials, currency, etc. These agreements effectively deprived the promised 'independence' of any substance. Thus, for the former French colonies in sub-Saharan Africa, access to international sovereignty was premised on remaining in the franc zone.[7]

As a result, most former French colonised countries south of the Sahara remained part of the two distinct CFA franc currency areas (see Figure 5.1), overlapping with the former French West African Federation (AOF in French) and the former French Equatorial Federation (AEF in French).

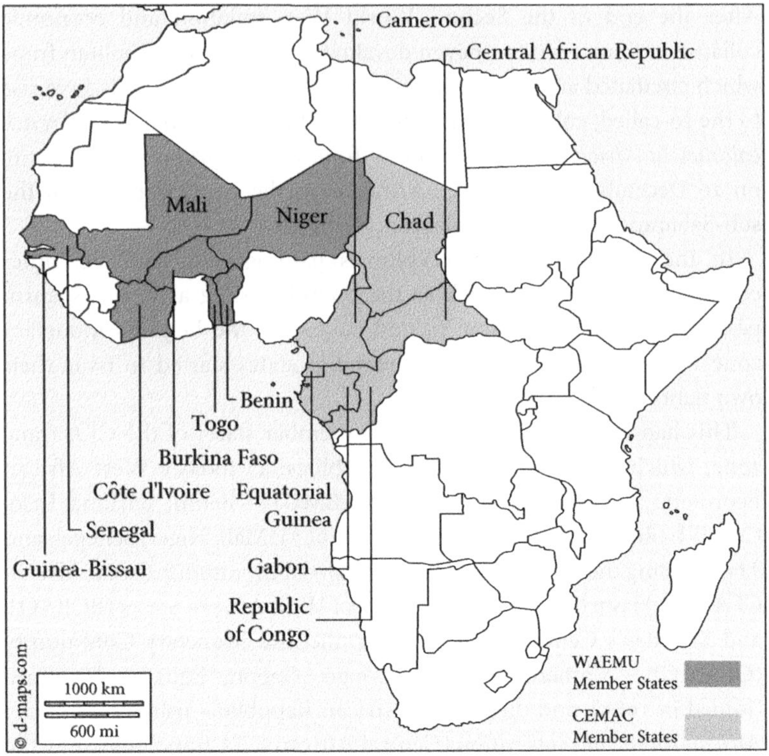


*Figure 5.1* Map of CFA Franc Zones: WAEMU and CEMAC member states

The working of these two CFA franc currencies is based on the following four principles:

I) A fixed exchange rate parity between the CFA francs and the French currency (French franc until 1999 and the euro since).[8] At its birth in 1945, 1 CFA franc was exchanged for 1.70 French franc. In 1948, it exchanged with 2 French francs. Since then, the CFA franc would remain stable vis-à-vis the French franc until it was devalued by 50 per cent in 1994. From 1999, the CFA franc has been pegged to the Euro at a fixed rate of 656 to 1.[9]

II) Freedom of movement of capital and transfer of income within each monetary union and between them and the France/euro area.[10]

III) Convertibility guarantee of the CFA franc at a fixed rate. In other words, the French Treasury promises to lend reserves in its own currency to the BCEAO and the BEAC whenever they lack sufficient foreign exchange.

IV) Centralisation and pooling of the CFA franc member states' exchange reserves in the French Treasury.[11] According to the monetary cooperation agreement between France and each of the two currency blocs, the member states have to 'pool their external assets in a foreign exchange reserve fund',[12] which is then deposited for each central bank in a current account (*compte d'opérations*) at the French Treasury. Initially, the deposit rate was 100 per cent, before being lowered to 65 per cent from the mid-1970s, and 50 per cent from the mid-2000s. The pooled reserves function as a guarantee for the convertibility ensured by the French Treasury. In return, the French Treasury[13] exercises budgetary and accounting controls through its representation in the organs of each central bank. For example, France has two seats on the BEAC's Board of Directors, equally to all member countries – including a veto right which became implicit over time. In addition, 'the BEAC's Statute establishes a three-member College of Censors. France appoints one member ex officio'.[14]

These arrangements resulted in a *double monetary union* (see Figure 5.2) that prioritises 'stability' over monetary sovereignty. The double character originates in the fact that each member state's monetary

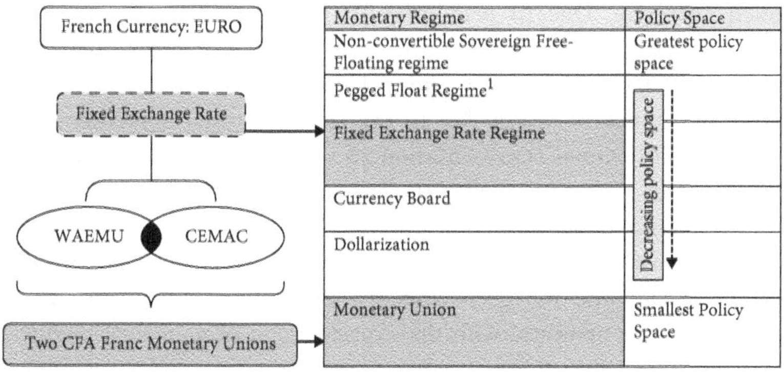


*Figure 5.2* The CFA Franc Double Monetary Union

[1] For an extensive discussion of the difference between fixed and pegged exchange rate regimes see Flassbeck (2001) as well as Mundell (2000).

policy space is restricted twice: first, by being part of a monetary union (WAEMU or the CEMAC), and second, via the fixed exchange rate between the CFA franc and the euro.

Figure 5.2 depicts a range of monetary regimes and their respective policy space after Tcherneva,[15] and positions the CFA franc *double monetary union* accordingly. It should also be noted that the two CFA francs are not freely convertible with each other, even though they are linked through a fixed peg to one another – completing a triangular fixed peg regime (black shaded area).

The greatest restriction in individual country monetary sovereignty results from entering a classic monetary union (WAEMU and CEMAC). Such a choice implies, on the one hand, the transfer of decision-making regarding monetary policy to a supranational level. It therefore represents the greatest decrease in policy space, even if each country is still part of the decision-making process and has equal input. The literature on optimum currency areas discusses scenarios in which joining a monetary union can be highly beneficial for its members despite the restriction in monetary sovereignty. On the other hand, the reduction in policy space due to a fixed currency represents a loss in monetary sovereignty as they could not rely on their exchange rate to adjust to economic shocks.[16] Entering a fixed currency regime means that the central bank of the anchoring currency (here, the Bank of France until 1999; the European Central Bank (ECB) since) is indirectly setting the monetary policy for the fixed currency. Due to principles II, III, and IV (see page 134), the specific arrangements of the CFA franc are more restrictive than other fixed currency regimes. However, it does not qualify as a classic monetary union due to the lack of formal agreements, as well as institutional representation of CFA franc member states in the decision-making bodies of the euro. I will hence refer to it in the following as a 'quasi-monetary union'.

Such drastic restrictions in any country's monetary sovereignty resulting from the above conceptualised double monetary union are justified in the literature with the expected gain of *monetary stability*, which supposedly offsets the loss in policy space and sovereignty. The next section will introduce the theoretical argument of 'monetary stability' versus monetary sovereignty and looks at the real economic effects of the CFA franc blocs on its member states' economies.

## STABILITY: WHAT REAL ECONOMIC PARAMETERS ARE BEING STABILISED?

Despite the longevity of the CFA franc regime, it is still uncertain whether the fixed exchange rate is beneficial to its member countries in real economic terms. Strong political support for the CFA franc arrangement comes from the Ivorian President, Alassane Ouattara, who called the CFA franc a 'solid and well-managed currency'[17] which stabilises African economies. 'Today, the West African Economic and Monetary Union is the most stable monetary zone in the world'.[18]

Despite the fact that the word 'stability' is widely used, and everyone might have an intuitive understanding in economic terms, it is far from clear what is actually being stabilised in the CFA franc member states – price levels, employment, growth, or other parameters? What real economic effects are connected to the stability of exchange rates and inflation?

Mainstream economic theory promises three main benefits from a fixed exchange rate regime:

1) Exchange rate stability leads to low inflation and price stability, which enables higher economic growth.
2) An increase in solidarity and regional integration between member states.
3) Increasing economic attractiveness and long-term planning ability: a fixed peg currency regime and its resulting price stability incentivises investment and long-term economic development.

In the following three subsections I will look at each of these theoretical promises and analyse their distributional effects: Who within the economies of the CFA franc and trading partners benefit from the fixed exchange rate?

### *Inflation Stability or the Loss of Trade Competitiveness*

The following section will explore the case of low inflation in the CFA franc zone and whether it really enhances economic growth. I will theoretically lay out the mechanism through which a fixed currency regime influences inflation. This will highlight the necessity to disaggregate inflation by sectors (tradable goods including all products and services which are exported or traded, and non-tradable goods comprising domestically produced goods which are not exported as well as services produced and consumed domestically) in order to understand the impact of changing relative prices on wealth distribution and power dynamics, as well as its relation to the systemic overvaluation of the CFA franc. Those relative price shifts – facilitated through the fixed exchange rate regime – result in a dual distributional mechanism: a) the shift in relative prices leads to CFA franc domestic consumption moving away from domestically produced goods towards imported goods, and b) the resulting currency overvaluation leads to a loss in competitiveness of domestically produced goods aimed at export markets.

Inflation describes the decline in purchasing power of a given currency and can be reflected in the increase of prices over time. The relative movement of prices within a given economy is subject to many factors including wage policy, productivity growth, and fiscal and monetary policies. The theoretical channel through which a fixed peg leads to price stability and in extension to beneficial macroeconomic outcomes is the following:

> In order to stabilise and ensure the credibility of the exchange rate parity, France and the ECB controls the supply of money for its own currency and, in extension, for the fixed CFA franc as well. Inflationary pressures arising from within the CFA franc member states are prevented because they are subjected to close macro-prudential monitoring based on principles III and IV (see below) to ensure lower fiscal deficits.[19] Due to the prevention of inflationary pressure arising from within the CFA, franc countries, investors, and other economic agents only need to trust[20] the anchor currency and its monetary policy (here France and the euro). In such a framework, economic uncertainty can be reduced, which should positively affect the profitability of investments via lower transaction costs and reduced exchange rate volatility, as well as a higher growth rate of GDP.[21]

Supporters of the CFA franc defend such theoretical channels by referring to the observed low and stable inflation of around 3 per cent, compared to 9 per cent average inflation[22] in other sub-Saharan African countries.

However, the fixed exchange rate regime sets in motion a complex spiral of change in the relative prices of goods within the CFA franc using economies. The phenomenon arising is called 'dual inflation', and describes the divergence of inflation rates for tradable goods and non-tradable goods leading to a relative price increase of domestically produced goods.[23]

The source of dual inflation is the widening gap in productivity growth rates between the tradable and non-tradable goods sectors. 'If the productivity growth differential between the tradable and non-tradable goods sectors is larger'[24] in the CFA franc using countries than in the euro area, the relative price of non-tradable to tradable goods will be rising faster in former than in the latter area.

The intuition can be understood with the example of the declining traditional clothing industry in WAEMU countries (non-tradable sector) due to used clothing imports (tradable sector) from OECD countries. The productivity in the tradable sector of imported cloths increased faster than the productivity of WAEMU non-tradable clothing services. More imported cloths[25] can be offered at cheaper prices: the price of imported used clothing is between 50 and 80 per cent cheaper than imported new cloths,[26] which correlates with the significant decline in traditional clothing manufacturing since the 1990s[27] in sub-Saharan Africa, particularly in Benin and Togo.

The difference in productivity increase in the non-tradable and tradable sector results in the following redistributive mechanism:

1) The relative price of imported cloths (tradable sector) decreases in comparison to domestic non-tradable cloth manufacturing, which becomes relatively more expensive. This leads to a shift in real economic consumption behaviour where households chose to consume relatively less traditional clothing and more imports. The real economic effect is, hence, a redistribution of economic profits away from domestic CFA franc production and towards importers.

If the relative price of domestic non-tradable goods increases, the purchasing power of the population decreases in real terms. 'Under a fixed exchange rate regime, [the divergence in productivity growth rates] will result in CPI inflation and real exchange rate appreciation'.[28] A direct link is therefore established between the choice of a fixed exchange rate regime, dual inflation,[29] and a systemic tendency of currency overvaluation.[30] The second distributional mechanism is, hence, the real economic effect of a systemically overvalued currency:

2) The overvaluation of the CFA franc means that the relative price of its export goods is higher than that of comparable exporting nations.[31] CFA franc using countries therefore lose out on international competitiveness and their trade benefits will remain systemically underperforming.

Figure 5.3 depicts the real effective exchange rate (REER) movement of the CFA franc using countries, as well as France/euro. From this simple descriptive data one important trend becomes apparent: while the absolute levels of the REER have been varying over time and across countries, the trend is one of constant overvaluation. Escaping the mass collapse of multiple fixed and quasi-fixed exchange rate regimes between 1990 and 2000,[32] the CFA franc was devalued once vis-à-vis its anchor currency in 1994, which amounted to 50 per cent of its former value. Figure 5.3 shows clearly that even though today's overvaluation has not reached pre-1994 levels, it only took four years (1997) for each CFA franc member country's REER to surpass the anchor currency, the euro, and to continue a path of appreciation since. The overvaluation towards the US dollar is even more striking, given that the euro has been appreciating by 40.7 per cent[33] against the US dollar between 2002 and 2020.

Those descriptive observations find supporting evidence in an IMF working paper by Ngouana (2012),[35] which explores the counterfactual scenario of the CFA franc appreciation under a) the euro fixed peg and b) a SDR peg.[36] That paper supports the finding of a systemic overvaluation of the CFA vis-à-vis the French franc and, since 1999, the euro which re-evolved even after the 50 per cent devaluation in 1994. The model predicts that under a SDR peg low inflation could be ensured, while simultaneously preventing systemic overvaluation and enhancing international competitiveness. Those findings are an important contribution to the literature on the impact of the CFA franc fixed currency on economic parameters opposing findings which neglect the negative impact of the CFA franc regime because their models do not find statistical significance.[37]

Ngouana's (2012) proposal to replace the fixed peg to the euro with a basket peg is heavily influenced by an observed shift in trade pattern away from France and the EU and towards other trading partners.

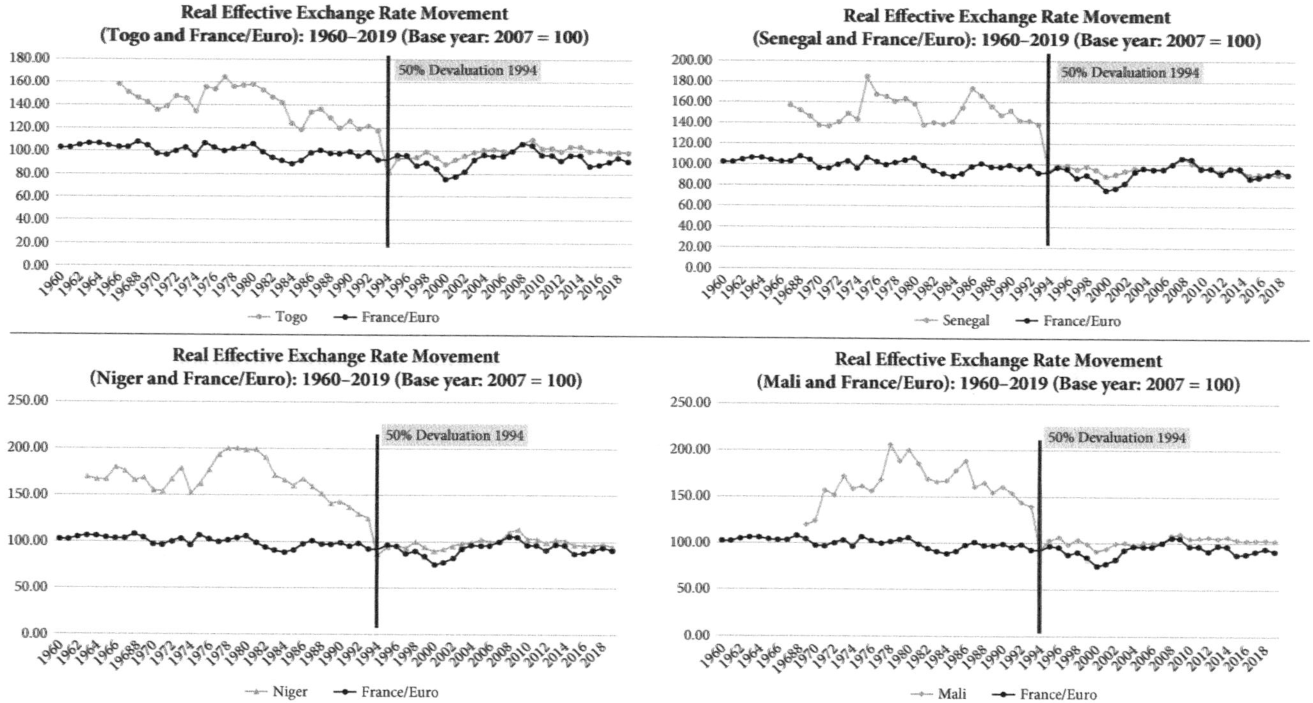


*Figure 5.3* Real Effective Exchange Rate (REER) Movement (CFA Franc member countries and France/Euro): base year 2007 = 100[34]

Source: The World Bank, Data, Real Effective Exchange Rate Index, last access 20.12.2020.

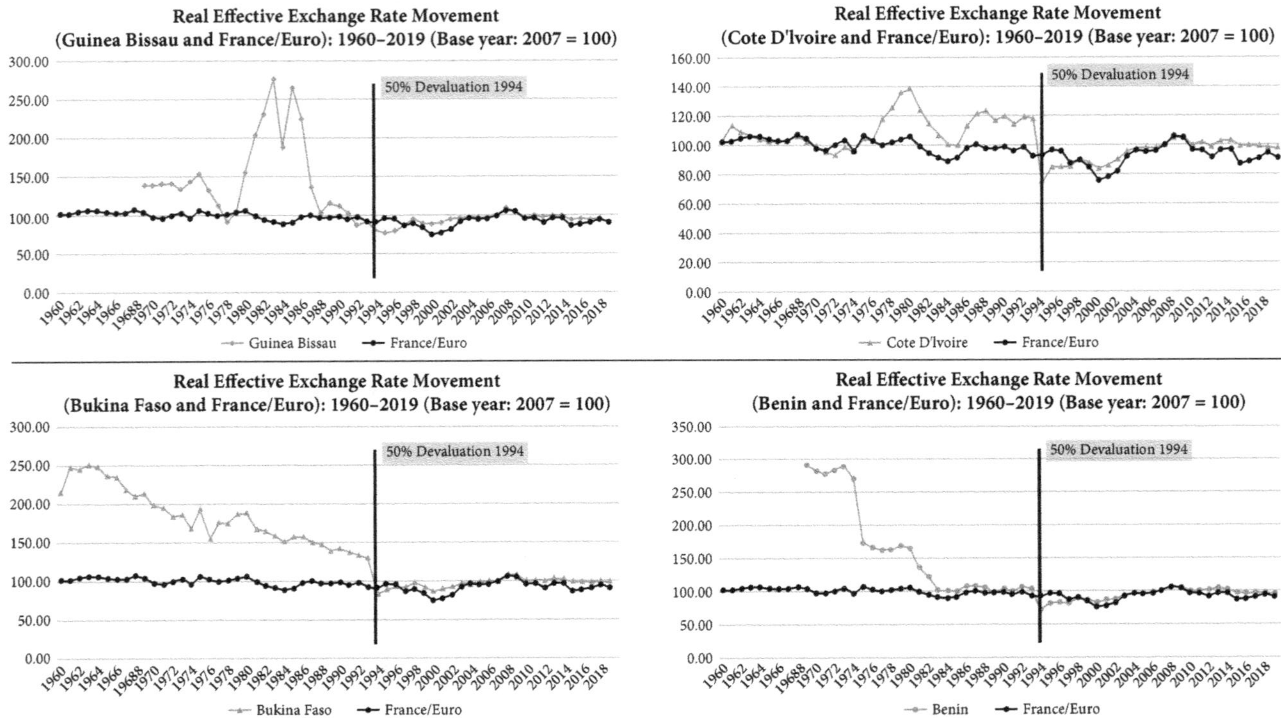


*Figure 5.3* (*continued*)

Until the 1970s, France, as the main trading partner, was the prime beneficiary of the CFA franc overvaluation. The French colonial empire created the CFA franc currency zones as a political motive to foster economic control over its colonised territories in times of war and change, especially after the Second World War. With the emergence of new trading partners over the past 30 years the trade patterns of the CFA franc region have drastically shifted: in 1980 the CFA franc countries engaged 54.2 per cent of their trade with the countries of today's euro area, of which 31.2 per cent was with France alone, but this share has dropped significantly. In 2010 Europe only accounted for half its previous trade (26.1 per cent) and France lost two-thirds of its trade share from thirty years ago (down to 10.4 per cent).[38] 'This trend, which is expected to continue further, is another argument in favour of the adoption of a more flexible exchange rate regime. While the dollar remains the invoicing currency for many international exchanges outside the Eurozone, products from the Franc zone are losing their competitive edge'.[39] The real loss in economic competitiveness and hence in trade and income is therefore carried by the CFA franc using economies.

To summarise: 1) The euro area and CFA franc countries trade increasingly less, while 2) CFA franc countries shift more trade (industrial and raw materials, but also financial services and debt) towards countries where their goods are denominated in US dollars, which has become more expensive due to the appreciation of the euro against the dollar. The preservation of the fixed peg vis-à-vis the euro is therefore a direct subsidy for international importers at the expensive of CFA franc economies. Nubukpo (2017) provides precise figures on the loss of competitiveness resulting in the reduction in economic growth:

> Our results suggest that the continual overvaluation of the real effective exchange rate [in the WAEMU] over the period 1985–2014 resulted in a loss of economic growth of 0.32 percentage points and an increase in volatility leading to a reduction of growth of 0.86 percentage points.[40]

Taking the argument even further, we can identify strong links between the overvaluation of a currency and the deterioration of workers' conditions, work safety, technological progress, and investment in R&D.

'It is precisely the pressure stemming from overvaluation – i.e. from low import prices and tough competition in the export markets – that acts as a sanction against unjustified claims of workers and other sectors of society. With an overvalued exchange rate, the adjustment pressure of the world market (i.e. of globalisation) is artificially but voluntarily increased'.[41]

The findings suggest that the primary beneficiaries of the redistribution are: a) import supplying countries – historically dominated by France and the EU and, lately, China, Maghreb states and the US and b) the upper classes of CFA franc using countries who enjoy luxury imports at relatively cheaper prices. The losers are: a) workers in all CFA franc using countries, and b) small and medium enterprises which produce for domestic as well as export markets. Those distribution affects often get lost in aggregated GDP figures. The GDP per capita figures on the other hand tell a very different story and hint at underlying inequalities: real GDP per capita has been falling in all CFA franc states over the past forty years according to some estimations.[42] In 2018, Côte d'Ivoire's real GDP per capita was 31 per cent lower than its best level, obtained in 1978. The second strongest economy in WAEMU – Senegal got back to its best level achieved in 1961 only in 2015. Niger's real GDP per capita in 2018 was 44 per cent lower than its best level in 1965. The former Portuguese colony Guinea-Bissau recorded its best level of real GDP per capita in 1997, the year it joined WAEMU. Twenty-one years later, this indicator had declined by 18 per cent!

Therefore, by praising the benefit of low inflation stability from a fixed peg regime one neglects the resulting distributive effects.

### *Solidarity, Regional Integration, and Stabilising Inflexibility*

As conceptualised above, the fixed peg regime binds the fourteen CFA franc countries and France in a quasi-monetary union. The arrangement is more restrictive than a normal fixed exchange rate regime because of principles III and IV, but it is not strong enough to be classified as a classic monetary union in the stricter sense. The relationships between the two CFA francs and the euro are based on the 23 November 1998 Decision of the Council of the EU. It determines that there is no formal link, including no formal declaration of solidarity mechanism, between CFA franc using countries and the European monetary authorities, etc.

The 1998 Decision concerns only France, as a 'guarantor' of the CFA franc convertibility.[43]

Under a free floating monetary sovereign regime, the exchange rate can, in principle, be instrumentalised in times of crisis to selectively support the needs of the country, capitalising on the relative change in price for imports and exports. Entering a quasi-monetary union restricts this function significantly. This does not mean that joining one could not hold benefits, but the costs need to be weighted accordingly. The literature on optimum currency areas suggests that monetary unions can offer support via common policy which – under ideal circumstances – could lead to a better coordination in the presence of asymmetric shocks.

Hence, two possible scenarios could justify a fixed exchange rate regime: 1) the economies of the fixed currency (CFA franc zones) and the economies of the anchor currency experience the same economic cycles and are hence in need of the same exchange rate policy at the same time. Or, in case (1) does not apply, increased solidarity and trade integration could offset the loss in monetary sovereignty for the CFA franc zones (scenario 2).

The stage setting for scenario (1) is based on the following observation: exchange rate policy always reflects the needs of the real economy and mirrors the economic cycle based on countries' production pallet.

Among the euro area's main export goods are high technology products with high R&D intensity.[44] The main exported goods include planes, helicopters and/or spacecraft, cars, pharmaceuticals, scientific instruments, and electrical machinery.

In comparison, WAEMU countries produce primarily low value-added primary goods, such as raw zinc and copper, gold, raw cotton, nuts, and tropical agriculture. Furthermore, the fraction of high technology goods produced in WAEMU countries is significantly lower than in the euro area. Figure 5.4 shows the high-technology products as a share of total exports for WAEMU countries and the euro area. The three biggest economies in the WAEMU – Cote d'Ivoire, Senegal, and Burkina Faso – have had spikes of high-technology goods exports in the past twelve years, but the overall picture is one of strong differences. Over the past five years, the average of high-technology export by WAEMU countries has not surpassed one fifth of that of the euro area.

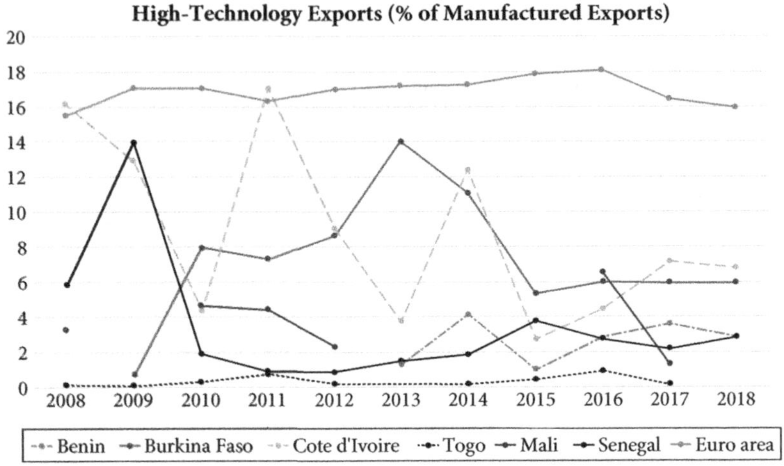


*Figure 5.4* High-Technology Exports (WAEMU countries and the Euro Area: 2008–2018)[45]

The main observation is hence: the pallet of produced goods of the euro area and the CFA franc zone represents two opposite ends of a spectrum ranging from low value-added primary commodities to highly complex manufactured goods. The impact is twofold: first, the central debate in development economics around the deterioration of the terms of trade of developing countries, lower prices for their primary commodity exports compared to their manufactured imports,[46] has contributed key insights into a postcolonial world where trade dependencies and structural inequality persist. A more nuanced discussion on the relevance of those structural imbalances and the prohibited long-term development of CFA franc countries will follow below. Second, the structurally different goods produced by the euro area and the CFA franc zone experience different economic shocks, fluctuations, and demand cycles; therefore, they require different exchange rate policy responses at different times.

The prices of primary unprocessed goods face 'problem[s] of short-term instability of primary commodity prices, which is greater than that of prices for non-primary tradable commodities'.[47] Owing to potentially rapid changes of supply and demand resulting in price shifts, countries producing those goods need a short-term adjustment of the exchange rate[48] to absorb shocks. In case of a good year of harvest, external commodity price shocks, etc., a short-term adjustment tool to devalue the currency is helpful to stimulate domestic consumption rather than import consumption. A short-term devaluation of the currency would decrease the relative price of domestic products in comparison to imported goods. Therefore, local farmers will be able to sell more of their products at a slightly cheaper price and export at competitive prices. In such a scenario, the good harvest will be able to generate surplus to either invest or to save for less ideal years. In the opposite scenario, when a harvest is poor, or a natural catastrophe has occurred, it is helpful to overvalue the currency on short notice to encourage imports to prevent a supply shortage which could lead to starvation or multiple supply crises. Since the two currency unions are pegged to the euro, the ECB is indirectly in charge of their monetary policy, but the latter is primarily concerned with the Eurozone economic cycle, which does not necessarily correlate with the economic cycles of the two CFA franc monetary blocs. The reason lies in the opposite characteristics of the European product range, which consists of high value-added products with very little price volatility.

The asymmetric terms of trade[49] between the Eurozone and the CFA zones are too diverse to be addressed by one monetary policy. The results are crises of hunger, overproduction and waste as well as structural dependencies.[50] The first dramatic crisis for CFA franc using countries which could have been prevented or at least attenuated with the tool of an adjustable exchange rate occurred in the second half of the 1980s. In the forefront – during the 1980s –

> The autonomous powers of the African central banks in determining monetary policy were [...] restrained by 'stability clauses' which granted the French minister of finance rights of consultation and veto over the formulation and implementation of monetary policy in the franc zone member countries.[51]

Those stability clauses towards the BCEAO and the BEAC led to an augmented demand of credits from private markets. The result was an inflationary credit expansion. When these financial developments were additionally hit with real economic deterioration in the terms of trade due to falling world market prices of raw materials, '[t]he real revaluation of the FCFA ultimately caused not only foreign trade but also domestic economic activity to collapse'.[52] Not only were the CFA franc institutions one of the sources of inflating credit demand on private markets, but they also proved ineffective in dealing with the crisis. 'The franc-zone model now proved counter-productive, as the initial inflationary potential gave way to flagging real economy, only exacerbated by the ability to adjust exchange rates. This was a situation in which devaluation would have offered the only way out'.[53] The results were domestic consolidation and structural adjustment programmes under the French government, the World Bank and the IMF. None of these programmes addressed the institutional setting of the CFA franc in their policy restructuring.

Summarising, there is little evidence that the monetary policy by the Bank of France/ECB has been equally beneficial to the very different production pallets. On the contrary, historical examples highlight a dominating passivity of the Bank of France/ECB in times of much needed monetary policy intervention to prevent economic crisis in CFA franc economies.

Regarding scenario 2, within a monetary union and the absence of exchange rate movements as a tool to absorb shocks, labour migration provides theoretically an alternative means of restoring equilibrium between labour markets and economies.[54] In times of asymmetric shocks, it allows unemployed workers to move to places which did not experience the shock and find employment. In theory, migration within monetary union is a sign of increased regional integration and functions as an alternative to absorb shocks.[55] In practice however, the potential for migration is limited between CFA franc using countries but especially restricted between the CFA franc zones and Europe. While freedom of capital movement is part of the statutory agreements, freedom of labour is not considered. Therefore, the theoretical channel to absorb real economic asymmetric shock via labour migration is institutionally prevented.

And lastly, the Covid-19 pandemic has shown that solidarity in times of crisis is not sufficient. On March 15, 2020 – at a time where the Covid-19 virus pandemic was spreading rapidly – the EU adopted export restrictions[56] on medical protective equipment to all non-EU countries, including CFA franc countries. Applying the insights from the overvaluation of the CFA franc, those export restrictions forced CFA franc countries to pay a relatively higher price to other suppliers in times of a severe health crisis, forcing public debt to increase further.

In summary, economies bound together by a fixed peg regime do not benefit from a similar exchange rate policy, nor has increased solidarity and trade integration offset the loss of monetary sovereignty.

*Economic Attractiveness and the Failed Promise of Long-term Development*

The last theoretical promise of a fixed currency regime is all about an increase in credibility, which should lead to more investment and long-term development. I will argue that this promise has not been delivered for two reasons: 1) the fact that the CFA franc was devalued once due to overvaluation, which never the less continued, did not create trust in the sustainability of the fixed exchange rate. International capital markets count on a further devaluation, the only question is when. Due to this fact, the CFA franc countries are subject to short-term investment and cyclical capital flight. The second argument goes deeper into an institutional argument: 2) the monetary regime and the CFA franc institutions support neocolonial path dependencies, maintaining the current global division of labour.

Only eighteen years after the CFA franc got devalued by 50 per cent, Gnansounou and Verdier-Chouchane (2012) published a paper on 'When Should the Franc CFA be Devalued Again?'. The combination of the experience of the 1994 devaluation due to overvaluation, and its possible reoccurrence, allows for justified doubt that international investors still trust the arrangement enough for long-term investment. On the contrary, we can observe that '[t]he CFA franc [...] encourages massive capital outflows'[57] Ndiaye (2012) analysed the effect of capital flight on economic growth in the CFA franc zone between 1970 and 2010. They found that real capital flight was positive and significant, with a magnitude of approximately $86.8 or $80.1 billion dollars, representing 122.1 per cent or 112.6 per cent of GDP, and 5.3 times or 4.9 times foreign direct investment.[58] According to another study, capital flight – consisting of private wealth being transferred outside of its country of origin, foreign direct investment being withdrawn, as well as sovereign transfers in exchange for reserves – puts CFA franc countries in the position of a global net lender rather than a debtor, despite the status of many of its member as least developed nations.[59]

Furthermore, overvaluation hampers domestic credit creation and enforces international financial dependency. As the BCEAO and the BEAC are committed to maintain a fixed peg, given the low diversification of production in many CFA countries, credit expansion will feed more imports – which will ordinarily deteriorate the current account balance, and deplete foreign exchange. Credit creation, in a context of countries with structural trade deficits and a commitment to a fixed peg, can expand only if countries receive external financial flows. In the WAEMU, all countries, except for Cote d'Ivoire, have structural trade deficits and very low domestic savings (2018: Senegal 24 per cent; Guinea-Bissau 8.8 per cent of GNI). With such weak domestic financial possibilities, the peg can be maintained only through increasing financial dependency towards international financial institutions. The result is a banking sector dominated by French, Moroccan and 'Pan-Africanist' banks[60] which underperform in their credit supply.[61] 'The credit-to-GDP ratio stands around 25 per cent for the WAEMU, and 13 per cent for the CEMAC, but averages 60+ per cent for sub-Saharan Africa, and 100 per cent+ for South Africa'.[62]

The literature on economic complexity indicators has shed light on one key economic relationship: while it is easy for countries which already have a diversified and complex production pallet to switch between products, the transition from producing primary less-complex goods to more advanced complex goods is incredibly difficult. But it is especially impossible if there is no domestic financing structure that provides credit for enterprises trying to develop more complex industries. Those investments might be connected with a higher risk of failure due to being exposed to highly competitive markets, but it is the only way to diversify and climb up the ladder of economic complexity. Here, further work must be done, employing methodology from economic complexity indicators and network theory to understand the neocolonial path dependency of production patterns in the CFA franc zones. Unfortunately, Kamrany et al. words from 1972 seem devastatingly timely:

> [T]he banking system [in the WAEMU] does not play an effective role toward capital accumulation, since its operating rules are basically aimed at financing trade flows and capital repatriations, rather than at stimulating monetisation, savings and local investments. Because the monetary and banking system are biased against indigenous savings and investments, they perpetuate the past system of economic production and are among the major institutional bottlenecks which limit indigenous opportunities in the region, especially in the traditional sector.[63]

## CONCLUSION: ONLY COSMETIC CHANGES FOR THE FUTURE

In light of the recently proposed currency reform which will replace one of the last colonial currency regimes – the West African CFA franc – with the newly introduced ECO, this paper has analysed the key monetary regime feature and its real economic effects: The fixed exchange rate vis-à-vis the euro which will be transferred into the ECO regime.

This paper has explored the three key promises of a fixed currency regime:

I) Lower inflation: It is achieved in the CFA franc zones, but comes at the high cost with dual inflation and a distributive effect which benefits importers and high-income classes within CFA franc states, and disadvantages for domestic production aimed at domestic demand as well as export markets.
II) Decreased coordination costs (via one monetary policy and increased solidarity and trade integration): The differences in production pattern among CFA franc and euro using countries reveal strong differences in exchange rate policy needs. The solidarity and regional integration between the two regions are not strong enough to offset CFA franc zone losses from a Europe-centred monetary policy.
III) Higher economic attractiveness and long-term development: Persisting overvaluation deteriorates the faith of international financial markets and fuels short-term investment and cyclical capital flight. The inability to bind long-term investment fosters the colonial production pattern of primary goods and raw materials because investment into diversifying and increasing the complexity of production does not find willing investors.

The above presented mechanism-based analysis concludes that all three theoretical promises from a fixed peg regime do not offset the loss in monetary sovereignty in the CFA franc region. Presented evidence suggests that upon entering the new ECO, the fixed regime should be replaced with a more flexible peg, similar to a SDR peg.

Exploring the structure of the double monetary union further, more work needs to be done on the optimality of the WAEMU and the CEMAC. Currently, two CFA franc reform proposals are on the table: the ECO as a replacement of the West African CFA franc (announced in 2019) and, second, the creation of the Economic Community of West African States currency (also ECO), which will include WAEMU members and seven other countries, including Nigeria.

Hence, both proposals aim at either preserving the underlying classic monetary union or even enlarging it by adding more countries. Unfortunately, just adding more countries into a single currency does not necessarily increase integration or solidarity, at worst it produces new internal power dynamics with new winners and losers.

Calling into question the optimality of today's WAEMU and CEMAC, the heterogeneity of inflation within the regions is huge and might not sufficiently qualify for a successful monetary union. For the period between 2014 and 2016, overvaluation ranging among WAEMU member states stood at between -7 per cent for Mali and +12 per cent for Guinea-Bissau.[64] Furthermore, the price volatility of goods, such as palm oil, cocoa beans, uranium, petroleum, fish meal, phosphate rock, cotton, and beef, across West African countries is far from uniform. The fear is, therefore, justified that by getting rid of the power dynamic with the Euro, where Europe's highly complex production pallet dominates the monetary policy needs of volatile primary goods and raw materials, the ECO will replace this dominance with a regional player: Nigeria. 'Nigeria alone represents 73.1 per cent of the zone's wealth, against just 26.9 per cent for the other fourteen countries. Clearly, there is a strong chance that satisfying the needs of Nigeria would be the chief preoccupation of monetary policy within the region'.[65]

The policy discussion should explore options for the breaking up the monetary unions and replacing them with 'an ambitious economic integration for the West African region based on mutually supportive national currencies'[66] to foster regional trade, develop regional financial systems, and diversify regional production patterns with the help of radical industrial policy. This would increase monetary sovereignty much further than the cosmetic change of a new name in the same cloths of the CFA franc.

## NOTES

1 I would like to express my deepest gratitude to Ndongo Samba Sylla whose intellectual guidance has been the greatest support. Thank you to El Hadji Malick Sow and Souleye Sow for being the first to engage and fascinate me over the CFA franc, resulting inequalities and real economic effects as well as Patrick Klösel for first discussions on theorising the subject. For wonderful feedback I am indebted to Marie Meyle, Carolina Alves and Costas Lapavitsas. Lastly, many thanks to the organisers of the conference *The Quest for Economic and Monetary Sovereignty in 21st Century Africa.*

2 Dieng, C., 2015. Idriss Déby appelle les pays africains à se débarrasser du Franc CFA. *Le Nouvel Afrik*, August 14.

3 The 15 ECOWAS (Economic community of West African States) member countries initially chose ECO (short for ECOWAS) for their single currency project. But Macron and Ouattara somehow decided to preempt it from them.

4 Ibrahima Jr., D., 2020. CFA Franc: France adopts the reform on the community currency (official). *Kapital Afrik*, December 11.

5 Kamrany, N.M., R. Tremblay, J.J. Stern, A.H. Kazmi, B. McCormick, and J.D. McQuigg, 1974. *A framework for evaluating long-term strategies for the development of the Sahel-Sudan Region. Annex 1: Economic considerations for long-term development.* Cambridge, MA: Center for Policy Alternatives, MIT, pp. 19–21.

6 Sylla, N.S., 2021. Fighting monetary colonialism in francophone Africa: Samir Amin's contribution. *Review of African Political Economy*, 48:167, pp. 32–49, 34. doi: org/10.1080/03056244.2021.1878123.s

7 *Ibid.*, 4

8 De Coustin, F., 2010. The franc zone. *Tech. rep. Banque de France.*

9 Gulde, A-M and Tsangarides, C.G., 2008. The CFA Franc Zone: Common currency, uncommon challenges. *International Monetary Fund Working Paper Series*, pp. 8–9.

10 Sylla, N.S., 2020. The Franc zone, a tool of French neocolonialism in Africa. *The Jacobin.* January 6.

11 Guia, G., 2008. *La France et l'Afrique Sub-Saharienne, 1957–1963. Histoire d'une décolonisation entre idéaux eurafriques et politique de puissance.* Bern, Switzerland: Peter Lang, p. 38.

12 Biankola-Biankola, M. and Nzauo-Kongo, A., 2020. International law and monetary sovereignty. The current problems of the international mastery of the CFA franc and the crisis of sovereign equality. *The International Law Research Quarterly*, 1(2), pp. 24–5.

13 *Ibid.*, 25.

14 *Ibid.*, 31.

15 Tcherneva, P.R., 2016. Money, Power, and Monetary Regimes. *The Levy Economics Institute Working Paper*, No. 861, p. 20.

16 Mundell, R.A., 1961. A Theory of Optimum Currency Areas. *The American Economic Review*, 51(4), pp. 657–65.

17 De Bassompierre, L., 2019. Ivorian president reiterates support for euro-pegged currency. *Bloomberg*, February 16.

18 Adetunji, J., 2019. Why abandoning the CFA Franc would be a risky operation. *The Conversation*, November 8.

19 Gulde, A-M. and C. Tsangarides, 2008. The CFA Franc Zone. Common Currency, Uncommon Challenges. International Monetary Fund (2008), pp. 8–9. Lower fiscal deficits have not always persisted in the history of the CFA franc zone, especially not during the 1980s, and from the mid-2010 for CEMAC countries.

20 Danladi, J.D., 2013. Inflation and sustainable output performance in the West African sub-region: The threshold effect. *American Journal of Economics*, 3(6), p. 252.

21 Feindouno, S. et al., 2020. *Zone franc, croissance économique et réduction de la pauvreté*. Ferdi, p. 8.

22 France diplomacy, franc zone, www.diplomatie.gouv.fr/en/country-files /africa/franc-zone/. [Last accessed 2.2.2021].

23 Mendoza, E.G., 2005. Real exchange rate volatility and the price of non-tradable goods in economies prone to sudden stops. *Economia* vol.6 n°1, p. 133.

24 Mihaljek, D. and Klau, M., 2003. The Balassa-Samuelson effect in central Europe: A disaggregated analysis. *Bank for International Settlement Working Paper Series*, No. 143, p. 1.

25 Brooks, A. and Simon, D., 2012. Unravelling the relationships between used-clothing imports and the decline of African clothing industries. *Development and Change* 43 (6), pp. 1265–90.

26 *Ibid.*, 1280.

27 *Ibid.*, 1279.

28 Mihaljek, D. and Klau (2003, 1)

29 Mendoza (2005, 133) finds that fluctuation in relative prices of non-tradable goods impacted managed and fixed currency regimes much stronger than in industrial and developing countries with floating currency regimes. In the example of Mexico, during its managed fixed exchange rate regime (1969–2000), '50 to 70 per cent of the variability in the Mexico-U.S. real exchange rate' was accounted for by fluctuation in relative prices of non-tradeable goods.

30 Uribe, M. and Schmitt-Grohe, S., 2017. *Open economy macroeconomics*. Princeton, NJ: Princeton University Press, Chapter 8.

31 Boughton, J.M., January 1992. The CFA franc: Zone of fragile stability in Africa. *International Monetary Fund. External Relations Department.*

32 Saqib, O.F., 2002. Interpreting currency crises: a review of theory, evidence, and issues. *Deutsches Institut für Wirtschaftsforschung (DIW) Discussion Papers*, No. 303, p. 3.

33 Feindouno, S. et al., 2020. *Zone franc, croissance économique et réduction de la pauvreté*. Ferdi, p. 5.

34 For visual simplicity and accounting for the introduction of the euro, the presented data here is: French franc REER until 1999 and Euro REER from 1999–2020.

35 Ngouana, C.L., 2012. Exchange rate volatility under peg: Do trade patterns matter? *IMF Working Paper*, 12/73.

36 The alternative peg regime here is special drawing rights (SDR), which is a weighted average of the main worldwide trading currencies – the US dollar, the euro, the Japanese yen, the British pound and, recently, the Chinese renminbi.

37 Feindouno et al., 2020, find a negative but not statistically significant impact of the fixed peg regime throughout their models. For an extensive discussion of why statistical significance is not enough to neglect potential real economic significance: see The Cult of Statistical Significance, in: Section on Statistical Education – JSM, pp: 2302–16; Bergstrom, Carl T. and Jevin D. West (2020): Calling Bullshit. The Art of Scepticism in a Data-Driven World, Penguin Random House, UK; Andrews, Donald W. K. (1989): Power in Econometric applications, in *Econometrica* 57 (5), pp. 1059–90; Ziliak and McCloskey, (2009), p. 2302; Bergstrom and West, (2020), p. 204; and Andrews, (1989), p. 1059.

38 Ngouana, C.L., 2012. Exchange rate volatility under peg: Do trade patterns matter? *IMF Working Paper*, 12/73), p. 8.

39 Gnansounou, S.U. and A. Verdier-Chouchane, 2012. Misalignment of the real effective exchange rate: When should the Franc CFA be devalued again? *African Development Bank Group Working Paper Series*, p. 166.

40 Nubukpo, K., 2017. Misalignment of exchange rates: What lessons for growth and policy mix in the WAEMU? *Oxford Global Economic Governance Programme Working Paper*, p. 126.

41 Flassbeck, H., 2001. The exchange rate: Economic policy tool or market price? *United Nations Conference on Trade and Development* 157, p. 32.

42 Pigeaud, F. and Sylla, N.S., Réforme du franc CFA: les députés français mal informés par leurs techniciens? Mediapart Blog. February 24, 2020. Available at: blogs.mediapart.fr/fanny-pigeaud/blog/220220/reforme-du-franc-cfa-les-deputes-francais-mal-informes-par-leurs-techniciens-0 [Accessed on 07 July 2021].

43 98/683/EC: Council decision of 23 November 1998 concerning exchange rate matters relating to the CFA Franc and the Comorian Franc, eur-lex.europa.eu/eli/dec/1998/683/oj.

44 Hausmann, R. et al., 2014. *The atlas of economic complexity: Mapping paths to prosperity*, Tech. rep. MIT Press, p. 22.

45 United Nations, Comtrade database through the WITS platform (2020).

46 Prebisch, R., 1950. *The economic development of Latin America and its principal problems, United Nations Department of Economic Affairs, Economic Commission for Latin America (ECLA)*. Lake Success, New York.

47 United Nations, Economic Development in Africa, 2003. Trade performance and commodity dependence. *Tech. rep. United Nations Conference on Trade and Development*, p. 13.

48 Bargawi, H. et al. Low-income countries and commodity price volatility. From Fragmentation to Coherence. In Thomas Cottier and Panagiotis Delimatsis, eds, 2011. *The prospects of international trade regulation.* Cambridge: Cambridge University Press.

49 Cartona, B. et al., 2015. Asymmetric terms-of-trade shocks in a monetary union: An application to West Africa. *Journal of African Economies*, 19 (5), pp. 657–90.

50 Friedmann, H., 2002. The political economy of food: A global crisis. *New Left Review*, 197, pp. 29–57.

51 Körner, H., 2002. The franc zone of West and Central Africa: A satellite system of European monetary union. *Intereconomics*, 37(4), pp. 198– 203.

52 *Ibid.*, 200.

53 *Ibid.*, 200.

54 International Monetary Fund, External Relations Department. *The CFA Franc: Zone of Fragile Stability in Africa*, January 1992.

55 Mundell, R.A., 1961. A theory of optimum currency areas. *The American Economic Review*, 51(4), pp. 657–65.

56 Vander Schueren, P. et al., 2020. EU and EU Member States impose COVID-19 related export restrictions on medical and protective equipment. https://www.mayerbrown.com/en/perspectives-events/publications/2020/03/eu-and-eu-member-states-impose-Covid-19-related-export-restrictions-on-medical-and-protective-equipment. [Accessed 7 July 2021].

57 Sylla, N.S., 2017. The CFA Franc: French monetary imperialism in Africa. *Review of African Political Economy blog*, 18 May 2017. http://roape.net/2017/05/18/cfa-franc-french-monetary-imperialism-africa/, [Accessed 7 July 2021].

58 Ndiaye, A.S., 2012. Une croissance économique forte et durable est-elle possible dans un contexte de fuite massive des capitaux en zone franc? Research Paper presented at African Economic Conference. Kigali, Rwanda, p. 28.

59 United Nations, Individual LDC fact sheets, Department of Economic and Social Affairs (2020).

60 BCEAO, 2019. Rapport Annuel 2018. *Commission bancaire union monétaire ouest-africaine*, (2019), 47.

61 Sing, Raju Jan/ Kpodar Kangni and Ghura, Dhaneshwar, 2012. Financial deepening in the CFA franc zone: The role of institutions. *IMF Working Paper*, 09/113, p. 12.

62 Sylla, N.S. (2017). The CFA Franc: French monetary imperialism in Africa. *Review of African Political Economy blog*, 18 May 2017. http://roape.net/2017/05/18/cfa-franc-french-monetary-imperialism-africa/ [Accessed 7 July 2021].

63 Kamrany, N.M., et al., 1974. *A framework for evaluating long-term strategies for the development of the Sahel-Sudan region. Annex 1: Economic considerations for long-term development.* Cambridge, MA: Center for Policy Alternatives, MIT.

64 Intra-community gaps for CEMAC are much larger ranging from an atypical overvaluation of the Central African Republic of +76 per cent and Equatorial Guinea with 12 per cent. See Feindouno S., et al., 2020. *Zone franc, croissance économique et réduction de la pauvreté,* Ferdi, 27/28.

65 Diagne, C.A.B., 2019. How francophone Africa's franc-backed CFA franc works and why it's controversial. *Quartz Africa,* August 2.

66 Sylla, N.S., 2021. Fighting monetary colonialism in francophone Africa: Amin's contribution, p. 2.

# 6
# The CFA Franc Under Neoliberal Monetary Policy: A labour-focused approach

*Hannah Cross*

## INTRODUCTION

The CFA franc has come to represent persistent neocolonial links with France that undermine a significant departure from colonial modes of development.[1] In a series of economic debates held in Dakar, inaugurated by Samir Amin, prominent economists and scholars brought the currency union to the forefront of political and economic struggle in the franc zone, where it was argued that 'money is the first instrument of sovereignty and the role of the CFA *vis-à-vis* the euro and French Treasury is one of the principal causes of economic difficulties in francophone countries'.[2] Expanding on the question of sovereignty, this paper will show how a neoliberal monetary regime, based on inflation targeting and central bank independence, shifted the existing pattern of foreign dominance over the economy. This policy framework brings a renewed democratic focus to critiques of the monetary regime in the franc and Eurozones, with impetus from those who have experienced the financial transformation of the state first-hand in official roles.[3]

What is often peripheral to discussion on global neoliberalism, democracy and neocolonial domination is their relationship to the power of the labouring classes which actually provides the links between them. The suppression of democracy is the consequence of an economic policy that aims to keep labour costs down, previously achieved in colonial practice and then sustained in changing forms of imperial dominance. The neoliberal project has institutionalised the existing imbalance of power between capital and labour in its reconfiguration of the state to contain labour.[4] To be clear, for observers of African regions' historical integration in the capitalist world economy, low-paid, precarious, or 'unfree' labour is not a novel pattern found in neoliberalism.[5] Nor has neoliberalism introduced the fundamental restrictions on autonomous development that the franc zone has faced since its inception. For Samir Amin, writing over fifty years ago, the aim for local control over reproduction of the labour force was part of the delinking project that also required local autonomy over the market, natural resources, technology, and investment, and this process needed the transformation of the franc zone's monetary structures.[6] Considering this history, this chapter examines, firstly, how the changing conditions of labour and subsequently of popular sovereignty are not distinct from monetary policy or epiphenomenal to it, but are part of its calculation. A background to labour struggle in the franc zone will illustrate that monetary policy is linked to the losses and gains of the labouring classes. The chapter subsequently examines the export of the Eurozone's macroeconomic framework to the franc zone, along with the CFA franc's peg to the euro, following both the 1994 devaluation and the abandonment of the French franc. This tightened monetary policy renewed the demand for alternatives, by which monetary sovereignty and its relation to the wider economy continues to be a necessary condition for broader social transformation.

## NEOLIBERAL MONETARY POLICY AND THE SUPPRESSION OF LABOUR

Rosa Luxemburg argued in 1899 that 'The fate of democracy is bound up, we have seen, with the fate of the Labour movement'. [7] Only the labour movement could achieve democracy, even though socialism was its primary goal. Social democracy in Europe had become oriented to imperialist policy, to the neglect of the international working classes. A century later, neoliberal policy was attacking social democracy and its redistribution of the benefits of imperialism to the bourgeoisie, eventually eroding the middle classes.

The abandonment in 1971–1973 of the fixed exchange rate system of convertibility of the dollar into gold embedded financial market intervention in the international monetary system, and this was combined with fiscal and monetary austerity policies that aimed to restrain wages. The resulting confrontations in Western Europe led to states' reversal of labour regulations, welfare, and employment benefits, and efforts to reduce industrial costs.[8] The indirect domination over the working class in Keynesian monetary policy would give way to direct subordination of workers. In turn, monetarism, associated with Hayek and Friedman's economic theory, rejected social democracy and argued that macroeconomic mismanagement and the acceptance of workers' demands generated excessively high inflation.

Monetarism broke with the consensus of states' responsibility to address unemployment and allow inflation to rise, moving the control of inflation to the centre of monetary policy. Milton Friedman's opposition to the targeting of unemployment was based on the idea that 'a lower level of unemployment is an indication that there is excess demand for labour that will produce upward pressure on wage rates'; while excess supply will produce downward pressure.[9] Workers were expected to price themselves into jobs in liberalised, flexibilised labour markets, exercising 'hard work and thrift'. Paul Volcker, leading the US Federal Reserve, announced the plan to fight inflation using an aggressive interest rate policy in 1979, encouraged by national banks' use of this mechanism in Germany, Japan and Switzerland. The Volcker shock showed that monetary policy, without wage, price, or credit controls, or supporting fiscal policy, could reduce inflation. Unemployment increased persistently and commercial bank credit expanded that did not circulate in the real economy but, instead, promoted the expansion of international finance, where US power was institutionally reconfigured.[10] The International Monetary Fund (IMF) adopted the inflation target[11] as the nominal anchor in many assistance programmes.[12]

Interest rate manipulation became the primary tool for monetary discipline under the 'new monetary policy consensus', a term used by Alfredo Saad-Filho (2005) and in Philip Arestis and Malcolm Sawyer's (2005) explanation of the neoliberal monetary policy that advanced in the early 1990s.[13] This policy draws on monetarism, new classical, and New Keynesian schools of thought. It is a policy approach that is based on nominal anchors, which have also included the gold standard, currency boards, and money supply targeting. It is a departure from Keynes' ideas, which prioritised output as well as price stability, and carried the objective of 'optimum level of employment', although wages still could be reduced by inflationary means.[14]

The Maastricht Treaty of the European Union, signed in 1992, assigned the Eurosystem the objective of maintaining price stability in the Eurozone, specified in 1998 in the European Central Bank (ECB) as 'a year-on-year increase in the Harmonised Index of Consumer Prices (HICP) for the euro area of below 2 per cent'.[15] The interest rate policy became the key policy instrument, in a 'one instrument-one target' framework, whether formally focused on an inflation target with a quantitative definition, or more broadly with a monetary policy that focused on price stability.[16]

At this time, there were major changes in central banks' laws in industrial and 'emerging market' economies. They gained authority over monetary policy, with legal responsibility for more than one country in the case of the ECB (Eurozone), the Central Bank of West African States (BCEAO) (West African Economic and Monetary Union [WAEMU]), and Bank of Central African States (BEAC) (Central African Economic and Monetary Community [CEMAC]). In these monetary unions, the hard exchange rate peg between countries led state authorities to surrender control over domestic monetary policy to the central bank. This transformation sought to prevent undisciplined wage bargaining and political agents from expanding the aggregate labour cost.[17]

A single inflation target, originally understood as a means of managing crisis, is excessively rigid between member countries of a central bank and also between regions.[18] In Europe's 'golden age', from 1947–1977, inflation averaged around 10 per cent. This might equally be expected of African countries that are reconstructing after a prolonged period of war or economic devastation. The movement of inflation suggests weighty demand and a lightened real value of debt.[19]

The effects of this monetary regime can fundamentally be understood as class-based, transferring wealth upwards at the expense of wage levels and labour conditions, which could improve with moderate inflation.[20] As manipulation of interest rates is the tool for low inflation, real interest rates tend to be higher, with an increase on costs of production, investment, and consumption, triggering public expenditure cuts. The singular focus on price stability can force the economy into a 'stabilisation trap', a 'low-level equilibrium with low growth, high unemployment, intractable problems of poverty and inequality'.[21] The reliance on wages as the adjusting variable will push wages down and cause persistent unemployment. Labour's share of national income declines and states lose the capacity for social compromise.[22] Hence, Greece's assertion of the principle of governing with the consent of the electorate was a 'profound shock' to the Troika (of the European Commission, the ECB, and the IMF); the Syriza government had dared to submit economic decisions to a democratic process.[23]

## LABOUR STRUGGLE IN THE CFA FRANC ZONE

The two CFA franc blocs[24] have economies and labour systems that were shaped differently by European colonialism from the late nineteenth century. Samir Amin described distinct regional patterns of integration into the world economy in colonial Africa.[25] In West Africa's *colonial trade economy*, pre-colonial trade networks were disrupted, mainly by France and Britain, and the region was restructured towards an export economy with commercial crop zones near to the coast and underdevelopment in the interior, underpinning coercive labour systems. The *Central Africa of concession-owning companies* did not have the population density and hierarchical social structures that had developed in West Africa. It was opened, mainly by Belgian and French colonisers, to private plunder of raw materials, moving towards the establishment of foreign-owned industrial plantation zones by the 1930s. In view of the lasting effects of colonial domination,[26] progressive forces emphasise the importance of a new sovereign project, delinked from the reproduction of patterns of underdevelopment and dependence.[27] Yet the politics of the franc zone have encouraged their continuity.

From 1960 to 1986, even if regular devaluations of the French franc and favourable prices of primary products enabled economic growth in some franc zone countries, monetary policy kept inflation rates abnormally low.[28] France's control over the zone loosened in the early 1970s, following protests from workers, students, and some African heads of state. In Senegal, the 'street fighting years' started in 1966 when anti-neocolonial students walked out to demonstrate against the ousting of Kwame Nkrumah in Ghana, and forced the government to legalise the students' unions. Following the repression of 1968's student strikes, trade unions joined in solidarity. The government was eventually forced to release arrested union leaders and increase the minimum wage by 15 per cent, while scholarships would be retained for the 1967–1968 academic year and universities would follow a principle of Africanisation. Later strikes in 1971 and 1973 were met with more authoritarianism and a loss of momentum for the revolutionary left, but these struggles did force a more open political system, with a significant role for the working class that is often downplayed.[29]

African leaders in this time of dissent threatened to leave the franc zone, opposing monetary arrangements that did not allow a negative balance in the operations account, which were oriented to the short-term needs of commodity marketing and export rather than industrialisation and development. The BCEAO and BEAC headquarters moved from Paris to Dakar and Yaoundé respectively, and gained African governors.[30] However, these reforms did not decolonise monetary policy or change its core operating rules. Economic and political violence from France against sovereign projects, or the benefits of the arrangements for the ruling elites, suppressed the possibility of liberation.[31] Moreover, the Organisation of Petroleum Exporting Countries' quadrupling of oil prices in the early 1970s created severe balance of payments problems. In WAEMU countries a domestic and external debt crisis by the early 1980s was compounded by the rise of interest rates following the Volcker shock. In the CEMAC countries, the discovery of oil disguised the crisis up to the late 1980s.[32]

Tariff protection, in response to firms' inability to match the prices of imported goods, was off the table in financial and academic circles, notwithstanding the rise of European protectionism, because, the argument went, they would impose 'efficiency costs' on the economy, be subject to corruption and rentierism, and would discourage foreign investment; similarly, capital controls to overcome their flight to France would 'promote greater capital flight'! Governments instead had to overcome their 'political failure' and impose austerity measures to restore macroeconomic equilibrium.[33] Neoliberal rationality was doubling down and, by the 1990s, most franc zone countries were under austerity programmes as farmers protested against the slashing of prices of export crops like cocoa, cotton, and coffee to almost half, and public sector workers' pay was frozen or cut.

These changes would not have been possible through democratic channels. In 1990, new institutional arrangements for the CFA franc would centralise banking supervision in regional banking commissions in West and Central Africa that would provide an 'agency of restraint' to preserve the currency's internal and external value.[34] France would impose technocrats like Oye M'Ba in Gabon and Alassane Ouattara in Côte d'Ivoire, who would insist 'the currency is a matter for experts and thus not a subject for democratic debate'.[35] France made an example of Benin by withdrawing financial support from the country and allowing salary arrears to accumulate in the civil service for nine months, forcing the ex-World Bank official Nicéphore Soglo into power.[36] The climate of austerity led Senegal's new government in 1993 to reduce salaries and cut state expenditure. Trade union groups refused to accept these sacrifices and pay for others' economic mismanagement, instead developing their support for each other and distancing themselves from political parties, hoping again to become the opposition that parties were failing to provide.[37]

The 1994 devaluation came soon after the death of President Félix Houphouët-Boigny of Côte d'Ivoire, one of its main opponents. It was seen as France's capitulation to the Bretton Woods institutions and a shift in power in the latter's favour. Three days of intensive meetings culminated in the change in parity promoted by the IMF and Ouattara, against the warnings of social explosion to President Mitterrand, led by Omar Bongo, Blaise Compaoré, Abdou Diouf, and Houphouët-Boigny.[38] Between 1948 and 1994, the CFA franc's parity to the French Franc was stable, though the French currency was regularly devalued. From 1 CFA franc equals 0.01 French franc, the CFA franc's value was halved in January 1994 to 0.02 French franc. This was not merely a remote economic decision with ripple effects on the economy, but an event that was directly and immediately absorbed by households. It created a wave of wage freezes and layoffs with retaliations from labour unions, while prices for pharmaceutical products and other imports soared. The governments of Côte d'Ivoire, Senegal, Benin, and Burkina Faso introduced temporary price controls on stock imports to prevent price-gouging and halt a sharp rise in inflation, while the IMF promised US$1.5 billion of aid to counter the impact of higher prices. France would set up a 'special development fund' and halve the debts of Gabon, Cameroon, the Republic of the Congo, and Côte d'Ivoire.[39] The IMF noted a growth in the franc zone of 0.8 per cent per year during 1994 to 96 after an annual decline of 2.6 per cent in the preceding years, inflation came down to single digits, and the balance of payments deficits and external public debts were contained. However, while terms of trade modestly improved, competitiveness gains were largely attributed to relative unit labour costs.[40]

In all countries, total wage costs diminished in relation to total public expenditure, declining from 43 per cent in 1993 to 32 per cent in 1997 in WAEMU countries, and from 50 per cent to 37 per cent in CEMAC countries in the same years.[41] This reduction in public wage expenditure extended to other sectors of employment and was combined with a loss of purchasing power. This deterioration in living standards vastly outweighed the mitigating measures taken by the IMF and France. Cameroon recorded positive macroeconomic results after the devaluation, but in 1996, almost half the population (55 per cent in rural areas and 22 per cent in urban areas) was consuming less calories per day than the Food and Agricultural Organisation's recommendation of 2400 calories.[42] People became half as rich and were often forced into unstable and exploitative forms of labour migration as a household survival strategy, with a new significance for the value of earnings from the US or Europe. The simultaneous disruption of international visa regimes led to the phenomenon of clandestine migration, which continues to mark economic shocks in Senegalese and other regional households.[43]

The trend over time has been a decline in incomes: in Côte d'Ivoire, average income in 2016 was under two-thirds that of the late 1970s, while Gabon's average income fell by half in the four decades after 1976. Guinea Bissau, rejoining WAEMU in 1997 when its average income was at its highest, saw a fall of 20 per cent by 2016.[44] Agricultural incomes were hit by the euro peg for exports. Burkina Faso, growing its cotton production sixfold between 1994 and 2006, saw marketing companies and peasants face severe losses when the euro strengthened against the dollar between 2004 and 2007. The appreciation of the euro also prevented food security such that, for example, Senegal's local rice was more expensive than imported rice from Thailand, which is priced in dollars. Thus, agricultural exports, as well as the potential for import substitution, were hit by the euro peg.[45]

## TIGHTENED MONETARY POLICY AND THE SEARCH FOR ALTERNATIVES

Following both the 1994 devaluation and the CFA franc's peg to the euro, the Eurozone's macroeconomic framework was exported to the CFA franc zone as a new anchor. This would leave governments dominated by French economic policies and the international price of commodities as these determine the currency's international value and exchange rate in US dollars.[46] Having ceded power to the international financial institutions (IFIs) in the previous decade, after 2002, macroeconomic surveillance in the franc zone included the demand for the wage bill not to exceed 35 per cent of budget revenues in WAEMU countries.[47] Intra-regional trade, which for CEMAC was less than 5 per cent of its total trade and for WAEMU around 10 per cent, was a secondary target.[48] The IFIs, European Commission and French Treasury view countries' own governments as the barrier to regional cooperation, claiming they are weak or lacking in political will, are not sufficiently promoting the market, and that their protectionism has stifled competition and prevented a single market of products, capital and labour mobility.[49] These ahistorical approaches obscure the uneven and combined development that has prevented diversification of production and has centred capital and labour mobility around export commodities.

Dependence on imported foods in both franc zone regions sparked rioting in 2007 and 2008 when prices of rice and grains soared by 50 per cent and more. The hunger riots were part of a wider pattern of protests against austerity, unemployment, and alienation of community land, intensified by food price hikes. Market deregulation, reduced grain reserves, and global financial speculation led to food crises.[50] This was acutely experienced in low-income countries, including in Côte d'Ivoire, the largest CFA economy. Riots in Abidjan led the government to cut taxes on household products. The government of Burkina Faso responded to the riots with emergency subsidies for fertilisers, seeds, and farming equipment, while Senegal introduced a special intervention programme to reduce dependency on imported rice.[51] In light of these countries' high dependence, a European Commission paper suggested that fiscal policies in the franc zone should have some flexibility, compared to the Economic and Monetary Union, and that fiscal programmes should respond to public opinion.[52]

Yet, in 2010 the BCEAO changed its decision-making bodies to establish committees for monetary policy and financial stability, revised the objectives of monetary policy, and expanded the set of operational tools, moving towards more rigidity and control. It became independent in relation to member states. Given the fact that the monetary base is often backed by foreign reserves by more than 70 per cent,[53] it looks like a currency board rather than a true central bank, with a primary focus on price stability, defined as the ECB's inflation target of 2 per cent, plus or minus 1 per cent over a 24-month period. Unlike the Eurozone, which has national roles in the supervision of financial responsibility, the CFA model establishes external discipline on financial and fiscal policy. As a counterpart to its so-called guarantee of convertibility, the French Treasury has a representative with voting rights in the organs of the BCEAO, which can barely diverge from the monetary policy of its anchor and, by extension, that of the ECB.[54]

While monetary stability has been promoted as a means of creating a stable environment for attracting foreign investment and promoting the integration of member countries, there has been major capital flight, especially in times of economic and political crises (see Chapter 5 by Carla Coburger). Foreign investment has favoured countries that are rich in oil and mineral resources, rather than responding to the stability of currencies while, at the same time, profits are repatriated to French investors.[55]

Currency unions with their pooling or surrender of state sovereignty are not inimical to democracy per se, but the neocolonial relationship with France and the mechanisms of neoliberal monetary policy prevent the state and the people from determining the allocation of social resources. However, in 2016, the BCEAO reported that financial, commercial, and transport activities had expanded in the region more recently and that subsidiaries of French banks had been losing their market shares to African banks that had an explicit regional approach, the largest of which was the 'pan-African' Ecobank.[56] South-South cooperation has extended in the past decade to include new considerations of regional monetary strategies to counteract the global financial and monetary system with its rigid conditionalities and narrow governance demands. The West African Monetary Zone, formed in 2000 and based in Accra, had plans to incorporate the regional franc zone countries with its members of Gambia, Ghana, Guinea, Nigeria, Sierra Leone, and Liberia, using the ECO as its currency. While it is not a neocolonial project, it is influenced by the neoliberal convergence criteria of the Eurozone and would include a targeted inflation rate below 5 per cent, a fiscal deficit ratio below 4 per cent, and a limitation of deficit financing by the central bank to 10 per cent. While it eases monetary policy, its central bank would remain focused on price stability in an inflation targeting framework, but it has since been postponed by political and economic instability.[57]

In line with the broader intellectual criticism of inflation targeting, African critics have argued during the last two decades that the CFA franc has adverse consequences for growth and employment levels. Côte d'Ivoire's former finance minister, Mamadou Koulibaly, launched an attack against the CFA franc at the start of the 2000s, arguing that, as a consequence, 'our industry is not competitive, we have low-skilled labour, our economy isn't diversified'.[58] Other critics include former international economic officials like Togo's Kako Nubukpo (ex-BCEAO), Senegal's Sanou Mbaye (ex-African Development Bank), and Guinea-Bissau's Carlos Lopez (ex-UN Economic Commission for Africa). In January 2017, there were anti-CFA demonstrations in African and European cities and calls to boycott French products.[59] Nubukpo has appealed for foreign exchange reserves to be mobilised through credit creation for projects in areas such as energy, telecoms, and other infrastructure, rather than be kept in the French Treasury.[60] Other recommendations are to have a sovereign currency as a basic condition for a regional market and a sustainable industrialisation process;[61] to peg the CFA franc to a basket of local currencies and soften draconian credit policies;[62] for commercial banks to have a role in financing long-term credits for productive investment;[63] and to coordinate between monetary policy and national budgetary policy.[64]

As a result of the growing criticism of the CFA franc, Alassane Ouattara and Emmanuel Macron, in December 2019, announced the 'replacement' of the latter with their own version of the ECO. However, their 'reform' is essentially cosmetic, as the core features of the neocolonial currency relationship – with a fixed peg to the euro, free transfer of capital and income, and the so-called French 'guarantee'– remain untouched. For Kako Nubukpo, the CFA franc will only be buried, and monetary sovereignty transferred, with an adjustable exchange rate regime; or if, instead, member countries do not enter into a single currency but introduce exchange rate agreements and advance the trade integration process with specialisation processes between economies.[65]

## REFORM AND EMANCIPATORY POLITICS

The CFA franc zone is associated with French neocolonial control. This continues to be symbolically and economically important, but the devaluation of the currency in 1994 also marked a reconfiguration of power in favour of the IFIs and international finance in line with the Eurozone's financial configuration. Ever similar patterns have emerged of austerity and the crushing of labour across a neoliberal world, in which few governments can succeed or be considered exemplary from the perspective of ordinary people. It is unhelpful to debate endlessly the degree to which low development indicators are caused by domestic or external politics, when these are best understood as a class relation that has been systematically isolated from the influence of elected governments.

Neoliberal monetary policy removed political power from economic policymaking by means of 'governance' mechanisms that reinforce an authoritarian nature to the economy as they ensure a programme that restricts welfare, public spending, wages, and employment for a supposed long-term goal of monetary and economic stability. However, restoring the monetary mechanisms of the Keynesian era will not go far enough to bring labour-centred development. Only a repoliticised, labour-centred approach will bring CFA economies beyond generations of capitalist exploitation of labour within the regions. This is why unearthing the emancipatory politics that are downplayed by history, and engaging with the left's attempts to rebuild itself in the present global wave of strikes and protests, will be central to substantive economic and monetary reform.

## NOTES

1 Agbohou, N., 1999, *Le franc CFA et l'euro contre l'Afrique*. Paris: Éditions Solidarité Mondiale; Olukoshi, A., 2001. *West Africa's political economy in the next millennium: Retrospect and prospect*. Dakar: CODESRIA Monograph Series, pp. 22–3; Sylla, N.S., 2017. The CFA franc: French monetary imperialism in Africa. *Review of African Political Economy blog*, 18 May 2017. http://roape.net/2017/05/18/cfa-franc-french-monetary-imperialism-africa/ [Accessed 7 July 2021].

2 Sy, C.S., 2013. La politique économique du Président Macky Sall: Continuité ou rupture? In Demba Moussa Dembélé, Ndongo Samba Sylla, and Henriette Faye, eds, *Déconstruire le discours neoliberal. Volume 1 des samedis de l'économie*. Dakar: Arcade and Fondation Rosa Luxemburg, p. 27.

3 See Nubukpo, K., 2010. Management of the CFA franc in West Africa: From an imposed extroversion to chosen extroversion? In Vishnu Padayachee, ed., *The Political Economy of Africa*. London: Routledge; Sylla, N.S., Emerger avec le franc CFA ou émerger du franc CFA? In Kako Nubukpo, Bruno Tinel, Martial Ze Belinga, Demba Moussa Dembélé, eds, 2016. *Sortir l'Afrique de la servitude monétaire: A qui profite le franc CFA?* Paris: La Dispute; Mbaye, S., 2012. Senegal falls behind the rest of Africa. *Le Monde Diplomatique* (English edition), February 12; Varoufakis, Y and Sakalis, A., 2015. One very simple, but radical idea: to democratise Europe. *Open Democracy*, October 25.

4 Fine, B. and Saad-Filho, A., 2017. Thirteen Things You Need to Know About Neoliberalism. *Critical Sociology*, 43(4–5), pp. 693–94.

5 Bernards, N., 2019. Placing African labour in global capitalism: the politics of irregular work. *Review of African Political Economy*, 46(160), p. 295; Miles, R., 1987. *Capitalism and unfree labor. Anomaly or necessity*. London: Tavistock; Cross, H., 2020. *Migration beyond capitalism*. Cambridge: Polity Press, p. 48.

6 Sylla, N.S., 2021. Fighting monetary colonialism in francophone Africa: Samir Amin's contribution. *Review of African Political Economy*, 48 (167), pp. 32–49.

7 Luxemburg, R., 2006. Reform or Revolution. In Paul Buhle, ed., *Reform or Revolution and other writings* [2nd edition 1908]. New York, Dover Publications Inc., p. 56.

8 Saad-Filho, A., 2010. Monetary policy in the neoliberal transition: a political economy critique of Keynesianism, monetarism and inflation-targeting. In Richard Westra, ed., *Political economy and global capitalism: The 21st century, present and future*. London: Anthem Press, p. 95.

9 Friedman, M., 1968. The Role of Monetary Policy. *American Economic Review*, 58(1), p. 7.

10 Konings, M., 2007. The institutional foundations of US structural power in international finance: From the re-emergence of global finance

to the monetarist turn. *Review of International Political Economy*, 51(1), pp. 54–5.

11 The IMF defines inflation targeting as a monetary policy framework involving 'the public announcement of numerical targets for inflation, with an institutional commitment by the monetary authority to achieve these targets, typically over a medium-term horizon'. According to this definition, only Ghana, Uganda and South Africa implemented such a framework. IMF, *Annual Report on Exchange Arrangements and Exchange Restrictions 2019*: Washington, D.C.: 2020, pp. 6, 8. The present chapter adopts a less restrictive definition. As we'll see the two central banks of the franc zone both have a mandate of price stability and target an annual rate of inflation below 3 per cent.

12 Goodfriend, M., 2007. How the world achieved consensus on monetary policy. *Journal of Economic Perspectives*, 21(4), p. 56.

13 Saad-Filho, A., 2005. Pro-poor monetary and anti-inflation policies: Developing alternatives to the new monetary policy consensus. Centre for Development Policy and Research, SOAS, Discussion Paper 2405, p. 11; Arestis P. and Sawyer. M., 2005. New consensus monetary policy: A critical appraisal. In Philip Arestis et al., eds, 2005. *The New monetary policy: Implications and relevance.* Cheltenham: Edward Elgar.

14 Mattick, P., 1978. *Economics, politics and the age of inflation.* Michigan, MI: University of Michigan, p. 37.

15 Quoted by Strauss-Kahn, M-O., 2003. Regional currency areas: A few lessons from the experiences of the Eurosystem and the CFA franc zone. *Regional currency areas and the use of foreign currencies*, Vol. 17, pp. 43–58, 44. https://www.google.com/url?sa=t&rct=j&q=&esrc=s&source=web&cd=&cad=rja&uact=8&ved=2ahUKEwjYlpL-rdHxAhUZgfoHHUgeD-oQFjACegQIGBAD&url=https%3A%2F%2Fwww.bis.org%2Fpubl%2Fbppdf%2Fbispap17.pdf&usg=AOvVaw1ARETxr2niOMxAoGjvbUio

16 Arestis P. and Sawyer, S., 2008. A critical reconsideration of the foundations of monetary policy in the consensus macroeconomics framework. *Cambridge Journal of Economics*, 32(5), p. 761; Otmar Issing, O., 2011. Lessons for monetary policy: What should the consensus be? IMF Working Paper.

17 Collignon, S., 2006. Natural unemployment, the role of monetary policy and wage bargaining: A theoretical perspective. Working Paper No. 133, Centre for European Studies p. 17.

18 Mattick, *Economics, Politics and the Age of Inflation*, p. 38.

19 Agbohou, 2016. *Le franc CFA et l'euro contre l'Afrique*, p. 223; Tinel, B. Le fonctionnement et le rôle des comptes d'opérations entre la France et les pays africains. In Kaka Nubukpo et al., eds, *Sortir l'Afrique de la servitude monétaire: A qui profite le franc CFA?* Paris: La Dispute, p. 101.

20 Krugman, P., 2014. Oligarchy and Monetary Policy. *The New York Times*. April 6. http://krugman.blogs.nytimes.com/2014/04/06/oligarchy-and-monetary-policy/?_r=0 [Accessed on July 7 2021].

21 Saad-Filho, A., Monetary policy in the neoliberal transition, p. 109; Seccareccia, M. and Khan, N., 2019. The illusion of inflation targeting: Have central banks figured out what they are actually doing since the global financial crisis? An alternative to the mainstream perspective. *International Journal of Political Economy*, 48(4), p. 375.

22 Stockhammer, E., 2014. The euro crisis and contradictions of neoliberalism in Europe. Working Paper 1401, Post Keynesian Economics Study Group, p. 6.

23 Weeks, J., 2015. Greferendum: Once upon a time in Europe democracy broke out. *Open Democracy*, June 30. www.opendemocracy.net/can-europe-make-it/john-weeks/greferendum-once-upon-time-in-europe-democracy-broke-out [Accessed on July 7 2021].

24 The West African Economic and Monetary Union WAEMU is led by the Central Bank of West African States (BCEAO) in Dakar, Senegal, with centralised monetary policy for its eight member countries of Benin, Burkina Faso, Côte d'Ivoire, Guinea-Bissau (former Portuguese colony that joined in 1997), Mali, Niger, Senegal, and Togo. The Brazzaville Treaty 1964 formed the union that would eventually become the Central African Economic and Monetary Community (CEMAC). The Bank of Central African States (BEAC) is based in Yaoundé, Cameroon, with member states of Cameroon, Central African Republic, Chad, Equatorial Guinea (former Spanish colony that joined in 1985), Gabon, and Republic of the Congo. Comoros is also part of the franc zone and has a similar set of conditions but a different peg to the CFA countries.

25 Amin, S., 1972. Underdevelopment and dependence in black Africa – Origins and contemporary forms. *Journal of Modern African Studies*, 10 (4): 503–24.

26 A discussion of continuity and change can be found in: Cross, H. and Cliffe, L., 2017. A comparative political economy of regional migration and labour mobility in West and Southern Africa. *Review of African Political Economy*, 44 (153), pp. 381–98.

27 Amin S. and Bush, R., 2014. An interview with Samir Amin. *Review of African Political Economy*, 41 (S1), pp. S111–2; Sylla, Emerger avec le franc CFA ou émerger du franc CFA?, pp. 159–87.

28 Pigeaud, F. and Sylla, N.S., 2018. *L'arme invisible de la Françafrique: Une histoire du franc CFA*. Paris: La Découverte, p. 146.

29 Bianchini, P., 2019. The 1968 years: Revolutionary politics in Senegal. *Review of African Political Economy*, 46(160), pp. 188–89.

30 van de Walle, N., 1991. The decline of the franc zone: Monetary politics in francophone Africa. *African Affairs*, 90(360), p. 390.

31 Sylla, Fighting Monetary Colonialism, pp. 32–49

32 Olukoshi, *West Africa's Political Economy*, p. 20; Diouf, M, 2002. *L'Endettement puis l'ajustement. L'Afrique des Institutions de Bretton Woods*. Paris: L'Harmattan.

33 van de Walle, The decline of the Franc Zone, pp. 394–96.
34 Baudoin, L., 2006. Monetary and exchange-rate agreements between the European Community and Third Countries. European Economy, Economic Paper No. 255. Brussels: European Commission, Directorate-General for Economic and Financial Affairs, p. 23.
35 Sylla, The CFA Franc: French monetary imperialism in Africa. Blog article roape.net/2017/05/18/cfa-franc-french-monetary-imperialism-africa/
36 van de Walle, The Decline of the Franc Zone, p. 404; Sylla, The CFA franc,
37 Kanté, B., 1994. Senegal's empty elections. *Journal of Democracy*, 5(1), p. 107.
38 Airault, P., 2015. Le FCFA, c'est de l'or entre nos mains. Vous n'avez pas le droit de nous le retirer', *l'Opinion*, July 28.
39 Noble, K.B., 1994. French devaluation of African currency brings wide unrest. *New York Times*, February 23.
40 Hadjimichael, M. and Galy, M.A., 1997. The CFA Franc Zone and the EMU. WP/97/156. African Department: International Monetary Fund, p. 10.
41 Sané, M., 2001. Les effets économiques et sociaux de la dévaluation du franc CFA dans les pays de l'UEMOA. In Hakim Ben Hammouda and Moustapha Kassé, eds, *L'avenir de la zone franc: Perspectives africaines*. Paris and Dakar: CODESRIA-KARTHALA, p. 256.
42 Dieudonné, B.Y. Performances macroéconomiques au Cameroun et dévaluation du franc CFA, in *L'avenir de la zone franc: Perspectives africaines*, p. 190. https://www.econbiz.de/Record/performances-macro%C3%A9conomiques-au-cameroun-et-d%C3%A9valuation-du-franc-cfa-dieudonn%C3%A9-bondoma-yokono/10001638133
43 Cross, H., 2013. *Migrants, borders and global capitalism: West African labour mobility and EU borders*. Oxford, UK: Routledge, p. 138.
44 Pigeaud and Sylla, '*L'arme invisible de la Françafrique*', p. 141.
45 *Ibid.*, 146.
46 Claeys, A.-S. and Sindzingre, A., 2003. Regional integration as a transfer of rules: The case of the relationship between the European Union and the West African Economic and Monetary Union (WAEMU). Development Studies Association, Annual Conference, University of Strathclyde, September 10–12, p. 8
47 Hallett, M., 2008. The role of the euro in Sub-Saharan Africa and in the CFA franc zone. *Economic Papers*, 347. Brussels: European Communities, p. 18.
48 *Ibid.*, 12.
49 Hadjimichael and Galy, The CFA Franc Zone and the EMU, p. 2; Hallett, The role of the euro in Sub-Saharan Africa and in the CFA franc zone, p. 14; Banque de France, 2015. *Rapport Annuel de la Zone Franc*, p. 68.
50 Bush, R., 2010. Food riots: poverty, power and protest. *Journal of Agrarian Change*, 10(1), p. 121.

51 *Ibid.*, 122–3.
52 Hallett, The role of the euro in Sub-Saharan Africa and in the CFA franc zone, p. 23.
53 Banque de France. *Rapport annuel de la Zone franc. Vue d'ensemble*, 2012, p. 12.
54 Nubukpo, Management of the CFA franc in West Africa, p. 360; Lamine, Monetary and exchange-rate agreements between the European Community and Third Countries; Kireyev, A., 2015. How to improve the effectiveness of monetary policy in the West African Economic and Monetary Union, Working Paper WP/15/99, International Monetary Fund; Sylla, The CFA franc.
55 Mbaye, S., 2014. L'afrique francophone piégée par sa monnaie unique. *Le Monde Diplomatique*.
56 Banque Centrale des Etats de l'Afrique de l'Ouest. Rapport sur la politique monétaire dans l'UMOA. June 2016.
57 Fritz B. and Mühlich, L., 2014. Regional monetary co-operation in the developing world taking stock. Working paper, UNCTAD, p. 35; United Nations Conference on Trade and Development, Monetary Unions and Regional Trade in Africa. TD/B/EX. Geneva: UNCTAD Trade and Development Board, p. 2.
58 Monnier, O. and Dzawu, O.M., 2015. West Africa rebels against CFA franc, currency linked to colonial France. Analysts say it's a loveless marriage. *Mail and Guardian*, October 2.
59 Sylla, The CFA Franc
60 Airault, Le FCFA, c'est de l'or entre nos mains,
61 Dembélé, D.M., 2014. 20 Years after devaluation: What is the future for the CFA franc?' *Fahamu,* April 2. Available at: www.pambazuka.org /governance/20-years-after-devaluation-what-future-cfa-franc [Accessed July 07 2021].
62 Mbaye, Senegal falls behind the rest of Africa
63 In H.B. Hammouda and M. Kassé, Introduction, *L'avenir de la zone franc,* p. 11.
64 Nubukpo, K., Le franc CFA et le financement de l'émergence en zone franc, in *Sortir l'Afrique de la servitude monétaire*, pp. 132–3.
65 Nubukpo, K., 2020. The ECO and CFA franc: Four weddings and a funeral. *The Africa Report*, January 23.

# 7
# From Central Bank Independence to Government Dependence: Monetary colonialism in the Eurozone

*Thomas Fazi*

## INTRODUCTION

African monetary sovereignty has been a core component of the Pan-Africanist ideal of political unity, as expressed, for example, by Ghanaian President, Kwame Nkrumah, in the early 1960s, with the foundation of the Organization of African Unity (OAU).[1] While a deepened monetary and financial cooperation within the African continent is a legitimate goal, the specifics leading to this process matter as well as the forms under which this cooperation is supposed to happen. The long-term ambition of African authorities is to create regional single currencies – such a project exists for example in West Africa and in East Africa – which would pave the way at one point to a continental single currency (see the chapter by Elisabeth Cobbett). Sadly, these currency unions projects are modelled on the European Monetary Union (EMU), also called Eurozone.[2] This is indeed unfortunate, as the Eurozone is far from being a 'model' to be emulated elsewhere.

The main premise of this chapter is that current discussions on how to strengthen the economic and monetary sovereignty of African countries cannot afford to ignore the dramatic consequences that monetary unification has had on the countries of Europe. In order to design forms of monetary integration that would enlarge their policy space, such a union would have to be tailored to meet their specific challenges. Thus, African countries would be well-advised to learn from the shortcomings of the Eurozone rather than draw uncritical inspiration from it. It is especially important for them to realise that monetary unions are no panacea. On the contrary, depending on how they are designed, they can compromise national independence and democratic self-determination, including the capacity by national authorities to implement coherent development policies that have lasting effects for their populations.

Indeed, there exists, and has existed for a long time, an established consensus that countries that belong to a monetary union are rather limited in the scope as regards their national economic policy. As the British economist Wynne Godley famously wrote, 'the power to issue [one's] own money, to make drafts on [one's] own central bank, is the main thing which defines national independence. If a country gives up or loses this power, it acquires the status of a local authority or colony'.[3] Indeed, to the extent that the management of a country's fiscal policy depends on its control of monetary and exchange rate policy, and that fiscal policy is the central plank of any meaningful economic policy (from industrial policy to (full) employment policy), we can conclude that giving up (or losing) the power to issue one's currency effectively means giving up (or losing) the ability to efficiently manage *all* aspects of economic policy – particularly demand-side and welfare policies aimed at sustaining employment, equality, and societal well-being. This loss of economic sovereignty becomes self-evident in the face of a financial/economic crisis, such as an external shock of some kind.

The EMU, and specifically the economic underperformance and high unemployment rates of its member countries vis-à-vis other advanced countries in the decade following the financial crisis of 2007–2008, testifies to this very clearly. When the financial crisis hit, member states, because they did not have the possibility to 'print the currency' to buy their own bonds (and thus control interest rates) or a central bank willing to act as lender of last resort, found themselves defenceless in the face of market speculators – or so-called bond vigilantes – which caused bond yields (interest rates) to skyrocket in a number of countries,[4] particularly those of the so-called periphery (Portugal, Ireland, Italy, Greece, and Spain, often referred to, with clear racist undertones, as the PIIGS). This gave rise to the so-called European 'sovereign debt crisis' or 'euro crisis'. Indeed, these countries became exposed to the very real risk of sovereign default, or 'national insolvency'. As Merkel stated in late 2011, '[t]he top priority is to avoid an uncontrolled insolvency, because that wouldn't just hit Greece, and the danger that it hits everyone, or at least a number of other countries, is very big'.[5]

For almost three years – from late 2009 to mid-2012 – the European Central Bank (ECB) refused to intervene (in any meaningful manner) to support euro area government bond markets, leaving member states at the mercy of financial speculation and forcing them to pursue harsh austerity measures to meet growing interest payments and, in some cases (Ireland, Portugal, Greece, Spain), to go cap-in-hand to the so-called *troika* – a tripartite committee with representatives from the European Commission, the ECB, and the International Monetary Fund (IMF) – for financial assistance, conditional upon even harsher austerity measures. These countries were essentially put into 'controlled administration'.

This was presented in the mainstream media and by policymakers as a 'natural' consequence of the fact that the countries in question had accrued excessive debt levels, which had caused them to 'lose the confidence of investors'. In fact, there was nothing natural about it. As we will see, to the extent that Eurozone countries continue to be subject to the 'market discipline' of bond vigilantes – and to the risk of national default/insolvency – this is uniquely a consequence of the defective architecture of the Eurozone (as well as the actions of EU institutions).

Monetarily sovereign governments that issue debt in their own currency – that is, all advanced countries with the exception of the Eurozone members – can never become insolvent or be forced to default on their public debt. That's because they can always roll over their debt by issuing new debt as the old debt matures – which is what most countries do – or they can even extinguish the existing debt by issuing new fiat money; that is, by 'monetising' the debt. A corollary of this is that, in a country that issues its own currency, the central bank, as a buyer of last resort, can always set the interest on its government bonds regardless of the country's deficit or debt levels, as Japan has been demonstrating for years;[6] simply put, if financial markets refuse to buy the country's bonds or ask for excessively high yields, the central bank can always step in and buy the bonds itself with newly 'printed' money, thus setting a ceiling on the interest rates. In such a context, there is little, if anything, bond markets can do to put pressure on an elected government.

This, of course, does not apply to countries that are part of the EMU: they effectively use a foreign currency, the euro. Much like a state government in, say, the US or Australia, Eurozone countries borrow in a currency which they don't control: they can't set interest rates nor can they roll over the debt with newly issued money and thus, unlike currency-issuing countries that issue debt in their own currency, they are subject to risk of default. This means that their ability to manage their public debts, and to engage in deficit spending, depends on their ability to issue debt to the private markets (and on the goodwill of the ECB, as we will see). This situation 'is reminiscent of the situation of emerging economies that have to borrow in a foreign currency', as Belgian economist Paul De Grauwe noted a few years back.[7]

Much of the euro area's problems – including the fact that it experienced a 'sovereign debt crisis' in the first place – can be attributed to this 'original sin': the member states' relinquishing of their monetary sovereignty to a supranational authority. That said, it could be (and has been) argued that the various policies undertaken by governments throughout the euro crisis were the result of choices willingly (if not happily) made by the national governments themselves – including the choice to turn to the *troika* for financial assistance – and that, to the extent that these decisions were taken under duress, the latter was solely caused by the defective architecture of the EMU rather than by the arbitrary decisions of any given actor.

In this sense, it might appear out of place to speak of 'monetary colonialism' – a term which implies some form of agency on behalf of the EMU's dominant institutions, particularly its issuing institute, the ECB – and specifically an arbitrary use of the latter's powers for illegitimate ends. Indeed, it is widely believed that, to the extent that the ECB contributed to the worsening of the euro crisis (for example by delaying the launch of its asset purchase, or quantitative easing (QE), programme), it did so purely because it was bound by the EMU's rigid rules-based framework; conversely, at the opposite end of the spectrum of opinions, to the extent that the ECB, particularly under the leadership of Mario Draghi, succeeded in stretching the EMU's rules (for example by eventually launching its QE programme in 2015), it is claimed that this was done with the sole intent of 'completing' the EMU and making it more resilient to crises.

Contrary to both these claims, this article aims to demonstrate that the ECB did indeed engage in an *arbitrary and illegitimate use of its monopoly currency-issuing powers* with the aim of coercing governments to comply with the overall political-economic agenda of the EU (and of the dominant actors there within). I will focus specifically on the following episodes: the ECB's delayed response to the European 'sovereign debt crisis' (2009–2012, or ongoing depending on the point of view); the signing of Ireland's bailout programme with the *troika* (2010); the resignation of Italian prime minister Silvio Berlusconi and his replacement by the 'technocrat' Mario Monti (2011); the shutdown of the Greek banking system (2015); and the bond market turbulence that accompanied the formation of the Five Star Movement-League government in Italy (2018–2019).

## HOW THE ECB 'ENGINEERED' THE 'EUROPEAN SOVEREIGN DEBT CRISIS'

On the heel of the global financial crisis (GFC), euro area bond markets were the target of intense speculation. The ECB took three years to finally quell it. In the summer of 2012, it announced its Outright Monetary Transactions (OMT) programme, under which it pledged, if necessary, to engage in unlimited purchases of government bonds on secondary bond markets in order to preserve 'an appropriate monetary policy transmission and the singleness of the monetary policy' – or, more simply, as ECB president Mario Draghi, who succeeded Jean-Claude Trichet in 2011, famously put it, 'to do whatever it takes to preserve the euro'. By declaring that 'no ex ante quantitative limits are set on the size of Outright Monetary Transactions', the ECB sent a clear signal to the markets. The implication was that if markets demanded excessively high interest rates the ECB would step in and buy the bonds itself, theoretically putting an end to the speculators' game. Unsurprisingly for anyone that understands the power of central banks, which I briefly outlined above, Draghi's announcement succeeded in immediately bringing down bond yields in affected countries – without even having to actually activate a single OMT programme (which entails 'strict and effective conditionality'; that is, austerity and neoliberal 'structural reforms' on behalf of the country that applies for one, which testifies to the fact that the OMT programme falls very short of transforming the ECB into a full-fledged lender of last resort, a point we will return to).

By then, however, the damage was done: the lives of millions of people across Europe – particularly in the countries of the periphery – had already been ravaged by brutal austerity policies that had been presented as a 'painful but necessary evil'[8] to shore up public finances, restore market confidence, and bring down bond yields. Which begs the question: why did the ECB wait so long to intervene? The delay is usually attributed to treaty obligations and to Trichet's dogmatic adherence to old monetary theories, as well as to the complex politics of compromise that characterises the Eurozone's decision-making process and, in particular, Germany's long-standing refusal to engage in any form of debt mutualisation.

There is some truth to this. However, it is now becoming increasingly clear that the European 'sovereign debt crisis' of 2009–2012 was largely 'engineered' by the ECB (and Germany) to impose a new order on the continent in the form of a self-imposed shock doctrine. Indeed, former ECB president Jean-Claude Trichet made no secret of the fact that the central bank's refusal to support public bond markets in the first phase of the financial crisis was aimed at pressuring Eurozone governments into consolidating their budgets and implementing (neoliberal) 'structural reforms'.[9] As Adam Tooze noted, '[t]he role of bond markets in relation to the ECB and the dominant German government was less that of a freewheeling vigilante, than of state-sanctioned paramilitaries delivering a punishment beating whilst the police looked on'.[10] In a number of countries, though, the ECB went much further than simply 'looking on' (or turning the other way) as financial markets beat governments into compliance. Early into the crisis, it had already become clear that the ECB had moved beyond its purely monetary prerogatives (or lack thereof) and had taken on the form of a 'full-blooded political actor engaging in a strategy aimed at forcing EU political leaders to embrace fiscal rectitude', as Jacob Kirkegaard of the Peterson Institute for International Economics wrote in 2011.[11]

## MONETARY BLACKMAIL: THE CASE OF IRELAND

An early example of this was in Ireland in 2010. Following the country's massive banking crisis of 2007–2008, the Irish government, in consultation with the ECB, made the controversial decision, in 2009, to offer a blanket guarantee to the country's highly indebted banks (and, indirectly, to their foreign creditors, which included British, German, French, and American banks). By March 2010, however, it had become clear that the government was unable to meet its mounting obligations to provide cash to the banks – in particular the Anglo Irish Bank, which had been nationalised in 2009. Thus, in consultation with the ECB, Dublin drafted a new deal with the bank, 'promising' to pay Anglo Irish the bailout cash through regular instalments (known as 'promissory notes') of €3.1 billion a year. The bank in turn would be able to use that 'sovereign promise' to access the ECB's Emergency Liquidity Assistance (ELA) – a special funding provided to institutions with liquidity problems. The operation became very contentious, as it basically shifted the banks' private debts onto the government's balance sheet. By September 2010, government support for the six guaranteed banks had risen markedly to 32 per cent of GDP, but the banks were still unable to raise finance on the markets. Moreover, by that point, Ireland's biggest banks had borrowed more than €80 billion from the ECB to pay back private creditors.[12]

At that point the ECB stepped in. In mid-November, Jean-Claude Trichet, then president of the ECB, sent a series of 'secret' letters to the Irish government – subsequently disclosed in 2014 following an appeal by the European Ombudsman[13] – in which he threatened to cut off ELA funding to the Irish banking system unless the government immediately applied for a bailout and agreed to a programme of austerity and bank recapitalisation. Ireland's request needed to include a commitment to undertake 'decisive actions in the areas of fiscal consolidation, structural reforms and financial sector restructuring', the letter added, despite the fact that the crisis in Ireland had been caused by private – not public – debt. A failure to accept these conditions would have resulted in the ECB cutting off ELA support for the Irish banks – which would have effectively caused the collapse of the Irish banking system. Soon afterwards, the government started negotiations with the ECB and the IMF for a €64 billion bailout.[14] Furthermore, over the course of 2012, the ECB repeatedly insisted that the promissory notes had to be repaid in full and refused the government's proposal to swap the notes with a long-term (and less costly) bond until 2013. In addition, the ECB insisted that no debt restructuring (or bail-in) should be applied to the nationalised banks' bondholders.

In many ways, the Irish bailout provided the blueprint for all future 'rescue programmes', whereby the European political-financial elites rewrote the history of the financial crisis, transforming a crisis of the markets – and in more general terms of neoliberalism – into a crisis of public spending, and then used this narrative to push through policies designed to re-engineer European societies and economies according to an even more radical neoliberal framework, even at the cost of resorting to financial and monetary blackmail and threatening to crash a member state's banking system (or actually crashing it, as we will see further on).

## A MONETARY COUP: THE REMOVAL OF SILVIO BERLUSCONI

In 2011, the ECB's policy of financial and monetary blackmail reached new heights. This time the country on the receiving end was Italy. On August 5 of that year there was a stir over the news that Italian government bond yields had risen above Spain's for the first time in more than a year.[15] This was widely interpreted as a sign of the markets' doubts about Rome's ability to meet its debt obligations. (In other words, the commentary followed the now-conventional wisdom about the Eurozone crisis: that it was all about legitimate market concerns over excessive government debt). That same day, ECB president Jean-Claude Trichet and his anointed successor, Mario Draghi, sent an extraordinary letter to the Italian government which was intended to remain secret, although it was subsequently leaked.[16] The letter claimed that Italy's post-crisis deficit-cutting plan was 'not sufficient', and set out detailed demands aimed at 'a major overhaul of the public administration'.

This included 'the full liberalisation of local public services'; 'large scale privatisations' (even though citizens had recently overturned through a referendum the government's attempts to privatise the country's water services); 'reducing the cost of public employees by strengthening turnover rules and, if necessary, by reducing wages'; 'reform [of] the collective wage bargaining system'; 'more stringent [...] criteria for seniority pensions'; and even 'constitutional reform tightening fiscal rules'. All this, of course, was needed 'to restore the confidence of investors'. Giulio Tremonti, Italy's then minister of Economy and Finance, later privately told a group of European finance ministers that his government had received two threatening letters in August: one from a terrorist group, the other from the ECB. 'The one from the ECB was worse', he quipped.[17]

At that point, the government pledged far-reaching reforms and deeper budget cuts. Nonetheless, interest rates continued to rise, eventually leading, on Saturday, November 12, to the resignation of Prime Minister Silvio Berlusconi. That same day, President Giorgio Napolitano appointed Mario Monti to form a so-called *governo tecnico* ('technical government' in Italian). Monti was a technocrat, not a politician. He had been a European commissioner and an international advisor to Goldman Sachs since 2005 (a position he resigned from just a few days before being sworn in). This marked the beginning of yet another chapter in the Eurozone crisis: the rise of the technocrats. Monti was sworn in as prime minister on November 16, just a week after having been appointed a senator for life.

In most accounts, the Italian government crisis was portrayed as the 'natural' response of financial markets to Berlusconi's handling of the economic crisis, in line with the dominant narrative of the European 'debt crisis'. However, it was clear from the start that there had been very strong international pressures at play. A number of commentators argued at the time that Angela Merkel, and especially the ECB, had played a pivotal role in Berlusconi's resignation. Over the years, evidence has surfaced to support such suspicions. In 2015, former Spanish Prime Minister, José Luis Zapatero, recounted to the Italian daily, *La Stampa*, the events that took place at the G20 meeting in Cannes between 3–4 November 2011, just a few days before Berlusconi's resignation:

> I will never forget what I saw at the G20 meeting in Cannes. I went there fearing that Spain was in the sight of the proponents of austerity but I was wrong: the target was Italy. Berlusconi and Tremonti were under immense pressure to accept an IMF bailout. But they staunchly refused. Shortly afterwards, I heard Monti's name mentioned in the corridors. I found it very strange. Was it a coup d'état? I don't know, all I can say is that […] the proponents of austerity wanted to decide Italy's economic policies in place of the government. It is definitely a case that needs to be studied.[18]

In light of Zapatero's startling declaration, it is safe to posit that it is probably not a coincidence that in the days following the G20 meeting there was a steep rise in Italian bond yields. This is considered by many to be a result of the fact that the ECB stopped or reduced its purchases of Italian bonds.[19] We can't be certain – back then the ECB wasn't in the habit of disclosing the countries involved in its weekly bond purchases, and in any case yields had been rising since mid-October – but it is telling to note that the following week the ECB stated that it had purchased about €4.5 billion in sovereign bonds, which is less than half of what it had acquired a week earlier (leading various analysts to conclude that the 'missing bonds' were indeed Italy's, and that the move was aimed at putting pressure on the Italian government, in a perfect example of the 'politics by other means' employed by the ECB in its handling of the crisis).[20] This was belatedly acknowledged even by Mario Monti himself, who claimed in a 2017 interview that in late 2011 'Draghi decided to stop the purchases of Italian government bonds, which had kept the Berlusconi government afloat in the summer and autumn of 2011'.[21]

Regardless of the details of the event in question, it is by now increasingly clear that the ECB 'forced Silvio Berlusconi to leave office in favour of unelected Mario Monti', by making his ousting the precondition for further support by the ECB for Italian bonds and banks, as even the *Financial Times* recently acknowledged.[22] It is hard to imagine a more disturbing scenario than a supposedly 'independent' and 'apolitical' central bank resorting to monetary blackmail in order to have an elected government removed from office and impose its own political agenda (outlined in the August 2011 letter), though this appears to be exactly what happened in Italy in 2011, leading some observers to suggest that the EU was on track to 'becom[ing] the post-democratic prototype and even a pre-dictatorial governance structure against national sovereignty and democracies'.[23] This exemplifies what Wynne Godley meant when he wrote that '[i]f a country gives up or loses' the power to issue its own money, it effectively 'acquires the status of a local authority or colony'.

## DENYING DEMOCRACY AND ECONOMIC REASON: THE SHUTTING DOWN OF THE GREEK BANKING SYSTEM

An even more explicit demonstration of this took place in Greece in 2015. On that occasion the ECB was exposed for what is really is: a fully-fledged political body with the power to bring a country to its knees – and the willingness to use it. As is well known, after the left-wing party

SYRIZA – led by Alexis Tsipras, which had campaigned on a radical anti-austerity platform – came to power in Greece in January 2015, a dramatic political standoff ensued between the Greek government and the EU authorities as the former attempted to renegotiate the country's public debt, fiscal policy, and reform agenda, and reverse the austerity policies that – ever since the first *troika* bailout package (and related 'economic and adjustment programme') in 2010, which was followed by a second bailout package in 2012 – had caused so much damage to the country. The standoff came to an end in the summer of that same year when the Greek government ultimately capitulated and accepted the onerous terms of yet another loan agreement conditional on further austerity and deregulation measures, effectively putting an end to the Greek 'rebellion'.

SYRIZA's capitulation is generally blamed on the obstinate refusal of the leading European states (first and foremost, Germany) to allow a peripheral country such as Greece to deviate from the fiscal-economic status quo, fearing a domino effect and, perhaps, even more importantly, to accept any losses on the loans extended by their banks to the Greek government. However, the most pernicious role was played by the ECB. Indeed, in Europe's war against the new Greek government, the first shots were fired by the central bank. On February 4, just nine days after the election, the ECB deprived the Greek government of one of its main lines of credit, by ruling that it would no longer allow Greek banks to access 'normal' ECB liquidity by offering as collateral Greek government bonds that were officially rated 'junk' – an exception granted to those countries undergoing a *troika* financial aid programme. From that moment on, the banks would have to rely on the more expensive Emergency Liquidity Assistance (ELA). The excuse offered by the ECB was that it was 'currently not possible to assume a successful conclusion of the [financial aid] programme review'.

It was an extraordinary decision for a number of reasons: not only was the new Greek government only one week old and still had three more weeks to extend the loan agreement with the creditors and the *troika* but, even more worryingly in terms of its economic consequences, the ECB's move set in motion a bank run that dramatically accelerated the capital flight that was already underway in the country. Months of very tense negotiations followed, during which the Greek government's proposals were all dismissed by the *troika*, further exacerbating the outflow of capital and causing the asset value and market capitalisation of Greek banks to plummet. The situation came to a head in June 2015. Even though the negotiations officially broke down on June 25, a week before – on June 18 – information was leaked out to the media (presumably by representatives of the ECB itself) that, with the massive haemorrhage and deposit outflow from Greek banks, the latter might not be able to open their doors to the public on the following Monday, June 22. As Mario Seccareccia, an economist at the University of Ottawa, notes, there is only one explanation for leaking such incendiary statements to the media in the midst of the negotiations: a desire 'to create a state of frenzy in Greece even before the collapse of the talks'.[24]

On June 25, the Tsipras government rejected the 'final offer' put forward by the *troika* for a new loan to allow the government to roll over a payment of €1.55 billion owed to the IMF, and two days later, in a strategic move to strengthen its hand in future negotiations, it announced that it would be holding a referendum on the terms of the offer, to be held on July 5. To facilitate the democratic process, the government asked the Eurogroup – the informal gathering of Eurozone finance ministers – to agree to a further extension of the loan agreement from June 30 to July 30. The Eurogroup turned the request down. Worse even, the following day, on June 28, the ECB refused Greece's central bank the right to increase its ELA facility, leaving the Greek government no choice but to shut down the nation's banks, impose capital controls, and restrict individual withdrawals to €60 per day, at an enormous cost to Greek business and citizens. The people of Greece were therefore 'denied the right to deliberate in calm conditions before the referendum, with the closed banks a constant reminder of the power of the ECB to hold a nation to ransom', as Yanis Varoufakis, the Greek finance minister at the time of the negotiations, observed.[25]

Despite the exceptional circumstances – or arguably because of them – the Greek people rejected en masse the austerity package demanded by the *troika*. Nonetheless, the Greek government did a political *volte-face* and accepted the terms of the EU, which were actually even more punitive than those that it had previously rejected. Obviously, for reasons that we cannot discuss here, Tsipras was not ready to face the economic and political consequences of a prolonged closure of the country's banking system, and even less so a rejection of the bailout package, which would have arguably left the Greek government little choice but to default, exit the Eurozone, and launch a national currency (though, to be fair, Greece's euro membership was never explicitly or officially at issue in the referendum).

In this sense, the ECB's behaviour played a crucial role in ultimately bringing the Greek government to heel, in what clearly amounted to a strictly political move for which no technical justification can be found. As Seccareccia writes, the ECB cut off liquidity to the Greek banks 'even though it knew fully well that this was not primarily because of a solvency problem for Greek banks but overwhelmingly it was a *systemic liquidity* problem arising from the growing uncertainty and fears on the part of the public reflected in the progressive hoarding of liquid funds' – fears that were 'undoubtedly compounded by the actions of the ECB itself':

> Hence, instead of seeking to support and promote the smooth operation of the payments system of one of its member states that, at no time, had officially proposed to exit from the Eurozone (in fact, it was the German leaders who were strategising a 'temporary' Grexit), the ECB actually cut off its liquidity assistance deliberately *in order to destabilise further the Greek payments system and force the SYRIZA government into accepting the harsh austerity measures* [...]. Clearly the ECB played a cruel political game of destabilising the Greek economy to further the ends of the current political and technocratic elite of the Eurozone.

Indeed, in the Eurozone it is no longer a case of the central bank being independent from governments (a questionable principle in itself), but rather of *the governments being dependent on the central bank*. As Paul De Grauwe says: 'In a stand-alone country, if the sovereign is in trouble it is always the sovereign which prevails and forces the central bank to provide the necessary liquidity. In the Eurozone it is the other way round: it is the ECB which prevails over the sovereign. That is a governance structure which is unacceptable and cannot be sustained in the long run'.[26] This is an almost historically unprecedented situation; in fact, one would be hard-pressed to find another instance in history in which a central bank deliberately crashed its country's banking system in order to force its political agenda upon an elected government.

Interestingly, once the Greek parliament accepted the terms of the new austerity package, the ECB not only resumed its liquidity assistance but, for the first time, extended its quantitative easing purchases to Greek government securities. The ECB's behaviour during the Greek crisis was so preposterous that, unsurprisingly, its legality has been called into question. It is interesting to note that the ECB itself commissioned external legal opinions to examine the lawfulness of its actions, but has repeatedly refused to release these to the public, citing 'attorney-client privilege'[27] – a fact that may be reasonably interpreted as an indication that the legal opinions in question were not supportive of its decisions, or at least that they contain views that the ECB does not want to publicise. According to the eminent EU Law expert, Andreas Fischer-Lescano, the ECB has no case for withholding such information from the public.[28]

## THE POLITICAL USE OF THE SPREAD: THE RISE AND FALL OF ITALY'S 'POPULIST' GOVERNMENT

We saw how, in 2011, the ECB effectively forced Silvio Berlusconi to leave office by allowing interest rates on Italy's government bonds to rise above the safety level, and by making his ouster the precondition for further support by the ECB for Italian bonds. Similarly, it would appear that, once again, the ECB manipulated Italy's bond market during the negotiations for the formation of the now-defunct Five Star Movement-League 'populist' government, in office from June 2018 to September 2019. The two 'anti-establishment' and eurosceptic parties – which emerged as winners in the extraordinary vote of March 4, 2018, which resulted in an unprecedented collapse of the political establishment that has ruled Italy for the last quarter century – reached an agreement after months of tense negotiations that took place under conditions of severe bond market instability that strongly influenced the outcome of the negotiations, resulting in the pre-emptive 'domestication' of the new government.[29] None of this was fortuitous.

It all began in the last week of May, when the designated prime minister, Giuseppe Conte, submitted for approval to the Italian president, Sergio Mattarella, as required by the Italian constitution, the list of ministers chosen for the new government, which included the economist Paola Savona – an establishment man through and through who was nonetheless known for his critical stance vis-à-vis the current European architecture – in the key role of economic minister. That same day, the credit rating agency Moody's announced that it had put Italy's rating on review for a possible downgrade, citing the country's political uncertainty. At that point, Italy's rating was Baa2, two notches above 'junk' status, the level at which the ECB can no longer accept a country's bonds as collateral for 'normal' (non-ELA) bank liquidity, thus forcing the country in question to accept whatever punitive conditions requested by the ECB to continue providing emergency liquidity to its banking system (as we saw in the cases of Ireland and Greece). It's yet another example of the way in which the Eurozone's complex institutional architecture was designed to give a semblance of neutrality to decisions that are entirely political in nature; for example, by shifting the blame for the loss of access to central bank liquidity onto the poor policies of member states, or the 'technical' assessment of rating agencies, when in fact, as we have amply noted, a country's solvency (credit worthiness) depends entirely on the policies of the ECB itself. The episode under examination provides a great case in point.

Following Moody's announcement, a sell-off of Italian bonds began. By the end of the day, a Friday, the spread between Italian and German government bonds – the benchmark commonly used to assess the 'risk' of the former – exceeded 200 basis points,[30] meaning that Italian bonds now carried a 2 per cent higher interest rate than German bonds. During the weekend – in an astonishing move that raises a series of legal and political problems that I have discussed elsewhere[31] – Italian president Mattarella announced that he would be vetoing the nomination of Paola Savona as economic minister, citing his excessively euro-critical stance as the cause of the market's negative reaction and claiming that his appointment would 'constitute a real risk for the savings of our fellow citizens and for Italian families'. (Savona was eventually replaced by Giovanni Tria, a committed pro-EU economist, in a telling demonstration of how easily a nominally 'populist' government can be pre-emptively neutralised in the Eurozone).

In line with the dominant narrative, the steep rise in bond yields was presented by Mattarella as a 'natural' consequence of the financial markets' hostility to the new government. In fact, as we have established, there was nothing natural about it: technically, a central bank always controls interest rates on the bonds issued in its currency. At the very least, it shows that, despite the various institutional innovations introduced by Mario Draghi, such as the OMT and quantitative easing

(QE) programmes, the ECB is still far from having evolved into a 'normal' central bank. While the ECB, through its QE programme, does indeed intervene on the sovereign bond markets of member states, and on a massive scale for that matter, it does so on the basis of fixed (or marginally flexible) quotas, based on each country's contribution to the ECB's capital (the capital key), meaning that it cannot boost its acquisitions of bonds for a specific country to quell market speculation. Or better, it can only do so through its OMT programme which, as we have seen, entails 'strict and effective conditionality', such as that imposed on Greece and other countries – that is, austerity and neoliberal 'structural reforms' – explaining why no country has yet applied for an OMT programme.[32] Thus, even assuming that the bond market turbulence that accompanied the formation of the Italian government was solely the result of the ECB's institutional constraints, or non-intervention, we would, at the very least, be in the presence of a highly dysfunctional system, which continues to subject governments to the 'market discipline' of so-called bond vigilantes – to the point of allowing the latter to even censor individual ministers. However, as in other instances, even in this case the ECB went much further than simply 'doing nothing'.

In early June, data released by the ECB revealed that, just like it had done in 2011, between April and May – right in the middle of the negotiations for the formation of the new government – the central bank scaled back the monthly proportion of Italian government bonds bought in the context of its QE programme, bringing it down to 15 per cent of the total, the lowest proportional allocation to Italy since the bond-buying programme began in 2015.[33] More specifically, the ECB underbought Italian bonds (by €362 million) and overbought German bonds (by more than €2 billion), relative to the two countries' capital key.[34] Understandably, various analysts and commentators accused the ECB of deliberately contributing to widening the spread between Italian and German bonds with its actions in order to increase the pressure on the prospective eurosceptic government.[35] ECB spokesman Michael Steen responded that the bank's buying decision are 'never about politics' and claimed that the change was necessary to accommodate a large German redemption, and that it acted in line with its stated rules on purchases.

However, there was no need for the ECB to bind itself so tightly to that logic. Its rules on reinvesting maturing bonds state that this must be done 'in a flexible and timely manner in the month they fall due, on a best effort basis, or in the subsequent two months, if warranted by market liquidity conditions. The published monthly net purchase volumes per jurisdiction may therefore fluctuate owing to the timing of these reinvestments'.[36] In other words, the ECB's rules do allow, for reasons of liquidity, a degree of flexibility relative to each country's capital key when dealing with redemptions. Indeed, the bank had previously strayed from the capital key during times of political strife, overbuying the bonds of certain countries precisely in order to avoid market turbulence. Thus the ECB would have been perfectly justified in postponing the redemption of the German bonds and even increasing its proportional purchases of Italian bonds to keep the spread down or at least mitigate its rise, and thus allow the democratic process in Italy to proceed as smoothly as possible – or at the very least fulfil its mandate of ensuring financial stability in the euro area.

But that is not what the ECB is there for, as should be clear by now. In fact, as mentioned, it did the exact opposite, fully aware – we can reasonably presume – of the consequences: it's hard to believe that the ECB didn't anticipate that overbuying German bonds while at the same time underbuying Italian bonds, thus reducing the purchases of the latter relative to the former, wouldn't have a pronounced effect on the two countries' yields, thus widening the spread and exacerbating market tensions. As *Bloomberg* commented, 'it's hard to completely shake the feeling that Italian politics informed the ECB's buying decisions in May'.[37] Interestingly, once the government (now pre-emptively tamed) was sworn in, in early June, the ECB boosted its bond purchases once again, thus stabilising markets.

The strategy worked: in August 2019, Italy's 'populist' government fell after League leader Matteo Salvini dropped out of the alliance with the Five Star Movement (M5S), thus paving the way to the formation of a new, staunchly pro-establishment government, as the M5S reached an agreement to form a new executive with the pro-EU, liberal-centrist Democratic Party. One of the main reasons cited by Salvini for pulling the plug on the government was the insistence of economic minister Giovanni Tria on complying with the EU's strict budgetary framework, and his refusal to raise Italy's budget deficit, as demanded by Salvini to make room for the League's proposed tax cut.[38] One may argue that, by appointing a man loyal to the EU to the most important government post of all, the Ministry of Economy and Finance – in charge of carrying out all the major economic negotiations with the EU through the ECOFIN (Economic and Financial Affairs Council) and the Eurogroup – president Mattarella (and, indirectly, the ECB) effectively put the government into 'controlled administration' before it was even born, thus ensuring that it would not pose a threat to the status quo, and sealing its fate in the process.

## CONCLUSIONS

In this chapter I have attempted to show that the euro area's problems extend far beyond the fact that it displays the typical pitfalls of all monetary unions, that it is not an optimal currency area or that it lacks federal-level stabilisation mechanisms (though all these facts are true). The reality is much more disquieting: over the course of the past decade, the Eurozone has evolved from a dysfunctional but formally democratic monetary union into an historically unprecedented and globally unparalleled inter/supranational governance structure where governments are disciplined and punished through a complex array of institutional mechanisms, where the formal democratic process itself is systematically subverted through financial and monetary blackmail – first and foremost, at the hands of the ECB, as we have seen – to the point that one may reasonably question whether euro area member states can still be considered democracies, even according to the narrow 'bourgeois' understanding of the concept. Frankly, it is hard to see how a system of democratically unaccountable institutions, such as the European Commission and the ECB, are able to arbitrarily decide the policies of elected governments – or even forcibly remove them from office – and how they could qualify as being democratic.

In fact, I would argue that we are in the presence of an extreme form of capitalist authoritarianism that is structurally post-democratic to its very core – worse even, that is moving from post-democracy to pre-dictatorship.[39] I would also argue, as I have discussed elsewhere, that this was not an unintended consequence of the 'mistakes' committed along the road – in good faith, it is often claimed – by the architects of EMU; on the contrary, constraining national democracies was one of the euro's principal aims all along.[40] For this reason, any belief that the EU can be 'democratised' and reformed in a progressive direction is a pious illusion. This would require an impossible alignment of left movements/governments that are yet to emerge at the international level. On a more fundamental level, a system that was created with the specific aim of constraining democracy cannot be democratised. It can only be rejected. And, certainly, it should not be emulated elsewhere.

African countries should consider carefully whether a Eurozone-type of monetary integration is the best way to go for them. Against the narrow and sometimes dubious economic advantages associated with monetary unions (lower transaction costs, increased regional trade, and more macroeconomic stability), they should factor in the potential negative implications of losing the power to issue their own currency – decreasing economic, financial, and political sovereignty, as well as a shrinking democratic space.

## NOTES

1 Consciencism. Dr Kwame Nkrumah Speaks in Addis Ababa in 1963. Available at: consciencism.wordpress.com/history/dr-kwame-nkrumah-speaks-in-addis-ababa-in-1963/, para. 23 [Accessed on July 7 2021].
2 Piccolino, G., 2019: Looking like a regional organization? The European model of regional integration and the West African Economic and Monetary Union (WAEMU), *Cambridge Review of International Affairs*. doi: 10.1080/09557571.2019.1634676; Sylla, N.S., 2020. Moving forward to African monetary integration: Lessons from the CFA franc. *Africa Development,* Volume XLV, No. 2, pp. 39–58.
3 Godley, W., 1992. Maastricht and all that. *London Review of Books*, 14 (19).
4 Mallet, V. and Spiegel, P., 2010. Doubts grow over 'peripheral' Eurozone nations, *Financial Times*, November 9.
5 Concern over Greek debt crisis reaches new heights. *The Irish Times*, 13 September 2011.
6 Bank of Japan, 2019. Price Stability Target of 2 Per cent and quantitative and qualitative monetary easing with yield curve control. https://www.boj.or.jp/en/mopo/outline/qqe.htm/ [Accessed on July 7, 2021].
7 De Grauwe, P., 2011. The Governance of a Fragile Eurozone. CEPS Working Document No. 364, CEPS.
8 See, for example, the interview with Mario Draghi by Brian Blackstone, Matthew Karnitschnig, and Robert Thomson. Europe's Banker Talks Tough. *The Wall Street Journal*, 24 February 2012.

9 See Bastasin, C., 2012. *Saving Europe: How National Politics Nearly Destroyed the Euro*. Washington, D.C.: Brookings Institution Press.

10 Adam Tooze, A., 2017. Notes on the global condition: Of bond vigilantes, central bankers and the crisis, 2008–2017. Author's blog (adatooze.com), November 7.

11 Kirkegaard, J., 2011. The next strategic target: De Gaulle's EU legacy. *VoxEU*, November 30.

12 Lewis, M., 2011. When Irish eyes are crying. *Vanity Fair*, March.

13 The exchange is viewable at https://www.ecb.europa.eu/press/html/irish-letters.en.html [Accessed on June 7 2021].

14 Peter O'Dwyer, P., 2018. Irish taxpayers carried biggest burden after bank bailouts. *The Times*, September 15.

15 Hughes, J. and Mallet, V., 2011. Italian bond yields rise above Spain's. *Financial Times*, August 5.

16 The letter is viewable in its entirety at: www.corriere.it/economia/11_settembre_29/trichet_draghi_inglese_304a5f1e-ea59-11e0-ae06-4da866778017.shtml [Accessed on July 7 2021].

17 Quoted in Walker, M., Forelle, C., and Meichtry, S., 2011. Deepening crisis over euro pits leader against leader. *The Wall Street Journal*, December 30.

18 Interview with José Luis Zapatero by Francesco Olivo. Zapatero: Macché populisti. Sono dei socialdemocratici. *La Stampa*, 23 March 2015.

19 See, for example, Babad, M., 2011. Did ECB hasten Berlusconi downfall by holding back? *The Globe and Mail*, November 15.

20 *Ibid.*

21 Interview with Mario Monti by Federico Fubini. Monti: Renzi è un disco rotto, ripete accuse a impatto zero. *Corriere della Sera*, 14 July 2017.

22 C. Klein, M.C., 2017. The euro is not a punishment system. *Financial Times*, November 9.

23 Elsner, W., 2012. Financial capitalism: At odds with democracy. *RealWorld Economics Review*, 62, p. 158.

24 Seccareccia, M., 2015. The ECB and the betrayal of the Bagehot rule. *Economia e Politica*, August 12.

25 Quoted in DiEM25, 2017. *#TheGreekFiles. Why ECB independence is impossible without greater transparency*, February 1.

26 Interview with Paul De Grauwe by Alexandre Trentin, 2018. We have to change the system – the Italian crisis makes this clear. *Finanz und Wirtschaft*, June 1.

27 DiEM25, *#TheGreekFiles*.

28 Quoted in DiEM25, *#TheGreekFiles*.

29 Fazi, T., 2019. The revenge of the elites. *Spiked*, October 4.

30 André Sapir, A., 2018. *High public debt in euro-area countries: Comparing Belgium and Italy*. Policy Contribution Issue No. 15, Bruegel, p. 12.

31 Fazi, The revenge of the elites.

32 The capital key rule has been temporarily suspended in the wake of the COVID-19 pandemic.

33 Ashworth, M., 2018. The ECB Deserves This Bout of Political Hot Water. *Bloomberg*, June 5.
34 *Ibid.*
35 *Ibid.*
36 European Central Bank, Additional information on asset purchase programme. Press release, 26 October 2017.
37 Ashworth, The ECB Deserves This Bout of Political Hot Water.
38 Fazi, The revenge of the elites.
39 Elsner, Financial capitalism.
40 Fazi, T. and W. Mitchell, 2018. The EU cannot be democratised – here's why. *Brave New Europe*, February 8.

# 8

# Geopolitics of Finance in Africa: Birth of financial centres, not monetary unions

*Elizabeth Cobbett*

## INTRODUCTION

The question this chapter addresses is at which scale of governance is formal monetary sovereignty across the African continent most likely to be fixed. There are three possibilities: formal monetary sovereignty at the national level, regional economic communities (RECs) formation of monetary unions (MUs), and a single continental currency adopted through an African Monetary Union (AMU). As the scale of monetary authority moves from the national towards the continental platform of governance, greater is the need for political collaboration and powerful supranational financial institutions, such as an African Central Bank (ACB).

While 'monetary sovereignty' has never been expressly recognised by leading financial international institutions, such as the International Monetary Fund, as a legal concept,[1] Hirsch[2] reminds us that there is a recognised connection between state sovereignty and the right to issue money. Yet, under European imperialism, control of national financial decisions and flows were denied to African colonial states.[3] African states did not have the power to issue a national currency, there were no national central banks, and the ruling elites did not have the right to issue money, nor to buy and hold domestic debt. In other words, they had no formal monetary sovereignty.

This changed as most African states[4] took control of issuing and managing currencies, central symbols of modern nation-state sovereignty,[5] upon independence. But, postcolonial African states obtained sovereignty at the dawning of a new age of financial globalisation. They entered a global economy progressively shaped by the resurrection of global finance which, like a phoenix, rose from the ashes of the capital controls of the Bretton Woods system.[6] The monetary and fiscal policies of newly independent African states were adversely shaped by the broader context of financial globalisation and high interest rates, accompanied by an ideological shift from Keynesian to monetarist Friedmanian economics in North America and Western Europe. Faced with balance of payments difficulties, international financial institutions (IFIs) instructed African states to reduce their financial imbalances through internal adjustment measures, such as by developing stricter debt management, privatising public services, legislating central bank independence, and improving their credit worthiness. In other words, formal, *de jure* monetary sovereignty did not bring *de facto* control. While Pistor[7] argues that if sovereignty were tied to effective control over money, rather than to control over territory and people, most states would fail the test of sovereignty, this was little consolation to African states who needed effective power to pursue development.

The African Union (AU) proposes the creation of an African Monetary Union (AMU) as a collective response to the challenges posed by global financialisation. In this case scenario, formal monetary sovereignty would move from the national scale of governance to the continental. The goal here is to increase political economic power for all African states through a centralised monetary sovereignty managed by the future African Central Bank (ACB). The Abuja Treaty, or African Economic Community (AEC) Treaty, signed in 1991, calls for an ACB to be established by 2028 as part of the range of African Continental Financial Institutions (ACFI), including an African Investment Bank, a Pan-African Stock Exchange, and an African Monetary Fund, supporting the African Monetary Union (AMU). The creation of the AMU, in this plan, will be achieved through incremental joining of monetary unions established in the Regional Economic Communities (REC). This plan for continental monetary sovereignty echoes the European template of progressively moving towards deeper political economic commitments, finalising in a single currency.

While this strategy sounds reasonably straightforward and the path clear cut, there are two major issues. First, there is no empirical case, nor evidence, of a single currency being adopted through the stitching up of sub-regional (or sub-continental in the case of Africa) monetary unions. As this chapter will demonstrate, MUs are rare because they require determined political will, including that to relinquish sovereignty plus economic readiness.

Second, plans for a future AMU ignore what is taking place empirically, that of a global financial geography organised through International Financial Centres (IFC). Hall and Wójcik[8] propose understanding IFCs through a networked geographical imagination. In this imagined network, global finance forms a deep-rooted archipelago-economy emphasising complex relations between different parts of financial centres and systems stretching across the globe. Select African governments – namely Morocco (North Africa), Lagos State, Nigeria (West Africa), South Africa (Southern Africa), and Kenya (East Africa) – are situating their business and finance hubs as part of this spreading archipelago-economy.

Within this framework, I argue that formal monetary sovereignty will, by and large, remain within national territories as the more powerful African public authorities reach out and embed financial networks within their economic hubs. Powerful African states are reaching out to embed financial networks within their economic hubs as they establish international financial centres (IFC). And to do this, they need to retain their monetary sovereignty and not delegate it to a sub-regional or continental level of public authority.

My argument is developed, in the first part of this chapter, by identifying the obstacles to the AU's goal to move formal monetary sovereignty to the continental scale through the formation of an AMU. I suggest that we can refer to monetary *dis-union* taking place across Africa.[9] There are three causes at play here. The first one is historical in nature, namely the legacy of imperialism and colonialism in relation to the economics and politics of monetary union in Africa. The second one, which is more current, but which also has historical origins, is the inherent complexity to provide any kind of collective good via public/state action necessary to tackle political economic barriers to monetary unions. This establishes the claim that an African monetary union (or regional ones) is extremely unlikely. A third reason that formal monetary sovereignty will most probably reside at the national level of governance – with recognition that sub-national public authorities are influential in shaping this process – is the progression of the global financial geography of International Financial Centres to emerging powers. In the second section, I therefore explain that Africa's financial architecture is being shaped in line with the geography of the globalisation of finance as it moves through multiple networks and private financial institutions organised in financial centres located in cities. This establishes African urban centres – Casablanca, Nairobi, Lagos, and Johannesburg – as continental foundations for the developing international monetary order as financial networks organise credit operations in selected geographical urban locations.[10]

## MONETARY DIS-UNION ACROSS AFRICA

### *African MUs are largely Colonial Institutions*

The 1991 Abuja Treaty roadmap identifies RECs as the building blocks to be 'stitched up' into a single continental African Economic Community (AEC). These include: the Arab Maghreb Union (AMU), the Economic Community of West African States (ECOWAS), the East African Community (EAC), and the Southern African Development Community (SADC). Drawing on the examples of the SADC and ECOWAS, this section argues that contemporary African monetary unions are rooted in colonial financial arrangements that present deep challenges as building blocks for further monetary integration.

In 1921, after the establishment of the South African Reserve Bank (SARB), the South African currency (initially British Sterling; since 1961, the Rand) became the sole medium of exchange and legal tender in South Africa, Bechuanaland (now Botswana), Lesotho, South West Africa (now Namibia), and Swaziland (now Eswatini). South Africa has dominated the region's political economy over the last one hundred and fifty years through its minerals-energy complex through control of migrant labour, mining, energy production, and global finance.[11]

As a system of accumulation, the minerals-energy complex was driven by state economic policies on behalf of Afrikaner capital in the post Second World War period, and its integration with English capital.[12]

This was built on the reshaping of indigenous social economic structures to the dominant organisation of mineral extraction towards the end of the nineteenth century, which effectively shifted South Africa's role and place in the international economic system.[13] This mineral revolution occurred because the Witwatersrand gold discoveries of 1886 coincided with the transition of the world financial system to a monetary system based on the gold standard, managed by British financiers and the state. These powerful economic, political, and ideological factors continue to underlie the dynamic of South African industrial policy, and economic policy more generally.[14]

The Rand Monetary Area (RMA) was established in 1974 between South Africa, Lesotho, and Swaziland. In 1986, it became the Common Monetary Area (CMA). Following its independence in 1990, Namibia formally joined the monetary union, under the 1992 Multilateral Monetary Area (MMA) treaty. All member states possess the right to issue sovereign national currencies within their respective territories, but must peg them at par to the Rand. This means that monetary policy is set by the SARB for Lesotho, Namibia, and Eswatini, and would be set for potential new members from the SADC. The SARB serves, first and foremost, the interests of South Africa and its minerals-energy complex political economy; its domestic objectives do not automatically benefit other MMA countries. Rather, members' domestic policies will ultimately be shaped by the floating exchange rate arrangement of the Rand with the rest of the world. And this is problematic as the Rand is volatile, given the country's historically deeply integrated position in global finance and the country's exchange controls on capital movements which restrict access to South African currency and the payments system.

Zimbabwe, to take a current example, has no political will to tie its economy and currency to the SARB. In June 2019, the government banned the multicurrency system and reintroduced the defunct Zimbabwean dollar, asserting that 'it had always been apparent to us that for true stability, stability upon which economic growth can be built, our own currency was necessary'.[15] From the perspective of sub-regional monetary integration, Zimbabwe's turbulent monetary history theoretically provided an opportunity for the country to align with the regional financial hegemon to address the ongoing economic crisis. And yet, Zimbabwe's Finance minister, Mthuli Ncube, clarified that his country would neither adopt the Rand as its main currency, nor join the MMA.[16] President Mnangagwa further explained that the country had approached the SARB with the intention of adopting the rand as its domestic currency,[17] but the conditions handed to Zimbabwe by the SARB were too constraining to make the choice realistic.

Turning to West Africa, monetary integration is complicated by legacies of imperial monetary structural powers in the region. These include Great Britain's African currency boards and sterling zone area, Portugal's escudo zone, and France's ongoing power in its former colonial empire.[18] The African franc zone survived after independence, unlike the other colonial monetary blocs which were broken up with the access of their members to formal political sovereignty. The African franc zone is currently composed of two monetary unions: The West African Economic and Monetary Union (WAEMU) and the Central African Economic and Monetary Community (CEMAC). Each monetary union has its own central bank and its own single currency. Although the CFA franc is the acronym of both currencies, its denomination is not the same for both.

In December 2019, the Côte d'Ivoire President, Alassane Ouattara, and the French President, Emmanuel Macron announced that the CFA franc in West Africa would be renamed the ECO. The ECO will remain pegged to the euro and will still be 'backed' by the French Treasury. This move to rename the CFA franc seems to have created confusion as the ECO (short for ECOWAS) was the name originally chosen for the single currency project for the fifteen countries of the Economic Community of West African States (ECOWAS), which includes the eight countries using the CFA franc. The Anglophone nations of Nigeria, Ghana, Gambia, Liberia, and Sierra Leone, along with Guinea, issued a communique in January 2020 condemning the WAEMU project to unilaterally rename the CFA franc as the ECO and to bypass policies in place to set up a West African currency. Nigerian Finance Minister Zainab Ahmed confirmed that the action contravened the decision of the Authority of the Heads of State and Government of ECOWAS to adopt the ECO as the future independent ECOWAS single currency.

Established in 1975, ECOWAS as a region remains poorly connected both internally and to the outside world.[19] Its regional single currency project dates from 1983. The initial option was to realise integration through two steps: the WAEMU would merge with the West African

Monetary Zone (WAMZ), a regional sub-grouping created in 2000 gathering the Gambia, Ghana, Guinea, Nigeria, and Sierra Leone. Liberia joined the WAMZ in 2010. The goal was to fast-track sub-regional integration and, to this end, the West African Monetary Institute (WAMI) was founded in 2001, with its headquarters in Accra, Ghana. The specific goal of the WAMI was to launch a common West African Central Bank (WCB) in preparation of a single currency in 2008. As this two-step approach did not work, the current option is that countries having achieved the 'criteria of convergence' will launch the regional currency.[20]

Two major reasons account for the several postponements of the launching of the ECOWAS currency since 2000. First, the members were ill-prepared, and not in optimal economic positions to create a single currency. Their central banks have had a hard time coordinating and elaborating a single, and common, monetary policy addressing possible future monetary shocks among the member countries.[21] Furthermore, the existence of parallel and competing monetary arrangements in the sub-region is identified as a major factor militating against the movement towards a single monetary zone.[22] According to some scholars, member countries of the WAMZ should not proceed towards a monetary union unless their economies converge substantially further.[23] Second, the WAEMU member countries have, hitherto, shown no sign of a willingness to break up their monetary ties with the French Treasury and the peg to the euro, a prerequisite for Nigeria. In the same vein, French officials contemplate extending further the franc zone in West Africa rather than letting it be dissolved in a regional monetary union where Nigeria would be the hegemon.[24]

## REQUIRED COLLECTIVE PUBLIC/STATE ACTION

Though the common history of destruction wrought by foreign countries binds Africans in common solidarity, the utopic goal of a single economic unit ignores what the historian, E. H. Carr,[25] calls 'the stuff of politics'. Utopia and reality are the two sides of politics. Utopianism is condemned for its naivety, and realism for its sterility. This constant interaction of these irreconcilable forces – the dream of a united Africa and, to take a recent example, the reality of the latest mid-August 2020 military coup in Mali – is the stuff of politics. As demonstrated above, the potentially conflictual character of monetary unions,[26] the considerable challenges in controlling and steering monetary integration, along with differences and asymmetries in economic development, and the antagonistic political ideologies of national governments across a continent of fifty-five countries has largely been ignored in the AMU blueprint. These factors make monetary unions, outside of imperial control, rare.

## MONETARY UNIONS ARE VERY RARE

Despite the extensive political economic difficulties in establishing and maintaining a monetary union, the successful launch of the Euro in 1999 appeared to offer a replicable template for the creation of MUs across the world.[27] It was expected that African countries could, and indeed should, emulate this illustration of sovereign collaboration, since integration is not only central to Pan-African ideals of continental unity,[28] it is key to reversing underdevelopment through continental economic fragmentation shaped by a history of imperial extraction to the metropoles. While the euro is evidence that monetary unions require tight political collaboration at the highest level, that it is a *sine qua non* along with convergence and collaboration on monetary policies,[29] it is also evidence that this condition is not guaranteed over the medium- or long-term.

A monetary union commonly has a single fiat currency with a single monetary authority. The International Monetary Fund (IMF) defines a currency union (CU), a term used interchangeably with 'monetary union (MU)', as 'an agreement among members of that union (countries or other jurisdictions) to share a common currency, and a single monetary and foreign exchange policy'.[30] MU membership entails the delegation of monetary and exchange rate policy to union level institutions. A common central bank becomes the single legal entity responsible for issuing currency across the monetary geographic area, as well as managing interest and exchange rates. The success of a common monetary policy depends on the operating political economic environment, the institutional framework adopted, and the choice and mix of the financial and monetary instruments used. To meet this goal, member states need to have similar preferences and be willing to fully cooperate. Most importantly, member states need to ensure that their national policies fully reflect these policies and that they also comply by the constraints of being in a MU.

These features mean that MUs are exceedingly difficult to establish. They require progressive pooling of sovereignty, identification of processes to overcome collective action problems, and agreements to manage differences in strategic areas of governance. A survey of proposed monetary unions, Cohen[31] observes, effectively reveals that there are simply not that many sovereign states willing or able to meet these conditions. Historical examples of successful monetary unions are, in effect, extremely rare.[32] Therefore, to talk about a single African currency in 2030,[33] as does the Agenda 2063 document, is certainly premature at best, but more probably idealistic at worst.

## MUS REQUIRE SOLUTIONS TO COLLECTIVE ACTION CHALLENGES

At the same time as the wave of independence movements was taking place across Africa in the 1960s, American political scientist Nye[34] asked a series of questions about whether, and how, regional integration could or should unfold across the world:

> Is it possible to integrate states into larger unions without the use of force? Should we think of a continuous 'federalising process' in which economic integration is a first step? Are there certain conditions under which economic integration of a group of nations automatically triggers political unity?[35]

Nye was, in all probability, thinking through the theoretical implications of the Treaty of Rome, the birth of the European Economic Community (EEC) in 1957, and 'the extent to which theories developed primarily upon the basis of the European experience can be generalised to other parts of the world'.[36] African leaders were asking a different, but fundamentally more challenging, set of questions. How can pan-African unity, the promotion of African interests, and socio-economic development become a reality while considering, at the same time, recently gained political liberation, national sovereignty, and a hostile global climate shaped by Cold War ideologies? Kwame Nkrumah argued that:

> Without necessarily sacrificing our sovereignties, big or small, we can here and now forge a political union based on defence, foreign affairs, and diplomacy, and a common citizenship, an African currency, an African monetary zone, and an African central bank. We must unite in order to achieve the full liberation of our continent.[37]

But how likely is it that fifty-five countries will unite? With large numbers, Olson[38] informs us that voluntary and rational self-interested actors will not necessarily be able to achieve a common group interest, such as pan-African economic integration, even if there is unanimous agreement about the public good to be obtained – reduced transaction costs, greater intra-African trade, economic growth, and greater leverage on the global arena through negotiating as a single voice – and the methods of achieving it. Three factors are responsible for this. First, members expect to receive smaller fractions of collective benefits the bigger the group is. Second, a small subset is needed to spearhead integration. France and Germany are frequently identified as forming this small subset as Strange reminds us in *Mad Money*.[39] Very large groups are less characterised by these small subsets. Third, organisational costs increase the larger the group is. In this respect, the fifty-five African countries form what Olson calls a large *latent* group. There are no two (or three) leading African states willing to collaborate to form of alliance from which to build the foundation for continental, or even regional integration. It would be very difficult to imagine a South African-Nigerian axis supporting continental integration.

## DECENTRALISED FINANCIAL GLOBALISATION: THE RISE OF AFRICAN FINANCIAL CENTRES

In the previous section I established that Africa's financial geography will not, in all likelihood, be shaped by sub-regional monetary unions, where formal monetary sovereignty moves to RECs. Nor is it likely that these RECs will connect together to form a single continental monetary union, relocating formal monetary sovereignty to the supranational scale of governance. Rather, in line with my main argument, I make the case that formal monetary sovereignty will remain, overall, in national territories. One main reason for this is that the more powerful African public authorities are situating their leading economic hubs as financial centres. This is more in the realm of geopolitical competition than a pan-African vision of deep economic integration. Yes, the African Continental Free Trade Area (AfCFTA) has come into effect, but this is the 'lightest' commitment to integration, far from the political commitment needed for a MU.

A financial centre can be understood as '[...] the grouping together, in a given urban space, of a certain number of financial services [...]. [And] as the place where intermediaries coordinate financial transactions and arrange for payments to be settled'.[40] Financial centres do not require formal monetary sovereignty at the national level, as witnessed by European centres such as Frankfurt, Paris, and Amsterdam, but the IFCs at the top of the European financial hierarchy are London and Geneva, both outside of the European Monetary Union. And, in the case of Europe, the centres were already well established before the euro became the single currency. This is in stark contrast to the African context where RECs have attempted to establish monetary unions before the growth of domestic financial centres. South Africa is the only case that resembles Europe, Johannesburg being an established financial centre before expanding into the Multilateral Monetary Area (MMA).

The great financial centres around the world – London, New York, Paris, Amsterdam, Berlin, Frankfurt, Tokyo, Hong Kong, and Singapore – are not static but rise, decline, and regenerate. These successful centres demonstrate the capacity of financial and political elites to absorb shifts in global economic production, economic recessions, financial crises, and shifts in the cycles of the global economy to promote their location as a site for global capital. And so it is with African states as they begin to direct regional and global flows through their business hubs.

Financial centres are not new to Africa. The geography of the production, distribution, and control of gold, for instance, placed Timbuktu as a vital node in medieval world trade and finance. To offer another example, the Kingdom of Kush, situated on the confluences of the Blue Nile, White Nile, and River Atbara, was one of the great ancient states of Africa and the inescapable economic, financial, and political centre for anyone doing business in the Nile Valley.[41] Africa is effectively home to some of the world's most ancient and powerful civilisations. Never isolated, these civilisations were part of dense webs with distant connections. As with other civilisations, the very constitution of African civilisations depended on these interactions. And finance was at their centre, as it is today. Yet, these histories of economic power and political prowess were not brought in as a key analytical element to factor in the process of forming new financial centres, underway across the continent. It is as if European imperial power and colonial rule drew a curtain to hide this history of power, wealth, trade, finance, gold, and cultural connectivity. And we scholars of political economy and African politics have largely left it drawn. Therefore, as the establishment of financial centres across the rest of Africa reflects the expansion of the globe's financial geography beyond established centres of capital in Europe, the Americas, Asia, the Middle East, and Russia, we need to remember that this urban formation is not new. What is different is that Africa is the last continent to enter/reproduce this current global financial geography to any meaningful extent, and actually make global capital 'global'.

## UNDERSTANDING THE RISE OF FINANCIAL CENTRES IN A WORLD OF FINANCIALISATION

Since the early 1990s, international financial markets, along with the entire banking sector, have been undergoing profound changes. The driving force behind this worldwide trend is habitually considered to be threefold: first, the advances made in the processing and the transmission of information; second, the trend towards the liberalisation of financial markets; and third, the growing and increasingly diversified demand for financial services. And, states' willingness to promote the cross-border movement of financial flows is crucial to this financial globalisation.[42] States do not only play a decisive role in reaching out and embedding financial markets within national regulatory frameworks,[43] they are also in the driving seat as financial globalisation takes place within their territories.[44]

In 'Money/Space', Leyshon and Thrift[45] point to the constitutive function of space as the nation state creates both commodity and credit money. Regimes of financial regulation always have a spatial dimension, even as they endeavour to escape geographical constraints. The international financial system, they argue, can be conceived as autopoietic or a self-referential system, where the centre is elusive; a mirage; or, as the authors call it, a 'nomadic state'. This financial system needs anchors, places where flows and communication lines converge, where information takes roots, grows, cross-fertilises, and is harvested. Financial centres are these embedded aspects of the system where analysis and interpretation take place.[46] This drive for the concentration of financial expertise and services underpins the birth of financial centres.[47] This is also referred to as 'economics of concentration', where global financial centres are complemented by smaller specialised centres in each time zone, even though technology allows financial actors to obtain information and transact on it virtually anywhere.[48]

Financial centres can thus be understood as decentralised sites of rule within the globalised world of financial markets. In this structure, while there are powerful IFCs, there is no definitive hub in global credit networks but, rather, a hierarchy of IFCs that endeavour to connect increasing numbers of individuals, firms, and governments across markets. This connectivity is central to their power. We can speak of a pattern of *leaderless* diffusion in financial geopolitics, very different from the concentrated power in the North Atlantic Bretton Woods system, with power in the international monetary system increasingly dispersed across the globe.[49]

In this sense, geographically, global finance forms a deep-rooted archipelago-economy[50] and a dense web of high-speed financial flows, materialising in specific geographics locations offering the necessary regulations and clusters of dense skills. European and North American financial centres have taken leading roles in producing and anchoring this web of flows with global reach. But, of the hundred IFCs listed in the 28th Global Financial Centres Index,[51] only a third are now located North America and Western Europe. Non-Western economies and their financial institutions are becoming increasingly central to the global financial provision of credit.[52] And African financial centres are the newcomers to this archipelago economy.

## AFRICAN FINANCIAL CENTRES

Whereas Asia's financial centres emerged in the post-crisis context of the 1990s, the region was simultaneously becoming the centre of global production and savings.[53] This is a very different trajectory from

Africa in the twenty-first century, where economies remain much more vulnerable to global forces as they endeavour to grow their economies in a very difficult economic climate. Yet, despite these challenges, some African states are altering their relationship to global capital by directing flows through their territory. Notable are the Lagosian State's Eko Atlantic, Morocco's development of Casablanca Finance City, and Kenya's aims for Nairobi to be East Africa's leading financial centre. The ambition of these African states is that their hubs will serve not only domestic economies, but also sub-regions and, potentially, continental Africa. These centres join South Africa as potential regional financial centres for West Africa, North Africa, and East Africa respectively.

Johannesburg is the undisputed IFC for Southern Africa, and with its sophisticated and deep financial services and experts, is recognised as an African leader. As much as the South African government and financial investors would like to see Sandton as the leading IFC for business on the whole continent, the city's position is changing as African states compete to set up new financial centres. In North Africa, for instance, Morocco, at the North Western edge of the continent, is gaining traction as an emerging hub interested in doing business and expanding into sub-Saharan Africa. Situated 'at the crossroads of continents', at the Northern westerly point of the continent, the Moroccan state positions Casablanca as a financial bridgehead between Europe and sub-Saharan Africa. Cairo has historically been an important business, financial, and cultural hub, but Egypt is more attuned to the Middle East than the rest of Africa. King Mohammed VI intends to turn the Morocco into the 'true' 'Hub of Africa'.[54] This strategy is part of discovering '[...] an untapped market in its own backyard: Africa'.[55] Launched in 2010, the Casablanca Finance City (CFC) is a strategic financial area for investments across the continent. The CFC is a key component of a comprehensive state vision, drawing on national worlding strategies[56] to establish the country as a global hub.

In West Africa, Nigeria is the clear economic hegemon. And within Nigeria, given its federal state system, it is Lagos State that is driving the integration of the megacity into global networks as it establishes its financial centre at the centre of West African networks. The new development of Eko Atlantic, built inside the Great Wall of Lagos, creates new urban space and is expected to underpin the city's role as financial epicentre of West Africa. This goal was vocalised by the Lagos

State Governor and the Office of Overseas Affairs and Investment – created in 2015: 'Lagos is one of three "command centres" for the African economy (along with Johannesburg and Nairobi.)'[57] The Lagos state designates 'Lagos as the most desirable investment destination in the world'.[58] The re-basing of Nigerian GDP has brought about global interest in the Nigerian Stock Exchange (NSE)[59] and is seen by Nigerian financial sector as an opportunity to brand itself as the gateway to African markets. The NSE is targeting market capitalisation growth through ECOWAS' West African Capital Markets Integration Council (WACMIC), which plans to integrate the Ghana Stock Exchange (GSE) and the Abidjan-based Bourse Régionale des Valeurs Mobilieres (BRVM)[61] – with an IFC for the WAEMU countries as a whole, and an affiliate based in Dakar – into a transnational investment cloud. West Africa's investment 'cloud' will be firmly anchored in Lagos, while enabling companies and investors in Nigeria to raise money for trades in stocks and bonds on other West African exchanges.

On the other side of the continent, African countries bordering the Indian Ocean see themselves as 'gateways' or entry points to the continent, particularly in line with China's Belt and Road Initiative (BRI). While Mauritius is the better known established offshore financial centre on the eastern seaboard of Africa, Nairobi is expected to be East Africa's new leading financial centre. As the largest and most advanced economy in East and Central Africa, the Kenyan government launched the all-encompassing Nairobi International Financial Centre (NIFC) plan as part of the country's Vision 2030. Positioning the country as East Africa's leading financial hub is central to this goal, and to this end the Kenyan state is leveraging China's presence in the Indian Ocean to reinforce Nairobi's role as the region's leading business hub. This relates both to tangible 'hard' infrastructure such as ports, roads, highways, and telecommunications that advantageously position Nairobi as a transportation hub, and to the 'soft' component of infrastructure relating to banking and finance regulations, the business environment, and other intangible institutional aspects that affect the formation of financial clustering.

In 2019, the African Development Bank, working with the African Securities Exchanges Association (ASEA), hosted the first capital market stakeholders' round table on the African Exchanges Linkage Project (AELP). The AELP is an initiative to facilitate cross-border trading and settlement of securities across participating bourses in Africa. ALEP drives financial integration along a geography of four cardinal points: the Nairobi Exchange (NSE), the Casablanca Exchange (CSE), the Johannesburg Exchange (JSE), and the Nigerian Exchange (NiSE). By choosing these exchanges as the continent's financial cornerstones, ALEP – and therefore the African Development Bank – confers a potential dominant leadership role to each of these countries and the capacity to become one of Africa's future key financial centres.

## CONCLUSION

This chapter asked the question: at which scale of governance is formal monetary sovereignty across the African continent most likely to be fixed. I have set out to establish that, while most African countries are committed to Pan-African ideals of cooperation, collaboration, and economic integration, the political economic barriers to realising an African Monetary Union seriously challenge this project. Many factors, including enduring legacies of monetary unions established during colonialism, the challenges in producing a common good – which would be the single African union – in a region of fifty-five countries, and the geography of global finance, organised through networks in anchored national territories, highlight the hurdles to achieving this goal. It is simply highly unlikely in the foreseeable future.

Instead, I argued that formal monetary sovereignty will, by and large, remain within national territories as powerful African public authorities reach out and embed financial networks within their economic hubs to establish financial centres. Johannesburg, the continent's established IFC, is being joined by the Nairobi Financial Centre, the leading centre for East Africa; Lagos, the undisputed economic and financial powerhouse of West Africa; and Casablanca Finance City, Morocco to determine a new financial geography for the continent. These developments indicate that African states are in the process of widening the world's financial structure of decentralised sites of finance to the region. These IFCs will help establish the continent's financial architecture, connecting with each other and smaller financial centres, while endeavouring to connect increasing numbers of individuals, firms, and governments across African markets.

## NOTES

1 Zimmermann, C.D., 2013. The concept of monetary sovereignty revisited. *European Journal of International Law*, 24(3), pp. 797–818.

2 Hirsch, F., 1969. *Money international: Economics and politics of world money*. New York: Doubleday & Co.

3 Cobbett, E., 2018. Gatekeepers of financial power: from London to Lagos. *Third World Thematics: A TWQ Journal*, 3(3), pp. 364–80.

4 This chapter recognises the very different colonial financial legacies within Africa; for instance, Great Britain's sterling zone, Portugal's escudo zone, and France's franc zone. The CFA franc zone continues as the West African CFA franc and the Central African CFA franc, two separate currencies 'guaranteed' by the French treasury and pegged to the euro. While change is on the horizon, countries within these two zones still do not have formal monetary sovereignty.

5 Helleiner, E., 1999. Historicizing territorial currencies: monetary space and the nation-state in North America. *Political Geography*, 18, pp. 309–39.

6 Cohen, B.J., 1996. Phoenix risen: The resurrection of global finance. *World Politics*, 48(2), pp. 268–96.

7 Pistor, K., 2017. From territorial to monetary sovereignty. *Theoretical Inquiries in Law*, 18(2), p. 491; Columbia Law School Center for Law and Economic Studies Working Paper No. 591.

8 Hall, S. and D. Wójcik, 2018. 'Ground Zero' of Brexit: London as an international financial centre. Geoforum.

9 Monetary *dis-union* does not rule out some forms of monetary cooperation. There are other types of monetary regimes, ranging in the degree to which countries are willing to cooperate, that can help states manage their national economies. A clear example is the Bretton Woods international monetary system, which attempted to avoid the rigidity of the previous international monetary systems while promoting inter-state cooperation.

10 Germain, R.D., 1997. *The international organization of credit: States and global finance in the world-economy*. Cambridge: Cambridge University Press, pp. 10–12; Germain, R.D., 2010. *Global politics and financial governance*. London: Palgrave, pp. 16–24.

11 Fine, B. and Rustomjee, Z., 1996. *The political economy of South Africa*. Boulder, CO: Westview Press.

12 Fine and Rustomjee, *The Political Economy*, p. 65.

13 Russell Ally, R., 1994. *Gold and Empire: The Bank of England and South Africa's gold producers, 1886–1926*. Johannesburg: Witwatersrand University Press, p. 1.

14 Fine, B., 2010. Engaging the MEC or a few of my views on a few things. *Transformation: Critical Perspectives on Southern Africa*, 71, p. 42.

15 Ncube, M., Professor. Currency: Taking back control. Ministry of Finance and Economic Development (n.d.). Available at: www.zimtreasury.gov.zw

/index.php?option=com_content&view=article&id=182:currency-taking-back-control&catid=83&Itemid=613, para.4 [Accessed on July 7 2021].

16 Chiwanza, T.H., 2019. Zimbabwe's Finance Minister says that the country cannot afford to adopt the Rand. The African Exponent, January 12. Available at: www.africanexponent.com/post/9647-zimbabwe-cannot-afford-to-adopt-the-rand-according-to-the-countrys-finance-minister [Accessed on July 7 2021].

17 Kuyedzwa, C., 2019. Mnangagwa tells Zimbabweans why the country did not adopt the rand. News 24, June 15. Available at: www.news24.com/fin24/Economy/Africa/mnangagwa-tells-zimbabweans-why-the-country-did-not-adopt-the-rand-20190615 [Accessed on July 7 2021].

18 Pigeaud, F. and Sylla, N.S., 2021. *Africa's last colonial currency: The CFA franc story*. London: Pluto Press.

19 Engel, J. and Jouanjean, M.-A., 2015. Political and economic constraints to the ECOWAS regional economic integration process and opportunities for donor engagement. EPS-PEAKS. Available at: assets.publishing.service.gov.uk/media/57a08997e5274a31e000017a/Political_and_Economic_Constraints_to_the_ECOWAS.pdf [Accessed on July 7 2021].

20 F. Bakoup. F. and Ndoye, D., 2016. Why and when to introduce a single currency in ECOWAS. *Africa Economic Brief*, 7(1), pp. 1–16.

21 Mati, S., Civcir, I., and Ozdeser, H., 2019. Ecowas common currency: How prepared are its members? *Investigación económica* 78(308), pp. 89–119.

22 Ernest Ebi, E., 2003. Regional currency areas: Lessons from the West African sub-region and Nigeria's policy stance. BIS Papers No. 17. In Bank for International Settlements (ed.), 2003. *Regional currency areas and the use of foreign currencies*, pp. 145–50

23 Harvey, S.K. and Cushing, M.J., 2015. Is West African Monetary Zone (WAMZ) a common currency area? *Review of Development Finance*, 5(1), pp. 53–63.

24 Sylla, N.S., 2020. The franc zone, a tool of French neocolonialism in Africa. *Jacobin*, January 6. Available at: www.jacobinmag.com/2020/01/franc-zone-french-neocolonialism-africa [Accessed on July 7 2021].

25 Carr, E.H. and Cox, M., 2001. *The Twenty Years' Crisis, 1919–1939: An introduction to the study of international relations*. New York: Palgrave, p. 94.

26 Cohen, B.J., 2003. Are monetary unions inevitable? *International Studies Perspectives*, 4(3), pp. 275–92; Henning, C., 1998. Systemic conflict and regional monetary integration: The case of Europe. *International Organization*, 52(3), pp. 537–73; Jonung L. and Jürgen Nautz, J., eds, 2007. *Conflict potentials in monetary unions*. Stuttgart: Franz Steiner.

27 Masson, P.R., 2008. Currency unions in Africa: Is the trade effect substantial enough to justify their formation? *The World Economy*, 31(4), pp. 533–47.

28 Honohan, P.L. and R. Philip Lane, 2000. Will the euro trigger more monetary unions in Africa? World Bank Policy Research Working Paper No. 2393; UNU-WIDER Working Paper No. 176.

29 Cohen, *Are monetary unions inevitable.*

30 Rosa, R., 2004. IMF Committee on Balance of Payments Statistics Currency Union Technical Expert Group (CUTEG), IMF Issues Paper (CUTEG) # 1 Definition of a Currency Union. Available at: www.imf.org/external/np/sta/bop/pdf/cuteg1.pdf, p. 1 [Accessed July 7 2021].

31 Cohen *Are Monetary Unions Inevitable.*

32 Guillaumont, P., Guillaumont, S, and Plane, P., 1998. Participating in African monetary unions: An alternative evaluation. *World Development*, 16(5), pp. 569–76

33 This date fluctuates in different AU documents

34 Nye, J.S., 1965. Patterns and catalysts in regional integration. *International Organization*, 19(4), p. 870.

35 Nye, Patterns and Catalysts in Regional Integration, p. 870.

36 *Ibid.*, 870.

37 Consciencism. Dr Kwame Nkrumah Speaks in Addis Ababa in 1963. Available at: consciencism.wordpress.com/history/dr-kwame-nkrumah-speaks-in-addis-ababa-in-1963/, para. 23 [Accessed on July 7 2021].

38 Olson, M., 1971. *The logic of collective action: Public goods and the theory of groups*. Cambridge, MA: Harvard University Press.

39 Strange, S.N., 1998. *Mad money: When markets outgrow governments.* Michigan, MI: University of Michigan Press.

40 Cassis, Y., 2010. *Capitals of capital: The rise and fall of international financial centres 1780–2009.* Cambridge: University of Cambridge Press, p. 2.

41 Hafsaas-Tsakos, H., 2009. The Kingdom of Kush: An African centre on the periphery of the bronze age world system. *Norwegian Archaeological Review*, 42(1), pp. 50–70.

42 Helleiner, E., 1994. *States and the Reemergence of Global Finance: From Bretton Woods to the 1990s.* Ithaca, NY and London: Cornell University Press, p. 58.

43 Germain, R.D., 2008. Financial governance in historical perspective: Lessons from the 1920s. Paper presented to the annual conference of the 2008 Canadian Political Science Association, University of British Columbia, www.cpsa-acsp.ca/papers-2008/Germain.pdf [Accessed July 7 2021].

44 Helleiner, *States and the Reemergence of Global Finance.*

45 Leyshon, A. and N. Thrift, 1997. *Money/Space: Geographies of monetary transformation.* London and New York: Routledge.

46 *Ibid.*

47 Cassis, Capitals of Capital.

48 Loong, L.H., 2001. Financial centres today and tomorrow: A Singapore perspective. International Monetary Conference, Singapore, June 4. Available at: www.bis.org/review/r010607c.pdf [Accessed on July 7 2021].

49 Cohen, B.J., 2008. The International Monetary System: Diffusion and Ambiguity, *International Affairs* (Royal Institute of International Affairs

1944-), 84 (3), Power and Rules in the Changing Economic Order (May, 2), pp. 455—70; italics in original.

50 Hall and Wójcik, 'Ground Zero' of Brexit.

51 Wardle, M. and Mainelli, M., 2020. The Global Financial Centres Index 28. Long Finance and Financial Centre Futures. Available at: www.longfinance.net/media/documents/GFCI_28_Full_Report_2020.09.25_v1.1.pdf [Accessed on July 7 2021].

52 Cobbett, E., 2011. The shaping of Islamic finance in South Africa: Public Islam and Muslim publics. *Journal of Islamic Studies*, 31, pp. 29–59; Germain, *Global politics and financial governance;* Helleiner, E. and J. Kirshner, eds, 2014. *The great wall of money: Power and politics in China's international monetary relations.* Ithaca, NY: Cornell University Press.

53 Lai, K.P.Y., F. Pan., M. Sokol, and D. Wójcik, 2020. New financial geographies of Asia. *Regional studies*, 54(2), pp. 143–48.

54 Morocco World News, 2017. Morocco, the new gateway to Africa? January 9. Available at: www.moroccoworldnews.com/2017/01/205567/morocco-new-gateway-africa [Accessed on July 7 2021].

55 Borzou Daragahi, B., 2015. Morocco looks south as Europe stagnates. *Financial Times*, January 14. Available at: www.ft.com/content/9a6f3350-971d-11e4-845a-00144feabdco [Accessed on July 7 2021].

56 Roy, A., and Ong, A., 2011. *Worlding cities: Asian experiments and the art of being global.* Chichester: Wiley-Blackwell.

57 Lagos Global (2018). Office of SDG & Investments. Lagos State Government. Available at: www.lagos-global.org/ [Accessed on July 7 2021].

58 Lagos Global. Foreign direct investment: Lagos deepens ease of doing business with one-stop-shop for investors. Lagos State Government, 13 April 2017. Available at: lagosstate.gov.ng/blog/2017/04/13/foreign-direct-investment-lagos-deepens-ease-of-doing-business-with-one-stop-shop-for-investors/ [Accessed on July 7 2021].

59 Onyema, O., 2014. Nigerian stock exchange: Corporate governance to reign supreme, 16 Oct. Available at: https://cfi.co/africa/2014/10/nigerian-stock-exchange-corporate-governance-to-reign-supreme/ [Accessed on July 7 2021].

60 Nigerian Stock Exchange, 2011. 'The NSE Market Segmentation', https://ngxgroup.com/ngx-download/the-nse-market-segmentation/ [Accessed on July 7 2021].

61 The BRVM is the regional stock market for all eight member states, including Benin, Burkino Faso, Guinea Bissau, Ivory Coast, Mali, Niger, Senegal, and Togo.

# PART IV
# Alternatives

# 9
# The Great Paradox: Liberalism Destroys the Market Economy: The pitfalls of the neoliberal recipe for African economic and monetary sovereignty

*Heiner Flassbeck*

Capitalism is an outstanding success story! Compare the living conditions of the majority of the people in the North and West today with those of 200 years ago. Nobody can seriously deny that there have been enormous successes over the past 200 years. At the same time, we know that these successes have by no means been uniform and steady, but were accompanied by enormous shocks and distortions that have repeatedly delivered blows to the system and with it to the well-being of working people.

It was mainly in the past seventy years, i.e. since the end of the Second World War, that the participation of the masses was realised on a large scale. But that applies mainly to the Western industrialised countries. In the developing world, the systematic participation of the mass of workers in the fruits of production is still the exception (which can be found above all in Asia), and not the rule. Consequently, in this seemingly successful system, in addition to great absolute poverty, there are still billions of people who live from hand to mouth and can barely keep their heads above water.

In this chapter, I will argue that the recipes propagated and used in Europe and the US since the 1970s are self-defeating. With a wrong theory of inflation and a lack of attention to the declining wage share, both regions have been unable to tackle the macroeconomic challenges of unemployment. The fact that many African governments continue to apply the same failed recipes to readjust their economies does not bode well for African economic and monetary sovereignty. For this sovereignty to grow Africa will need to emancipate itself from the traditional economic doctrines.

## 20 YEARS OF SUCCESS: BRETTON WOODS AND KEYNESIANISM

The post-war period, especially the twenty years from 1950 to 1970, produced outstanding results in terms of income development, employment, and employee participation. In Germany, for example, this phase is often called the German economic miracle and is ascribed to liberal politics. But this is a myth trying to glorify liberalism. The era of the Bretton Woods system was a time of great prosperity in the entire industrialised world, and some countries were more successful than Germany. But the developing countries associated with the system also benefited and developed better than before and later.[1]

This means that there must have been reasons for this global success story, which went far beyond German peculiarities and the actions of people in Germany. Some attribute the success to a one-off effect that was based on the 'need' to catch up after the global war. But this view is completely flawed. 'Catching up' and 'need' are not categories that can influence and explain concrete economic development in any way, as we can see in many countries of the Global South every day.

I will try to show that the economic conditions in the first decades after the Second World War explain this result. The basic investment conditions created by the Bretton Woods system were such that the dynamics of a market economy could develop driven by entrepreneurial investment. However, the widespread belief that the successes were related to the 'market-economy reforms' that Germany had pushed through against the spirit of the times is just as great an error as the belief in 'catch up demand' in the 1950s.[2]

Since then, the real growth rate has fallen steadily (Figure 9.1), even in Germany. Despite Germany being in a relatively good position because of its competitive advantage in Europe (achieved by wage dumping),

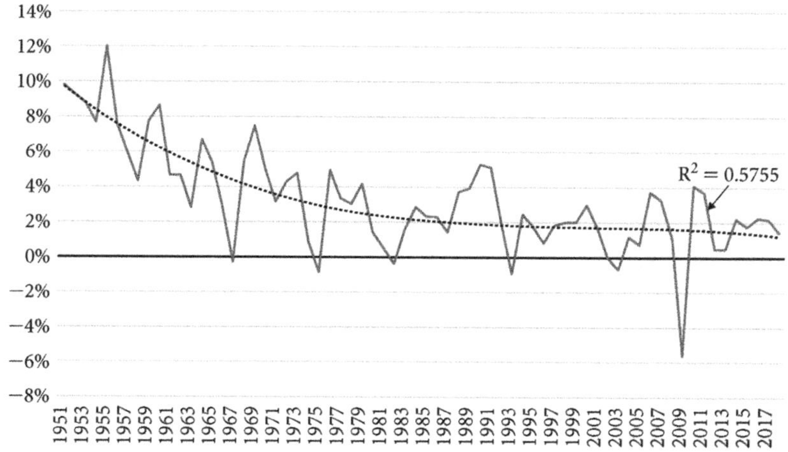


*Figure 9.1* Real GDP growth rate in Germany
Source: Bundesbank

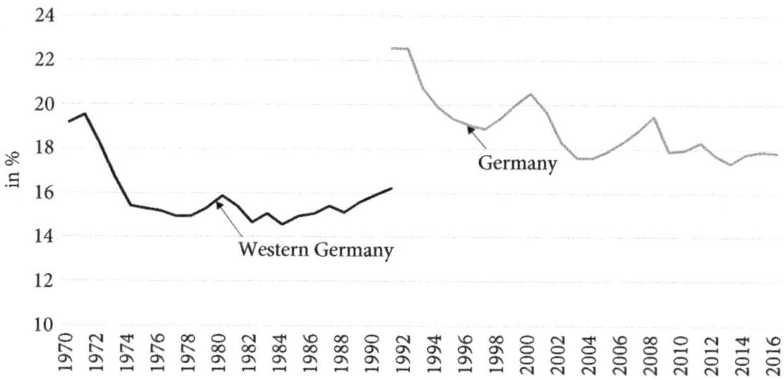


1) Gross fixed capital formation (new facilities) in relation to the gross value added
2) Agriculture, manufacturing and service sector excluding property/estate sector and public services

*Figure 9.2* Nominal investment ratio (1) of the corporate sector (2) in Germany
Source: German Statistical Federal Office, own calculations

it means that the situation for Europe as a whole became dramatically worse.

Looking at the investment activity of companies (Figure 9.2), the findings are also clear for Germany: since the end of the 1970s things have been going downhill. Apart from a small revival at the end of the 1980s and the consequences of German reunification – which brought entrepreneurial investment to a new level – a slowdown over time is undeniable. And this is despite the fact that since the turn of the 1980s economic policy has done everything it can to stimulate and stabilise private investment. The most important keyword here for Germany is the halving of taxes for companies.

There must, therefore, have been conditions in the Bretton Woods system which, in retrospect, created unique positive conditions for private investment. These conditions, which are usually completely overlooked, are macroeconomic in nature. Institutions ('the economic order') and functioning individual markets are one thing; favourable conditions for companies to invest are quite another.

## THE MACRO-REGIME IN BRETTON WOODS

The decisive empirical relationship is easy to understand (see Figure 9.3). In the first thirty years of the second half of the last century, the relationship between interest rates and growth (both nominal here) was exactly the opposite of that in the thirty years that followed. In the first thirty years, interest rates were almost always lower than the growth rate (which can also be seen as a kind of macroeconomic return on investment), and in the thirty years that followed they were almost always higher. This is demonstrated for the United States in Figure 9.3.

The same picture can be found for all major Western economies – except Great Britain, which did not experience an economic miracle during the Bretton Woods period and was therefore regarded as the 'sick man' of Europe. The Bretton Woods era was a time of favourable investment conditions. Paradoxically, the time of the neoliberal revolution thereafter brought about the opposite. Only after the great financial crisis of 2008/2009 did favourable investment conditions return – but now in a deflationary environment.

Dividing the decades accordingly, the result for Germany is clear (Figure 9.4). With the exception of the recession years 1966 and 1967 as well as 1974 and 1975, interest rates in the first phase were well below the growth rate.

During the neoliberal decades, the conditions changed dramatically; investment conditions were exactly the opposite of what one would have expected from the 'revival' of the market-economy. Apart from

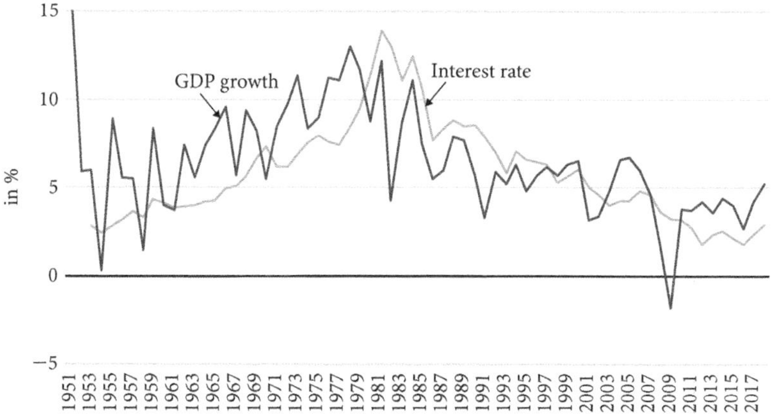


*Figure 9.3* Growth rate (1) and federal bond interest rate (2) in the USA
Source: FRED; FED.

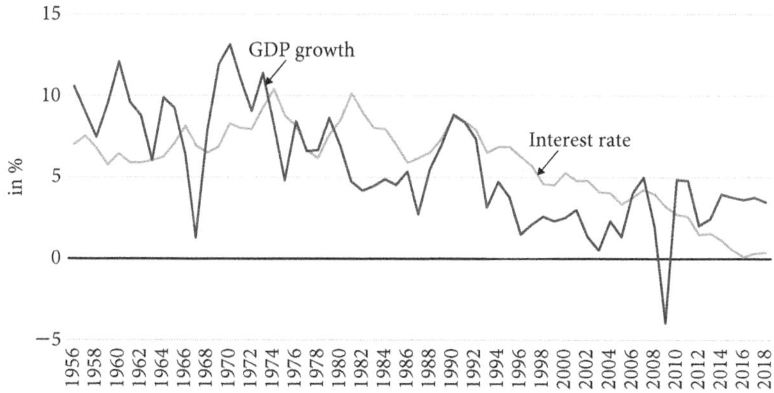


*Figure 9.4* Growth rate (1) and federal bond interest rate (2) in Germany
Source: German Statistical Federal Office; OCED; AMECO.

the years 1990 and 1991, the years of German unification (and a short episode in 2006 and 2007), the interest rate was always above the growth rate and, thus, measured against 'reasonable market conditions' were always too high. This applies in exactly the same way to France (Figure 9.5).

For France the picture is absolutely similar: France had low interest rates compared to GDP for the two decades from the beginning of the

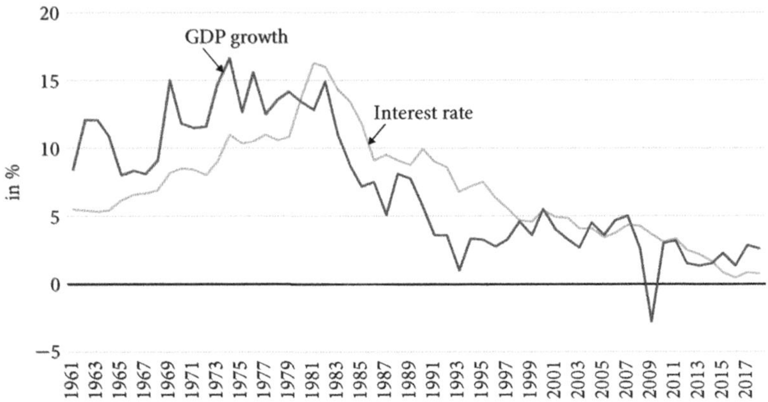


*Figure 9.5* Growth rate (1) and federal bond interest rate (2) in France
Source: AMECO; FRED.

1960s to the end of the seventies and high interest rates thereafter which led to a slowdown of growth and investment.

The neoliberal revolution that turned around economic policies in the 1980s in many Northern countries was by no means a success story. Real GDP growth has been declining throughout, and high unemployment became a permanent attendant of the market economy.

## THE BIG EXCEPTION

The only large country in the North that has been able to regain full employment time and again (before the Covid-19-shock hit) is the US. Here, too, growth momentum has slowed, but far less than in other countries (Figure 9.6).

The investment ratio in the US has not been falling as in other Northern countries, but has recovered enormously since 2008/2009. If one adds that the US has succeeded in reducing unemployment to a level that can be called full employment, even in this cycle (before Covid-19), the question arises what the US has done differently to that of other countries.

The answer has to be found on the fiscal side of economic policy. The US was the only country pursuing a very pragmatic economic policy in its effort to bring unemployment close to full employment levels in

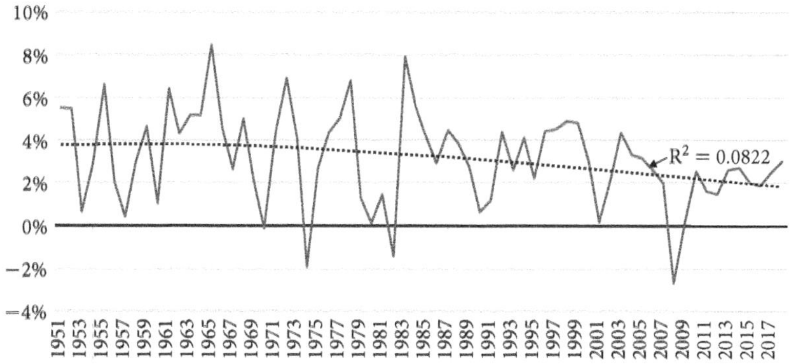


*Figure 9.6* Real GDP growth rate in the USA
Source: FRED

every upturn. As long as private market dynamics – driven by expansive monetary policy – were sufficient, the state held back. But this phase was already over in the mid-1970s.

After that period, massive government stimulus from fiscal policy became the rule, not the exception. Only during the phase of the so-called dotcom bubble in the second half of the 1990s, was the government able to get by without any new indebtedness of its own. At that time, private households increased their spending to such an extent that, on balance, they became indebted year after year and did not save (see Figure 9.7).

Unfortunately, the financial balances not available for most developing countries, are the most important analytical instrument at the macro level. They show the accounting identities at the macro level where a net saver has to have as its counterpart a net debtor. As the world as a whole cannot have a positive or negative savings balances, the four curves always add up to zero.[3] To illustrate this graphically, the current account is displayed inversely compared with the common use of the term: a current account deficit is a surplus of imports – goods and services financed by a net debt increase against the rest of the world.

In the US, as in other countries, companies were traditionally the counterpart for private households that spent less than they earned, but since the beginning of the 1980s that scenario no longer applies. In the new century the company sector became a net saver. As the US has exhibited a current account deficit for decades, the government has had to step in to stabilise the economy permanently. The gap between income and expenditure has been widening and, even before Covid-19,

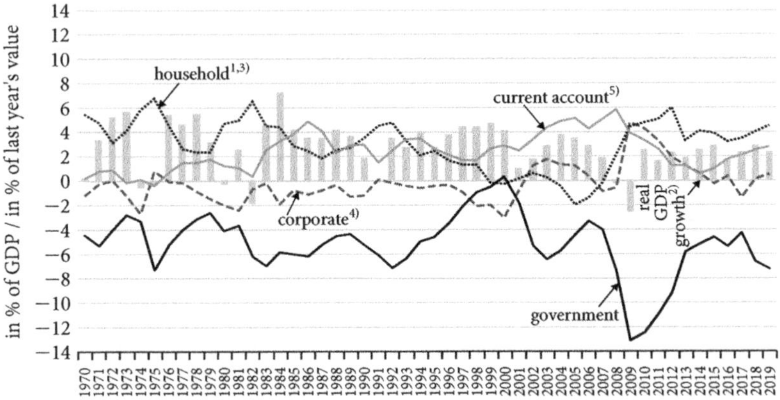


1) Disposable income minus consumption, net wealth transfers and net investments. 2) Rate of change of the real GDP compared with the previous year. 3) Including organisations without purpose for earning. 4) Non-financial and financial corporations. 5) The current account balance is inverted in this graph. Therefore, a current account deficit is displayed in the positive area of the chart to underline the zero-sum characteristic of the balances of the economic aggregates.

*Figure 9.7* Sectoral financial balances and growth rate of the USA
Source: AMECO

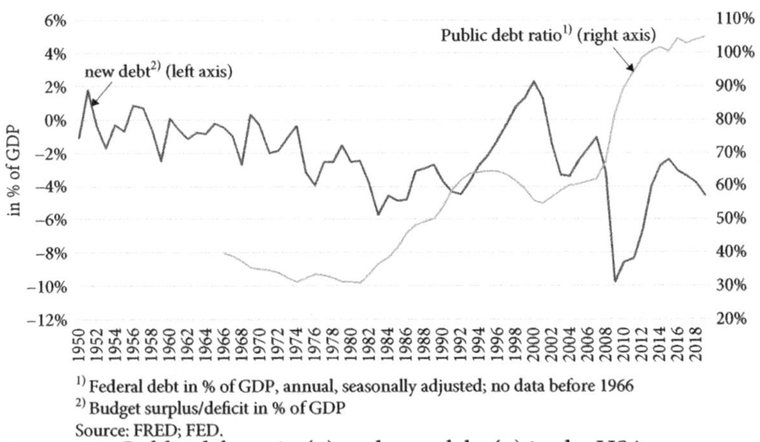


1) Federal debt in % of GDP, annual, seasonally adjusted; no data before 1966
2) Budget surplus/deficit in % of GDP
Source: FRED; FED.

*Figure 9.8* Public debt ratio (1) and new debt (2) in the USA
Source: FRED; FED.

when full employment had been reached, the state still had to increase its deficit. In 2019 the past fiscal year it was 3.9 per cent of GDP, or 700 billion US dollars (only for the central government) (Figure 9.8).

Total debt (as a percentage of GDP) has risen towards 110 per cent in 2019, and will rise far beyond this level after 2020. Contrary to the liberal and neoliberal belief, this is not a problem. It shows, however, that there can be no reasonable economic development without a permanently greater financial commitment on the part of the state if companies refuse – for whatever reason – to take on debt.

In a world dominated by monetarism and neoliberal labour market policies ('labour market flexibility') demand dynamics are systematically restricted and only the government can provide a remedy by aggressive demand policies. The government has to create the dynamics of the market economy in order to achieve ambitious employment goals. The United States has understood this and has developed an impressive pragmatism across both parties in terms of government debt. In Japan, too, the state has understood that companies that save and won't invest are creating a completely new situation and are making the state directly and indispensably responsible for demand management.

The European Commission and the European Council, with their dogma of a 'healthy' fiscal policy – driven largely by Germany – have left the ranks of rational governments behind. The result is persistently high unemployment. After the Covid-19-shock that brought about pragmatic fiscal policies there is a chance to revise the old dogma. But it is doubtful that the authorities are able to overcome their own prejudices.[4]

## DEVELOPMENT ECONOMICS OR THE RIGHT ECONOMICS FOR DEVELOPMENT?

All these considerations are extremely important for developing countries, in particular those in Africa. In developing countries, officials that were trained in the traditional centres of education where neoclassical economics dominate the teaching, very often run economic policies. Most politicians consider the main theoretical framework provided by the majority of economists and politicians in the North as a given. Why should anyone in a developing country dare to question policies that have been implemented for long periods of time, which seem beyond question or critique?

It is in this way that most economists of the developing countries accept the theories and the policy tools, which are rightly called the 'Washington Consensus'.[5] For a long time, the Washington Consensus was so dominant that it was almost impossible to question its apparently obvious 'rules'. Economists engaged in advising developing countries insisted that the 'structural conditions' of developing countries are different and have to be taken into account, but a different set of macroeconomic rules was not on their agenda.

One of the most important rules concerns monetary policy and how it should be implemented literally anywhere – local differences do not matter. For many decades, the IMF based its recommendations on monetarism. Monetarism had the practical advantage that its guidelines could be put into practice immediately. All that is necessary is a 'quantity of money' and a projection about growth potentials. However, the world is not as simple as monetarism has it. After a very short period in which it was dominant, many Western countries began to abandon its ideas completely. The United States even pioneered totally different approaches back in the 1980s.

Today, monetarism is not only dead, according to leftist economists, it has been completely abandoned by central banks all over the world. Neither the ECB, nor the FED, nor the Bank of Japan, nor the Bank of England still use monetarism as a basis for their policies. Unfortunately, to the developing world monetarism is still being sold as the only available and correct macroeconomic theory. The famous American phrase 'do as we say, but don't do as we do' still applies. The US government has fully abandoned monetarism, but the IMF nonetheless continues to preach and implement it all over the developing world. Developing countries need to address such a contradiction in international discussions – unless they prefer to remain the intellectual slaves of the Washington Consensus.[6]

The second example for this kind of spiritual slavery is the idea called 'structural reforms'. Despite the fact that nobody knows exactly what it is, it is used as a mantra in policy debates all over the globe. The most important component of these 'structural reforms' is always the same. It is as straightforward as it is monotonous: labour markets need be made more flexible. But are labour markets really flexible in the Western world, or in the North in general? If they have become more flexible of late, did the general situation improve? The clear answer is that making labour markets more flexible is not working at all. Just as in the case of monetarism, there is a strong contradiction between the narrative for the developing world and the one for the North.

My third point is the least well understood of all. The Washington Consensus demands that governments contain and cut their deficits. Something close to zero is seen as ideal. As shown above, things are far from that simple, because government deficits are connected to both trade balances and the savings positions of the economics sectors in each country.

These are questions that the developing countries need to ask. Do politicians and experts from the North implement their own theories at home? If not, why not, and if so, why do they fail? Unemployment remains unacceptably high in Europe. How can it be explained that Europe is still unable to bring unemployment down a decade after the financial crisis of 2008/09? Is it due to rigid wages? Is it due to inflexible labour markets in France, Italy, and many other countries? When the IMF tells developing countries that they have to make their labour market more flexible and cut wages, the developing countries should ask why cutting wages in Spain, Portugal, and Greece failed miserably to bring back growth and unemployment.

## THE THEORY OF INFLATION IS KEY TO DEVELOPMENT

As explained above, the traditional monetary theory holds that inflation is related to some form of money supply. But the only strong evidence ever found strongly supports otherwise. Inflation in the Western world is not related to any monetary aggregate, but it is closely correlated to wages, as Figure 9.9 clearly proves. The strongest correlation found over periods of twenty years is between unit labour costs and inflation. Unit labour cost measures the excess of nominal wages (per hour worked) over productivity (per hour).[7]If productivity increases by 5 per cent and nominal wages rise by 7 per cent, unit labour costs will rise in the long run by 2 per cent. All over the world, unit labour costs will move perfectly in line with inflation if sufficient time is allowed (Figure 9.9).

This is true for all regions of the world, for the US as well as for Europe and (as shown by UNCTAD) for developing countries. The lesson to be learned here is extremely simple and straightforward: inflation is not determined by any quantity of money but – in the longer term – by unit labour costs.

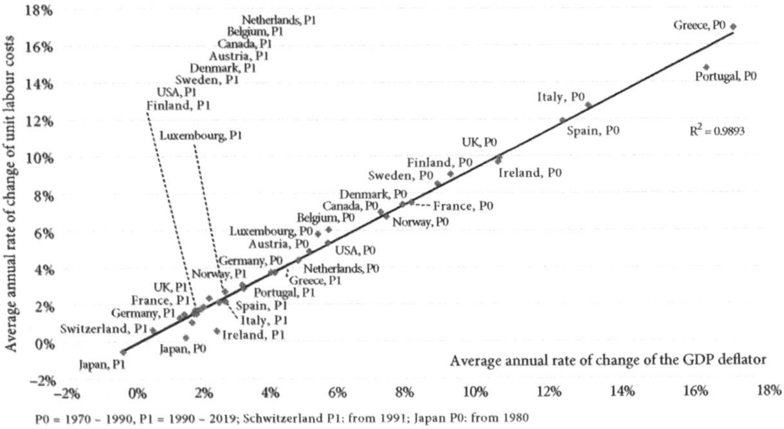


*Figure 9.9* Correlation between unit labour costs and inflation
Source: AMECO

## WAGES AND UNEMPLOYMENT

This evidence is of utmost importance: if unit labour costs determine inflation, wages cannot at the same time determine employment because real wages are no longer available as policy instrument. Time and again the developing countries are faced with the traditional textbook chart depicting the neoclassical supply and demand curve of the labour market, where real wages determine employment and unemployment. This is definitively erroneous. If falling nominal wages lead to falling prices in the medium- and long-term, real wages will not change and, if real wages do not change, they cannot determine the evolution of employment in the neoclassical sense (which means the long-term restructuring of production according to changes in prices of the factors of production).

No doubt, the neoclassical labour market theory is wrong. The wage inflation theory proves that monetary policy is powerless against the deflationary forces of falling costs in the overall economy, and sluggish demand from consumers. Deflation, diminished expectations, and the uncertainty of private households about their future income prevent private consumption from taking a lead role in a recovery. However, it is absolutely misleading to call such a situation a 'liquidity trap'. The trap is, in effect, much more a wage trap or an income trap than a liquidity trap. This trap is usually triggered by sharply rising unemployment that is unrelated to specific labour market developments, such as unreasonably high wage increases.

The financial crisis and the high unemployment that resulted provided the ideological justification for policies to cut wages and incomes again, although wages and incomes were already depressed before the outbreak of this crisis. High unemployment together with the attempts by workers 'to price themselves back into the flexible markets', as some neoclassical economists put it, created the conditions for the perfect storm that is still raging today, a full eight years after the outbreak of the financial crisis. After the Covid-19 shock, the situation is much worse – again, unemployment is rising, but this rise is totally unrelated to wages.

Monetary policy can bring interest rates to zero or even into negative territory and it can implement quantitative easing (QE). After this, the possibilities of monetary policy are exhausted. What is needed, therefore, are fiscal policies: huge stimulus programmes that overcome the reluctance of consumers to spend in the face of their uncertain outlooks on jobs and wages. Today, investment is restricted on a global scale by low demand, as a consequence of income expectations of private households during very high levels of unemployment. It is, in its most basic form, a consequence of a dysfunctional labour market in which it is possible for unemployment to sharply rise without wages being 'too high'.

Depressed wages stifle private consumption, and a lack of sufficient consumption prevents the economy from recovering, although some monopolistic companies in the digital world are making enormous profits. The only way out, without resorting to unconventional instruments such as income policies, lies in the direct improvement of labour market conditions, which can only be achieved by an extremely huge fiscal policy stimulus, but this is blocked for political reasons in many developed economies as in most of the developing world.

The traditional way to get around the brutal logic of destabilising labour markets is to hope for improved competitiveness of the economy as a whole, and to increase exports (or decrease imports). Indeed, if a wage cut quantitatively stimulates foreign demand more than it depresses domestic demand, a solution seems to be at hand. The problem is that all of us may well wish to be net exporters, but this will remain impossible as long as we do not find new planets which are willing to accept current account deficits and the uneasy positions of debtors. That is why the biggest country in the EMU, Germany, now faces a problem that is similar to the one of Japan. Germany has the highest current account surplus in the world, but its European partners are suffering; few are willing to accept further deficits and debtor countries ran out of steam all over the world. It is clear that the German mercantilist approach has hit the wall.

Due to many years of wages lagging productivity growth, Germany nowadays has the lowest wage share ever since the end of the Second World War. Its private households have persistent net savings. Due to the export boom, the company sector is sitting on enormous amounts of profits and is, therefore, also a net saver. This is the consequence of the export bonanza of the last decade. Unfortunately, as shown above, domestic investment, which would correspond to the high domestic net savings, is flat.

In Germany as in the US, the way out, without taking on new government debt, is to make the company sector accept its role of being the natural counterpart of high private net savings (Figure 9.10). But that would imply increasing wages and raising corporate taxes, both are taboo in the conservative policy framework. While this may sound perplexing and paradoxical to some, the macroeconomic logic (or, if

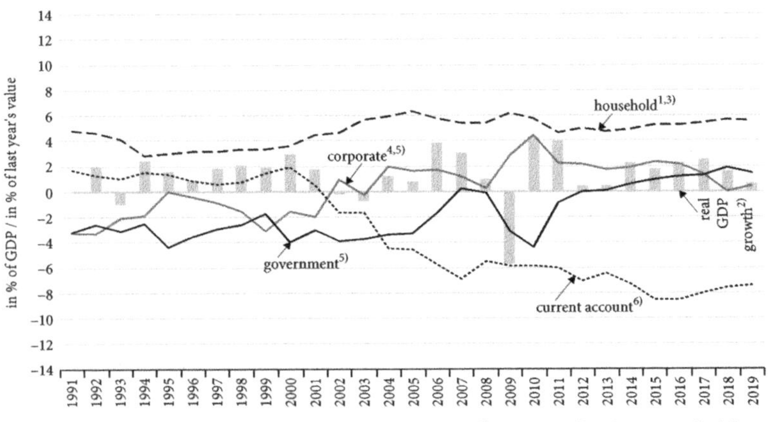


1) Disposable income minus consumption, net wealth transfers and net investments. 2) Rate of change of the real GDP compared with the previous year. 3) Including organisations without purpose for earning. 4) Non-financial and financial corporations. 5) 1995: transfer of ~100 billion euro debts of the privatization agency from the government to the corporate sector. 2000: transfer of 50.8 billion euro revenue from UMTS royalties from the government to the corporate sector. 6) The current account balance is inverted in this graph. Therefore, a current account surplus is displayed in the negative area of the chart to underline the zero-sum characteristic of the balances of the economic aggregates.

*Figure 9.10* Sectoral financial balances and growth rate of Germany
Source: AMECO.

you prefer, macroeconomic bookkeeping) behind it is irrefutable. If government debt is considered to be unsound and has to be kept in check, the company sector has to be both a net debtor and the main investor, as has been the case for most of the time after the Second World War.

What is happening in the Western world is the result of a downward pressure on wages over a period of decades. But if you ask Western policymakers about the reasons for their failure, they will talk about 'structural problems'. Is the structural problem in the Western world 'too high wages'? No. Wages are definitively too low, but economic policy is based on the same fallacious ideology everywhere.

The crucial message is that cutting wages does not lead to economic recovery. It makes things worse, not better. However, there is another possibility to improve competitiveness and to increase employment for a single economy. Instead of cutting wages, it is possible for countries to use a depreciation of their currencies. The result of a currency depreciation is similar to cutting wages, but without having the same negative effects on domestic demand. Countries can, to a certain extent, use depreciations as an instrument to increase employment. However, any depreciation of one currency implies the appreciation of the currencies of other countries. It is not possible for everyone to depreciate.

In addition, currency depreciation cannot be implemented like any other policy instrument, as the experiences of many developing countries show. Depreciations are tricky and normally associated with destabilising capital flows. Currency depreciations cannot be a general or a sustainable solution, neither for the developing nor for the developed world. In fact, depreciation only works – for some limited amount of time – if only one country does it and gets away with it. This is what happened in Europe. Germany *de facto* depreciated and all other countries suffered because of it.

## STABLE WAGE GROWTH AND STABLE MONETARY CONDITIONS

A new macroeconomic paradigm for development is urgently needed. It has to be based on the conviction that the neoclassical dogma is wrong. Growth always needs the stimulus of demand. Such stimulus cannot come from other countries, as the mercantilists believe. For the developed world and the developing world as a whole, the stimulus has to come from within. More than anything else, this means raising incomes for people in line with productivity and the inflation target.

Labour markets cannot and should not be 'flexible' in the neoclassical sense of the word. Flexible labour markets are a dangerous concept: cut wages and make labour markets flexible are excellent ways to destroy consumption and demand. Neither growth nor sustainable development and prosperity can be based on increasing the flexibility of labour markets. No sustainable growth is possible if the population does not have the means to consume what they produce.

Public debt is part and parcel of the overall savings-investment matrix of an economy. It has to be interpreted in the wider realistic context of the financial situation of other countries, as well as in the context of the financial situation of the domestic sectors. Cutting public expenditure with the purpose of cleaning up public budget deficits is only possible if someone else is willing to increase its deficits. Cutting public expenditure because the IMF tells you to do so will never work. The ideology about the 'correct' debt to GDP ratio has to be abandoned. There is no scientific basis to any such figures.

The general conclusion of all these considerations is simple: no positive change can be achieved within the framework of neoclassical and neoliberal ideology. The dogma that has been imposed upon developing countries, including African countries, has prevented the necessary change towards a new system in which the participation of the population at large is a crucial condition for long lasting success.

Monetary conditions in all developing countries need to be fixed in order to stimulate private investment. For example, price developments in Africa are absolutely chaotic in many countries (Figure 9.11a and Figure 9.11b). With very few exceptions, such as Morocco, the stability of inflation is crucial for investment. This is missing throughout Africa.

Closely associated with domestic monetary instability is interest rate volatility and exchange rate volatility. Figure 9.12a and Figure 9.12b show that interest rate developments in Africa are as chaotic as price developments.

Without stable monetary conditions, including stable exchange rates that are conducive for growth and investment, generating economic and societal progress remains impossible. Africa needs a monetary

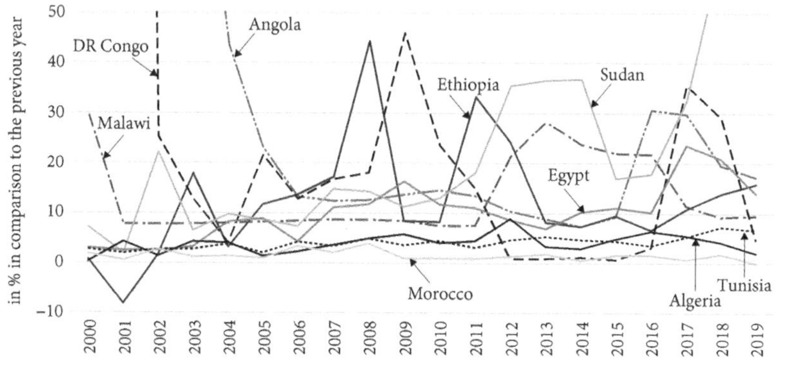


*Figure 9.11a* Inflation rates in African countries (1)

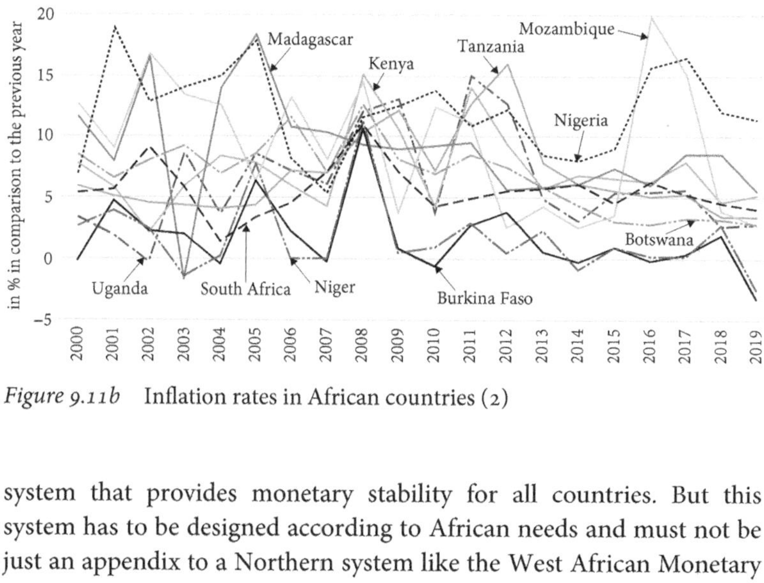


*Figure 9.11b* Inflation rates in African countries (2)

system that provides monetary stability for all countries. But this system has to be designed according to African needs and must not be just an appendix to a Northern system like the West African Monetary Union.[8] Currency pegs like this one, or national debts in dollars, made the countries dependent on the ideologically driven recipes from the institutions of the international financial framework.

'Structural reforms' are much less important than macroeconomic reforms. Developing countries have to consider my main point, namely that 'labour market flexibility' is a dangerous concept as it implies instability of inflation rates, instability of interest rates, and instability of exchange rates. The first thirty years of development after the Second

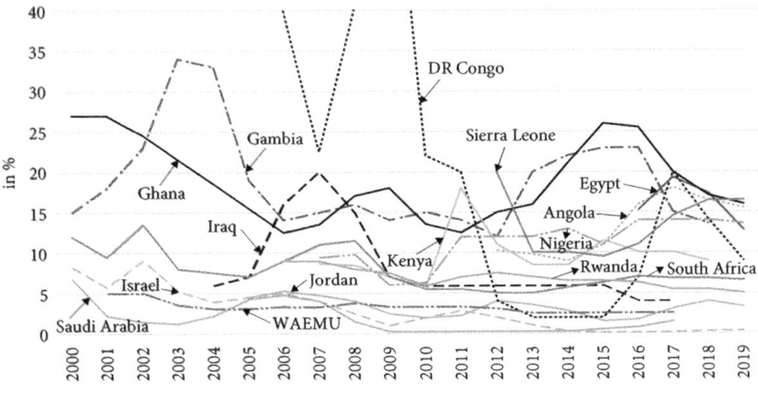


*Figure 9.12* Short-term interest rates in African and Near East countries

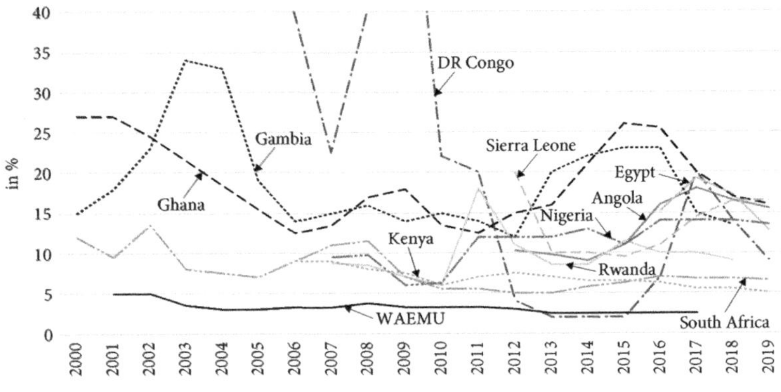


*Figure 9.12a* Short-term interest rates in African countries

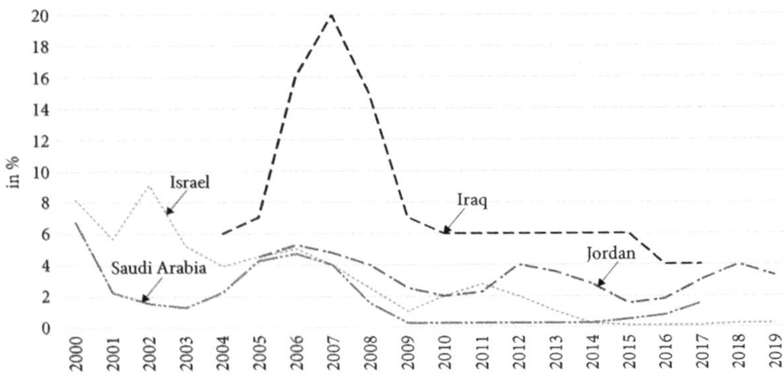


*Figure 9.12b* Short-term interest rates in countries of the Middle East

World War in the Western world reveals the outstanding importance of interest rates that are stable, and consistently lower than growth rates.

The conclusions to be drawn from the evidence and the economic logic is a simple one: without completely discarding both, the monetarist inflation theory and the neoclassical labour market theory, development policies cannot succeed. Without a new and relevant theory of economics, improvements in living standards, and a chance to overcome the current misery in many countries, is an illusion.

## NOTES

1 UNCTAD, ed., Evolving development strategies – Beyond the Monterrey consensus. Global Partnership and National Policies for Development, Trade and Development Report 2006. New York, NY: United Nations, pp. 41–71.

2 Flassbeck, H. and F. Spiecker, 2016. *Das Ende der Massenarbeitslosigkeit mit richtiger Wirtschaftspolitik die Zukunft gewinnen*. Frankfurt am Main: Westend.

3 Flassbeck, H. and Steinhardt, P.F., 2020. *Failed globalisation: Inequality, money, and the renaissance of the state*. Singapore: World Scientific.

4 Bibow, J. Global imbalances, Bretton Woods II, and Euroland's role in all this. In Jörg Bibow and Andrea Terzi, eds, 2007. *Euroland and the World Economy*. London: Palgrave Macmillan, pp. 15–42.

5 Flassbeck and Steinhardt, *Failed globalization*.

6 Ghosh, J. Wirtschaftliche Integration und globale Krise aus der Perspektive der Entwicklungsländer. In Heiner Flassbeck, Paul Davidson, James K. Galbraith, Richard C. Koo, and Jayati Ghosh, eds, 2013. *Handelt jetzt! das globale Manifest zur Rettung der Wirtschaft*. Frankfurt am Main: Westend, pp. 159–91.

7 Flassbeck, H., Spiecker, F, and Dudey, S., 2020. *Atlas der Weltwirtschaft 2020/21: Zahlen, Fakten und Analysen zur globalisierten Ökonomie*. Frankfurt am Main: Westend.

8 UNCTAD, ed., 2009. 'Reform of the International Monetary and Financial System'. In *Responding to the Global Crisis: Climate Change Mitigation and Development*, pp. 113–32. Trade and Development Report 2009. New York, NY: United Nations.

# 10
# Food Sovereignty, the National Question, and Post-colonial Development in Africa

*Max Ajl*

Across Africa, agriculture, land, peasants, food, seeds, and agrarian reform are centre stage in the theatres of capitalist accumulation and resistance. From colonialism and the birth of the capitalist world system, land and the commodities grown upon it have been central to accumulation on a world scale. The African continent, which spurred the creation of world systems theory, is now ground-zero for escalating agrarian dispossession and a 'new scramble' for its resources, alongside potentially genocidal mechanisms of population management for its people.[1] How might we make sense of new dependencies – financial, nutritional, and technological? Are African nations fated to remain constrained and immiserated? Will the fields, factories, cities, and slums of the global South forever haemorrhage value to the North? How do the African countryside and heterodox development theories help us understand how dependency is reproduced, how it might be challenged, and how agrarian change might thicken the gossamer shell of sovereignty?

This chapter explores linkages between food sovereignty, agroecology, dependency, and African heterodox theories of development. I analyse them with an eye towards how they might help draw up roadmaps to depart dependency relations and melt apart the manacles, from technology transfer and aid, to unequal exchange and persistent declines in the terms of trade for agricultural products, enchaining the creative, self-managed, and free play of production in the South. And I put the national question front-and-centre.

Agricultural trade is central to economic sovereignty, since continental agriculture has suffered from an excess of imports over exports over the last decade.[2] Furthermore, exports like cacao, coffee, and olive oil have extremely erratic prices, imperilling long-term planning.[3] They are subject to ebbs and flows largely outside the control of African states. Agricultural trade and production based on comparative advantage erodes rather than enhances economic sovereignty. Conversely, food sovereignty based on producing for a widened home market, with prices engineered around social needs and goals, could lead to greater macro-economic stability and economic sovereignty.

In these ways, the land question, threatened national liberation, and dependent insertion into a polarised world-system mold how African nations must understand and act to change the world. In particular, they must foreground the national frame to understand exploitation and underdevelopment. Following upon that, I focus on developing and nationally and environmentally embedding production and creating and using agricultural surplus beyond subsistence (not merely surplus value). I ground the discussion in regional theories of development/southern theory, auto-centred development, the heterodox agronomy of Slaheddine el-Amami, and the newer approaches of agroecology and food sovereignty.

This chapter's first section discusses the origins of dependency analysis. The second section discusses postcolonial dependency thought, explains self-reliant development more broadly, and presents the thinking of Slaheddine el-Amami, a Tunisian agronomist. The third section treats agroecology as it relates to surplus creation and decreasing import reliance. The conclusion shows how such research programmes and analyses mesh with a programme for smallholder agroecology/food sovereignty as a peripheral development path.

## DEPENDENCY: VALUE AND THE CONCRETE

Dependency theory emerged out of a radicalisation of the structuralist thought cultivated at the Economic Commission for Latin America and the Caribbean thought (CEPAL, in its better-known Spanish acronym). Clusters of researchers in Chile, a centre for continental economics, sought to understand the inability of Latin American countries' to lock in value and improve their peoples' lives. One of the lenses which brought their subjugation into clearest focus was the Prebisch thesis. This argued that, for a variety of reasons, primary commodities faced constantly deteriorating terms of trade against manufactured goods.[4] That is, if one widget traded for one bushel of coffee in 1940, in 1945 one widget would buy two bushels of coffee. Under such circumstances – all things being equal – it is better to make widgets than to grow and export coffee. Logically, CEPAL thought Latin America should make rather than import widgets: import-substitution industrialisation. Furthermore, it would be easier to manufacture widgets if there were a broader market in which to sell domestically crafted widgets: increased urban buying power.

As Latin America applied these policies, it began to industrialise. But it did not close the gap with Northern incomes. With the epochal eruption of the Cuban revolution, socialism burst over the horizon. Southern social scientists and economists were radicalised by the working-class and peasant revolt.[5] Indeed, one of the founders of Marxist Latin American dependency theory, Vania Bambirra, devoted volume after volume to Cuba and the 1960s wave of Latin American insurrection.[6]

Thus enchanted and empowered, these thinkers advanced an array of ways to understand dependency, focusing on internal class relationships and how they co-evolved with imperialism. Through the work of Ruy Mauro Marini, who peered at an industrialising Brazil and a broken and brutalised Brazilian rural and urban proletariat, they realised that one major mechanism of dependency was super-exploitation: paying workers so little that their salaries fell below the cost of their social reproduction, or what it would cost to reproduce their own labour power. In a sense, salaries cut into the well-being of the workers themselves, compressing consumption to famine-like levels.[7] Marini showed how dependency was not just about flows between nations, but fights between classes.

## DEPENDENCY IN AFRICA

Although Samir Amin defended his dissertation on dependency in 1957, African/Arab dependency thinking acquired its sharpest edge only after states, especially on the continent's Northern rim, had begun their attempts at industrialisation.

In the post-independence agrarian sector, countries either left colonial agrarian export structures in place, or tended to focus on what they considered the more productive farmers, those with enough land to mechanise and use all kinds of inputs and the modified seeds, hybrids, and chemical fluids of the Green Revolution; a 'programme of agricultural intensification' using industrial inputs and targeting medium and large farmers, 'for achieving national sufficiency in food grain production'.[8] Such farmers produced some cereals for domestic markets. But North Africa remained stuck within colonial channels of commodity crop exports: olive oil, dates, and later increasing amounts of fruits and vegetables. As did Africa more broadly, sending out cotton, coffee, and cacao. These germinating policies produced a disappointing harvest. While continent wide during the early post-independence period – through roughly, 1970 – countries were more or less self-sufficient, imports then began to rise continuously, almost irrespective of developmental regimes.[9]

Amongst the major causes of developmental lock-in was deliberate imprisonment. The US and other settler states furnished their own excess cereal grains to North Africa through non-market channels. What seemed like manna was the very opposite. The food flows were political engineering to constrain more wide-ranging agrarian revolution.[10] They were also meant to keep grain reliant states in check, afraid of the consequences of departing too much from US policies.

Furthermore, African states often engineered prices to ensure nascent urban working classes could labour cheaply in newly built factories, the better to outcompete imports of Northern industrial goods and to compete with other countries' exports on world markets. Technology and know-how became central to the subjugation and immiseration of the South, as industrialisation became a path to perdition rather than the promised land.

In this way, these countries became dependent in multiple senses, opening the way for multiple ways of understanding how they had become subjugated. In the broadest sense, they were increasingly outward-oriented, structured to complement the core rather than cater to their popular classes. Such obeisance took on many a form, morphing and shifting over time. We cannot necessarily reduce it to mere reliance on cereals (although this has been important throughout), reliance on commodity exports, or the gradations of industrial capacity. Rather, the fundamental constant reflects the Leninist thesis of a dominating-dominated-dyad: dependency 'consists of the transfer of surplus value from a less-developed total national capital to a more developed one'.[11] Cereal import dependency and food dependency are woven into an under-developmental or de-developmental matrix across Africa. But once one has identified the location and nature of a problem, one can move on to solutions. If agrarian crisis is the skeleton key to open up our understanding of pervasive socio-economic and environmental crisis, it may likewise unlock the door to a largely untested African development path in the twenty-first century.[12] Let us see how.

## AUTO-CENTRED DEVELOPMENT AND AFRICAN THEORIES

Africa has been a people's laboratory for some of the most impressive and lesser known thinking on how to break from dependency relationships. From the 1950s onward, partially due to Chinese support for African national liberation, the Chinese revolution had become enormously well known amongst continental theorists and planners.[13] For that reason, the Chinese example was an inspiration and insight for plans for balanced rural-urban growth, and criticisms of technology transfer soon abounded. Maneuvering within intellectual and political space opened up by the Chinese people, throughout the 1970s and the 1980s, the stars of figures such as Samir Amin, Mohammed Dowidar, Fawzy Mansour, A. M. Babu, Walter Rodney, and countless others in the firmament of African heterodox thought shone like beacons. They marked the path to liberation. As a result, the dependency school dominated development discussion on the left in Africa, offering a framework for understanding concrete situations of underdevelopment.[14]

As in Latin America, dependency's anatomies of postcolonial underdevelopment were devastatingly accurate. To some extent, unlike in Latin America, Africa, and the Arab region which it overlaps, have been able not merely to state why attempted development was stillborn, but to offer ways to reanimate the developmental process.[15] Above all, life and spirit came from their temporal and spatial closeness to that stunning example of postcolonial development, freed from imperialism by a countrywide people's war that turned the peasants into subjects of social revolution and the keystone of postcolonial planning: China.[16] In Tanzania, China trained postcolonial self-defence forces, and provided massive amounts of aid. And China's model of self-reliance was partially inscribed into, and a major influence on, the Arusha Declaration.[17] Relying on one's own resources became the basis for, at the very least, a new way of thinking about development – not the fool's errand of trying to copy the 'Western path' of modernisation and its hidden motors of colonialism, slavery, and genocide, but a new path based on building up the wealth of the domestic direct producers.[18]

China was not merely an inspiration because of its apparent success in a country previously subject to Western imperialism, or because of the efforts China made to help national liberation across the continent. In terms of domestic development, China did many things that any African country could do. It radically shifted the organisation of labour and broke apart large plots.[19] With labour rationalised, people were free to devote as much energy as needed to immediate labour on their own plots or cooperative lands. And because they could be sure they would be fed, they were also available to take on the onerous work of land restoration and hand dug water works to expand the quantity of land available for land constrained China to meet its peoples' needs without relying too much on imports. Most under-known, China often sought to formalise and improve people's knowledge through decentralised scientific experimentation, an emphasis on village level self-reliance and productivity increases, and proto-agro-ecological modes of intellectual-practical work based on exploring 'traditional' practices with an eye as to how they could be improved under a political system which worked to that end.[20]

The Chinese model was seriously studied. Based on their research, writers like Babu, Mansour, Dowidar, Amin, and Amami developed an extremely wide array of suggestions for an auto-centred model. Self-reliance meant thinking about converting political sovereignty into economic sovereignty. First, of course, this meant understanding what was awry. As they saw clearly, in one way or another, peasants were, at best, labour reserves left with small subsistence plots, while industrialisation was not really offering any kind of technological upgrading of peasant agriculture.[21] The self-reliant model meant shifting the logic of accumulation – qualitative use values rather than what the logic of the law of value demanded be produced. States and their peoples would try to weave together domestic industrial or manufacturing sectors with domestic peasantry to do the impossible – increase the productivity of each, feed the people, balance rural-urban growth, avoid headlong hyper-urbanisation, maintain national sovereignty, and find some way to extract a surplus for sovereign industrialisation. The model, of course, was China, which had commanding advantages of scale, but in other ways seemed a suitable course for such countries to copy. And such scale is also why pan-Arabism loomed large in most early national-popular thought.

Throughout Africa, the model remained essentially untried, even in its original heartland, Tanzania itself. But that did not prevent it from flourishing on an intellectual and continental scale, from Dar es Salaam to Dakar, where Amin and his collaborators worked together to think through the implications of the Chinese experiment for African and Arab sovereign development. That line of flight also radiated outwards, as Dakar was a hub for African social science. Amin's influence was particularly heavy in North Africa, where his monographs on Maghrebi development and futures circulated with speed, and were read with enthusiasm. In North Africa and France, Francophone young people could easily access his texts. And Maoism was warmly embraced across the left, and more quietly within state intellectual-agronomic research institutions. One of those figures took to thinking about auto-centred development and applied it through direct agronomic research: Slaheddine el-Amami, in the process prefiguring the wide array of work which now goes under the banner of agroecology.

## SLAHEDDINE EL-AMAMI'S PRESCIENT FOOD SOVEREIGNTY VISION

Slaheddine el-Amami emerges as a prescient and unique progenitor of a holistic and sovereign vision for environmentally sound rural development, based on building up from the strengths of traditional farming systems. This was very far from an antiquarian treasure hunt, but was instead a search into the past in the quest for a different modernity and a different future.

Amami's quiet penchant for Maoism was likely picked up from the Perspectives group, where he had been a close comrade of the

Maoist-influenced agronomist, Gilbert Naccache. Both sought to re-direct national agricultural planning, then primarily an imposition from above, into a patient process of accumulation from below. Indeed, both sought to emplace a radical land-to-the-tiller agrarian reform during the 1960s, the 'Ben Salahiste' cooperative experiment, helmed by the country's 'super-minister', Ben Salah, a former trade union leader.[22] But the top-down model prevailed until the 1967 US-Israeli aggression against the Arab states led to massive protests in Tunisia, rupturing the legitimacy of dirigiste planning and setting in motion a shift to state regulated capitalism.[23]

As the space for radical thought narrowed, with leftists in prison or exiled, Amami entered into state agricultural research institutions, coming eventually to head the Centre de Recherche en Génie Rural (CRGR). The state research institution became shield and cage. As a shield, it gave Amami an institutional position from which to research alternative technologies, and to call for better state policies for rural people in an Arab region where state directed development still reigned.[24] This took place within the authoritarian Habib Bourguiba regime. As a result, Amami was unable to call for the substantive shifts in political power needed to carry out such a programme.[25]

Within the CRGR, Amami wrote quietly and unobtrusively within the dependency paradigm, attentive to how Tunisia had put in place an ensemble of technologies utterly unsuited to its biomes, the amount of capital it had available for development projects, or the number of people who needed jobs.[26] He also was entirely aware of deteriorating terms of trade for Arab exports, and crafted programmes with that in mind.[27] His analysis exposed and proposed with every word. With every attack on the prevailing imported technological system, he forwarded ambitious alternatives, drafting blueprint after blueprint, nationwide planning schematics, local level investigations and proposals for sustainable alternatives, and appropriate forms of agricultural technology for a people-centred and auto-centred development strategy.

In what follows, I begin with one of Amami's broadest and densest works – a manifesto for local agronomic research, which he reprinted again and again. He dissected the national research structures and their connections to the larger dependent national technological style. Because he was debating and criticising agronomists who did not see as he saw, or as he thought things should be seen, he emphasised how the institutions produced an ideology which favoured technological choices that helped reproduce dependence.[28] He highlighted how Tunisian agronomists had barely studied those plants and animals that were the living technological inheritance of the producers of the past, which had been bred and selected for hundreds, if not thousands, of years to produce a species that was best suited for semi-arid and arid Tunisia.

He drew the connection between the kinds of thinking encouraged in the national schooling system, and the ways foreign corporations could turn Tunisia into an arena for profit. He began with an analysis of the engineering schools' contempt for the 'traditional' and the technologies to which the slur referred. In disdaining over a millennium of precolonial polytechnics, such contempt became 'in reality a colonial ideology favouring the supremacy of imported technology and wanting to disown any specificity to the colonised country'.[29] He insisted that colonialism and neocolonialism/postcolonialism were fettering the social relations of production. The disarticulation and rearticulation of agriculture was inseparable from colonial and neocolonial capitalism. First, the bequest from the past had been slowly shrunk: 'Just some pockets and enclaves have been preserved from colonial destruction and constitute the true national libraries of Maghrebi agricultural technology'.[30] Neocolonialism had broken apart the labour and attention heavy agricultural systems of old. It had not done so with an eye towards improving them to lighten that which broke backs. Second, the new system, through schooling, 'dangled the mirage of an urban life getting rid of centuries of prejudice and downgrading in which the rural world bathed. To "modernise" is to erase and surpass all of the traditional systems of managing natural resources [...]. The choice of techniques is almost never inspired by the local patrimony'.[31] Amami saw that Tunisia's development project hinged on an ideological buy-in, alongside a hefty dose of derision towards the rural world where most Tunisians lived.

Amami grounded his criticisms in a dependency-style relational account of how technology was a mechanism for value flow, from Tunisia to the wealthy world, from the periphery to the core. He focused on seeds and water works. He saw the very physical stuff of agriculture had become conduits for value outflow from Tunisia to the merchants and 'large foreign conglomerates' that monopolised supposedly improved seeds. Even the institutions in Tunisia for developing its agricultural capacity were functioning 'as a gigantic technological relay between the exterior and the interior'. Research focused on Green Revolution wheats. The institutions barely looked at barley, although it was adapted to aridity and [a crop] which covered half the Northern cereal lands and almost all the seeded lands of the Centre-South. Such plans discounted local heritage. State agricultural institutions barely fostered agronomic research into the animal species and plant landraces central to precolonial agriculture. In Tunisia, 'a zoologist who might be interested in the pasturing of camels will be ridiculed. The growing of cactus is paralysed by this prejudice that it is a symbol of underdevelopment. A tree as noble as the date palm is totally ignored', while research programmes that needed a minimum of a decade to produce results were disdained. Botanists and agricultural engineers in the post-independence era did little more than carry out descriptive inventories of the cactus landraces covering Tunisia.[32]

As a result, the Global South lacked the institutional mechanisms that had been the sine qua non for Global North productivity increases. In his framework, the national commodity offices, charged with overseeing entire commodity chains, whether for oils (the National Oils Office, ONH) or the Office of Cereals, had to link research to plans to embed research nationally. They also had to have national popular priorities, with decisions, programmes, schematics, grants, research, and funding reflecting those priorities and values:

> In order to advantageously and effectively use the research infrastructure, every decision and technical choice of the research organisms, including the importation of seeds and plants, the choice of agricultural material, development of zones, and also the technical content of planning objectives, all these operations and activities which are now actually carried out in a more or less improvised fashion, and without previous studies or experiments, must be condoned by the research organisms. The orientations and the technical choices will then be taken on rational bases and as a function of norms and trials elaborated in Tunisia and not artificially transferred.[33]

Amami had a great many possible treatments for the wound and stanching the value flowing out from it. His polymathic grasp of Tunisian agriculture allowed him to recommend solutions in sector after sector, remoulding every institution and project into a mechanism for an alternative system – national and popular at the same time. Research had to be collective, but the problem was clear. The non-stop replacement of precolonial indigenous polytechnics with imported technology were creating 'double agricultural dependence, downstream and upstream, [which] is the most alienating of the relationship of unequal development between the affluent countries and the underdeveloped countries'.[34] For Amami, agriculture – in days past the least alienated portion of the productive process – was becoming the most alien to the farmer herself. He saw the farmer becoming a kind of organic factory tied to transnational supply chains, inputs, and outputs subject to the fluctuations and price movements made by monopolies and monopsonies.

Here, I pause and extract a series of crucial elements from Amami's work. One, the question of scale. Amami began but did not end with thinking of the problem at the level of Tunisia as a nation state. This was not a nationalism that expressed the desire for inclusion within the capitalist system on a world scale, or ending the domination of the national capital of the periphery by the national capital of the core, but a nationalism which aspired to a sovereign national-popular path of development. Tests and trials to see what new plant breed or which technologies would be most suited for Tunisia would occur first *in* Tunisia, pursuant to domestic social choices. Furthermore, he did not simply reject foreign technological innovations. As with the Chinese experiment, his almost certain model, the idea was not to create a hermetically sealed technical sphere, but to selectively draw on other technologies when and where they were needed.[35] Amami was well aware, for example, that the water technologies of Tunisia drew on the accumulated wisdom of Andalusia. His was a cosmopolitan, not cloistered, sovereignty.[36] Nor was there any trace of atavism or prelapsarian romance. The use of the word 'library' to describe the repositories of knowledge within traditional farming systems was not accidental. It spoke to a way of thinking of using archives and the technology contained therein in the service of a different modernity. He also knew that technology was never innocent. It was not merely that Tunisia was dependent on imported technologies as part-and-parcel of protecting value flows. He also noted that the application of a 'model' – which assumed that Tunisian agriculture would ever look like the agriculture that French or US agronomists took as normative – would ensure that Tunisia would forever fall short of its capacities by denying its specificities. In dealing with living biomes and beings, creativity and ingenuity unfolded within limits.

Furthermore, Tunisia was simply a starting point. Amami knew that Tunisia had a dazzling variety of biomes, from the semi-arid plains of Sidi Bouzid to the cereal fields of the wetter North, to the oasis archipelago spotting a sea of pastoralism in the south, to the olive plantations blanketing the central coast. Different bioregions were best suited to different crops, and that specificity was not merely a question of the North versus Tunisia, but of territories within Tunisia itself. For that reason, he urged the decentralisation of research, given that scientists ought to conduct their experiments in proximity to the peoples and plants they were meant to serve. Furthermore, he focused on the relational constitution of core and periphery. He knew dependence was not a thing, but part of a 'relationship of unequal development', an understanding clearly drawn from the framework of uneven development on a world scale.[37] He was always thinking about the strategic deployment of the nation's resources to produce a closed national circulatory system, keeping use values within the country to the greatest extent possible, rather than bringing the country wholly into the global law of value where it would be sure to suffer. And given that such relationships, such flows of expertise and technology, were made, they could be unmade – the mandate Amami set for himself.

Much of Amami's work broadened, or had been a build up to these themes and synthetic conclusions, or was a plan for intensifying production to increase the surplus. He seldom applied a merely technical approach to such questions, although institutional pressures and restrictions weighed on his writings, such that he often covered calls for redistribution in the shroud of technicism. He always knew the problem of development was social.

## AGROECOLOGY

Some of what Amami wished to do was happening in parallel elsewhere across the Third World, especially in Latin America, through early work on traditional farming systems as an intellectual and genetic treasure which could be drawn on freely for people-centred and peasant-centred peripheral development. By the early 1990s, agroecology began to apply scientific experimentation to the processes underlying traditional farming systems, and to formalise these investigations in a coherent approach to rural development.[38]

Traditional farming systems, or farming systems which have not 'modernised' or industrialised, share six features. One, high levels of biodiversity, regulating the functioning of ecosystems and providing ecosystem services. Two, land, landscape, and water resource management conservation systems. Three, diversified farming systems, or polycultures. Four, resilient agroecosystems that can cope with disturbances and absorb the caprice of inconsistent and sometimes inclement weather. Five, they are nurtured by traditional methods, not purely book based knowledge systems and the technologies with which they are bound. And six, cultural values and forms of social organisation which ensure wide access to resources. Such systems integrate livestock and poly-cropping, and maintain *in situ* (on the farm) genetic diversity. Another important, but not universal, feature of these systems is their seamless weaving into a natural matrix. Agroecology overlaps with and grows outwards from these logics and focuses on closed metabolic cycles secured through a series of principles. First, recycling of biomass. Second, strengthening the 'immune system' of the larger farming system by promoting natural enemies of pests. Three, promoting healthy soil. Four, minimising the loss of water, energy, or nutrients by both conserving and regenerating soil, water, and biodiversity. Five, promoting species- and genetic-level diversity over time and space. And six, enhancing synergies amongst various ecological and biological processes.

Such systems work within rather than against the tendency of natural systems to grow polycultures and recycle wastes. In terms of yield, and thus potential surplus, the golden grail of productivist-oriented technologies may yield less on a per crop basis. But when evaluated on a per-unit area, they produce far more than the monocultures beloved of Western agricultural modernisation projects – at least on the periphery.[39] Furthermore, on marginal lands agroecology may also considerably outyield conventional systems, whether for cereals or agroforestry. They also fail far less frequently than do monocrops in reaction to climate change induced disasters, and better tolerate or bounce back from extreme weather events.[40] And they do so while strengthening rather than sapping environmental health, which keeps farms functioning.

Agroecology increases national production of exchange values and use values in multiple ways. First, within peripheral farming systems, it has the capacity to considerably increase national food/agricultural production. Second, it can do so using fewer or no capital intensive inputs, thus reducing import bills. Third, it protects ecological health and potentially increases the level of $CO_2$ in the soil, thereby increasing the national soil's capacity to resist floods and drought, the output of too intense or too intermittent rainfall, due to climate change.[41] Fourth, because it relies on building upon the knowledge that exists within existing *campesino* or smallholder communities, it does not rely on foreign experts or technical attaches, nor on the more pernicious forms of development aid. In these ways, agroecology and the food sovereignty project with which it is interwoven reduce or eliminate the dependency of peripheral social formations on core commodity and expertise flows. Furthermore, agroecology and food sovereignty, calling for agrarian reform, have a social logic which works against monocultural exports and the insertion of peripheral countries into the global division of labour in a subordinate position. Whereas agroecology and food sovereignty tend to operate on family farms or smallholder subsistence farms producing for familial, local, or regional consumption, all things being equal, large-scale and capital intensive farms tend to produce for export using more industrialised methods.[42] Because margins are higher, even with the same productivity on smallholder farms, there is a greater surplus, whether counted in terms of use values for domestic consumption or sales within the community. Reciprocally, given a greater surplus for non-farm use, markets for non-agricultural goods expand, which can facilitate sovereign industrialisation. Feeding the population and providing it with the manufactures it needs alongside just reward for labour, while caretaking the environment, is also what many understand as socialism.

In examining this unmarked nexus and its relation to sovereignty, the question is how national or sub-national food and agricultural systems – encompassing production, processing, and consumption – can contribute to economic autonomy and auto-centred sovereign projects, or the capacity for national decision-making according to a popular and non-capitalist law of value.[43] Three traits are relevant. First, such systems should be self-reliant, or non-import dependent. Countries that can supply their own subsistence needs are better positioned for economic sovereignty, since they need not expend hard currency on basic goods needed for survival. This is essentially the vision of food sovereignty. Second, such systems need to be articulated internally. In other words, they should be closed systems at the national level. If capital inputs, such as tractors or organic fertilisers, are needed on farms, they should be procured nationally, whether through effective nutrient recycling or national manufacturers, relying minimally on international markets, international prices, and international technology transfer. Third, they should use agroecology, which strengthens the farm level environment, while reducing the need for off farm capital inputs. All three traits reduce or eliminate food and agricultural imports. Countries that develop stronger economies are less likely to incur unpayable debt, and they cut off an avenue for external pressure and constraints over political decisions: the ability of powerful states to turn food into a weapon via embargo. Through applying such measures – not merely or even primarily by the state, but with the necessary use of the state as carapace and shield for the people to amass power and restructure their lives – agrarian revolution alongside the back-to-the-future of agroecology could provide the basis for an untested African peasant path to development.

## AGROECOLOGY, FOOD SOVEREIGNTY, AND SOVEREIGN DEVELOPMENT

As is clear, African agrarian systems and peripheral agrarian systems more broadly, alongside dominant food consumption patterns, are structured in ways that reinforce value flows from periphery to core. These patterns coexist and constitute hierarchical differences between overall consumption and the two ideal-typical components of the world system: the core and the periphery. Dependency manifests as: unequal exchange, compressed prices for primary goods, reliance on technology transfer or inputs, and ecologically unequal exchange. It is also socially reproduced time and again by the lack of sufficient social power in the hands of the working people.[44] Breaking dependency means moving away from the law of value towards more auto-centred systems of production. While food sovereignty does not use this language, it very much shares much of the horizon.

I have explored theoretical precursors and fellow travellers to the food sovereignty discourse, as well as those treating issues of sustainable manufacturing and industrialisation. I have done so by exploring the ideas of Slaheddine el-Amami, an outstanding theorist of postcolonial dependent development. My aim was only to implicitly show convergences between food sovereignty, agroecology, and Amami's pioneering thoughts. Still, there are many convergences: the call for the devolution of power to the powerless, the call for national food production to meet the nutritional needs of the nation, and the call for agriculture to be protector rather than predator of the environment. Agrarian reform was a more muted convergence, above all amidst Tunisia's censorious neocolonial dictatorship.[45]

Perhaps the most telling area of agreement was around the call for the use of local agricultural technologies, from seeds to rotations, to water harvesting technologies. The break from the Green Revolution/modernisation paradigm and the intellectual-practitioner turn or return to the peasant as the core of a sovereign project is the common basis and taproot of the North African theorists of development and those who, above all in Latin America, originated the theories of agroecology and the related idea of food sovereignty. Given agriculture's centrality to future development strategies in the periphery, returning agriculture to a mode of production that produces an energetic surplus and an ever increasing amount of use values for national populations is a central component of repairing the holes within national circulatory systems through which exchange values gush and flow. Every step taken in that direction, and every move to make agriculture into a sector for the production of use values, also works against the unequal exchange and price compression of agricultural products on a world scale – a central element in imperialist value transfers and social control.[46] In this way, we can see that a peasant path to peripheral development is, in fact, not merely untried in most of the world, and certainly most of Africa, but is, in fact, the only path that will allay rather than aggravate the environmental de-development of various industrial regimes of the 'development' project, and is the only one which does not rely on capital stocks that do not currently exist across the periphery.[47]

In the current context of the Afro-Arab region – and increasingly, Venezuela – where food dependency is not merely a mechanism of value transfer, or securing tropical foods for the core, but is, rather, potentially or presently a mechanism of political coercion, food sovereignty takes on even more enhanced value. Countries capable of feeding themselves have more freedom to refuse onerous trade deals, or assume a sovereign foreign policy position contradicting the interests of major cereal exporters within the world system.[48] Food sovereignty, as one expression of the politics of national and popular liberation, is linked to, but transcends, balance of payments constraints. It is connected to the broader agenda of peripheral political decision-making and political alliances which could lead to a non-hierarchical world. And, indeed, it is increasingly popular at least at the level of discourse in North Africa, where the agrarian question is slowly being forced back onto the development discourse.[49] In this way, as in others, the project for a sovereign Africa, including North Africa and the Arab region of which it is a part, has a rich heritage upon which to draw as it attempts to build up independent and sovereign projects – in this century, and beyond.

## NOTES

1 Rodney, W., 2012. *How Europe underdeveloped Africa.* Wantage: Fahamu Books/Pambazuka Press; Moyo, S., P. Yeros, and P. Jha, 2012. Imperialism and primitive accumulation: Notes on the new scramble for Africa. *Agrarian South: Journal of Political Economy,* 1(2), pp. 181–203; Shaw, A. and Wilson, K., 2019. The Bill and Melinda Gates Foundation and the necro-Populationism of 'climate-smart' agriculture. *Gender, Place and Culture,* 27(3), pp. 1–24. doi.org/10.1080/0966369X.2019.1609426

2 FAOSTAT, selected years.

3 FAOSTAT, 1992–2016; St Louis Fed.

4 Love, J.L., 1990. The Origins of Dependency Analysis. *Journal of Latin American Studies,* 22(1–2) pp. 143–68; Prebisch, R., 1949. *The Economic Development of Latin America and Its Principal Problems.* United Nations.

5 Bambirra, V., 1978. *Teoría de la dependencia: una anticrítica.* Ediciones Era.

6 Bambirra, V., 1978. *La revolución cubana: una reinterpretación.* Editorial Nuestro Tiempo; Bambirra, V., 1971, *Diez años de insurrección en América Latina* Ediciones Prensa Latinoamericana.

7 Marini, R.M., 1969. *Subdesarrollo y Revolución.* Mexico City: Siglo Veintiuno Editores.

8 Sharma, D., 2017. Techno-politics, agrarian work and resistance in post-green revolution. Punjab, India: Cornell University, Dissertation p. 1.

9 Arment, C.J., 2020. Food dependency in Sub-Saharan Africa: Simply a matter of 'vulnerability', or missed development opportunity? *Development and Change*, 51(2), pp. 283–323. doi.org/10.1111/dech.12532

10 Friedmann, H. and McMichael, P., 1989. Agriculture and the state system: The rise and decline of national agriculture. *Sociologia Ruralis*, 29(2), pp. 93–117; Friedmann, H., 1982. The political economy of food: The rise and fall of the postwar international food order. *American Journal of Sociology*, 88, pp. 248–86; Friedmann, H. The origins of Third World food dependence. In Henry Bernstein (author), Ben Crow (editor), Maureen Mackintosh (contributor), and Charlotte Martin (contributor), 1990. *Food Question: Profits versus People?* Routledge, pp. 13–31; Ajl, M., 2019. Farmers, Fellaga, and Frenchmen. Ithaca, NY: Cornell University, PhD thesis.

11 Dussel, E., 2002. *Towards an unknown Marx: A commentary on the manuscripts of 1861–63*. London: Routledge, p., 214; Lenin, V.I., 2017. *Imperialism: The highest stage of capitalism.* London: Resistance Books; I developed this interpretation of Lenin from Ajl, M., 2020: Lenin's colonial question in the 21st century. PRISM, June 18. Available at: www.prismm.net/2020/06/18/lenin-colonial-question-21st-century/ [Accessed March 25 2021].

12 Moyo, S., Jha, P., and Yeros, P., 2013. The classical agrarian question: Myth, reality and relevance today. *Agrarian South: Journal of Political Economy*, 2(1), pp. 93–119.

13 Alsudairi, M.T., 2020. Arab encounters with Maoist China: Transnational journeys, diasporic lives and intellectual discourses. *Third World Quarterly*, 42(3), pp. 1–22. doi: org/10.1080/01436597.2020.1837616

14 Palma, G., 1978. Dependency: A formal theory of underdevelopment or a methodology for the analysis of concrete situations of underdevelopment? *World Development*, 6(7–8), pp. 881–924; Kvangraven, I.H., 2020. Beyond the stereotype: Restating the relevance of the dependency research programme. *Development and Change*, 52(1). [Accessed August 22, 2020]. doi.org/10.1111/dech.12593

15 There were exceptions, like the Argentine geologist and expert in Latin America science policy, Amilcar Herrera, as it related to underdevelopment. But it appears that the Arab/(North) African dependency thinkers were thinking much more about developmental policy on the whole.

16 Fergany, N., 1987. Min al-kitāb al-aḥmar ila al-kitāb al-aṣfar: arḍ tajruba al-ṣīn al-tanmūwīyya [From the Red Book to the Yellow Book: Presentation of the Chinese Development Experience]. In Nader Fergany, ed., Al-tanmīyya al-mustaqila fi al-waṭan al-'arabī [Independent Development in the Arab Nation]. Beirut: Center for Arab Unity Studies, pp. 291–322; Abdallah, I.-S., 1980. Arab industrialization strategy based on self-reliance and satisfaction of basic needs. *IFDA Dossier*, vol. 16, pp. 1–12. Nyon, Switzerland: International Foundation for Development Alternatives; Babu, A.M., 2002. *The future that works: Selected writings of A. M. Babu.* Trenton: Africa World Press.

17 Lal, P., 2015. *African socialism in postcolonial Tanzania*. Cambridge University Press, pp. 51–59.

18 Amin, S., 2017. Revolution and liberation: 100 years since the October Revolution, 50 Years since the Arusha Declaration. *Agrarian South: Journal of Political Economy*, 6(2): vii–xi, doi.org/10.1177/2277976017737902; Shivji, I.G., 2008. Revisiting the debate on national autonomous development. In S. Adejumobi and A. Olukoshi, eds, *The African Union and New Strategies for Development in Africa*, pp. 177–206.

19 Aziz, S., 1978. *Rural Development: Learning from China*. London: Macmillan International Higher Education.

20 Schmalzer, S., 2016. *Red Revolution, Green Revolution: Scientific farming in socialist China*. Chicago, IL: University of Chicago Press; Ajl, M. Delinking's ecological turn: The hidden legacy of Samir Amin. In Ushehwedu Kufakurinani, Ingrid Harvold Kvangraven, and Maria Dyveke Styve, eds, 2021. Samir Amin and beyond: Development, dependence and delinking in the contemporary world. *Review of African Political Economy*, 48(167), pp. 1–7.

21 Amin, S., 1974. Accumulation and development: A theoretical model. *Review of African Political Economy*, 1(1), pp. 9–26. doi.org/10.2307/3997857

22 Ayeb, H., 2019. Entretien Avec Gilbert Naccache. OSAE (blog), December 20. Available at: www.osae-marsad.org/2019/12/20/entretien-avec-gilbert-naccache/ [Accessed March 25, 2021].

23 See my Chapter five. Ajl, Farmers, Fellaga, and Frenchmen; Hendrickson, B., 2013. *Imperial fragments and transnational activism: 1968 (s) in Tunisia, France, and Senegal*. Boston, MA: Northeastern University; on post-1969 capitalism, see Romdhane, M.B., 1981. L'accumulation du capital et les classes sociales en Tunisie depuis l'indépendance. Tunis: University of Tunis, Ph.D. dissertation; and in its rural dimensions, Ayeb, H. and Bush, R., 2019. *Food Insecurity and Revolution in the Middle East and North Africa*. London and New York: Anthem Press.

24 Ajl, M., 2020. Does the Arab region have an agrarian question? *Journal of Peasant Studies*. doi.org/10.1080/03066150.2020.1753706

25 Cf. Ajl, M., 2018. Delinking, food sovereignty, and populist agronomy: Notes on an intellectual history of the peasant path in the Global South. *Review of African Political Economy*, 45(155), p. 77.

26 For accounts of that process in Tunisia, see Fetini, H., 1981. Recherche Sur Les Deux Modèles Coopératif et d'import-Substitution 1960–1970: Effets et Rôle Dans La Restructuration de l'économie Tunisienne Postcoloniale. Tunis: University of Tunis, Al-Manar; Amrani, F., 1979. La Réforme Agraire. Tunis: FDSE, Dissertation.

27 El-Amami, S., 1976. Projets de Coopération Régionale En Matière de Recherche Scientifique et Technologiques, Conférence Des Ministères Des États Arabes Charges de l'Application de La Science et de La Technologie Au Développement, UNESCO, Rabat, August 16–25. Les Cahiers Du

CRGR. Tunis, Tunisia: CRGR, July 1976) 8, MoA, 76/37; Prebisch, R. *The Economic Development of Latin America*; Dietrich, C.R.W., 2017. *Oil revolution: Anticolonial elites, sovereign rights, and the economic culture of decolonization*. Cambridge University Press.

28 In some of these sections I draw on and rework portions of the following: Ajl, M., 2019. Auto-centered development and indigenous technics: Slaheddine El-Amami and Tunisian delinking. *Journal of Peasant Studies*, 46(6), pp. 1240–63.

29 El-Amami, S., 1982. Pour Une Recherche Agronomique Au Service d'une Technologie Nationale Intégrée. In *Tunisie: Quelles Technologies ? Quel Développement?* Éditions Salammbô: GREDET, p. 15.

30 El-Amami, S., 1983. Technologie et Emploi Dans l'Agriculture. In *Tunisie, Quelles Technologies ? Quel Developpement, GREDET* Tunis: Éditions Salammbô, p. 21.

31 El-Amami, Technologie et Emploi Dans l'Agriculture, p. 23.

32 El-Amami, Pour Une Recherche Agronomique, p. 16.

33 El-Amami, Technologie et Emploi Dans l'Agriculture, p. 19.

34 El-Amami, Technologie et Emploi Dans l'Agriculture, p. 19.

35 Schmalzer, *Red Revolution, Green Revolution.*

36 El-Amami, S., Al-Ray Bil-Tanqit nd al-Awam [The Drip Irrigation of Ibn al-Awam]. The Third International Symposium on the History of Science in the Arab Region, The First Specialized Conference, Kuwait, 1984; El-Amami, S., 1984. Les Aménagements Hydrauliques Traditionnels En Tunisie. Tunis: CRGR.

37 Amin, S., 1974. *Accumulation on a world scale: A critique of the theory of underdevelopment*. Monthly Review.

38 The following discussion draws from Rosset, P. and Altieri, M.A, 2017. *Agroecology: Science and politics*. Rugby: Practical Action Publishing.

39 Rosset, P.M. et al., 2011. The Campesino-to-Campesino agroecology movement of ANAP in Cuba: Social process methodology in the construction of sustainable peasant agriculture and food sovereignty. *The Journal of Peasant Studies*, 38(1), pp. 161–91; Sosa, B.M. et al., 2013, Agroecological revolution. The farmer to farmer Movement of the ANAP in Cuba. *Jakarta: La Vìa Campesina*; Badgley, C. and I. Perfecto, 2007. Can organic agriculture feed the world? *Renewable Agriculture and Food Systems*, 22(2), pp. 80–6. doi.org/10.1017/S1742170507001986; Badgley, C. et al., 2007. Organic agriculture and the global food supply. *Renewable Agriculture and Food Systems*, 22(2), pp. 86–108. doi.org/10.1017/S1742170507001640; Funes-Monzote, F., 2014. 2001 Fincas Integradas Ganadería-Agricultura Para Cultivar Biodiversidad, March 6.

40 Altieri, M.A. and Nicholls, C.I., 2017. The adaptation and mitigation potential of traditional agriculture in a changing climate. *Climatic Change*, 140(1), pp. 33–45; Holt-Giménez, E., 2002. Measuring farmers' agroecological resistance after Hurricane Mitch in Nicaragua: A case

study in participatory, sustainable land management impact monitoring. *Agriculture, Ecosystems & Environment*, 93(1–3), pp. 87–105. doi.org/10.1016/S0167-8809(02)00006-3

41 On questions of quantifying use values from a socio-ecological and environmental justice perspective, see Martinez-Alier, J., Munda, G., and O'Neill, J., 1998. Weak comparability of values as a foundation for ecological economics. *Ecological Economics*, 26(3), pp. 277–86.

42 Patnaik, U., 1996. Export-oriented agriculture and food security in developing countries and India. *Economic and Political Weekly*, 31(35/37), pp. 2429–49; Byerlee, D. and Deininger, K., The rise of large Farms in land-abundant countries. In Stein Holden, Keijiro Otsuka, and Klaus Deininger, eds, 2013. *Land Tenure Reform in Asia and Africa*. London: Palgrave Macmillan. doi.org/10.1057/9781137343819.0024; Carter, M.R., Barham, B.L., and Mesbah, D., 1996. Agricultural export booms and the rural poor in Chile, Guatemala, and Paraguay. *Latin American Research Review*, 31(1), pp. 33–65; Ayeb, H., 2019. Building food sovereignty in Tunisia. Food First, May 2. Available at: www.foodfirst.org/building-food-sovereignty-in-tunisia/ [Accessed March 25, 2021]. One partial exception, which I do not develop here, are large-scale cereal farms producing for domestic consumption using Green Revolution technologies.

43 Amin, S., 1990. *Delinking: Towards a Polycentric World*. London: Zed Books.

44 G. Shivji, I.G., 2017. The concept of 'Working People'. *Agrarian South: Journal of Political Economy*, 6(1), pp. 1–13. doi.org/10.1177/2277976017721318

45 I discuss this more in Ajl, Auto-centered development and indigenous technics: Slaheddine El-Amami and Tunisian delinking; Naccache, G., 2009. *Qu'as-tu fait de ta jeunesse: itinéraire d'un opposant au régime de Bourguiba, 1954–1979: suivi de récits de prison*. Paris: La Marsa. Cerf : Mots passants.

46 Patnaik, U. and Patnaik, P., 2016. *A Theory of Imperialism*. New York: Columbia University Press.

47 McMichael, P., 2011. *Development and social change: A global perspective*. New York: SAGE Publications; Jorgenson, A.A. and Rice, J., 2005. Structural dynamics of international trade and material consumption: A cross-national study of the ecological footprints of less-developed countries. *Journal of World-Systems Research*, 11(1), pp. 57–77.

48 Ayeb discusses this in the Tunisian case: Building Food Sovereignty in Tunisia.

49 E.g. Ayeb. Building Food Sovereignty in Tunisia.

# 11

# Being Poor in the Current Monetary System: Implications of foreign exchange shortage for African economies and possible solutions

*Anne Löscher*[1]

## INTRODUCTION: UNRELENTING CALLS FOR REFORM

It seems a striking – yet maybe unsurprising – regularity that after each phase of a major crisis, more and more call for the reform of the international monetary system. After Russia defaulted on its debt in 1998, which led to the near collapse of US-American Long Term Capital Management, Bill Clinton demanded a new monetary system.[2] After a series of defaults and financial crises in Latin-America and Asia, the then deputy managing director of the IMF, Anne O. Krueger, urged a reform of the debt restructuring mechanism and the role the IMF plays in it.[3] The number of critics of the international monetary system surged when financial turmoil also affected OECD countries with the outbreak of the international financial crisis in 2007–08 and the Covid-19 crisis.[4] However, these crises took place against the backdrop of a more long-term and serious crisis: the climate crisis. A recent report from Bank for International Settlement (BIS) and the Banque de France purports that 'the fight against climate change is taking place at the same time when *the post-World War II global institutional framework is under growing criticism*. This means that the unprecedented level of international coordination required to address the difficult (international) political economy of climate change is seriously compromised'.[5]

But economic, financial, and environmental crises are only a magnifying glass for the problems prevalent in 'normal' times. This chapter addresses the criticism targeting the international monetary system and sheds light on some reform proposals. It first critically appraises the current hierarchically structured monetary system with respect to peripheral, economically undiversified countries, whose political and economic position is predominantly shaped by colonialism. We focus on African economies in particular. This problem diagnosis is followed by an overview and discussion of different reform proposals – some more radical than others, such as the introduction of an equitable debt restructuring mechanism, the reform of the IMF, the introduction of a truly global currency, and the issuance of compound of several currencies such as bancor (see below).

## THE PITFALLS OF THE CURRENT INTERNATIONAL MONETARY SYSTEM

The main characteristic of the post Bretton-Woods institutional setting of the international monetary system is the hierarchical structuring of currencies along their real or expected liquidity, i.e. their degree of exchangeability at short notice at no loss. Currencies' liquidity levels correspond to their ability to fulfil the three functions of money: as a means of transaction, a means to store value, and a unit of account. Being the most important unit of account in international trade, debt contracts, and financial assets, the US dollar is on the top of this currency hierarchy, followed by the euro, yen, Chinese renminbi, the pound Sterling, Swiss franc, etc. Currencies of peripheral countries are positioned in the lowest ranks of this hierarchy, i.e. they enjoy the lowest degree of confidence and acceptance among economic agents. Peripheral countries are, therefore, dependent on income in key currencies to pay for imports, service external liabilities, and safeguard against external instabilities, though the conduct of exchange rate stabilisation policies to counter excessive volatility or to preemptively protect against sudden capital outflows.[6]

Foreign exchange dependence establishes the external constraint, that is the need to secure enough key foreign currencies when due, be it via exports or the influx of foreign capital. To manage this *external constraint* via exports has proven an almost insurmountable challenge for peripheral countries in the past, as their exports are predominantly primary commodities commodities, a state described as *commodity dependence.*[7] But primary commodities are a poor source for stable foreign exchange revenues: they are not only subject to a higher degree of volatility, but their terms-of-trade vis-à-vis manufactured goods also follow a long-term downward trend[8] – despite attempts to counter this in cartels like OPEC, diverse rare metal cartels (IBA for bauxite or CIPEC for copper),[9] and the recent cocoa cartel between Ghana and the Ivory Coast.[10]

But lacking capacity to generate foreign exchange rooted in low levels of industrialisation and unequal exchange is just one side of the problem, while how existing funds are spent is another. Precious foreign exchange reserves are diminished by illicit financial outflows and the repatriation of revenues by transnational corporations.[11] In fact, since the 1980s there has been a net capital flow from the Global South to the Global North.[12] Foreign exchange reserves are also wasted on massive prestigious infrastructure projects ('white elephants') with little positive, or even negative, socio-economic effects.[13] Furthermore, inequality is on the rise globally and nationally. The rising shares of the 'well offs' translates into a higher share of imported luxury goods, which diminishes a country's foreign exchange reserves.[14] Last, but not least, service on external debt accounts for a big share of what foreign exchange is used for in peripheral countries. According to World Bank data, in 2019 the external debt service as percentage share of exports and primary income stands at, on average, 15.4 per cent for low and middle incomes, though in some countries the figures are twice as high, such as in Zambia (31.3 per cent), Ethiopia (28.9 per cent), and Angola (26.8 per cent).[15]

Where net exports are insufficient to satisfy the need for foreign exchange, external debt has to be issued to manage the external constraint. The latter comes predominantly in the form of portfolio capital flows, which are more mobile and short-term – as elaborated in the literature on international financialisation.[16] These processes started in the 1980s and 1990s in Latin-America, Asia, and Soviet-Bloc states,[17] and continued from 2006 onwards in African economies, when the Seychelles was the first to issue foreign currency denominated bonds on international capital markets, and bond markets in local currency further developed across the continent.[18]

This greater reliance on portfolio flows increases peripheral countries' vulnerability vis-à-vis international financial capital flows and exacerbates financial subordination.[19] It necessitates strategies to attract foreign capital via investor-friendly policies: capital accounts have to be deregulated, high interest rates offered, and safe exit-options[20] provided to incentivise foreign capital inflows into the country. These measures exacerbate the subjugation under external economic conditions imposed by the financial cycle, which spillover to the domestic economy in the form of domestic recessions and financial instability. The increased mobility of capital, combined with the deregulation of capital accounts including the flexibilisation of exchange rates, has opened up an opportunity for both domestic and international financial investors to reap profits from trading currencies as means of speculation via carry trade transactions that make use of inter-temporal arbitrage.[21] Though the share of assets in peripheral currencies held in international portfolios is small in nominal terms, it is relatively large in comparison to the size of the issuing economies.[22]

With peripheral currencies' integration in financial portfolios as targets for speculation, their exchange rates are subject to unmanageable volatility. Where the exchange rate is the 'chink in the armour of modern-day macroeconomic policymakers',[23] this has significant implications for monetary sovereignty.[24] Here the mechanics of the *financial Dutch Disease*[25] play out: inflows of foreign capital into a small open economy with flexible exchange rates and a shallow monetary system fuel the expectation of appreciation of the local currency – a self-fulfilling prophecy.[26] These inflows are rooted in speculative carry trade transactions, or primarily finance extractive industries, such as the real estate and the finance sector.[27] The appreciation of the domestic currency is accompanied by growing concerns of an eventual depreciation – be it because of domestic sterilisation policies[28] or a sudden *flight-to-quality* of financial investors into safe havens, such as government bonds of centre countries, in reaction to a lingering global recession or changes in the US policy rate – the primary initiator of global financial cycles.[29] Once the *animal spirits* turn pessimistic, the fall in confidence in the currency ensues capital outflows, with a sudden depreciation of the exchange rate, a depletion of reserves, and sudden increases in interest rates as result. While depreciation inflates external debt in real terms and reduces the purchasing power of the local population, the high real interest rates introduce domestic recessionary pressure.[30] When capital outflows result in balance of payments difficulties, countries turn to the IMF for emergency loans, and austerity, as condition, deepens the recession because it reduces public spending and hence effective demand.[31]

A high degree of volatility of the exchange rate rooted in portfolio finance and currency speculation introduces politically unmanageable domestic boom-bust cycles, hence financial instability and domestic recessions. Exchange rate volatility is detrimental to domestic economic development as it harms the export sector,[32] and with it a country's capacity to generate foreign exchange, which increases uncertainty, concerning private investments and considerably narrows policy space, which is the backbone for economic diversification towards high-value manufactured export goods, i.e. reliable sources for foreign exchange.[33] Furthermore, notoriously unstable exchange rates are both rooted in and contribute to a low position in the international currency hierarchy.[34]

But the current monetary system does not only have deleterious effects on small peripheral countries alone. Robert Triffin elaborated the contradictions implied in the post Bretton-Woods monetary order: when a nationally issued currency serves as international currency, the issuer of the key currency has the privilege and obligation to run large current account deficits and to pursue loose monetary policies to supply the world economy with liquidity. This, however, gets in the way of its autonomous economic policies and eventually undermines confidence in its currency – where the latter might eventually lead to a portfolio restructuring towards other currencies, or gold.[35] As consequence, the US turned from the biggest creditor to world's biggest debtor country, with deficits accumulating to $488.5 billion in 2018 alone.[36] While the US served as a growth engine for at least three decades by importing other countries' exports, jobs were created and profits were reaped elsewhere.[37]

The current monetary system also implies long-term recessionary pressure, as John M. Keynes pointed out almost a century ago:[38] it creates an incentive to run current account surpluses, as this allows a higher degree of policy space and ensures high living standards as export industries create jobs and income. Apart from the impossibility of all countries running current account surpluses, this matter of affairs also yields a deflationary pressure on the world economy, given that exchange rates are flexible. The current monetary system leads to competition for outlets of export goods and, consequently, a race to the bottom in an attempt to lower prices for the export goods, with a recessionary tendency as result. As an example: because Chinese goods play such an important role in the US economy, the (hypothetical) appreciation of the renminbi as result of current account surpluses of China vis-à-vis the US, also leads to a higher price level in the US. The FED responds by increasing the policy rate, which has a recessional effect on the US and global economy as the US imports less, consequently providing less global liquidity. As China goes into recession too, because of the drop in outlets for its exports, it cannot make up for the lowered demand by importing more US goods.[39] Even for exporters of manufactured goods, the dependence on the US dollar is impossible to circumvent: if they decided to export less to the US (as they lose confidence in the US dollar due to high American debt levels), this would imperil their own growth prospects as jobs in the export sector would get destroyed. But if they continued to export to the US, the US liabilities would accumulate even more, potentially further depreciating the US dollar and, consequently, their own foreign reserves. The only remaining viable solution would then be to demand US imports.[40]

## THE BURDEN IS UNEQUALLY DISTRIBUTED

The monetary system in its present form cements the global division of labour, i.e. it makes the alignment of living standards impossible and implies economic instability with recessional tendencies, namely a race-to-the-bottom. Peripheral countries are confronted with chronic balance of payments difficulties and the subjugation of policymaking under global conditions imposed by financial capital flows implying unmanageable macroeconomic instabilities and high interest rate levels. These factors, rooted in the current monetary system, impede industrialisation, or even contribute to deindustrialisation, i.e. aggravating the difficulties to generate sufficient foreign exchange. Here, the self-perpetuating nature of macroeconomic imbalances inherent in the monetary world order become apparent.

African economies are no exception. Economic diversification has declined in recent decades in many African economies, with few exceptions, such as Mauritius, Senegal, Mali, Zimbabwe, Ghana, and Ethiopia.[41] Persistently high, even increasing levels of external debt, attest to the increasing difficulties in generating enough foreign exchange.[42] This external debt is particularly expensive for African debtors due to prejudiced peer rating practices where assumptions of Africa's perceived particularness translate into higher risk premia.[43] This form of unjustified generalisation is well documented in an article on Eurobond issuances in Africa: 'potential investors [. . .] have to bear in mind that *Africa is not a risk-free asset* [...] investors should watch for across the continent when contemplating buying into a sovereign bond'[44] – a comment hard to imagine in a European context where macroeconomic heterogeneity and discrepancies are as great as on the African continent, as became obvious during the euro crisis. The tendency to assess financial assets as riskier when they originate in the African continent results in a higher risk premium – the 'Africa premium'[45] – independent of country specifics.[46]

What is more, the current monetary system implies 'a net transfer of resources from [. . .] peripheral countries to the major economies issuing the global reserve currencies'.[47] Stabilisation and safeguarding funds needed by peripheral countries are held in sovereign bonds issued in centre countries such as the US, Japan, the UK, and, since 2011, China.[48] Peripheral countries' need to hold foreign exchange finances centre countries deficits, which have low or stagnant growth rates and finance their excess consumption from debt.[49] As these bonds bear very low interest, the opportunity costs of having to hold these bonds are enormous.[50] What is more, countries with current account deficits face the *transfer problem*, i.e. they have to go through massive depreciation of their currency, aggravating balance of payments difficulties, and possibly inducing domestic recessions, in order to become net exporters.[51] Hence, Keynes emphasised that it is impossible to achieve free capital movement, flexible exchange rates and sustained growth at the same time. In a system of flexible exchange rates and free capital movement, the burden of adjustment is carried by the debtor country, hence the economically weaker country which creates a deflationary pressure.[52]

Another expression of how the current monetary setting perpetuates global inequality and a strong centre-periphery divide, respectively, is represented by the role the IMF plays. While the G7 countries are able to autonomously conduct monetary policies, the IMF is in charge of disciplining the rest of world; small peripheral countries in particular. This was visible prior and during the international financial crisis: the IMF did not forecast it, nor did it intervene in the US or other OECD countries from where the crisis sprang. The IMF was criticised for its double standards, where peripheral countries are punished for protectionist measures, but centre countries responsible for far more harmful financial shocks rippling through the entire global economy remain untroubled.[53]

Self-perpetuating monetary asymmetries are apparent in the differences in macroeconomic policy space, too. When countries in the Global North experience balance of payments difficulties, their currency positions allow them to resort to solutions far less detrimental to policy space and national interests. Central banks at the centre can act as a lender of last resort for their financial institutions, or establish SWAP lines among themselves, while harsh conditions – massively curbing policy autonomy and hence monetary sovereignty – in exchange for emergency loans are imposed on peripheral countries.[54] The FED, for instance, pursued a two-tiered strategy distinguishing between core central banks and a bunch of emerging market economies,[55] in which the core central banks were treated as peers, with permanent and unlimited access to dollar liquidity SWAP lines. The peripheral countries' central banks were subject to restricted access in respect to time and the extent of available liquidity. SWAP lines can be a relief when peripheral countries experience balance of payments difficulties due to capital outflows in times of crisis, such as the recent Covid-19 shock.[56] However, this privilege is granted to very few countries in the Global South, which are largely excluded from such backstop reassurances.[57]

As a solution to the problems inherent in the current monetary system, a plethora of solutions have been recommended in the literature. What follows is a non-exhaustive overview of reform proposals aimed at a better coping with balance of payments difficulties and domestically decoupling from the financial cycle, or to eradicate that cycle altogether.

## REFORM PROPOSALS TO MANAGE BALANCE OF PAYMENTS DIFFICULTIES

### *Debt Restructuring Mechanism*

Some critics of the current monetary system point to the lack of a transparent and coherent multilateral agreement on moratoriums in case of balance of payments difficulties and arrears. Debt restructuring processes are often arbitrary and favourable for the Paris Club, i.e. the major creditor governments. As debtors currently bear the brunt of costs in case of defaults, the current state implies a moral hazard problem which encourages imprudent lending.[58] A new sovereign debt restructuring mechanism could include rescheduling debt repayments until a country runs a current account surplus (as was agreed on in the context of Germany's reparation payments after the Second World War), capital controls (see below), haircuts, etc.; and could be more like national bankruptcy procedures for corporations, as was envisioned by the UN assembly in 2014 – but without consequences.[59] The former IMF economist, Peter Doyle, suggests reforming the IMF's approach, in line with a pre-emptive insolvency mechanism as practiced in the US banking sector, to avoid fire sales of a country's debt titles and its assets, which act as accelerants in debt crises.[60] More radical authors call the legitimacy of external debt coming from current account deficits fundamentally into question.[61]

### *Reparation Funds*

With the devastating socio-economic effects of colonialism (or colonial continuities) and the climate crisis in mind, voices calling for reparations payments become louder.[62] While colonialist extractivist exploitation has set former colonies on the path of commodity dependence, the climate crisis imperils foreign exchange income when climate related natural disasters destroy crops or productive capital; or when climate policies reduce the demand of fossil fuels, which constitute more than 90 per cent of exports in countries like Angola, Nigeria, and Algeria.[63] At the UN Conference of the Parties' resolution in 2009, a fund of $100 billion was promised to be mobilised by 2020. However, not only is the agreed amount too small given the challenges ahead, it also comes in the form of aid (with potential conditionality) and so far only about 6 per cent of the promised amount has actually been disbursed so far.[64]

### *Capital controls*

Other authors demand the application of capital controls to slow down capital flight. This policy measure has long been excluded from peripheral countries' policy repertoires, since open capital accounts were a mainstay of the Washington Consensus, and fiercely demanded in World Trade

Organization Uruguay Round by centre countries.[65] Capital controls allow governments to regulate sudden in or outflows of financial capital in times of changing global financial conditions. Capital controls can encompass the taxation of capital flows (e.g. the Tobin tax), the imposition of a minimum of reserve requirements, outright limits to in or outflows, a minimum investment time span, etc.[66] Capital controls were applied in some Asian and Latin-American countries in reaction to the crises in the 1990s (e.g. Chile and Malaysia), in 2007/08 (e.g. Iceland, Brazil, and China), and the Covid-19 crisis,[67] and are still the norm in Ethiopia – though this is currently changing.[68] Capital controls are dismissed by mainstream economists for being ineffective, as they can be circumvented by over invoicing of trade.[69] However, more convincing is that the grown dependence on portfolio capital implies that policymakers have to act in accordance with investor preferences, meaning that the former shirk the policy option not to deteriorate their refinancing position on international capital markets via reputational losses.

## REFORM PROPOSALS TO SHIELD THE DOMESTIC ECONOMY FROM THE INTERNATIONAL MONETARY SYSTEM

### *Making a currency less susceptible to the adverse effects of the financial cycle*

Other reform proposals aim at reducing the adverse transmission mechanism from capital flow fluctuations to domestic factors. Paula et al. suggest the building up of local currency bond markets to buffer exchange rate volatility.[70] This was a strategy pursued by a number of Asian governments as a reaction to the Asian crises in the 1990s, which were rooted in short-term foreign exchange debt to finance long-term investments denominated in domestic currencies,[71] and underlies the World Bank's 'cascade approach' to mobilise private finance for development.[72] However, though they were praised for overcoming the *Original Sin* (the inability to issue debt in domestic currencies at reasonable rates), the local currency bond markets did not overcome foreign exchange dependence. Authors have argued that local currency bond markets increase vulnerability vis-à-vis capital flows. They come at shorter maturities and higher interest rates to compensate for the exchange rate risks attached to them.[73] Deregulation of the capital account and other policies aiming at improving convertibility to build up investor confidence forego the establishment of local currency bond markets. These accompanying measures impose discipline as they continue to rely on foreign exchange debt issued in international capital markets. Reputational losses due to denied convertibility would lead to capital flight and restricted capital market access. That local currency bond markets actually aggravate peripheral countries' vulnerability in times of crises was demonstrated by the Covid-19 crisis.[74]

Other proposals aim to improve peripheral currencies' position in the currency hierarchy through monetary unions. The rationale behind this is that monetary unions enhance cooperation, lower transaction costs, and generate synergy effects among member countries, rendering the economic area stronger.[75] The resulting gains in investor confidence could increase the currency's liquidity premium; that is, a better position in the international currency hierarchy compensating for the voluntarily renounced loss in policy autonomy. The fifteen ECOWAS countries' plan to issue a single currency was motivated by such hopes. However, the dangers implied in monetary unions marked by strong economic asymmetries, and by a lack of fiscal union, were demonstrated in the Eurozone,[76] and could be repeated in the ECOWAS single currency project once it is realised.[77] That monetary unions do to necessarily improve a currency's acceptance is demonstrated by the euro, which is not more international than the currencies it replaced, taken together.[78]

### *The MMT perspective*

Another strategy to avoid the adverse effects of external financial instability is to try to minimise exposure to external finance. Proponents of Modern Monetary Theory (MMT), also known as Neo-Chartalists,[79] insist on the importance of monetary sovereignty. They highlight that a currency issuing government does not have any intrinsic financial constraint on its own currency.[80] It has, therefore, the capacity to directly finance productive capacity enhancing and employment generating projects. Excessive money, threatening to cause inflation in the face of real resource constraints, can be mopped up through tax collection in the domestic unit of account. To increase monetary sovereignty, and hence reduce foreign exchange dependence, sovereign debt should be denominated in domestic currency. Combined with capital controls, exchange rates should be floating in order to increase the scope for monetary and fiscal policy to pursue domestic goals, such as growth and full employment. Economic development should be based on local resources – especially labour – following an industrial development strategy. The latter is supported by development banks and credit guidance. Job guarantee programmes financed in local currency aim to solve the pressing issue of mass unemployment. To avoid that this additional income aggravates current account deficits because they would increase imports, employment generation measures have to be accompanied by import substitution, tariff protection and taxes. Given the specificities of peripheral countries, some MMT authors concede that some level of foreign exchange denominated external debt is unavoidable, especially for those suffering chronic current account deficits.[81]

## REFORM PROPOSALS TARGETING THE FINANCIAL CYCLE ITSELF

### *Regulations to dampen the financial cycle*

Yilmaz Akyüz, among others, emphasises that peripheral countries carry the brunt of financial crises, such as in 2007/08, though they did nothing to cause it. Consequently, some demand reforms to prevent financial crises by regulating financial markets in centre countries; i.e. by reversing the deregulation policies since the 1980s, which ascribed governments the reduced role to bail out financial agents of systemic importance.[82] Regulating internationally, if not globally, is necessary because of regulatory arbitrage and international spillovers from the adverse effects of deregulation. An internationally agreed on regulatory system – i.e. regulations that are not historically dominated by OECD countries as is the case with the Basle Accords – would make regulation less dependent on individual politicians' discretion. However, there are also certain dangers: a one size fits all regulation is not suitable to address existing asymmetries. Also, negotiations on such regulations might be dominated by, and in favour of, powerful industrial countries.[83] Charles Goodhart[84] highlighted that financial regulation which only targets parts of the monetary system can aggravate the problem of financial instability: when regulation deepens the split between the unregulated and regulated financial institutions, it will likely trigger a substitution flow into the unregulated, riskier, and more destabilising sectors.

### *SDRs as counter-cyclical global currency*

Other reform proposals demand the introduction of a truly international currency, devoid of the perils coming with a monetary order arranged around a currency which is subject to national monetary policies. As an alternative to the US dollar as an international unit of account, reformers suggest the expansion and redesign of the use of the IMF's special drawing rights (SDR). Here, the IMF is ascribed the role of a technocratic supplier of counter-cyclical liquidity using SDR to ensure a facilitated and unconditional access to multinational relief. The IMF would hence turn from being a pro-cyclical institution with double standards to a counter-cyclical provider of liquidity, and thus buffer financial cycles. The additional liquidity in the form of SDRs might serve as a kind of buffer to restore confidence in the banking sector and financial markets. The aim is to ease temporary foreign exchange crunches in bear phases of the international financial cycles and, therefore, surmount the limited policy space that developing countries face in times of crises.[85]

However, the SDR's underlying currency basket is criticised for being reflective of this power imbalance towards the Global North. Its composition has little connection to the current world economy: SDRs consist of the US dollar (42 per cent), the euro (about 31 per cent), the renminbi (11 per cent), the yen (8 per cent), the pound sterling (8 per cent).[86] This composition does not reflect the share in world trade as the currencies of Brazil, India, and Russia, for instance, are not included.[87] An inclusion of currencies issued in the Global South in the SDR currency basket could improve their position in the currency hierarchy and weaken the strong centre-periphery divide in the monetary system.

### *International Clearing Union*

The introduction of an international currency – the *Bancor*, composed of a currency basket of thirty of the most important currencies – was also included in the Keynes plan drafted for the negotiations on the post Second World War monetary order.[88] The Bancor was part of a wider institutional setting, consisting of a system of fixed exchange rates and an International Clearing Union (ICU) overseeing international transactions, where the Bancor served as unit of account to settle international liabilities. The ICU functions as a sort of central bank of central banks, administering all international transactions for countries that have an account with the ICU.

Primary aims are the establishment of a less crisis prone and equilibrating monetary system. Keynes envisioned a monetary system that distributed the burden evenly among creditors and debtors. Surplus countries are incentivised to lend to deficit countries via a penalty interest – a measure Keynes weakened in the later versions of his proposal, presumably in the hope of obtaining the US's support, which was the major creditor at the time.[89] Financial stability would be achieved through eradicating the possibility of currency speculation and sudden capital flights: the Bancor only serves as unit of account among central banks and the ICU, and is not accessible to private agents; exchange rates are fixed with the Bancor currency basket. The fixed exchange rates are adjustable, however, incorporating countries' inflation rates and wage levels in regular intervals. These adjustments aim to ensure a stable purchasing power so that inflation is not exported. By preventing sudden movements of financial capital, the Keynes plan aimed to prevent liquidity difficulties and the resulting lack of demand in crises, the expansion of liquid assets while preserving the existing assets' values, and a heightened degree of transparency of capital movements for the purpose of capital controls and the clamping down on tax evasion. What is more, comparative advantages based on an undervalued currency were to be eradicated.[90]

José A. Ocampo's[91] adoption of Keynes' proposal to the current institutional setting where SDR serve as Bancor and the Bank of International Settlements as ICU re-raises the issue of the feasibility of the ICU. Interestingly, the workings of the ICU would be similar to that of SWAP lines established between centre central banks, where liabilities in key currencies are cleared. It becomes clear that such liability clearing mechanisms are possible even in the current setting – given the political will. Though requiring international diplomatic agreement, such an international unit of account, independent of a single country's national monetary policies and exchange rates, would imply much lower costs for foreign exchange dependent countries, while promising financial stability.[92]

## DISCUSSION AND CONCLUSION: REFORMS AND MONETARY SOVEREIGNTY

Colonial continuities, international financialisation, and climate vulnerability establish and aggravate monetary dependency: while colonial continuities indirectly (e.g. via commodity dependence rooted in colonial heritage and the unreliable and volatile foreign exchange income associated with it) and directly (e.g. via intuitional settings such as the CFA-Franc)[93] curb monetary sovereignty, international financialisation increases the exposure to vulnerabilities connected to an open capital account.[94] Climate vulnerability increases monetary dependence by increasing the costs for external debt, introducing financial instability, and deteriorating a country's capacity to achieve a positive current account balance.[95] Increasing monetary sovereignty should be an important policy goal, as monetary sovereignty is a mainstay of development,[96] understood here as the bettering of living conditions of a country's population within a global capitalist system.

The reform proposals addressed here are connected to questions of monetary sovereignty to a varying degree. Reforms aiming at the improvement of peripheral countries' position facing balance of payments difficulties, namely reforms of the debt mechanisms, reparation payments, and the (re)normalisation of capital controls improve policy autonomy of peripheral countries – however only temporarily. Debt relief such as the Highly Indebted Poor Countries Initiative (HIPC) and aid only had temporary effects in the past, with over-indebtedness and balance of payments difficulties prevailing.[97] What is more, in countries highly dependent on international capital markets, reputational losses among investors due to debt relief and capital controls can prove costly, as market participants would demand higher premia on assets issued by these countries in the future.[98]

The second set of reform aims to achieve policy autonomy by decoupling from the international monetary system, or cushioning its effects on the domestic economy. Mainstream responses would be the deepening of domestic financial markets, to avoid that balance of payments transactions impact the exchange rate, and creating monetary unions to improve a currency's position in the currency hierarchy. While financial deregulation can backfire when it reduces political leverage to the management of the boom-bust cycle (this time domestic ones), the membership in monetary unions externalises policy decisions and trades policy autonomy for an uncertain marginal improvement of the currency's acceptance. An ECOWAS currency union would improve monetary sovereignty on the one hand, as it would end France's control over the monetary policies in the CFA Franc zone. But, on the other hand, it would also imply a loss in monetary sovereignty as monetary policies are outsourced to supranational institutions. The proposal by MMT authors to reduce the dependence on foreign exchange by following domestically focused development strategies sheds light on the importance for peripheral countries to increase their degree of monetary sovereignty, which is not an easy feat given global monetary asymmetries.

The third strand of reform proposals primarily targets the financial cycle, which seems more effective to achieve lasting improvements to monetary policy space in the periphery. Weakening or eradicating the financial cycle and its boom-bust mechanisms would prevent spillover effects to peripheral countries, adverse to their macroeconomic policy space as described above. To definancialise via tighter regulation at the centre is difficult as unregulated sectors might be disproportionately advantaged, and fire sales might fuel financial instability. More promising is the reform of the IMF, to become an institution bestowed with the task to counter-cyclically manage international liquidity via SDR as truly international currency. The last and most radical proposal is to establish an ICU that administers international transactions at fixed but adjustable exchange rates. This would imply that monetary sovereignty is not hampered by the considerations of exchange rate adjustments counteracting policy decisions.

The basic observation of this chapter is that the international monetary system is lopsided and needs reforming. It gives a summary of what self-reinforcing factors lying in the international monetary system contribute to the cementation of economic imbalances, foremost financial sovereignty, and thereby power structures. It curbs policy space for governments in the periphery and prevents the improvement of living standards for its population. While centre countries enjoy a high degree of autonomy and are less affected by international fluctuations, financial, ecological, and pandemic crises highlighted the adverse effects of being a peripheral country with a high degree of susceptibility to external instabilities with extremely limited policy space. Given the poor performance of the international monetary system in respect to equitable development, which requires stability and policy space for all, the number of critics from various institutional backgrounds is unsurprising. Though an in-depth discussion of the reform proposals is not possible within the scope of this chapter, it is clear that the reform proposals put forward here appear more promising the more thoroughly they turn the current monetary system inside out.

## NOTES

1 I would like to thank Franziska Müller and the editorial team for their helpful comments. The remaining errors are all mine, though.

2 Davidson, P., 2017. Globalization and an international monetary clearing union. In Oscar Ugarteche, Alicia Payana, and Maria Alejandra Madi, eds, *Ideas Towards a New International Financial Architecture.* St. Andrews: WEA Books, p. 159.

3 Krueger, A., 2002. A new approach to sovereign debt restructuring. Washington, D.C.: International Monetary Fund. Available at: www.imf.org/en/Publications/Pamphlet-Series/Issues/2016/12/30/A-New-Approach-to-Sovereign-Debt-Restructuring-15722 [Accessed March 25, 2021].

4 For example, Zhou, X., 2009. Reform the International Monetary System, *BIS Review.* Beijing: People's Bank of China; Stiglitz, J.E. et al., 2009. Report of the Commission of experts of the President of the United Nations General Assembly on reforms of the international monetary and financial System, interim draft. New York: United Nations Organization; UNCTAD, 2009. Trade and development report. Geneva, New York: United Nations. Available at: unctad.org/en/Pages/PublicationArchive.aspx?publicationid=2167 [Accessed March 25, 2021]; D'Arista, J., 2009. Setting an agenda for monetary reform. *PERI Working Papers.* Available at: scholarworks.umass.edu/peri_workingpapers/166 [Accessed March 25, 2021]; Prasad, E.S., 2014. *The dollar trap: How the U.S. dollar tightened its grip on global finance.* Princeton, NJ, and Oxford: Princeton University Press; Gallagher, K., J.A. Ocampo, and U. Volz, 2020. Special drawing rights: International monetary support for developing countries in times of the COVID-19 crisis. *The Economists' Voice* 17(1). doi: 10.1515/ev-2020-0012

5 Bolton, P. et al., 2020. The green swan, p. 7, available at: www.bis.org/publ/othp31.htm, emphasis added [Accessed March 25, 2021].

6 A sharp depreciation of the domestic currency as result of large capital outflows would ensure the twin crisis of the domestic currency and the domestic banking sector leading to financial and economic crises. See: Akyüz, Y., 2013. *The financial crisis and the Global South: A development perspective.* London: Pluto Press; Paula, L., Fritz, B., and Prates, D.M., 2017. Keynes at the periphery: Currency hierarchy and challenges for economic policy in emerging economies. *Journal of Post Keynesian Economics*, 40(2), pp. 183–202. doi: 10.1080/01603477.2016.1252267

7 Sindzingre, A., 2019. Financing the developmental state: Tax and revenue issues. OEC, 'Economic Complexity Ranking of Countries, 2013–2017. Available at: www.oec.world/en/rankings/country/eci/ [Accessed March 25, 2021].

8 Harvey, D. et al., 2010. The Prebisch-Singer Hypothesis. Four centuries of evidence. *The Review of Economics and Statistics*, 92(2) pp. 367–77; Nissanke, M., 2011. Commodity markets and excess volatility. Sources and Strategies to Reduce Adverse Development Impacts. Available at: www.common-fund.org/wp-content/uploads/2017/06/CFC_report_Nissanke_Volatility_Development_Impact_2010.pdf [Accessed March 25, 2021].

9 Mingst, K.A. 1976. Cooperation or illusion: An examination of the intergovernmental council of copper exporting countries. *International Organization*, 30(2), pp. 263–87. doi: 10.1017/S0020818300018270

10 Wexler, A., 2020. Cocoa cartel stirs up global chocolate market. *Wall Street Journal*, January 31. Available at: www.wsj.com/articles/new-cocoa-cartel-could-overhaul-global-chocolate-industry-1157826160 [Accessed March 25, 2021].

11 In the case of Zambia, see Fischer, A.M., 2020. Haemorrhaging Zambia: Prequel to the current debt crisis. *Developing Economics* (blog). Available at: developingeconomics.org/2020/11/24/haemorrhaging-zambia-prequel-to-the-current-debt-crisis/ [Accessed March 25, 2021].

12 Kregel, J.A. 2017 The clearing union principle as a basis for financial regional arrangements in developing countries. In UNCTAD Debt vulnerabilities in developing countries: A new debt trap? Volume II: Policy Options and Tools, p. 63.

13 Robinson, J.A. and Torvik, R., 2005. White Elephants. *Journal of Public Economics*, 89(2), pp. 197–210. doi:10.1016/j.jpubeco.2004.05.004

14 For the case of Kenya, see Import liberalization in Kenya. In Jean-Marc Fontaine, ed., 1992. *Foreign Trade Reforms and Development Strategy*. London and New York: Routledge. doi: 10.4324/9780203979235-18

15 World Bank, Total Debt Service (% of Exports of Goods, Services and Primary Income) | Data, January 2021. Available at: data.worldbank.org/indicator/DT.TDS.DECT.EX.ZS [Accessed March 25, 2021].

16 Bortz, P.G. and Kaltenbrunner, A., 2017. The international dimension of financialization in developing and emerging economies. *Development*

*and Change*, 49(2), pp. 375–93. doi: 10.1111/dech.12371; Bonizzi, B., 2013. Financialization in developing and emerging countries. *International Journal of Political Economy*, 42(4), pp. 83–107. doi: 10.2753/IJP0891-1916420405

17 Grabel, I., 1996. Marketing the Third World: The contradictions of portfolio investment in the global economy. *World Development*, 24(11), p. 1761. doi: 10.1016/0305-750X(96)00068-X; Gabor, D., 2013. The financialisation of the Romanian economy: From central bank-led to dependent financialization. FESSUD studies (Financialisation, economy, society and sustainable development (FESSUD) Project. Available at: econpapers.repec.org/paper/fesfstudy/fstudy05.htm [Accessed March 25, 2021].

18 Kvangraven, I.H., The changing character of financial flows to Sub-Saharan Africa. In A.V. Gevorkyan and O. Canuto, eds, 2016. *Financial Deepening and Post-Crisis Development in Emerging Markets: Current Perils and Future Dawns*, pp. 223–45. doi: 10.1057/978-1-137-52246-7_11; Löscher, A., 2019. The birth of African Eurobond markets. Its causes and possible implications for domestic financial markets. Berlin: FMM Conference: The Euro at 20. Available at: www.boeckler.de/pdf/v_2019_10_25_loescher.pdf [Accessed March 25, 2021].

19 Kaltenbrunner, A. and Painceira, J.P., 2018. Subordinated financial integration and financialisation in emerging capitalist economies: The Brazilian experience. *New Political Economy*, 23(3), pp. 290–313. doi: 10.1080/13563467.2017.1349089; Bortz and Kaltenbrunner, The International Dimension, 2017; Bonizzi, B., 2013. Financialization in developing and emerging countries. *International Journal of Political Economy*, 42(4), pp. 83–107. doi: 10.2753/IJP0891-1916420405; Powell, J., 2013. Subordinate financialisation: A study of Mexico and its non-financial corporations. University of London: PhD dissertation, SOAS; Grabel, Marketing the Third World.

20 Such safe exit options when holding local currency come, for instance, in the form of de-risking by central banks' strategies to act as swapper-of-last-resort – an important component of what Gabor coined the Wall Street Consensus. Gabor, D., 2018. Understanding the financialisation of international development through 11 FAQs. Heinrich Böll Stiftung, North America; for Brazil: Macalós, J.P.S., 2017. Foreign exchange swaps: A near substitute for international reserves in peripheral countries? The Case of Brazil. Berlin: 21st FMM Conference. Available at: www.boeckler.de/pdf/v_2017_11_10_macalos.pdf [Accessed March 25, 2021]; for Mexico: Powell, J., 2013. Subordinate Financialisation.

21 In carry trade transactions, foreign exchange is borrowed to invest in short-term investments in peripheral countries. This is done in the hope of an appreciation of exchange rate (which is often a self-fulfilling prophecy when the volume of carry trade is large) which, together with the extremely high interest rates, often proves very profitable. Bortz and Kaltenbrunner, The International Dimension.

22 Bortz and Kaltenbrunner, the International Dimension, p. 380.

23 Barry Eichengreen, B., 2004. *Capital Flows and Crises*. Cambridge, MA: The MIT Press, p. 100.

24 For a definition of monetary sovereignty, see: Wray, L.R., 2015. *Modern Money Theory: A Primer on Macroeconomics for Sovereign Monetary Systems*, 2nd ed. London: Palgrave Macmillan.

25 The *Dutch Disease* describes the negative effects arising from a sudden influx of foreign capital as result of the discovery of natural resources, which leads to an overvaluation of the local currency and a decline of exports as result. Corden, W.M., 1984. Booming sector and Dutch disease economics: Survey and consolidation. *Oxford Economic Papers*, 36(3), pp. 359–80. doi: 10.1093/oxfordjournals.oep.a041643

26 On the role of expectations in exchange rate determination, see: Kaltenbrunner, A., 2017. Financialised internationalisation and structural hierarchies: A mixed-method study of exchange rate determination in emerging economies. *Cambridge Journal of Economics*, 42(5), pp. 1315–41. doi: 10.1093/cje/bex081; Kaltenbrunner, A., 2015. A post Keynesian framework of exchange rate determination: A Minskian approach. *Journal of Post Keynesian Economics*, 38(3), pp. 426–48. doi: 10.1080/01603477.2015.1065678

27 Bortz and Kaltenbrunner, The international dimension, p. 386.

28 Sterilisation policies consist of buying up foreign exchange in exchange for domestic currencies by domestic central banks in an attempt to sterilise the appreciation of the exchange rate.

29 Rey, H., 2018. Dilemma not trilemma: The global financial cycle and monetary policy independence. Working Paper, National Bureau of Economic Research. doi: 10.3386/w21162

30 Grabel, Marketing the Third World; Andrade, R.P. and Prates, D.M., 2013. Exchange rate dynamics in a peripheral monetary economy. *Journal of Post Keynesian Economics*, 35(3), pp. 399–416. doi: 10.2753/PKE0160-3477350304

31 Akyüz, Y., 2012. *The financial crisis and the Global South: A development perspective*. London: Pluto Press.

32 Serenis, D. and Tsounis, N., 2013. Exchange rate volatility and foreign trade: The case for Cyprus and Croatia. *Procedia Economics and Finance*, volume 5, pp. 677–85. doi: 10.1016/S2212-5671(13)00079-8

33 Amsden, A., 'The wild ones. Industrial policies in the developing world. In Narcís Serra and Joseph E. Stiglitz, eds, 2008. *The Washington Consensus Reconsidered: Towards a New Global Governance*. Oxford: Oxford University Press; Chang, H.J. 2002. *Kicking away the ladder: Development strategy in historical perspective*, 1st edition. London: Anthem Press; Sindzingre, A., 2007. Financing the developmental state: Tax and revenue issues. *Development Policy Review*, volume 25(5); Nissanke, M., 2011. Commodity markets and excess volatility.

34 Paula, Fritz, and Prates, Keynes at the Periphery, p. 11.

35 Bordo, M. and McCauley, R.N., 2017. Triffin: Dilemma or myth? BIS Working Papers, Bank for International Settlements. Available at: ideas.repec.org/p/bis/biswps/684.html [Accessed March 25, 2021].

36 Reuters, 2019, U.S. current account deficit hits 10-year high; Firms bring back more foreign profits, March. Available at: www.reuters.com/article/us-US-economy-currentaccount-idUSKCN1R81R5 [Accessed March 25, 2021].

37 Davidson, Globalization and an International Monetary Clearing Union

38 Ocampo, J.S., 2010. Special drawing rights and the reform of the global reserve system. Intergovernmental Group of 24, Initiative for policy dialogue. Available at: g24.org/wp-content/uploads/2016/01/Special-Drawing-Rights-and-the.pdf [Accessed March 25, 2021].

39 Davidson, Globalization and an International Monetary Clearing Union, p. 153f.

40 Schulmeister, S., 2009. Globalisierung Ohne Supranationale Währung: Ein Fataler Widerspruch, ifo-Schnelldienst, no. 16/2009.

41 OEC, Economic Complexity Ranking of Countries 2013–2017.

42 Kvangraven, The Changing Character of Financial Flows to Sub-Saharan Africa, pp. 223–45.

43 As represented in economic research by the 'African dummy'. See Englebert, P., 2000. Solving the mystery of the AFRICA Dummy. *World Development*, 28(10), pp. 1821–1835. doi: 10.1016/S0305-750X(00)00052-8

44 Allen, K., 2017. African nations turn to bond markets for finance needs. *Financial Times*, September 15. Available at: www.ft.com/content/08d5c562-994f-11e7-b83c-9588e51488a0; emphasis added [Accessed March 25, 2021].

45 Soto, A., 2020. African nations say they're being ripped off by Wall Street, *Bloomberg.Com*. Available at: www.bloomberg.com/news/articles/2020-09-08/borrowing-costs-make-africa-s-stars-victims-of-the-neighborhood [Accessed March 25, 2021].

46 Olabisi, M. and Stein, H., 2015. Sovereign bond issues: Do African countries pay more to borrow? *Journal of African Trade*, 2(1-2), pp. 87–109. doi: 10.1016/j.joat.2015.08.003. This is aggravated when climate vulnerability is added: Buhr, B. et al., 2018. Climate change and the cost of capital in developing countries. London and Geneva: SOAS University of London.

47 Ocampo, Special Drawing Rights and the Reform of the Global Reserve System, p. 4.

48 Ugarteche, O, 2017, A New international financial architecture: The regional versus the global View? In Oscar Ugarteche, Alicia Payana, and Maria Alejandra Madi, eds. *Ideas towards a new international financial architecture*. Place of publication not identified: College Publications, pp. 175–208.

49 Alami, I., 2018. Money power of capital and production of 'new state spaces': A view from the Global South. *New Political Economy*, 23(4), pp. 512–29. doi: 10.1080/13563467.2017.1373756

50 Rodrik, D., January 2006. The social cost of foreign exchange reserves. Working Paper, Working Paper Series, National Bureau of Economic Research. doi: 10.3386/w11952; Kregel, J.A., 2006. Negative net resource transfers as a Minskian hedge profile and the stability of the international financial system; Cheltenham: Edward Elgar Publishing.

51 Krugman, P., 1999. Balance sheets, the transfer problem, and financial crises. *International Tax and Public Finance*, 6(4), pp. 459–72. doi: 10.1023/A:1008741113074

52 Davidson, Globalization and an international monetary clearing union, pp. 143–75.

53 Akyüz, The financial crisis and the Global South.

54 Ugarteche, A new international financial architecture.

55 Namely Brazil, Mexico, South Korea, and Singapore. Alami, Money power of capital, p. 525.

56 Gabor, D., 2020. Critical macro-finance: A theoretical lens. *Finance and Society*, 6(1), pp. 45–55.

57 Mühlich, L. et al., 2020. The global financial safety net tracker: Lessons for the COVID-19 crisis from a new interactive dataset, GEGI Policy Brief 010. Boston: Global Development Policy Center. Available at: www.bu.edu/gdp/2020/11/30/the-global-financial-safety-net-tracker-lessons-for-the-Covid-19-crisis-from-a-new-interactive-dataset-2/ [Accessed March 25, 2021].

58 Akyüz, *The financial crisis*, 29ff.

59 Stichelmans, T., 2015. Why a United Nations sovereign debt restructuring framework is key to implementing the post-2015 sustainable development agenda. Eurodad briefing paper for European legislators and decision-makers; see also Krueger, A New Approach to Sovereign Debt Restructuring.

60 Doyle, P., 2019. A preemptive sovereign insolvency regime. *Financial Times*, March 14. Available at: www.ft.com/content/deb5c9f0-1faf-3024-8d69-a99938313 57c [Accessed March 25, 2021].

61 See, for example, Cencini, A., 2017. The sovereign debt crisis: The case of Spain. *Cuadernos de Economía*, 40(112), pp. 1–13. doi: 10.1016/j.cesjef.2017.02.001; Schmitt, B., 2014. The formation of sovereign debt. Diagnosis and remedy. SSRN Scholarly Paper. Rochester, NY: Social Science Research Network. doi: 10.2139/ssrn.2513679

62 Lynn, S. and C. Thorbecke, 2020. What America owes: How reparations would look and who would pay. *ABC News*, September 27. Available at: abcnews.go.com/Business/america-owes-reparations-pay/story?id=72863094 [Accessed March 25, 2021]; Sheller, M., 2020. The case for climate reparations – *Bulletin of the Atomic Scientists* (blog), November 6. Available at: thebulletin.org/2020/11/the-case-for-climate-reparations/ [Accessed March 25, 2021]; Bolton et al., The Green Swan, p. 15.

63 OEC, Economic Complexity Ranking of Countries (2013–2017).

64 Khan, Z.H., 2019. COP-25 reminder: Where Is the compensation for the climate vulnerable. *Six Degrees* (blog), November 30. Available at: www

.sixdegreesnews.org/archives/27757/cop-25-reminder-where-is-the-compensation-for-the-climate-vulnerable [Accessed March 25, 2021].

65 On the changing stance of the IMF on capital controls, see: Fritz, B. and Prates, D.M., 2014. The new IMF approach to capital account management and its blind spots: Lessons from Brazil and South Korea. *International Review of Applied Economics*, 28(2), pp. 210–39. doi: 10.1080/02692171.2013.858668

66 Singh, K., 2019. Recent experiences with capital controls. Madhyam Policy Brief. Available at: www.madhyam.org.in/recent-experiences-with-capital-controls/ [Accessed March 25, 2021].

67 For example, Grabel, I. and K.P. Gallagher, 2015. Capital controls and the global financial crisis: An introduction. *Review of International Political Economy*, 22(1), pp. 1–6. doi: 10.1080/09692290.2014.931873 [Accessed March 25, 2021].

68 Since December 2019, Ethiopia is under a new IMF programme. The current prime minister, Abiy Ahmed, has recently taken the first steps to open up Ethiopia's capital account. See also Gavin du Venage, 2020. Ethiopia's Reformist Leader Abiy Ahmed Woos Private Sector Investors to Fuel Economic Growth, The National, January 28. Available at: www.thenationalnews.com/business/economy/ethiopia-s-reformist-leader-abiy-ahmed-woos-private-sector-investors-to-fuel-economic-growth-1.970398 [Accessed March 25, 2021].

69 De Grauwe, P. and M. Polan, 2001. Increased capital mobility: A challenge for National macroeconomic policies. In Horst Siebert, ed., *The world's new financial landscape: Challenges for economic policy*. Berlin , New York: Springer, pp. 177–94.

70 Paula, Fritz, and Prates, Keynes at the Periphery.

71 Hardie, I. and L. Rethel, 2019. Financial structure and the development of domestic bond markets in emerging economies. *Business and Politics* 21(1), pp. 86–112. doi: 10.1017/bap.2018.11

72 Gabor, D., 2019. Securitization for sustainability. Does it help achieve the sustainable development goals? Washington, D.C.: Heinrich Böll Stiftung North America.

73 Bortz and Kaltenbrunner, The International Dimension.

74 Hofmann, B. Shim, I, and Hyun Song Shin, 2020. Emerging market economy exchange rates and local currency bond markets amid the Covid-19 pandemic. BIS Bulletin No. 5. Available at: www.econpapers.repec.org/paper/bisbisblt/5.htm [Accessed March 25, 2021].

75 Grauwe and Polan, Increased capital mobility.

76 Stiglitz, J.E., 2016. *The Euro: How a common currency threatens the future of Europe*, New York: W.W. Norton & Company.

77 For the challenges of the regional single currency project in West Africa, see: Bakoup F. and Ndoye, F., 2016. Why and when to introduce a single currency in ECOWAS. Africa Economic Brief. African Development Bank Group. Available at: www.afdb.org/fileadmin/uploads/afdb/Documents

/Publications/AEB_Vol_7_Issue_1_2016_Why_and_when_to_introduce_a_single_currency_in_ECOWAS.pdf [Accessed March 25, 2021].

78 Ilzetzki, E., Reinhart, C.M., and Rogoff, S., 2020. Why is the euro punching below its weight? National Bureau of Economic Research. doi: 10.3386/w26760

79 For example, Wray, L.R., 2007. *Modern money theory: A primer on macroeconomics for sovereign monetary systems.* London: Palgrave; Kaboub, F., 2007, Institutional adjustment planning for full employment. *Journal of Economic Issues*, 41(2), pp. 495–502.

80 The 'applicability' of MMT in peripheral countries is a hot issue. For some authors, MMT lacks relevance as a policy guide in this latter context (see for example: Aboobaker, A. and E. Ugurlu, 2020. Weaknesses of MMT as a Guide to Development Policy. *UMass Amherst Economics Working Papers.* Available at: www.scholarworks.umass.edu/econ_workingpaper/292 [Accessed March 25, 2021]. For others, MMT is more than a set of specific policy advices. It's an analytical perspective which helps to explain colonial monetary relations, and criticises mainstream economic theories such as 'optimal currency area' and fiscal budget constraints underlying austerity measures. See *Sylla, N.S. (forthcoming)* "Modern Monetary Theory as an analytical framework and a policy lens: An African perspective" in *L. R. Wray and Y. Nersisyan (eds), Elgar Companion to Modern Money Theory, Edward Elgar.*

81 Sylla, N.S., 2020. Modern monetary theory in the periphery. Rosa Luxemburg Stiftung. Available at: www.rosalux.de/en/news/id/41764/modern-monetary-theory-in-the-periphery [Accessed March 25, 2021].

82 Ugarteche, A new international financial architecture.

83 Akyüz, *The financial crisis and the Global South: A development perspective.*

84 Goodhart, C., 2008. The boundary problem in financial regulation. *National Institute Economic Review*, 206(1), pp. 48–55. doi: 10.1177/0027950108099842.

85 Akyüz, *The financial crisis and the Global South*; Taylor, L., 1998. Capital market crises: Liberalisation, fixed exchange rates and market-driven destabilisation. *Cambridge Journal of Economics*, 22(6), pp. 663–76. doi: 10.1093/cje/22.6.663

86 IMF, 2019. Factsheet: Special Drawing Right (SDR). Available at: www.imf.org/en/About/Factsheets/Sheets/2016/08/01/14/51/Special-Drawing-Right-SDR [Accessed March 25, 2021].

87 Ugarteche, A new international financial architecture.

88 Keynes, J.M., 1986. Proposal for an international currency (or clearing) union. In John Keith Horsefield, ed., *The International Monetary Fund 1945–1965: Twenty years of international monetary cooperation.* Washington, D.C. IMF, pp. 3–18. The Keynes plan was eventually dismissed in favour of the White plan, which established the Bretton-Woods system (1944–1971), including the establishment of IMF and the World Bank:

Davidson, Globalization and an international monetary clearing union; Ugarteche, A new international financial architecture

89 Keynes, Proposal for an international currency, paragraph 17; Keynes, Proposal for an international clearing union, paragraph 7.

90 Davidson, Globalization and an International Monetary Clearing Union.

91 Ocampo, Special drawing rights; Jan Kregel adopted it for the regional level. Kregel, The Clearing Union Principle.

92 Akyüz, *The Financial Crisis*, p. 20.

93 Koddenbrock, K. and Sylla, N.S., 2019. Towards a political economy of monetary dependency: The case of the CFA franc in West Africa. *MaxPo Discussion Paper*. Available at: https://pure.mpg.de/pubman/item/item_3152726_2/component/file_3152727/mpifg_mpdp19_2.pdf

94 Because of the high interest rate levels and exchange rate volatility associated with the exposure to the financial cycle. Bortz and Kaltenbrunner, The International Dimension.

95 Buhr et al., 2018. Climate change and the cost of capital in developing countries. London and Geneva: SOAS Imperial College London; Bolton et al., The Green Swan.

96 Chang, *Kicking Away the Ladder*; Amsden, The wild ones.

97 However, critics say that the debt relief was by far not extensive enough and was conditioned to liberalisation measures. Therefore it failed.

98 Cline, W.R., 2001. The Management of Financial Crises. In Horst Siebert, ed., *The world's new financial landscape: Challenges for economic policy*. Berlin and New York: Springer, pp. 55–81.

# 12

# The German Push for Local Currency Bond Markets in African Countries: A pathway to economic sovereignty or increased economic dependency?

*Frauke Banse*

Debts in foreign currencies can be a great burden for developing and emerging countries (DECs). Entire economies are export oriented for servicing debt in hard currencies, exchange rate volatilities create huge stress for public and private budgets, and dependencies on external monetary policies create great uncertainties.

Issuing bonds in local currencies is seen by many – from critical NGOs to the G20 – as a useful tool to reduce some of these vulnerabilities. Dependency on foreign currencies would be reduced; fluctuations in local currencies would threaten the debt service less; countries would be less prone to exogenous shocks.[1] Hence, one could argue, bonds in local currencies can help reduce the external orientation of DECs and create greater political leeway.

The potential reduction of exchange rate risks and the reduction of exogenous shocks is underlined by big donor countries: since 2007, the G8, and later the G20, have had local currency bond markets (LCBMs) in DECs on their agenda, and support their establishment – especially in Africa.

Viewed in isolation, the general case for local currency debt appears convincing at first glance.

Seen in its broader context though, the positive connection between economic sovereignty and local currency bonds melts away; instead, there are changing patterns of economic dependency and increased social inequality, not least due to the requirements of markets for these bonds, and the interests behind their establishment.

This article aims to explore this context in its geopolitical and geoeconomic dimension. It first looks at the commodity character of the bonds, and the fact that they need markets to function. Given the peripheral position of the countries in question, it consequently explores the external interests in establishing LCBMs, mainly those of the G20. It will take a closer look at the outstanding activities of diverse German state institutions in supporting LCBMs, with particular attention to Africa. This is followed by a discussion on how the recycling of surplus money and an increased economic footprint in Africa might have played a role for these German institutions. The article concludes with an underlining of the class character of German surplus recycling, and a short discussion on the entry points for international solidarity.

## LCBMS ARE PART OF THE GLOBAL FINANCIAL MARKETS

Bonds represent not only a debt relation, but are also securities and therefore commodities. As a commodity, these bonds need a market to be sold and traded, buyers are required to invest in this commodity, and the investments have to generate profit. In order to attract vast resources, these markets are designed for external, international investors too. The consequences of this international market character appear to have been overlooked by the above-mentioned positive references to LCBMs. The volatile behavior of the involved international investors and the measures taken to buffer it lead to far reaching political consequences, radically effecting social justice and development policies.

So-called 'patient' domestic investors, such as domestic pension funds or domestic insurance companies that are less tempted by short term speculation and capital flight, are crucial to ensure relatively stable debt-relations for peripheral countries. They are meant to root LCBMs domestically, functioning as an anchor to minimise the risks of foreign capital flight in times of crisis.[2] To ensure that bonds in local currency are purchased domestically in relevant quantities, these domestic investors need to be created and their base enlarged.[3]

In order to offer diversified investment areas and risk profiles to attract institutional investors, both domestic and international, new forms of asset classes are meant to be created. Accordingly, public infrastructure – roads, bridges, ports, but also education or health – are turned into profitable asset classes.[4] LCBMs are crucial for these investments as they contribute strongly to the liquidity of these assets (see below).

These requirements link LCBMs directly to the privatisation of public infrastructure and social services. This privatisation appears on the side of investors (e.g. privatised pension systems) as well on the asset side (e.g. privatised public services). It turns the aspiration to domestically denominated debt into a project supporting large-scale commodification and rising social inequality,[5] aggravated by focusing only on those infrastructures being 'marketable' or 'bankable', and not on those most needed.[6]

The investment risks in African countries are considered to be high, leading not only to structurally high interest rates for bonds nominated in domestic currencies.[7] Additionally, to attract the 'global pool of private finance'[8] required to fill an assumed and probably exaggerated annual gap of $130–170 billion (US) per year to finance African infrastructure,[9] the investment risks need to be reduced considerably by the state.

These de-risking measures include most favourable general investment laws and regulations for foreign investors, blending mechanisms with the public entities taking specific risks by, for instance, taking over the riskiest tranches of a securitised infrastructure investment. De-risking measures also involve contractual templates for public-private partnerships (PPPs), ensuring investors that social, political, climate, or liquidity risks will be covered by the public hand.[10]

Additionally, the exchange rate risks of external investors are mitigated by the hedging activities of the central bank, which requires vast amounts of foreign reserves.[11] Finally, this de-risking measure by means of foreign exchange reserves exposes the independence from hard currencies by LCBMs as a myth.

For attracting the 'global pool of private finance'[12] for public infrastructure investment in DECs, domestically well-rooted LCBMs, as an anchor for deeper and more 'mature' domestic financial markets, are crucial for the general goal of liquidity.[13] The architects using these global 'trillions'[14] of infrastructure finance, such as the World Bank or the G20, understand the risks of volatile global financial investment flows. Hence, they also warn to be cautious with external investments at an early stage of establishing an LCBM.[15]

There are, however, severe doubts whether this anchoring works at all, despite the social consequences or the reality of investment streams outlined above. All de-risking measures taken at the domestic level, whether they are adapted investment laws, adapted contracts, or far- reaching guarantees, might be useless in attempting to keep foreign capital inside the country. The behaviour of global investors is not only influenced by domestic regulations and changing conditions such as currency depreciations, but also by global conditions of financing,[16] underlining the structural embeddedness of DECs in global capitalism.[17] Deep, open, and liquid domestic financial markets connect the peripheral economies directly with the global boom-bust cycles, systemic risks, and the disciplining power of global financial markets, as observed in the vast capital flight during the Covid-19 virus crisis.[18]

Marginalised in the discussion around LCBMs is the structural need for taking up debt. Drafts to implement LCBMs[19] call for better debt sustainability and improved public debt monitoring. However, they tend to neglect the effects of the volatilities mentioned above and the related consequences of default under the disciplining pressure of global financial markets.[20] Structural causes of rising public debt, such as a permanent current account deficit, the dominance of foreign direct investment, and closely related legal and illegal financial outflows, remain largely unmentioned.[21]

## THE FUNCTION OF LCBMS IN FINANCIAL CAPITALISM AND GERMANY'S ROLE

While government bond markets may be seen as 'the cornerstone of domestic financial markets',[22] domestically rooted LCBMs in DECs, as discussed above, may be seen as a major element for a 'resilient'[23] and open global financial system.[24] They are meant to attract the 'global pool of private finance'[25] in times of low interest rates in high income countries with generally scarce profitable investment options. As put by Andreas Dombret, former member of the Executive Board of the Deutsche Bundesbank, the German central bank: '[LCBMs] broaden the spectrum of investments for international investors and facilitate their global search for diversification'.[26]

The first known attempt to push for LCBMs in peripheral countries was in 2007 during the G7/8 summit under German presidency. It was interrupted by the global financial crisis but lead to an LCBM action plan of the G20 in 2011, under the French presidency, with the strong support of Germany in the sub-Group.[27]

Several multinational organisations, led by the World Bank and the IMF, took part in the implementation of the 2011 G20 action plan. They were strongly supported by the Deutsche Bundesbank (the German Central Bank) as the only institution of an individual member state.[28] Regarding the role of the Bundesbank, Andreas Dombret notes: 'At the global level, the G7 finance ministers and central bank governors agreed in 2007 that developing local currency bond markets (LCBMs) deserved more political support. The Bundesbank backed this process in close cooperation with the Federal Ministry of Finance and played a major part in drawing up the G8 Action Plan, which was endorsed in May 2007. Since then, the Bundesbank has, with the International Monetary Fund and the World Bank group, co-hosted three international workshops dealing with ways to implement the G8, and now the G20, recommendations'.[29]

While other individual countries' institutions of the G20 are also involved in the establishment of LCBMs, such as the British DFID,[30] Germany appeared to play – at least in the beginning of the process, and especially in the African context – a leading role in the multilateral implementation process, with the Bundesbank as the main agenda setting institution of an individual member state. In this context, Daniela Gabor speaks of 'a renewed global push, *led by Germany* in the G20, to extend the reach of financialised globalisation'.[31]

Furthermore, the German development bank, Kreditanstalt für Wiederaufbau (KfW), is clearly visible in its engagement for LCBMs.[32] According to a well-informed, anonymous source, it was also the KfW which included LCBMs systematically in the conception of the German driven G20 Compact with Africa (CwA).[33] With the advent of the CwA in 2017, the G20 investment plan for Africa, under German presidency, a plan to implement LCBMs in Africa was set.

The CwA was authored by the IMF, the WB, and the AfdB, but due to the German presidency of G20, written by the Ministry of Finance in Berlin. Its main agenda is to support (foreign) investment and infrastructure finance in Africa. It suggests several reforms to be implemented by African countries invited to join the CwA. Along with other neoliberal policy recommendations, the CwA focuses strongly on the creation and deepening of domestic financial markets with LCBMs as one core recommendation.[34] This goes along with the creation or enlargement of domestic institutional investors, the creation of new, safe asset classes, and far reaching de-risking policies as discussed above.[35] A central aspect of risk mitigation is ensuring liquidity of LCBMs.[36] Accordingly, Matthias Dombret emphasised, with regard to the LCBM initiative of the G20: '(. . .) one main objective of this initiative is to strengthen the liquidity of those [LCB] markets (. . .)'.[37] Hence, next to primary markets – the market where these bonds are issued – secondary markets are of crucial importance to ensure that investors can buy and sell bonds whenever deemed necessary.[38] Given that liquidity is a precondition for LCBMs to attract (foreign) investors, they are less constructed to hold stable, 'patient', foreign capital. More crucially, 'these markets facilitate short-term gains for institutional investors chasing returns across the globe'.[39] Instead of 'strengthen[ing] national and global stability',[40] as it is put by the Bundesbank, LCBMs question this fragile stability even further.

## THE RATIONALE OF GERMANY'S GLOBAL ENGAGEMENT FOR LCBMS

But why are German financial and development institutions particularly engaged in establishing LCBMs in Africa? It is only recently that Germany's role in deepening financial markets in the periphery has attracted scholarly attention.[41] Peter Volberding (2021), for instance, concludes that the German development bank KfW has been a key driver in establishing on a global scale what he calls *marketised development financial instruments*. Volberding points out that the KfW's projects of market-based development finance need deep financial markets in order to achieve the expected results.[42] This requirement might provide one explanation for the KfW's engagement for establishing LCBMs.

From his perspective, Volberding detects mainly institutional (and ideological) reasons for the KfW being the driving developmental bank applying market-based development projects.[43] He has good reason to claim that KfW's behavior mainly followed an institutional logic, such as finding solutions for specific funding problems of their programmes. Nonetheless, regardless of his valuable details and conclusion, the institutional perspective disguises a broader view to proactive institutions of the capitalist state.

However, available data provides insights on the economic and geopolitical benefits for the German state and German capital fractions by the establishment of LCBMs, especially in the African context. How these contradict, reinforce, parallel, precede, or follow intra-institutional processes, described by Volberding for the KfW, are very relevant to further determine the relationship between the state and different capital fractions. Unfortunately, this connection cannot be explored in more detail within the scope of this paper.

Yet, relations between state policies and capital interests in reference to the implementation of LCBMs have been created by the involved institutions themselves. The former director of the financial stability department of the Deutsche Bundesbank, Bernd Braasch, in his plea for LCBMs, states that 'more diversified domestic financial systems strengthen the ability of countries to absorb an increasing volatility of international capital flows and therefore dampen the need or incentive to reintroduce capital controls (. . .)'.[44] The economic advantages of 'mature' LCBMs for external investors, be it for portfolio investors or direct investors, are high. For an economy like Germany, with large trade surpluses, the avoidance of capital controls would be a major advantage for any form of investment.

The export orientation of the German economy has accelerated over the last decade. This acceleration was not least based on wage suppression, outsourced labour, and capital-friendly tax policies. This led to high profits for German enterprises. Meanwhile, domestic investment and consumption remained low and the labour share of income declined more than elsewhere,[45] stressing the domestic class character of this export-based growth model. This form of accumulation also changed the mode of finance in Germany, a dynamic of international relevance.

Germany's financial system has for a long time been described as bank based, with companies and their house banks closely related on a long-term basis. Interestingly, with the expansive export strategy and the high yields of profits coming with it, this system seems to have changed drastically, with big companies being much more independent of their banks by self-financing, or even becoming lenders in their own right.[46] However, these high corporate profits have not led to increased capital investments. Instead, corporate lending grew significantly.[47] According to Jacoby, by far the largest component of Germany's capital account are portfolio outflows.[48] The German banks' power decreased vis-à-vis these financially potent companies, partly compensating their losses at home with a stronger financialisation and internationalisation of their business model, also lending to the financial sector itself. This process accelerated in the global financial crisis.[49]

Germany might not be known for hosting many big institutional investors. However, given also these restructurings of the past years, a specific interest of the German state and German capital fractions in financial infrastructure and legal arrangements enabling market-based finance on a global scale with higher yield perspectives than in industrialised countries might have grown.

Furthermore, LCBMs, as a cornerstone to change financial systems in DECs towards market-based systems, are also hugely beneficial to German export capital in terms of easing market access. Germany not only exports more goods and services than it imports, it provides credit to enable external trading partners to buy these, increasing the likelihood of indebted trading partners[50].

Deeper financial markets in Africa would not only ease capital movements for direct or portfolio investments, but also the provision of consumer credits. These are, for example, needed for the German car industry in the African market for new cars, a market that is far from being saturated.[51] According to the head of the German-African business association (Afrikaverein der deutschen Wirtschaft), the focus for German car firms in Africa will be on e-mobility.[52] This market is growing very slowly at home and thus contains great risks for the envisaged restructuring of the industry, including the costs for research and development. The German push for LCBMs and, consequently, for market-based finance in Africa could thus also enable African consumers to buy German products, such as new cars.[53] This would not only help recycle German surplus money, but also improve market access via consumer credits. Volkswagen financial services, so far operating in South Africa, could be one example of this.[54]

Digital payment systems, closely connected to the non-banking sector and depending on market-based finance and therefore liquid markets as discussed above,[55] are also used by German companies. This can again be observed in the example of VW, but also of Siemens and SAP in Rwanda: VW recently started the production of electric cars in Rwanda and offers a car sharing service based on digital payment systems. Both the production of electric cars as well as car sharing services, are meant to be implemented in other African countries.[56] The infrastructure for e-mobility in Rwanda is provided by Siemens; German software provider SAP also participates in the common German initiative.[57]

While the advantages of open and 'mature' financial markets apply to all external investors, and the increased search for investable assets in times of low interest rates is a global phenomenon,[58] German companies are particularly awash with surplus money. What is more, the German state can use its specific engagement in reforming financial systems towards market-based finance, based on LCBMs, to enter markets with, so far, little German investment. This applies particularly to African countries. Continent-wide, German FDIs rank 12th in comparison to other countries of origin, an exception given to all other global investment areas.[59] In its German Africa Guidelines (Afrikapolitische Leitlinien), the government states that it places its activities on the continent in relation to other states active in Africa: 'Also with regard to the *engagement of other states* we want to be a responsible partner for Africa and collaborate in mutual interest.'[60]

With the German-driven Compact with Africa and its related projects[61], Germany enters into territories that have been dominated by former colonial powers, France and Britain, and which are now also under the growing influence of China and others. Interestingly, nine of the twelve CwA countries are francophone; six of them belong to the CFA franc zone with its lasting colonial monetary restrictions.[62] Their CwA membership can be interpreted as an attempt to step out of postcolonial ties, being reflected also in the establishment of LCBM more generally.

LCBMs, as a cornerstone for open market-based financial systems, can be very attractive for African governments too. While entering into a dependency at very high economic, political, and social costs, financing via global financial markets can appear as loosening the old colonial ties.[63] Furthermore, it can assure election winning infrastructure projects and sovereign (debt) finance in local currencies, without official conditionalities. PPPs additionally provide options that project risks taken over by the state do not appear at the states' budget for the time the project is being realised, even though PPPs tend to be a great budgetary burden at a later stage.[64]

The requirements for far-reaching investor protection and de-risking (see above), as well as high interest payments, then come along as structural demands of the market rather than conditioned by a donor. Meanwhile, these structural demands make debt cancellations ever more difficult because the creditors are diverse and the markets are very sensitive to threats of default.[65]

Geopolitical struggles around infrastructure and its modes of finance are increasing.[66] The External Investment Plan (EIP) of the European Union, for example, can be seen as a reaction to the Chinese Belt and Road Initiative.[67] The same is true of the infrastructure policies of the US in reaction to China.[68] Market-based finance via blended finance, or PPP for instance, features prominently in the financing of global infrastructure.[69] Besides its direct negative implications for accessibility and social equality, these projects are much more likely to attract investors in deep, mature, domestic financial markets as these markets ensure liquidity. LCBMs built the anchor for this form of financial deepening. Germany not only has a geopolitical interest in countering the infrastructure activities of countries such as China – in conflictual cooperation with other European countries – but also supports the interests of its strong infrastructure-providing companies such as Siemens, SAP, and others. Blended finance and PPP can be seen as crucial instruments for those.

## INTERNATIONALIST PERSPECTIVES

As outlined above, LCBMs can be seen as a crucial element of market-based development finance. Some stress the intertwined interest of increased market-based development finance with those of, for example, European workers. The private pensions of these workers are seeking profitable and safe investments – to be found also in de-risked African infrastructure. This leads, so the argument, to a win-win situation: The savings of European workers are invested in, for example, a road in Dar es Salaam, publicly de-risked and profit generating to secure their pensions. Tanzanian citizens, on the other hand, get a new road that might not have been built otherwise[70]. However, others question this assumed win-win-situation, stressing that the road should be accessible for all without generating any profit. Those critiques link the interest of European workers to the privatisation of infrastructure in Africa at the expense of African citizens.[71]

Again, in isolation, an immediate interest of future pensioners for safe and profit generating investment cannot be denied. However, this argument obfuscates the class character of the push for market-based development finance as such.

The example of Germany's external surplus, based on wage repression (including a pension reform that indirectly reduces the employers share via the partial privatisation of the pension system), low corporate taxes, and increasing profit margins, underlines this. It is reflected in a strongly grown social inequality since the early years of the twenty-first century an inequality most visible in terms of wealth distribution[72].

In average terms, German citizens belong to the richest group in Europe. Regarding the distribution of wealth, however, indicated for example in median household wealth, households in Germany are poorer than those in Spain and are only slightly wealthier than the median households in Greece or Poland. What is more, many German households do not have any wealth at all.[73] In the Eurozone, Germany displays the greatest difference between the median and mean household wealth, in other words between the average household wealth and its distribution.[74] Estimates of individual wealth inequalities in Germany had to recently be corrected by the DIW Berlin (the German Institute for Economic Research). In a study it unraveled an even higher social inequality in Germany than previously assumed.[75] This contributes to a globally skyrocketing social inequality[76] and adds to the 'global pool of private finance'[77] seeking diversified and profit generating assets for the wealth to increase ever more.

Overall, the argument about pensioners' interests in a profit generating investment abroad (for example in a road in Tanzania) ignores the fact that market-based pensions are risky and costly for the individual, as they undermine collective forms of social security systems. This point also creates the image of a shared interest of European citizens in market-based development finance, while obscuring its underlying social and economic conflicts, briefly discussed in this article for the case of Germany.

## CONCLUSION

The above discussion shows that the promise of increased economic sovereignty by introducing LCBMs in Africa is unlikely. The dominant way of designing and implementing LCBMs in Africa allows global finance, foreign direct investors, and geopolitical actors to act ever more freely on the African continent. This implies not only high social, public and economic costs, but also old and new dependencies – from financial markets, export markets for foreign revenue needed for de-risking measures, and from donor countries providing guarantees. At the same time LCBMs might offer greater access to finance that is less dependent on postcolonial conditionalities. Furthermore, not least due to rising social inequality in African countries themselves, LCBMs might provide African middle- and high-income households investment opportunities, otherwise only available in hard currency.

As has been shown, the discussed interests involved in establishing LCBMs in Africa underline the close connection between diverse domestic economic structures, policies, and class struggles, as well as their related international dynamics and institutional logics. They therefore offer a valuable starting point to elaborate on options for international solidarity and confronting market-based development finance. In order to do so, it is crucial to first analyse the class fractions that are benefitting from 'deeper domestic financial markets' in Africa, which are in support of the new development agenda. Second, we may analyse class struggles in Africa – providing potential for resistance against this financial deepening across the continent – and ask how these are interlinked with, likewise contradictory, class struggles in countries pushing for financial globalisation, such as Germany or other European countries.

The potential for establishing solidarity links between workers and other progressive movements might be linked to the subjection of finance to democratic, people-centred needs in struggles around housing markets, pension systems, public services, and other contested areas.

## NOTES

1 See, for example: Berensmann, K., Dafe, F., Lindenberg, N., and Volz, U., 2015. Financing Global Development: The Role of Local Currency Bond Markets in Sub-Saharan Africa. Briefing Paper 11, Berlin. German Development Institute; G8, 2007. G8 Action Plan for Developing Local Bond Markets in Emerging Market Economies and Developing Countries. Finance Minister Meeting, Potsdam, May 19, 2007. Available at: www.g8.utoronto.ca/finance/g8finance-bond.pdf [Accessed January 18, 2021]; for the NGO side see: C2017, 2017. The G20's Compact with Africa: Some damaging initiatives for sustainable development, p. 1. Available at: https://www2.weed-online.org/uploads/c20_finance_wg_compact_with_africa_june_2017.pdf [Accessed January 17, 2021].

2 AfdB, IMF and WB, 2017. The G20 compact with Africa. G20 Finance Ministers and Central Bank Governors Meeting, March 17–18. Baden-Baden, Germany, p. 38. Available at: www.compactwithafrica.org/content/dam/Compact%20with%20Africa/2017-03-30-g20-compact-with-africa-report.pdf [Accessed October 17, 2020]; Dombret, A., 2011. Local currency bond markets and international capital flows. BIS central bankers' speeches. Available at: https://www.bis.org/review/r111128b.pdf [Accessed July 29, 2021].

3 AfdB, IMF and WB, The G20 compact with Africa, p. 34.

4 *Ibid.* pp. 27, 35; G20, 2018. Overview of Argentina's G20 Presidency 2018. Building Consensus for Fair and Sustainable Development. Buenos Aires. Available at: g20.argentina.gob.ar/en/overview-argentinas-g20-presidency-2018 [Accessed January 17, 2021]; Gabor, D., 2021: The Wall Street Consensus. *Development and Change*, Vol. 52(3), pp. 429–459. doi: https://doi.org/10.1111/dech.12645.

5 *Ibid.*, p. 38; Gabor, D., 2018. Goodbye (Chinese) shadow banking, Hello market-based finance: Debate: Shadow Banking or Market-Based Finance? *Development and Change*, 49(2), pp. 394–419. doi: 10.1111/dech.12387. Banse, F., 2019. Compact with Africa – der deutsche Beitrag zur Investitionsliberalisierung und Finanzialisierung in Afrika. Prokla, 49(1). doi.org/10.32387/prokla.v49i194.1770

6 UNCTAD, 2018. Trade and Development. Power, platforms and free trade delusion. New York and Geneva, Chapter IV.

7 Musthaq, F., 2020. Development finance or financial accumulation for asset managers? The perils of the global shadow banking system in developing countries. *New Political Economy*. doi: 10.1080/13563467.2020.1782367. For a critical discussion on the risk calculations and related interests for African bonds, see: Olabisim, M. and Stein, H., 2015: Sovereign Bond Issues: Do African Countries Pay More to Borrow? *Journal of African Trade*, No 1/2015, pp. 87–109. doi:10.1016/j.joat.2015.08.003.

8 AfdB, IMF and WB, The G20 compact with Africa, p. 29.

9 AfDB, 2018. African Economic Outlook 2018. African Development Bank. Available at: www.afdb.org/fileadmin/uploads/afdb/Documents/Publications/African_Economic_Outlook_2018_-_EN.pdf [Accessed December 20, 2019].

10 AfdB, IMF and WB, The G20 compact with Africa, p. 25; World Bank, 2017. Forward look: A vision for the World Bank Group in 2030. Progress and Challenges. Available at: www.devcommittee.org/sites/www.devcommittee.org/files/download/Documentation/DC2017-0002.pdf [Accessed May 12, 2020]; Gabor, The Wall Street Consensus; Banse, Compact with Africa, pp. 79–98.

11 Musthaq, Development finance or financial accumulation for asset managers? p. 12f.

12 AfdB, IMF and WB, The G20 Compact with Africa, p. 29.

13 *Ibid*, p. 3; Dombret, Local currency bond markets and international capital flows, p.3.

14 WB, no date. Maximizing Finance for Development (MFD). Available at: https://www.worldbank.org/en/about/partners/maximizing-finance-for-development#3, [Accessed February 1, 2020].

15 AfdB, IMF and WB, The G20 Compact with Africa, p. 33.

16 Gabor, D., 2020. The Liquidity and sustainability facility for African sovereign bonds: A good ECA/PIMCO idea whose time has come? Draft Paper, p. 23; Jäger, J. and Küblböck, K., 2011. Entwicklungsfinanzierung im Umbruch – Entwicklungsstaaten im Aufbruch? *Journal für Entwicklungspolitik*, No. XXVII, 2-2011, p. 7.

17 Becker, J., 2008. Der kapitalistische Staat in der Peripherie: politökonomische Perspektiven. *Journal für Entwicklungspolitik*, XXIV, No. 2-2008, pp. 10–32.

18 Barbosa, N. et al., 2020. Letter: The threat is greatest for developing and emerging countries. *Financial Times*, March 25, 2020. Available at: www.ft.com/content/35053854-6d17-11ea-89df-41bea055720b [Accessed March 20, 2020].

19 AfdB, IMF and WB, The G20 Compact with Africa, p. 31.

20 Roos, J., 2019. *Why not default? The political economy of sovereign debt.* Princeton: Princeton University Press; Erlassjahr, Brot für die Welt, Misereor and Oxfam, 2020. Debt relief as a response to the Covid-19-induced recession. Online Discussion, 25.9.2020, Available at: www.youtube.com/watch?v=pWcJ9atl8Uk [Accessed September 27, 2020].

21 For the highly indebted Zambia, see: Fischer, A., 2020. Haemorrhaging Zambia: Prequel to the Current Debt Crisis. A Critical Perspective On Development Economics. Available at: https://developingeconomics.org/2020/11/24/haemorrhaging-zambia-prequel-to-the-current-debt-crisis/ [Accessed January 17, 2021]; generally, see UNCTAD, 2019. State of Commodity Dependence, pp. 2ff. Available at: https://unctad.org/en/PublicationsLibrary/ditccom2019d1_en.pdf [Accessed May 29, 2020];

UNCTAD, 2016: Economic Development in Africa. Report 2016 Debt Dynamics and Development. Finance in Africa. Available at: https://unctad.org/en/PublicationsLibrary/aldcafrica2016_en.pdf [Accessed April 30, 2020]; Banse, F., 2021. Private Sector Promotion for Development? An Analysis of German and European Development Policies in Africa. Available at: https://www.brot-fuer-die-welt.de/fileadmin/mediapool/blogs/Mari_Francisco/Banse_Privatinvestitionen_Analyse99.pdf[Accessed September 1, 2021].

22 IMF, WB, EBRD and OECD, 2013. Local currency bond markets. A diagnostic framework, p. 3. Available at: www.oecd.org/daf/fin/public-debt/Local-Currency-Bond-Markets-Diagnostic-Framework-2013.pdf. 2013 [Accessed May 29, 2020].

23 FSB, 2015. Transforming shadow banking into resilient market-based finance. FSB. Available at: www.fsb.org/wp-content/uploads/shadow_banking_overview_of_progress_2015.pdf [Accessed January 17, 2021].

24 Gabor, Goodbye (Chinese) shadow banking, Hello market-based finance, p. 408.

25 AfdB, IMF and WB, The G20 Compact with Africa, p. 29.

26 Dombret, Local currency bond markets and international capital flows, p. 2

27 G20, 2011. Action plan to support the development of local currency bond markets. Available at: www.g20.utoronto.ca/2011/2011-finance-action-plan-currency-111015-en.pdf [Accessed January 17, 2021].

28 WB, 2012. Supporting the Development of Local Currency Bond Markets. Interim Progress Report on Implementing the G20 Action Plan on the Development of Local Currency Bond Markets. Available at: https://documents1.worldbank.org/curated/pt/275781468335977188/pdf/705030WP0Suppo0Box370043B000PUBLIC0.pdf [Accessed July 29, 2021].

29 Dombret, Local currency bond markets and international capital flows, p. 1.

30 Giraudo, M.E., Kaltenbrunner, A., Kvangraven, I.H., Metz, C., Okot, A., and Perraton, J., 2020. The Rise of Domestic Debt Markets in Africa. What Shapes Them? Who benefits? Draft paper. University of Leeds, Unversity of Sheffielt, University of York, US-NY. p. 15.

31 Gabor, Goodbye (Chinese) shadow banking, Hello market-based finance, p. 398.

32 See for example ALCB Fund, no date. Supporting the Development of African Capital Markets. Available at: https://www.alcbfund.com/ [Accessed January 17, 2021]; EC, 2019. Summaries of the EU External Investment Plan. Guarantees. Available at: https://ec.europa.eu/international-partnerships/system/files/181213-eip-28-guarantees-brochure-final_en.pdf [Accessed June 10, 2020].

33 AfdB, IMF and WB, The G20 Compact with Africa, p. 29.

34 *Ibid.*, p. 31

35 See for further elaboration on the Compact with Africa in Banse, Compact with Africa; Banse, Private Sector Promotion for Development?

36 AfdB, IMF and WB, The G20 Compact with Africa, p. 33.

37 Dombret, Local currency bond markets and international capital flows, p. 3

38 AfdB, IMF and WB, The G20 Compact with Africa, p. 34; see also Bundesbank, 2013. The financial system in transition: the new importance of repo markets, pp. 57–71. Available at: https://www.bundesbank.de/resource/blob/707406/9c08446930bd174887fe4432992f26ec/mL/2013-12-repo-markets-data.pdf [Accessed January 17, 2021]; Gabor, The Liquidity and Sustainability Facility for African Sovereign Bonds; Musthaq, Development Finance or Financial Accumulation for Asset Managers?; Potts, S., 2017. Deep finance: sovereign debt crises and the secondary market 'fix'. *Economy and Society*, Vol. 46, No. 3–4, pp. 452–475. doi: 10.1080/03085147.2017.1408215.

39 Musthaq, Development finance or financial accumulation for asset managers?, p.15.

40 Dombret, Local currency bond markets and international capital flows, p. 1.

41 Gabor, Goodbye (Chinese) Shadow Banking, Hello Market-Based Finance; Banse, Compact With Africa; Volberding, P., 2021. *Leveraging financial markets for development. How KfW revolutionized development Finance.* Cham: Palgrave Macmillan.

42 Volberding, Leveraging financial markets for development. pp. 12ff.

43 *Ibid.*, pp. 9, 124ff.

44 Braasch, B., 2012. The world needs to develop missing markets. *Financial Times*, January 25, 2012. Available at: www.ft.com/content/7987d8f3-faob-3271-b8a9-1e6f5e306b9a. [Accessed March 4, 2019].

45 Braun, B. and Deeg, R., 2019. Strong Firms, Weak Banks: The Financial Consequences of Germany's Export-Led Growth Model. *German Politics*, 29(3), pp. 2ff. doi: 10.1080/09644008.2019.1701657; Klein, M.C. and Pettis, M., 2019. Trade Wars are Class Wars. How rising Inequality distorts the Global Economy and threatens International Peace. New Haven, CT and London: Yale University Press, pp. 155ff.; Jacoby, W., 2020. Surplus Germany. *German Politics*, 29(3), pp. 10ff. doi:10.1080/09644008.2019.1707188.

46 Braun and Deeg, Strong firms, weak banks, p. 9.; see also Sablowski, T., Towards the americanization of European finance? The case of financeled accumulation in Germany. In Panitch, Leo and Martijn Konings, eds, 2009. *American empire and the political economy of global finance.* Hampshire/New York: Palgrave macmillan, pp. 135–158.

47 Braun and Deeg, Strong firms, weak banks, p. 9.

48 Jacoby, Surplus Germany, p. 13; see also Bundesbank, 2020. Germany's international investment position at the end of 2019. Press Release 30.9.2020. Available at: https://www.bundesbank.de/en/press/press-releases/germany-s-international-investment-position-at-the-end-of-2019-846024 [January 17, 2021]. The Bundesbank notes furthermore that German FDIs are mainly a boosting of capital account abroad or direct investment loans to affiliated enterprises (*ibid*).

49 Braun and Deeg, Strong Firms, Weak Banks, pp. 13f.

50 Handelsblatt, 2019. Deutschland erzielt erneut weltgrößten Leistungsbilanzüberschuss. *Handelsblatt*, September 13, 2019. Available at: www.handelsblatt.com/politik/deutschland/ifo-institut-deutschland-erzielt-erneut-weltgroessten-leistungsbilanzueberschuss/25012390.html [Accessed April 17, 2020].

51 Handelsblatt, 2019. Volkswagen startet Pilotprojekt mit Elektroautos in Ruanda. *Handelsblatt*, October 22, 2019. Available at: www.handelsblatt.com/unternehmen/industrie/autobauer-volkswagen-startet-pilotprojekt-mit-elektroautos-in-ruanda/25141588.html [Accessed April 17, 2020]; Ibukun, Y., 2020. VW, Nissan chase African new-car market where financing is rare. *Automotive News Europe*, January 13, 2020. Available at: europe.autonews.com/automakers/vw-nissan-chase-african-new-car-market-where-financing-rare [Accessed February 24, 2020].

52 Kannengießer, C., 2019. Afrika-Verein der deutschen Wirtschaft, über deutsche Wirtschaftsinteressen in Afrika. Tagesschau, 2019. Available at: www.tagesschau.de/multimedia/video/video-623065.html [March 17, 2020].

53 Ibukun, VW, Nissan chase African new-car market where financing is rare; on the securitization of micro credits see Söderberg, S., 2013. Universalising financial inclusion and the securitisation of development. *Third World Quarterly*, 34(4), pp. 593–612. doi.org/10.1080/01436597.2013.786285.

54 See: www.vwfs.co.za/ [Accessed February 24, 2020].

55 Gabor, D. and Brooks, S., 2017. The Digital Revolution in Financial Inclusion: International Development in the Fintech Era. *New Political Economy*, 22(4), pp.7ff. doi.org/10.1080/13563467.2017.1259298.

56 Handelsblatt, Volkswagen startet Pilotprojekt mit Elektroautos in Ruanda.

57 *Ibid.*; BMZ, 2018. Digitales Verkehrskonzept. BMZ und deutsche Unternehmen starten Mobilitäts- und Ausbildungspartnerschaft 'Moving Rwanda'. Available at: www.bmz.de/de/presse/aktuelleMeldungen/2018/februar/180228_pm_015_BMZ-und-deutsche-Unternehmen-starten-Moving-Ruanda/index.jsp [Accessed January 17, 2021]. See for further discussion Banse, Private Sector Promotion for Development?.

58 See, for example, McNally, D., 2011. *Global slump. The Economics and Politics of Crisis and Resistance.* Oakland Spectre.

59 Kappel, R., 2020. Die Neujustierung der deutschen Afrikapolitik. Institut für Afrikastudien, Leipzig, p.11. Available at: www.ssoar.info/ssoar/handle/document/66470 [Accessed April 15, 2020]; see also UNCTAD, 2018a. World Investment Report 2018. Investment and New Industrial Policies. New York/Geneva, p. 38.

60 Bundesregierung (2019): Eine vertiefte Partnerschaft mit Afrika. Fortschreibung und Weiterentwicklung der Afrikapolitischen Leitlinien der Bundesregierung, p.3, translation and italics FB. Available at: https://www.auswaertiges-amt.de/blob/2204146/61736c06103e9a28e328371257ee34f7/afrikaleitlinien-data.pdf, [Accessed July 29, 2021].

61 Banse, Private Sector Promotion for Development?

62 The countries being part of the CwA include, so far: Benin, Burkina Faso, Côte d'Ivoire, Egypt, Ethiopia, Ghana, Guinea, Morocco, Rwanda, Senegal, Togo, and Tunisia. Available at: www.compactwithafrica.org/content/compactwithafrica/home/compact-countries.html [Accessed February 24, 2021].

63 See also Sylla, N.S. and Koddenbrock, K., 2019. Financialization in the West-African monetary union. *African Agenda*, 22(2), pp. 7–9. Available at: http://twnafrica.org/wp/2017/wp-content/uploads/2019/06/WAEMU.pdf [Accessed January 17, 2021].

64 Romero, M.J., 2015. What lies beneath? A critical assessment of PPPs and their impact on sustainable development. Available at: eurodad.org/files/pdf/1546450-what-lies-beneath-a-critical-assessment-of-ppps-and-their-impact-on-sustainable-development-1450105297.pdf [Accessed June 3, 2020].

65 See Erlassjahr, Brot für die Welt, Misereor and Oxfam; Roos, Why Not Default?; see also Potts, Deep finance: sovereign debt crises and the secondary market 'fix'.

66 See, for example, Politi, J., 2018. G20: US and China clash on developing world infrastructure. *Financial Times*, November 29, 2018. Available at: www.ft.com/content/35305b50-deb2-11e8-b173-ebef6ab1374a [Accessed January 15, 2021].

67 Tröster, B., Küblböck, K., and Grumiller, J., 2017. EU´s and Chinese raw materials policies in Africa: Converging Trends? *Kurswechsel*, No. 3/17, Wien: ÖFSE, p. 74; see also Banse, Private Sector Promotion for Development?

68 Thrush, G., 2018. Trump Embraces Foreign Aid to Counter China's Global Influence. *New York Times*, October 14, 2018. Available at: www.nytimes.com/2018/10/14/world/asia/donald-trump-foreign-aid-bill.html [Accessed January 17, 2021]; Lui, Y. and Ng, E., 2018. To solve China's Belt and Road financing problem, Hong Kong looks to infrastructure loan-backed securities. *South China Morning Post*, October 15, 2018. Available at: www.scmp.com/news/article/2168671/solve-chinas-belt-and-road-financing-problem-hong-kong-looks-infrastructure [Accessed January 17, 2021]; Gabor, D., 2018. The World Bank pushes fragile finance in the name of development. *Financial Times*, October 29, 2018. Available at: www.ft.com/content/1b9d5aa0-9aa9-316d-b154-d2582c1dc093 [Accessed January 17, 2021];

69 AfdB, IMF and WB, The G20 Compact with Africa, pp. 27ff., 35ff.; G20, Overview of Argentina´s G20 Presidency; WB – World Bank (2017): Forward Look: A Vision for the World Bank Group in 2030; see also Gabor, The Wall Street Consensus.

70 See Kim, J.Y., 2017. Speech by World Bank Group President Jim Yong Kim: Rethinking development finance. Available at: www.worldbank.org/en/news/speech/2017/04/11/speech-by-world-bank-group-president-jim

-yong-kim-rethinking-development-finance, [Accessed January 17, 2021]; Arbouch, M. and Canuto, O. and Vazquez, M., 2020. Africa's infrastructure finance. G20 Insights. Available at: www.g20-insights.org/policy_briefs/africas-infrastructure-finance/ [Accessed January 17, 2021]; G20, Overview of Argentina´s G20 Presidency 2018.

71 Alexander, N., 2017. Beware the Cascade-World "Banck" to the Future. *Heinrich Böll Foundation,* May 23, 2017. Available at: justgovernance.boellblog.org/2017/05/23/beware-the-cascade-world-banck-to-the-future/ [Accessed June 24, 2020].

72 WSI (no date). Soziale Ungleichheit: Fragen und Antworten. Available at: www.wsi.de/de/soziale-ungleichheit-fragen-und-antworten-15098.htm [January 17, 2021].

73 Klein, M.C. and Pettis, M., Trade Wars are Class Wars, p. 163; see also ECB, 2020. Household Finance and Consumption Survey. Wave 2. Statistical Tables, p.3. Available at: www.ecb.europa.eu/home/pdf/research/hfcn/HFCS_Statistical_Tables_Wave2.pdf?58cf15114aab934bcd06995c4e91505b [Accessed January 17, 2021].

74 De Grauwe, P. and Yuemei J., 2013. Are Germans really poorer than Spaniards, Italians and Greeks? *Voxeu*, April 16, 2013. Available at: voxeu.org/article/are-germans-really-poorer-spaniards-italians-and-greeks. 2013 [Accessed January 17, 2021].

75 DIW, 2020. MillionärInnen unter dem Mikroskop: Datenlücke bei sehr hohen Vermögen geschlossen – Konzentration höher als bisher ausgewiesen. *DIW-Wochenbericht*, No. 29/2020. Available at: https://www.diw.de/de/diw_01.c.793802.de/publikationen/wochenberichte/2020_29_1/millionaerinnen_unter_dem_mikroskop__datenluecke_bei_sehr_ho___geschlossen______konzentration_hoeher_als_bisher_ausgewiesen.html [Accessed January 17, 2021]; Handelsblatt, 2020. Studie: Reichste zehn Prozent besitzen gut zwei Drittel des Vermögens. *Handelsblatt*, July 15, 2020. Available at: www.handelsblatt.com/politik/deutschland/vermoegensverteilung-studie-reichste-zehn-prozent-besitzen-gut-zwei-drittel-des-vermoegens/26006588.html?ticket=ST-4904720-5Ee9hkduuQbp2bvi12hQ-ap5 [Accessed January 17, 2021].

76 Oxfam, 2020. Time to care. Unpaid and underpaid care work and the global inequality crisis. *Oxfam.* Available at: www.oxfam.de/system/files/2020_oxfam_ungleichheit_studie_englisch_time-to-care.pdf. [Accessed January 17, 2021].

77 AfdB, IMF and WB, The G20 Compact with Africa, p. 29.

# Notes on Editors

**Maha Ben Gadha** is Economic Program Manager at the North Africa office of the Rosa Luxemburg Foundation in Tunis, holds a Master in Industrial economics, from the University of Paris 13, and a Master of Financial Analyst from Clermont Ferrand University. She was advisor to the Tunisian Presidency after the 2011 revolution, her current work in RLS consists in supporting and developing networks of relevant actors in economic policymaking, unions, social movements in the region engaged in rethinking progressive political strategies and alternative economic models to translate the demand for social justice into feasible transformative projects and solidarity actions between and within the Global South.

**Fadhel Kaboub** is Associate Professor of Economics at Denison University and President of the Global Institute for Sustainable Prosperity. He has held research affiliations with the Levy Economics Institute, and the John F. Kennedy School of Government at Harvard University. He is an expert on Modern Monetary Theory, the Green New Deal, and the Job Guarantee. His work focuses on public policies to enhance monetary and economic sovereignty in the Global South, build resilience, and promote equitable and sustainable prosperity.

**Dr. Habil. Kai Koddenbrock** is a research group leader in International Relations and International Political Economy at the 'Africa Multiple' Cluster at the University of Bayreuth, Germany. He is working on the history and present of finance, imperialism and economic sovereignty in the Global South. He has published a monograph on the critique of humanitarian aid and peacekeeping in the DR Congo and is currently editing a book on 'Capital claims: Power and finance in the 21st century' with Benjamin Braun, with whom he also coordinates the research network 'Politics of money'.

**Ines Mahmoud** is a lecturer at the University of Applied Arts in Vienna where she teaches on the social study of money and debt. She is a research student at the Oxford Department of International Development and holds an LLM in International Economic Law from the University of Birkbeck. Ines has previously worked as a regional programme manager of the economic and migration programme of the North Africa Office of Rosa Luxemburg Stiftung, as well as the Middle East Forum of Open Democracy. Her research interest focuses on the political economy of North Africa.

**Ndongo Samba Sylla, PhD,** is a Senegalese development economist. He has previously worked as a technical advisor at the Presidency of the Republic of Senegal. He is currently a Research and Programme Manager at the West Africa office of the Rosa Luxemburg Foundation (Dakar). His publications cover topics such as Fair trade, labour markets in developing countries, social movements, democratic theory, economic and monetary sovereignty. He recently coauthored *Africa's Last Colonial Currency: The CFA Franc Story* (Pluto Press 2021).

# Notes on Contributors

**Max Ajl** is a postdoctoral fellow at the Rural Sociology Group at Wageningen University and an associate researcher at the Tunisian Observatory for Food Sovereignty and the Environment. He is an associate editor at *Agrarian South*. His book, *A People's Green New Deal*, was published in 2021 with Pluto Press.

**Frauke Banse** is a senior researcher in International Political Economy at the University of Kassel, Germany. She is a regular advisor to labour unions and NGOs, and works on financial markets and German Africa policy.

**Elizabeth Cobbett** is lecturer at the University of East Anglia, UK. Her current research project, *Growth of African Financial Systems*, maps the emerging geography of finance across the continent, and is the focus of her forthcoming monograph: *The Political Economy of African Financial Centres: The New Realm of Global Finance.*

**Carla Coburger** is a research assistant at the ESRC's Rebuilding Macroeconomic Network at the National Institute for Economic and Social Research, London, and is part of the European Research Network on Social and Economic Policy (EReNSEP)

**Hannah Cross** is a senior lecturer in International Relations at the University of Westminster and chair of the Editorial Working Group of the Review of African Political Economy.

**Harry Cross** is an Assistant Professor at Prince Mohammad Bin Fahd University in Dhahran, Saudi Arabia. He holds a PhD in Political Economy and Financial History from Durham University in the UK.

**Radhika Desai** is a Professor at the Department of Political Studies; director of the Geopolitical Economy Research Group, University of Manitoba, Winnipeg, Canada; and president of the Society for Socialist Studies. She proposed a historical materialist approach to understanding world affairs in her *Geopolitical Economy: After US Hegemony, Globalization and Empire* (2013).

**Thomas Fazi** is an Anglo-Italian writer, journalist and translator. He is the author of several critically acclaimed books in English and Italian, including *The Battle for Europe: How an Elite Hijacked a Continent – and How We Can Take It Back* (Pluto, 2014) and *Reclaiming the State: A Progressive Vision of Sovereignty for a Post-Neoliberal World* (Pluto, 2017), co-written with Bill Mitchell, an appraisal of nation states in the global age. He regularly writes for numerous English language publications about European and Italian affairs, of which he is considered a foremost expert, and has a good following on social media.

Professor **Heiner Flassbeck** advises governments, political parties and other institutions in macroeconomic affairs. Prior to that he served from 2003 to 2012 as Director of the Division on Globalization and Development Strategies of the United Nations Conference on Trade and Development (UNCTAD). He was the principal author and the leader of the team preparing UNCTAD's Trade and Development Report. Prior to joining UNCTAD, Professor Flassbeck was chief economist in the German Institute for Economic Research between 1988 and 1998, and State Secretary (Vice Minister) from October 1998 to April 1999 at the Federal Ministry of Finance responsible for international affairs, the European Union and IMF.

**Francis Garikayi** is a Ph.D. Researcher in Economics at the Open University. He is interested in structural transformation and African economic development.

**Anne Löscher** is a Ph.D. candidate working on the macroeconomics of the climate crisis with focus on low-income countries and their integration in the international financial system. She holds an M.Sc in Empirical Economics and Policy Consulting as well as Economics with Reference to Africa from the University of London.

**Fatiha Talahite** is an economist, senior researcher at the CNRS, member of the Center for Sociological and Political Research in Paris (Cresppa). She joined the CNRS in 1995, first at the Clersé (Lille 2 University) then at the CEPN (Paris 13 University). Previously, she was assistant professor at the University of Oran in Algeria, where she studied. Her many publications include the transformation of the Algerian economy since the socialist period, the reforms and the institutional changes of the 1990s and 2000s, as well as the gender economy, both theoretical and applied to the Arab and Muslim world.

# Index

Thanks to our Patreon Subscribers:

*Lia Lilith de Oliveira*
*Andrew Perry*

Who have shown generosity and comradeship in support of our publishing.

Printed and bound by CPI Group (UK) Ltd, Croydon, CR0 4YY

15/09/2026

14962452-0002